AF564583

Economics of Money and Banking

Economics of Money and Banking

Anand Prakash

Economics of Money and Banking

ISBN 978-93-5111-805-3

Published in 2016 in India by

RANDOM PUBLICATIONS

4376-A/4B, Gali Murari Lal, Ansari Road
New Delhi-110 002
Phone : +9111-43580356, 011-23289044, 011-43142548
e-mail: sales@randompublications.com,
info@randompublications.com, randomexports@gmail.com

Reprinted 2026

Type Setting by : Friends Media, Delhi-110089
Digitally Printed at : Replika Press Pvt. Ltd

Preface

The importance of money reflects the most fundamental nature of a modern economic system. In a society without extended division of labor, in which every family produces almost all that they consume, there would be little need for money.

The quantity theory of money states that there is a direct relationship between the quantity of money in an economy and the level of prices of goods and services sold. According to QTM, if the amount of money in an economy doubles, price levels also double, causing inflation (the percentage rate at which the level of prices is rising in an economy). The consumer therefore pays twice as much for the same amount of the good or service. Another way to understand this theory is to recognise that money is like any other commodity: increases in its supply decrease marginal value (the buying capacity of one unit of currency). So an increase in money supply causes prices to rise (inflation) as they compensate for the decrease in money's marginal value.

In simple words, Banking can be defined as the business activity of accepting and safeguarding money owned by other individuals and entities, and then lending out this money in order to earn a profit. However, with the passage of time, the activities covered by banking business have widened and now various other services are also offered by banks. The banking services these days include issuance of debit and credit cards, providing safe custody of valuable items, lockers, ATM services and online transfer of funds across the country/ world.

This book aims to apply economic principles and models to understand the role of money and banking in the economy and to critically evaluate current debates on competition and regulation in the banking sector.

– Author

Contents

1

Measuring the Money Supply in Economy

The concept of the quantity theory of money (QTM) began in the 16th century. As gold and silver inflows from the Americas into Europe were being minted into coins, there was a resulting rise in inflation. This led economist Henry Thornton in 1802 to assume that more money equals more inflation and that an increase in money supply does not necessarily mean an increase in economic output. Here we look at the assumptions and calculations underlying the QTM, as well as its relationship to monetarism and ways the theory has been challenged.

QTM IN A NUTSHELL

The quantity theory of money states that there is a direct relationship between the quantity of money in an economy and the level of prices of goods and services sold. According to QTM, if the amount of money in an economy doubles, price levels also double, causing inflation (the percentage rate at which the level of prices is rising in an economy). The consumer therefore pays twice as much for the same amount of the good or service. Another way to understand this theory is to recognise that money is like any other commodity: increases in its supply decrease marginal value (the buying capacity of one unit of currency). So an increase in money supply causes prices to rise (inflation) as they compensate for the decrease in money's marginal value.

THE THEORY'S CALCULATIONS

In its simplest form, the theory is expressed as:

$$MV = PT \text{ (the Fisher Equation)}$$

Each variable denotes the following:

M = Money Supply

V = Velocity of Circulation (the number of times money changes hands)

P = Average Price Level

T = Volume of Transactions of Goods and Services

The original theory was considered orthodox among 17th century classical economists and was overhauled by 20th-century economists Irving Fisher, who formulated the above equation, and Milton Friedman. (For more on this important economist, see *Free Market Maven: Milton Friedman*.)

It is built on the principle of "equation of exchange":

Amount of Money × Velocity of Circulation = Total Spending

Thus if an economy has US$3, and those $3 were spent five times in a month, total spending for the month would be $15.

QTM Assumptions

QTM adds assumptions to the logic of the equation of exchange. In its most basic form, the theory assumes that V (velocity of circulation) and T (volume of transactions) are constant in the short term. These assumptions, however, have been criticized, particularly the assumption that V is constant. The arguments point out that the velocity of circulation depends on consumer and business spending impulses, which cannot be constant.

The theory also assumes that the quantity of money, which is determined by outside forces, is the main influence of economic activity in a society. A change in money supply results in changes in price levels and/or a change in supply of goods and services. It is primarily these changes in money stock that cause a change in spending. And the velocity of circulation depends not on the amount of money available or on the current price level but on *changes* in price levels.

Finally, the number of transactions (T) is determined by labour, capital, natural resources (*i.e.*, the factors of production), knowledge and organisation. The theory assumes an economy in equilibrium and at full employment.

Essentially, the theory's assumptions imply that the *value* of money is determined by the *amount* of money available in an economy. An increase in money supply results in a decrease in the value of money because an increase in money supply causes a rise in inflation. As inflation rises, the purchasing power, or the value of money, decreases. It therefore will cost more to buy the same quantity of goods or services.

Money Supply, Inflation and Monetarism

As QTM says that quantity of money determines the value of money, it forms the cornerstone ofmonetarism.

Monetarists say that a rapid increase in money supply leads to a rapid increase in inflation. Money growth that surpasses the growth of economic output results in inflation as there is too much money behind too little production of goods and services. In order to curb inflation, money growth must fall below growth in economic output. This premise leads to how monetary policy is administered. Monetarists believe that money supply should be kept within an acceptable bandwidth so that levels of inflation can be controlled. Thus, for the near term, most monetarists agree that an increase in money supply can offer a quick-fix boost to a staggering economy in need of increased production. In the long term, however, the effects of monetary policy are still blurry.

Less orthodox monetarists, on the other hand, hold that an expanded money supply will not have any effect on real economic activity (production, employment levels, spending and so forth). But for most monetarists any anti-inflationary policy will stem from the basic concept that there should be a gradual reduction in the money supply. Monetarists believe that instead of governments continually adjusting economic policies (*i.e.*, government spending and taxes), it is better to let non-inflationary policies (*i.e.*, gradual reduction of money supply) lead an economy to full employment.

QTM Re-Experienced

John Maynard Keynes challenged the theory in the 1930s, saying that increases in money supply lead to a decrease in the velocity of circulation and that real income, the flow of money to the factors of production, increased. Therefore, velocity could change in response to changes in money supply. It was conceded by many economists after him that Keynes' idea was accurate.

QTM, as it is rooted in monetarism, was very popular in the 1980s among some major economies such as the United States and Great Britain under Ronald Reagan and Margaret Thatcher respectively. At the time, leaders tried to apply the principles of the theory to economies where money growth targets were set. However, as time went on, many accepted that strict adherence to a controlled money supply was not necessarily the cure-all for economic malaise.

WHAT IS MONEY?

Money is not necessarily legal currency (notes and coins). Money is any asset (or assets) that the public in general accepts as capable of performing certain functions (the functions of money). The social agreement (or acceptance) is the most important requirement. Money is believed to improve economic efficiency and social welfare.

- *Barter:* Barter is the direct exchange of commodities without the use of money (exchanging commodities for commodities). Barter is less efficient than monetary exchange (selling one commodity for money and buying another using that money). The exchange is not possible unless there is a "double coincidence of wants" (*i.e.*, the wants of the two parties match exactly), a condition not easy to satisfy. Time and other real costs of completing a transaction (transaction cost) are therefore higher with barter. There are other difficulties with barter as well.
- *The Functions of Money:* Money fulfills three basic functions as:
  1. A medium of exchange (as payment for goods and services);
  2. A unit of account (as a yardstick for measuring value or price); and

3. A store of value (as an asset in terms of which the storage of wealth is possible).

As a generally acceptable medium of exchange, money is perfectly liquid and eliminates the need for a double coincidence of wants. The ease with which an asset can be converted into a medium of exchange is called liquidity.

The suggestion that money must be designated as legal tender is not appropriate since the confidence of the public, not government enforcement, ultimately decides which assets will be used as money. Transaction costs can be lowered by using media of transaction such as traveller's cheques or credit cards. The medium of exchange function does not imply the store of value function, as there other interest rate-bearing assets than money (or cash) which may function better as stores of value.

MONETARY STANDARDS

A society's monetary standard is the basis of its monetary arrangements and includes rules, regulations, and customs regarding the issue and use of money. Broadly, two monetary standards are found in history: commodity standards and fiat-money standards. Under a commodity standard the monetary unit is defined as a commodity such as gold (a physical asset) in a specified quantity and often quality.

The physical commodity itself, or minted coins made from it or papers convertible into the commodity, were used as circulating media (actually used in transactions). Under a fiat-money standard (paper-money standard), the circulating media are the legal tender (notes and coins whose monetary worth is determined and guaranteed by the taxing and borrowing powers of the government), and have virtually no commodity value. No monetary standard is perfect, but fiat-money standards have become more popular and widespread.

GOLD STANDARD

Gold has been the commodity most often used as money. Many countries have used versions of a gold standard in which the exchange rate is fixed to the price of gold. Canada had a gold standard from 1854 to 1914 and from 1926 to 1931. Before 1914, many countries in the West were on a classical gold standard according to which their currencies were convertible into gold on demand. Under this system, the price of gold was fixed and exchange rate fluctuations were limited.

In a pure gold standard circulating notes are fully (100 per cent) backed by gold. The ability of governments and monetary authorities to manipulate the money supply (the power of discretionary monetary policy) is very limited, and hence it is easy to maintain price stability. However, the limited power of monetary policy and other inflexibilities under a pure gold standard may exacerbate economic problems in a recession.

- *Bimetallism:* A monetary system based on two metals, such as gold and silver, is called bimetallism. The exchange rate between the two metals is fixed. Changes in the relative market value of the two metals can lead to the operation of Gresham's Law, which states that "Bad money drives good money out of circulation."
- *Canada's Early Paper Money:* Canada's early experience with paper-money standards (for example, when playing cards and pieces of cardboard were used as circulating media) were not happy, in particular when the paper money was not fully backed by redemptions. Under the paper standard known as Army Bills, the circulating media were redeemed in full. Prior to Confederation in 1867 the private notes issued by private banks were believed to be the best way to satisfy the need for money. Circulating coins appeared only in 1858. By 1866 provincial notes were introduced. Government effectively had monopoly over small denomination notes while the private banks circulated larger denomination notes. Following Confederation, dominion notes replaced provincial notes, and the first Bank Act was introduced. In the mid 1930s the Bank of Canada was created, and the Bank of Canada notes replaced the dominion notes and private bank notes.
- *Fiat Money and Central Banks:* As the adoption of fiat-money standards became widespread in the twentieth century, the importance of central banks increased. A central bank (*e.g.*, Bank of Canada) is a national bank which is owned by the public sector and is responsible for the conduct of monetary policy. It acts as the banker for the federal (central) government, and entertains a certain degree of independence from the government.

MEASURING THE MONEY SUPPLY IN ECONOMY

The amount of money available in the economy is called the money supply or money stock. Money may include many assets other than currency in circulation (notes and coins), and therefore, the measurement of its supply is not simple.

Some Helpful Concepts of Money

- *Types of Banks and Deposits:* Banks are a group of deposit-taking financial institutions which include chartered banks (*e.g.*, Bank of Montreal, Bank of Nova Scotia), and near banks such as trust companies and credit unions. Depositors lend their funds to the banks Therefore, the deposits are assets to the depositor and liabilities to the institution.

The deposits are of four types:

- Current accounts and personal chequing accounts;

- Savings deposits;
- Term deposits; and
- Money market mutual funds.
- *Cheques and Cheque Clearing:* A cheque is a written order for a bank to transfer a specific amount of funds from the writer's account to someone else. In a system of many banks, a large number of transactions are done every day using cheques which require the transfer of funds between the banks and changes in the balances of accounts. In Canada this is done by the Canadian Payments Association, which operates an automated cheque-clearing system (a clearing house). Computer technology has increased the speed of cheque clearing, but at all times some cheques are in transit. As a result, the double counting of money held by financial institutions is unavoidable. Therefore, an estimate called private sector float is used to adjust for the amount of double counting.

Definitions of the Money Supply

Empirical definitions used in Canada, from the narrowest to the broadest, are listed below:

- Currency in Circulation, *i.e.*, the notes and coins outside the banking system.
- M1. The currency in circulation plus current, demand, and personal chequing accounts at chartered banks, net of the private sector float.
- M2. M1 plus non-personal notice deposits and personal savings deposits at chartered banks.
- M2+. M2 plus notice and term deposits at near banks, generally at trust and mortgage loan companies.
- M3. M2 plus non-personal fixed-term deposits at chartered banks plus the Canadian dollar value of foreign currency deposits of residents booked in Canada.

Some Possible Refinements: Still broader measures of the money supply may be constructed which include some liquid assets such as Canada Savings Bonds, unused portions of credit card balances, and consumer or residential mortgage credit. Each of the money supply definitions measures the aggregate value of many different types of assets. Divisia Indexes have been developed to take into account the degree of liquidity of different assets included in the definitions of money supply.

Why So Many Monetary Aggregates? The link between the money supply and key macro aggregates such as GDP and price level has evolved over time because of financial innovations and deregulation. In response to new developments in the financial sector and the economy, the Bank of Canada has introduced a series of monetary aggregates. These aggregates are crucial variables in the analysis of economic performance and monetary policy effectiveness.

Seasonal Adjustment: Seasonal adjustments, calculated to smooth seasonal variations of money supply aggregates, are less necessary as we move from narrow to broad definitions.

INFLATION AND SOCIAL WELFARE

Inflation is an increase in the general level of prices. Inflation reduces the purchasing power (real value) of money and decreases social welfare through a redistribution of income and other harmful effects. Social costs result because inflation upsets the debtor-creditor relationship; influences the government revenue motive for inflation; creates a deadweight loss for society; leads to the additional cost of distinguishing nominal from real magnitudes; increases menu costs, poses problems for accounting in historical and current values; and generates uncertainty associated with higher and volatile prices.

THE BASIC FUNCTION OF MONEY

The basic function of money is to enable buying to be separated from selling, thus permitting trade to take place without the so-called double coincidence of barter. In principle, credit could perform this function, but before extending credit, the seller would want to know about the prospects of repayment. That requires much more information about the buyer and imposes costs of information and verification that the use of money avoids.

If a person has something to sell and wants something else in return, the use of money avoids the need to search for someone able and willing to make the desired exchange of items. The person can sell the surplus item for general purchasing power — that is, "money" — to anyone who wants to buy it and then use the proceeds to buy the desired item from anyone who wants to sell it.

The importance of this function of money is dramatically illustrated by the experience of Germany just after World War II, when paper money was rendered largely useless because of price controls that were enforced effectively by the American, French, and British armies of occupation. Money rapidly lost its value. People were unwilling to exchange real goods for depreciating currency.

They had to resort to barter or to inefficient money substitutes. Price controls reduced incentives to produce. The result was to cut total output of the economy in half. The German "economic miracle" just after 1948 reflected partly a currency reform by the occupation authorities that replaced depreciating money with money of stable value and, at the same time, eliminated all price controls, thereby permitting a money economy to replace a barter economy.

Separation of the act of sale from the act of purchase requires the existence of something that will be generally accepted in payment — this is the "medium of exchange" function of money. But there must also be something that can serve as a temporary store of purchasing power, in which the seller holds the proceeds in the interim between the first sale and the subsequent purchase, or from which the buyer can extract the general purchasing power with which to pay for what is bought. This is the "asset" function of money.

VARIETIES OF MONEY

Anything can serve as money that habit or social convention and successful experience endow with the quality of general acceptability, and a variety of items have so served — from the wampum (beads made from shells) of American Indians to cowries (brightly coloured shells) in India, to whales' teeth among the Fijians, to tobacco among early colonists in North America, to large stone disks on the Pacific island of Yap, to cigarettes and liquor in post-World War II Germany. The wide use of cattle as money in primitive times survives in the word pecuniary, which comes from the Latin *pecus*, meaning cattle.

Metallic Money

The use of metals as money has occurred throughout history. As Aristotle observed, the various necessities of life are not easily carried about, and hence people agreed to employ in their dealings with each other something that was intrinsically useful and easily applicable to the purposes of life, for example, iron, silver, and the like. The value of the metal was at first measured by size and weight but, in time, governments or sovereigns put a stamp upon it, to save the trouble of weighing and to make the value known at sight.

The use of metal for money can be traced back to Babylon more than 3000 years before the birth of Christ, but there were earlier standards. Standardisation and certification in the form of coinage, as referred to by Aristotle, did not occur except perhaps in isolated instances until the 7th century. Historians generally assign to Croesus, King of Lydia, a state in Anatolia, priority in using coined money. The first coins were made of electrum, a natural mixture of gold and silver, and were crude, bean-shaped ingots bearing a primitive punchmark certifying to either weight or fineness, or both.

The use of coins enabled payment to be by "tale," or count, rather than weight, greatly facilitating commerce. But this in turn encouraged clipping (shaving off tiny slivers from the sides or edges of coins) and sweating (shaking a bunch of coins together in a leather bag and collecting the dust that was thereby knocked off) in the hope of passing on the lighter coin at its face value. Gresham's law (that "bad money drives out good" when there is a fixed rate of exchange between them) came into operation, and heavy, good coins were held for their metallic value, while light coins were passed on to others.

The coins became lighter and lighter, and prices higher and higher. Then payment by weight would be resumed for large transactions, and there would be pressure for recoinage. These particular defects were largely ended by the "milling" of coins (making serrations around the circumference of a coin), which began in the late 17th century. A more serious matter was the attempt by the sovereign to benefit from the monopoly of coinage. In this respect, Greek and Roman experience offers an interesting contrast.

Though Solon, on taking office in Athens in 594 BC, did institute a partial debasement of the currency, for the next four centuries, until the absorption of Greece into the Roman Empire, the Athenian *drachma* had an almost constant silver content (67 grains of fine silver until Alexander, 65 grains thereafter) and became the standard coin of trade in Greece and in much of Asia and Europe as well. Even after the Roman conquest, the *drachma* continued to be minted and widely used.

The Roman experience was very different. Not long after the silver *denarius*, patterned after the Greek *drachma*, was introduced in about 212 BC, the prior copper coinage (*aes*, or *libra*) began to be debased until, by the time the empire began, its weight had been reduced from one pound to half an ounce. The silver *denarius* and the gold *aureus* (introduced about 87 BC) suffered only minor debasement until the time of Nero (54 BC), when almost continuous tampering with the coinage began.

The metal content of the gold and silver coins was reduced, and the proportion of alloy was increased to three-fourths or more of its weight. Debasement in Rome (as ever since) used the state's profit from money creation to cover its inability or unwillingness to finance its expenditures through explicit taxes. But the debasement in turn raised prices, worsened Rome's economic situation and contributed to the collapse of the empire.

History of Paper Money

The history of money shows repeated innovations that changed the objects used as money. Carrying large sums in gold, silver, or other metal was inconvenient and risked loss or theft. China was the first to use paper money, more than 1000 years ago. By the late 18th and early 19th centuries, paper money and bank notes spread widely. The bulk of the money in use came to consist not of actual gold or silver but of fiduciary money — promises to pay specified amounts of gold and silver.

These promises were initially issued by individuals or companies as bank notes or as the transferable book entries that came to be called deposits. Although deposits and bank notes began as claims to gold or silver on deposit at a bank or with a merchant, this later changed. Knowing that everyone would not claim his or her balance at once, the bank or merchant could issue more claims to the gold and silver than the amount held in safekeeping. It could invest the difference or lend it at interest. In periods of distress, when borrowers did not repay their loans or in case of overissue, the bank might fail.

Gradually, the government assumed a supervisory role. It specified legal tender, defining the type of payment that legally discharged a debt when offered to the creditor and that could be used to pay taxes. It set the weight of coins and their metallic composition. Later, it replaced fiduciary paper money promising to pay gold or silver with fiat paper money — that is, notes that are issued on the "fiat" of the sovereign government, are specified to be so many dollars or pounds, or yen, and are legal tender but are not promises to pay something else.

The first large-scale issue in a Western country occurred in France in the early 18th century. The French revolutionary government issued paper money in the form of assignats from 1789 to 1796. The American colonies and later the Continental Congress issued bills of credit that could be used in making payments. These early experiments gave fiat money a deservedly bad name. The money was overissued, and prices rose drastically until the money became worthless or was redeemed in metallic money (or promises to pay metallic money) at a small fraction of its initial value.

Subsequent issues of fiat money in the major countries during the 19th century were temporary departures from a metallic standard. In Great Britain, for example, the government suspended payment of gold for the outstanding bank notes during the Napoleonic Wars (1797-1815). To finance the war, the government issued fiat paper money. Prices in Great Britain doubled as a result, and gold coin and bullion became more expensive in terms of paper. To restore the gold standard at the former gold price, the government deflated the price level by reducing the quantity of money. In 1821, the gold standard was restored. Similarly, in the United States during the Civil War, the government suspended convertibility of Union currency (greenbacks) into specie, and resumption did not occur until 1879. At its peak in 1864, the greenback price of gold, nominally equivalent to $100, reached more than $250.

Episodes of this kind, repeated in many countries, convinced the public that war brings inflation, and the aftermath of war brings deflation and depression. This sequence is not inevitable. It reflected nineteenth century experience under metallic money standards. Typically, wars required increased government spending and budget deficits. Governments suspended the metallic (gold) standard and financed their deficits by borrowing and printing paper money. Prices rose.

The end of wartime spending and inflation left the price of gold far above its pre-war value. To restore the metallic standard at the prewar price of gold in paper money, prices quoted in paper money had to fall. The alternative was to accept the increased price of gold in paper money by devaluing the currency. After World War I, Great Britain and the United States deflated, but many other countries devalued their currencies against gold. After World War II, all major countries accepted the higher price level and most devalued to avoid deflation and depression. Since the cost of producing paper money is far below its exchange value, forgery is common. The development of copying machines made forgery easier, necessitating changes in paper, use of metallic strips and other devices to make forgery more difficult. The use of machines to identify, count, or change currency increases the need for tests to identify genuine currency.

THE NATURE AND DEVELOPMENT OF MONEY

Many analyses of money begin with some story about the evolution of money from sea shells, to precious metals, to bank deposits and finally to modern "fiat" money. Why do economists begin monetary analysis with a potted history? Perhaps it is to focus attention on the essential characteristics, or nature, of money. To be sure, we will never "know" the origins of money for at least two important reasons. First, the origins are lost "in the mists of time"—almost certainly in pre-historic time.

It has long been speculated that money predates writing because the earliest examples of writing appear to be records of monetary debts—meaning that the closely intertwined chronology of the development of writing and money will make it impossible to find a written history. Second, recent scholarship indicates that the origin of writing, itself, is exceedingly complex—it is not so simple to identify what is "writing". Similarly, it is not clear what we want to identify as money. Like writing, money is social in nature and it consists of complex social practices that include power and class relationships, socially constructed meaning, and abstract representations of social value.

As Hudson (2004) rightly argues, ancient and even "primitive" (tribal) society was no less complex than today's society. Economic relations, including what we might want to identify as monetary relations, were highly embedded within complex social structures that are very difficult to uncover and understand from our cultural and historical vantage point. As a result, trying to uncover "the" origins of money is almost certainly an impossible or at least misguided endeavor unless it is placed within the context of a theoretical framework. When we attempt to discover the origins of money, we are identifying institutionalised behaviours that appear similar to those today that we wish to identify as "money". This identification, itself, requires an underlying economic theory about the nature of, and role played by, money.

For example, the barter story usually told by orthodoxy highlights the medium of exchange and store of value functions of money. A natural propensity to truck and barter is taken for granted. Attention is diverted away from social behaviour and towards individual utility calculation. Social power and economic classes are purged from the analysis, while "the market" is exalted. The story focuses on transactions-cost reducing innovations, except where government interferes, creating inefficiencies to be overcome. And this story is consistent with the neo-classical worldview, because the orthodox economist sees exchange, markets, and relative prices wherever she looks.

For the orthodox economist, the essential difference between "primitive" and modern society is that these early societies are presumed to be much simpler—relying on barter or commodity monies. Hence, economic relations in earlier society are more transparent; innate propensities are laid bare in the Robinson Crusoe economy for the observing economist. Gradually more complex financial practices emerge—to reduce transactions or evade government-imposed constraints—as money is naturally transformed from a commodity to fiat notes and finally to electronic charges stored in computers that introduce an increasingly opaque veil concealing primordial urges.

On the surface, this appears to be an "evolutionary" approach that recognises human agency in the transformation from barter to fiat money. However, the orthodox economists turn money into a "natural" phenomenon free from essential social relationships.

Although economists allow that money is a human invention assuming different forms in different times and places, they adopt an evolutionary perspective that de-emphasizes money's contingency and its ultimate foundation in social convention. As capitalist economies became more complex, money 'naturally' assumed increasingly efficient forms, culminating in the highly abstract, intangible money of today.

The story typically begins with a double coincidence of wants that spurs barter, leading to specialisation and the development of the market. The market, itself, is relatively free of social relations, because efficiency conditions require participants to ignore social status and other socio-cultural and individual idiosyncrasies as utilities are maximized and costs minimized. It is "natural" to choose a convenient medium of exchange to facilitate these impersonal transactions. The value of each marketed commodity is denominated in the medium of exchange through the asocial forces of supply and demand.

Not only is money asocial, but it is also neutral as it greases the wheels of commerce. The ideal medium of exchange is a commodity whose value is intrinsic—free from any hierarchical relations or social symbolism. As markets become more complex, money is transformed to minimize transactions costs through time. For example, precious metals like gold replace other commodities because their intrinsic characteristics can reduce transactions costs; paper notes are then issued on the basis of gold reserves, economising on scarce bullion.

From this viewpoint, it is regrettable that nations have abandoned the use of intrinsically valuable metallic money in favour of "fiat" monies that have no "natural" value. Some economists advocate return to a gold standard, but most accept that this is (at least) politically infeasible. Hence, it is necessary to remove as much discretion as possible from monetary and fiscal authorities, to try to ensure that modern fiat money operates in a manner similar to that of commodity money. Monetary growth rules, prohibitions on treasury money creation, balanced budget requirements, and the like (not to mention currency boards and dollarisation for developing nations), are all attempts to remove discretion and thereby restore the natural, asocial, neutered, monetary order. Even some "pure credit" heterodox theorists argue that government is, or should be, in the same situation as any other "individual", with liabilities that have to compete in financial markets, constrained by the quantity of money they can tax or borrow to finance their spending.

Thus, for many analysts, social relations are hidden behind money's veil. Carruthers and Babb provide one of the most incisive analyses of the asocial nature of money in orthodox theory. They quote Hilferding affirmatively:

In money, the social relationships among human beings have been reduced to a thing, a mysterious, glittering thing the dazzling radiance of which has blinded the vision of so many economists when they have not taken the precaution of shielding their eyes against it.

Simmel put it even more concisely: money transforms the world into an "arithmetic problem". The underlying relations are "collectively 'forgotten about'" in order to ensure that they are not explored. Doubters need only examine how money is introduced as little more than an afterthought into modern macroeconomic ("arithmetic") analyses (and recall Friedman's 1969 famous presumption that money is simply dropped by helicopters).

The (intended?) effect of neutering money is to hide the social relations behind a natural (transactions costs reducing) veil of asocial market exchange. To uncover those social relations, we will argue that the heterodox economist cannot begin analysis of money with market exchange. While heterodox economists try to avoid the orthodox "economistic" blinders, tracing the origins of money necessarily requires selective attention to those social practices we associate with money—knowing full well that earlier societies had complex and embedded economies that differ remarkably from ours.

I believe that the credit money and state money approaches, properly integrated, can provide the starting point. The key concept is debt (or, credit, if we look at it from the other side of the coin)—not "market exchange". The credit approach brings the debt/credit relation to the forefront of analysis, while the state money approach emphasizes the social nature of the money of account in which credits and debts are denominated.

The credit approach locates the origin of money in credit and debt relations. The analysis is inherently social—at the very least it requires a bilateral relation between debtor and creditor. The unit of account is emphasized as the numeraire in which credits and debts are measured. The store of value function could also be important, for one stores wealth in the form of others' debts. On the other hand, the medium of exchange function and the market are de-emphasized; indeed, one could imagine credits and debits without markets and without a medium of exchange. However, it is not sufficient to pose a "social relation" between debtor and creditor, for one could argue that the Robinson Crusoe and Friday story also involves a bilateral "social" relation with a mutually agreed-upon choice of a numeraire. One obvious difference, however, is that the credit/debt relation is persistent—until the debt is retired—while the Crusoe-Friday relation is extinguished with the exchange. There is thus an explicit and lasting social relation between creditor and debtor that could include hierarchy and power.

Those who adopt the credit approach go further, identifying the social nature of the money unit of account and, indeed, the social processes that generate creditors and debtors. We must carefully avoid imposing 21st century social relations on ancient peoples, replacing "trucking and bartering" with a natural propensity to lend and borrow. Indeed, the evidence suggests that one would not have voluntarily become a debtor, a reluctance also suggested by the etymology of the words associated with debt—see below. Hence we should not automatically presume that credit emerged from mutually beneficial negotiations; we might even say that there is nothing "natural" about credit/debt—rather, this relation develops and evolves as a result of complex social, historical, and economic forces.

Innes suggested that we can locate the origins of credit and debt relations in the elaborate system of tribal wergild designed to prevent blood feuds. Wergild fines were paid by transgressors directly to victims and their families, and were established and levied by public assemblies. A long list of fines for each possible transgression was socially developed (not as a result of negotiation between perpetrator and victim), and a designated "rememberer" would be responsible for passing it down to the next generation. Note that each fine was levied in terms of a particular item that was both useful to the victim and more-or-less easily obtained by the perpetrator. The transgressor's family would be held responsible for payment, and the fines would be enforced by the community.

As Hudson reports, the words for debt in most languages are synonymous with sin or guilt, reflecting these early reparations for personal injury. Originally, until one paid the wergild fine, one was "liable", or "indebted" to the victim. We still think of a traffic fine as an "obligation" to pay, and speak of the criminal's "debt to society". Thus, we should not imagine an economy of independent agents voluntarily lending and borrowing to maximize utility. Rather, the debt/credit relation was involuntarily and socially created and imposed to "pacify" the victim (to make peace, and from which comes our verb "to pay").

Hudson also makes it clear that the words for money, fines, tribute, tithes, debts, man-price, sin, and, finally, taxes are so often linked as to eliminate the possibility of coincidence. It is almost certain that wergild fines were gradually converted to payments made to an authority. This could not occur in an egalitarian tribal society (in which payments were made to victims, not authorities), but had to await the rise of some sort of ruling class. As Henry argues for the case of Egypt, the earliest ruling classes were probably religious officials, who demanded tithes (ostensibly, to keep the gods happy). Alternatively, conquerors required payments of tribute by a subject population. Tithes and tribute thus came to replace wergild fines, and fines for "transgressions against society" (that is, against the crown), paid to the rightful ruler, could be levied for almost any conceivable activity. Eventually, taxes would replace most fees, fines and tribute (although this occurred surprisingly late—not until the 19th century in England). These could be self-imposed as democracy swept away the divine right of kings. "Voluntarily-imposed" taxes proved superior to payments based on naked power or religious fraud because of the "democratic" nature of the decision to impose them "for the public good".

The notion that taxes "pay for" provision of "public goods" like defence or infrastructure added another layer of justification, as did the occasionally successful attempt to convert taxes from a "liability" to a "responsibility". In any case, with the development of "civil" society and reliance mostly on payment of taxes rather than fines, tithes, or tribute, the likely origin of such payments in the wergild tradition has been forgotten.

At this point, we move from the credit approach to the state money approach. We have seen how the debt/credit relation was transformed with the rise of an authority able to impose debts on subjects (and later, by "citizens" who collectively imposed debts on themselves). The question is: how did this debt become monetised? The key innovation lay in the transformation of what had been the transgressor's debt to the victim, denominated in specific items to be used for "pacification", to a universal "debt" or tax obligation imposed by and payable to the authority in terms of a socially recognised numeraire. This required standardisation of the imposed obligations in terms of a unit of account—almost certainly a tortuous transformation.

At first, the authority might have levied a variety of fines (and tributes, tithes, and taxes) in kind, in terms of goods or services to be delivered, one for each sort of transgression (as in the wergild tradition). When all payments are made to the single authority, however, this would become cumbersome. Unless well-developed markets already existed, those with liabilities denominated in specific goods or services could find it difficult to make such payments. Or, the authority could find itself blessed with an overabundance of one type of good while short of others.

Denominating payments in a unit of account would simplify matters—but would require a central authority. As Grierson realised, development of a unit of account would be conceptually difficult. It is easier to come by measures of weight or length—the length of some anatomical feature of the ruler (from which, of course, comes our term for the device used to measure short lengths—the "ruler" used to measure a foot), or the weight of a quantity of grain. By contrast, development of a money of account used to value items with no obvious similarities (weight, height) required more effort. Hence, the creation of an authority able to impose obligations transformed wergild fines paid to victims to fines paid to the authority, and at the same time it created the need for and possibility of creation of the monetary unit.

Orthodoxy has never been able to explain how individual utility maximizers settled on a single numeraire. While use of a single unit of account results in efficiencies, it is not clear what evolutionary processes would have generated the numeraire (even Selgin—one of the biggest supporters of the approach—admits that Austrians have not provided a convincing explanation; Klein and Selgin 2000). According to the conventional story, the higgling and haggling of the market is supposed to produce the equilibrium vector of relative prices, all of which can be denominated in the single numeraire. However, this presupposes a fairly high degree of specialisation of labour and/or resource ownership—but this pre-market specialisation, itself, is hard to explain. (Bell, Henry, and Wray 2004) Once markets are reasonably well developed, specialisation increases welfare; however, without well-developed markets, specialisation is exceedingly risky, while diversification of skills and resources would be prudent. Further, even if this specialisation problem can be finessed, no evolutionary process that would generate a single unit of account has been identified. It seems exceedingly unlikely that either markets or a money of account could have evolved out of individual utility maximizing behaviour.

It has long been recognised that early monetary units were based on a specific number of grains of wheat or barley. As Keynes argued in his research on ancient monies, "the fundamental weight standards of Western civilization have *never* been altered from the earliest beginnings up to the introduction of the metric system" These weight standards were then taken over for the monetary units, whether the *livre, sol, denier, mina, shekel,* or later *the pound*. This relation between the words used for weight units and monetary units generated speculation from the time of Innes and Keynes that there must be some underlying link. Hudson (2004) explains that the early monetary units used in the temples and palaces of Sumer in the third millennium BC were created initially for internal administrative purposes: "the public institutions established their key monetary pivot by making the shekel-weight of silver (240 barley grains) equal in value to the monthly consumption unit, a 'bushel' of barley, the major commodity being disbursed".

Hence, rather than the intrinsic value (or even the exchange value) of precious metal giving rise to the numeraire, the authorities established the monetary value of precious metal by setting it equal to the numeraire that was itself derived from the weight of the monthly grain consumption unit. This lends support to the argument that the unit of account was socially determined by the central authority (temple, palace, royal court, representative government) rather than the result of individual optimisation that propelled the search for a numeraire to replace simple barter.

Does the origin of money as a social unit of account used to measure obligations matter? Is money a social institution, or is it best characterised as a convenient medium of exchange? While Institutionalists and some Post Keynesians have long viewed money as an institution, indeed, as the most important institution in a capitalist economy, most heterodox economists have not delved deeply into this. (Important exceptions include Dillard 1980 and Minsky 1986, and the sociologist Ingham 2000, 2004a, 2004b)

However, if we are to understand the nature of money, it is important to uncover the social relations that are obscured by this institution. The credit money and state money approaches help to lift that veil by shedding light on the nature of money. In the next three sections, we look at each of these approaches and then point the way towards an integration with the better-known endogenous money approach.

THE CREDIT THEORY OF MONEY

Credit theories of money, also called debt theories of money are concerned with the relationship between credit and money. Proponents of these theories, such as Alfred Mitchell-Innes, will sometimes emphasize that credit and debt are the same thing, seen from different points of view. Proponents assert that the essential nature of money is credit (debt), at least in eras where money is not backed by a commodity such as gold. Two common strands of thought within these theories are the idea that money originated as a unit of account for debt, and the position that money creation involves the simultaneous creation of money and debt. Some proponents of credit theories of money argue that money is best understood as debt even in systems often understood as usingcommodity money. Others hold that money equates to credit only in a system based on fiat money, where they argue that all forms of money including cash can be considered as forms of credit money.

The first formal *Credit theory of money* arose in the 19th century. Anthropologist David Graeber has argued that for most of human history, money has been widely understood to represent debt, though he concedes that even prior to the modern era, there have been several periods where rival theories like Metallism have held sway.

MONETARY THEORY OF CREDIT

Schumpeter made a useful distinction between the "monetary theory of credit" and the "credit theory of money". The first sees private "credit money" as only a temporary substitute for "real money"—possibly a "natural" money that is free of social relations. Final settlement must take place in real money, which is the ultimate unit of account, store of value, and means of payment.

Exchanges might take place based on credit, but credit expansion is strictly constrained by the quantity of real money.

Ultimately, only the quantity of real money matters so far as economic activity is concerned. Most modern macroeconomic theory is based on the concept of a deposit multiplier that links the quantity of privately created money (mostly, bank deposits) to the quantity of high powered money, HPM. This is the modern equivalent to what Schumpeter called the monetary theory of credit, and Friedman (or Karl Brunner) is a good representative. The real money that is the basis of deposit expansion should be controlled, preferably by a rule that will make modern fiat money operate more like the metallic money of the hypothesised past.

The credit theory of money, by contrast, emphasizes that credit normally expands to allow economic activity to grow. This new credit creates new claims on HPM even as it leads to new production. However, because there is a clearing system that cancels claims and debits without use of HPM, credit is not merely a temporary substitute for HPM. Schumpeter does not deny the role played by HPM as an ultimate means of settlement, he simply denies that it is required for most final settlements.

Like Schumpeter, Innes focused on credit and the clearing system, mocking the view that "in modern days a money-saving device has been introduced called *credit* and that, before this device was known all purchases were paid for in cash, in other words in coins." Instead, he argued "careful investigation shows that the precise reverse is true". Rather than selling in exchange for "some intermediate commodity called the 'medium of exchange'", a sale is really "the exchange of a commodity for a credit". Innes called this the "primitive law of commerce": "The constant creation of credits and debts, and their extinction by being cancelled against one another, forms the whole mechanism of commerce..." He explains:

By buying we become debtors and by selling we become creditors, and being all both buyers and sellers we are all debtors and creditors. As debtor we can compel our creditor to cancel our obligation to him by handing to him his own acknowlegment [sic] of a debt to an equivalent amount which he, in his turn, has incurred.

The market, then, is not viewed as the place where goods are exchanged, but rather as a clearinghouse for debts and credits: credits and debits are the focus, not market exchange. Indeed, Innes rejected the typical analysis of the medieval village fairs, arguing that these were first developed to settle debts, with retail trade later developing as a sideline to the clearing house trade. Even if Innes goes too far in this claim, it is useful in emphasizing debts and credits and clearing as primary, with trade in goods and services of subsidiary interest—one of the ways in which one becomes a debtor or creditor (or clears debts). Innes viewed the creditor-debtor relation (not the barter exchange) as the fundamental social relation lying behind money's veil. Further, there is no "natural" relation-free money that lies behind the credits and debts. Indeed, for Innes even HPM, including gold coins, is credit money—for reasons discussed in the next section.

The credit approach as advanced by Innes and Schumpeter provides a more useful vision of monetary operations of a capitalist, "market", economy than does the orthodox view of money serving as a lubricating medium of exchange. The monetary production economy as described by Marx, Veblen, and Keynes is dominated by a complex web of financial relations that were characterised by Minsky as "money now for money later" propositions. Money is not a veil that should be stripped away to observe the essential characteristics of the "market economy". Rather, the money of account and those credit-debt relations are the key institutional relations of the capitalist economy.

THE STATE THEORY OF MONEY

Now, however, the problems of metallism and the idea of money as credit, and in turn the functional finance implications, are well understood. Besides the contributions of Knapp and Innes to these areas, what did they think about private credit money creation? There is, given their focus on metallism and other issues of the time, relatively little on private money creation in their work. The past century, as mentioned, has seen the development of more or less a full understanding of the implications of the ideas of Knapp and Innes. However, there have been numerous relatively small crises in the past century (just since the 1980s: Savings and Loan in the US, the Japanese asset price bubble, LCTM, banking crises in Finland, Sweden, Asia, Russia, Argentina, Ecuador, Uruguay, and throughout Europe) and two massive economic crises that have had much or most of their basis in the private credit money creation realm of the economy. In other words, although a great deal of the suboptimal performance (sustained unemployment, lack of investment in infrastructure, education, and health care) has been due to a failure to understand and apply readily implementable state money and functional finance insights, there has also been another major source of economic suffering, resulting from the non-state-money side of the economy. The worldwide private credit money system has caused untold suffering and misery for millions.

State Money and Approach

Goodhart (1998) makes a useful distinction between the metalist, orthodox, approach and the chartalist—or state money—approach. The latter emphasizes that money evolves not from a pre-money market system but rather from the "penal system" based on the ancient practice of wergild. Hence, it highlights the important role played by "authorities" in the origins and evolution of money. More specifically, the state (or any other authority able to impose an obligation) imposes a liability in the form of a generalised, social unit of account—a money—used for measuring the obligation.

This does not require the pre-existence of markets, and, indeed, almost certainly predates them (as discussed above). Once the authorities can levy such obligations, they can name what fulfills the obligations by denominating in a social unit of account those things that can be delivered, in other words, by pricing them. This resolves the conundrum faced by methodological individualists and emphasizes the social nature of money and markets—which did not spring from the minds of individual utility maximizers, but rather were both socially created.

Note that the state can—in theory—choose anything to function as the "money thing" denominated in the money of account: "Validity by proclamation is not bound to any material" and the material can be changed to any other so long as the state announces a conversion rate. In practice, the state needs to choose something that cannot be readily counterfeited. The state chooses the unit, names the thing accepted in payment of obligations to itself, and (eventually) issues the money-thing it accepts.

In (almost) all modern developed nations, the state accepts the currency issued by the treasury (in the US, coins), plus notes issued by the central bank (Federal Reserve notes in the US), plus bank reserves (again, liabilities of the central bank)—together, HPM. The material from which the money thing issued by the state is produced is not important (whether it is gold, base metal, paper, or even digitised numbers at the central bank). No matter what it is made of, the state must announce its nominal value (that is to say, the value at which the money-thing is accepted in meeting obligations to the state) and accept it in payments made to the state.

The state money approach might appear to be inconsistent with the credit money approach described in the previous section because it is not obvious that state money represents a credit/debt relation. Indeed, some critics of the state money approach imagine that markets operating on the basis of private credits and debits denominated in a money of account pre-existed the state or authorities. The state is then supposed to have inserted itself into the private money system, taxing and borrowing the *private credit money* for use in public expenditures. The state's own money initially consists of "commodity money"—precious metal coins whose value is determined by embodied bullion—*not* a credit money. Later, somehow, the state manages to dupe the public into accepting "fiat money" that is neither fish (debt) nor fowl (precious metal). Again, close control over the issue of intrinsically valueless state money is necessary to prevent inflation or hyperinflation.

In contrast, Innes insisted that when the state spends, it becomes a debtor (as he said, "by buying we become debtors") as it issues state money. Hence, even state money is credit money, however, as we will see, it is a special kind of credit, "redeemed by taxation". For the government, a dollar is a promise to 'pay', a promise to 'satisfy', a promise to 'redeem,' just as all other money is. Innes argued that even on a gold standard it is not gold that government promises to pay:

It is true that all the government paper money is convertible into gold coin, but redemption of paper issues in gold coin is not redemption at all, but merely the exchange of one form of obligation for another of an identical nature.

Whether the government's IOU is printed on paper or on a gold coin, it is indebted just the same. What, then, is the nature of the government's IOU? This brings us to the "very nature of credit throughout the world", which is "the right of the holder of the credit (the creditor) to hand back to the issuer of the debt (the debtor) the latter's acknowledgment or obligation".

The holder of a coin or certificate has the absolute right to pay any debt due to the government by tendering that coin or certificate, and it is this right and nothing else which gives them their value. It is immaterial whether or not the right is conveyed by statute, or even whether there may be a statute law defining the nature of a coin or certificate otherwise.

Hence, we can integrate the state money and credit money approaches through the recognition of the "very nature of credit", which is that the issuer must accept its own IOUs when presented (as when bank notes are returned to the issuing bank for redemption if conversion is promised, or to pay a debt owed to the issuing bank).

What, then, is special about government? The government's credit "usually ranks in any given city slightly higher than does the money of a banker outside the city, not at all because it represents gold, but merely because the financial operations of the government are so extensive that government money is required everywhere for the discharge of taxes or other obligations to the government."

The special characteristic of government money, then, is that it is "redeemable by the mechanism of taxation": "[I]t is the tax which imparts to the obligation its 'value'.... A dollar of money is a dollar, not because of the material of which it is made, but because of the dollar of tax which is imposed to redeem it". This tax liability is imposed by the government on a sufficient proportion of the population that there is a nearly universal demand for the government's own liabilities—which are necessary to pay taxes.

By contrast, orthodox economists accept a "metalist" position, arguing that until recently, the value of the government's money was determined by the gold used in producing coins or by the gold backing paper notes. However, in spite of the attention paid to the gold standard, it was actually in place for only a short period. Typically, the money-thing issued by the authorities was not gold-money nor was there any promise to convert the money-thing to gold.

Indeed, as Innes insisted, throughout most of Europe's history, the money-thing issued by the state was the hazelwood tally stick: "This is well seen in medieval England, where the regular method used by the government for paying a creditor was by 'raising a tally' on the Customs or on some other revenue getting department, that is to say by giving to the creditor as an acknowledment of indebtedness a wooden tally." Other money-things included clay tablets, leather and base metal coins, and paper certificates. Why would the population accept otherwise "worthless" sticks, clay, base metal, leather, or paper? Because these were evidence of the state's liabilities that it would accept in payment of taxes and other debts owed to itself. The key power of the state was its ability to impose taxes: "[t]he government by law obliges certain selected persons to become its debtors.... This procedure is called levying a tax, and the persons thus forced into the position of debtors to the government must in theory seek out the holders of the tallies or other instrument acknowledging a debt due by the government." Contrary to orthodox thinking, then, the desirability of the money-thing issued by the state was not generally determined by intrinsic value, but by the nominal value set by the state at its own pay offices.

Nor was the government's money forced onto the public through legal tender laws. It is certainly true that governments often do adopt legal tender laws, but these are difficult to enforce and hence often ineffective. The power of government to impose a tax and to name what will be accepted in tax payment is sufficient, and certainly trumps legal tender laws.

Once the state has created the unit of account and named what can be delivered to fulfill obligations to the state, it has generated the necessary pre-conditions for development of markets. As Innes argued, credits and debts probably preceded markets, and indeed, created the need for markets. The quintessential debt is the tax obligation, which then creates the incentive for private credits and debts and then for markets—because those without the means of paying taxes could use markets to obtain those means. Evidence from Babylonia suggests that early authorities set prices for each of the most important products and services—perhaps those accepted to meet obligations to the authorities.

Once prices in money were established, it was a short technical leap to creation of markets. This stands orthodoxy on its head by reversing the order: first money and prices, then markets and money-things (rather than barter-based markets and relative prices, and then numeraire money and nominal prices). The next step was the recognition by the authority that it could issue the money-thing to purchase the mix it desired, then receive the same money-thing in the tax payments by subjects/citizens. This would further the development of markets because those with tax liabilities but without the goods and services the authority wished to buy would have to produce for market to obtain the means of paying obligations to the state. There need not be any conflict between credit money and state money approaches. The state provides the unit of account in which private credits and debts are denominated. The state denominates tax liabilities in that same money unit, and names what can be delivered in tax payment. The modern state issues HPM—its liability that is accepted in tax payment—as it spends. The private sector not only uses HPM for tax payment, but also for net clearing of private debts. The state even accepts some private liabilities in payments to the state, although ultimate clearing takes place in the state's HPM. In the next section we turn to the endogenous money approach, and a more detailed look at the role played by HPM in net clearing.

The Endogenous Money Move Towards

Beginning in the early 1970s there has been a revival of the endogenous money approach that had been followed by the Banking School of the early 19th century as well as by Marx several decades later. (It could be argued that most economists before WWII accepted some version of endogenous money, and that the exogenous approach gained dominance only with the development of the neo-classical synthesis.

See Wray 1990.) This culminated in the "horizontalist" approach to money advanced by Moore (1988) that emphasizes the non-discretionary nature of reserves. This effectively reverses the "deposit multiplier" of the money and banking textbooks, arguing that "loans make deposits" and "deposits make reserves".

The focus is on the private decisions made by banks and their customers, which determine the supply of loans and deposits, hence, the supply of credit money that "endogenously" expands to meet the needs of trade. The central bank can only "exogenously" set the short-term interest rate (federal funds rate in the US, repo rate in the UK) at which it supplies reserves "horizontally" on demand to banks. Finally, the endogenous money approach rejects even long-run neutrality of money, arguing that the creation of money is tied to the fundamental processes of a capitalist economy, thus, money *always* matters. These points are all well-established in the Post Keynesian literature and do not require further elaboration here.

The links between the endogenous money approach and the credit money approach discussed above should be obvious. The difference is really one of emphasis, with the endogenous money approach focusing more upon bank and central bank decision-making and interactions, while the credit approach has been more interested in identifying the nature of credit/debt relations. The fundamental property of all credit, according to Innes, is that its issuer must accept it; the endogenous money equivalent is the Banking School reflux principle: excess bank deposits return to banks to retire loans.

There certainly is no conflict between the endogenous money emphasis on the monetary role played by bank liabilities and the credit money claim that bank money is debt. The endogenous money approach also recognises that today's HPM is the debt of the government (treasury and central bank), although it is not clear that all followers of this approach would agree with Innes that all money—even gold coin—is debt.

What has largely been neglected in the endogenous money literature is the role of the state and the impact of fiscal operations on banks and the central bank. At least in the horizontalist version, the role of the state is limited to the central bank's ability to set the overnight interest rate, which requires that it passively accommodate bank demand for reserves. Indeed, the index to Moore's 1988 book does not even list entries for fiscal policy, treasury, or taxes, and discussion of the connection between fiscal and monetary policy is limited to a brief argument that governments in the Third World are generally biased towards low interest rates because they are typically the largest borrower in any economy.

By implication, government is seen to be in the same position as any other economic agent, financing its spending either by running down deposit balances, or through borrowing from financial institutions. Hence, relations between the state money approach and the endogenous money approach remain relatively unclear. It is somewhat surprising that fiscal effects on reserves are largely ignored in the endogenous money literature, because these are potentially many times larger than the quantities of reserves added or drained by central bank operations. Some of those who adopt the endogenous money approach have even argued that central bank behaviour should be analysed separately from fiscal operations, as the central bank is formally independent of the treasury in many nations.

In reality, however, the central bank's desire to set and hit overnight rate targets means that it cannot be independent of the treasury—in the sense that any undesired impact of fiscal operations on banking system reserves must be immediately and completely offset by central bank operations. All else equal, treasury spending leads to a credit to banking system reserves while tax payments lead to a debit, thus, treasury deficits lead to net credits. In practice, daily operations of the treasury would almost always generate either net credits or net debits even if the budget were balanced over the course of the year for the simple reason that tax payments on any given day would differ from government spending on that day. Hence, the treasury and central bank have created complex procedures that allow them to closely coordinate activities to minimize effects on reserves. These reserve effects of fiscal operations have been a central concern of the Chartalist literature.

None of this really requires revision of the horizontalist, or more generally the endogenous money, approach that is consistent with both the credit and the state money approaches. According to the state money approach, the state chooses the unit of account (the dollar, for example) in which the privately-issued credit moneys are denominated. The state also chooses which moneys it will accept in payment of taxes. In modern sovereign nations with their own domestic, floating, currencies, this is always an inconvertible, high powered, money (liabilities of the treasury and central bank). Private banks help in clearing between the government and the private sector, since most taxes are "paid" using bank accounts and most recipients of treasury checks deposit them into private banks.

In these operations, the private banks act as intermediaries making payments to the government on behalf of their depositors, and crediting depositors with government payments. The central bank and treasury then coordinate activities to offset undesired impacts on bank reserves, allowing the central bank to exogenously set and hit the overnight rate target. The high powered money accepted by the state in such countries is always a credit money, a liability of the treasury or central bank, and hence operates according to Innes' fundamental law of credit—or the law of reflux cited by the followers of the endogenous money approach. That is to say, state liabilities (HPM) are destroyed when they return to the state, mostly in tax payments or bond purchases by the non-government sector.

Still, we are left with a question: must an endogenous money approach adopt a chartalist, or state money, approach? An endogenous money approach could possibly locate the origins of money in barter, or in a primordial "free market" economy free from government intrusion (as in Parguez and Seccareccia 2003). As discussed above, it is not so important to finally uncover the "true" origins of money, but rather, to explicate the "nature" of money.

The question is whether a hypothesised stateless but monetary economy sheds any important light on the nature of the modern money we use. Does it help us to understand the "horizontal" monetary policy of modern central banks? Does it reveal the social relations important to the operation of modern capitalist economies? Is our understanding enhanced by presuming that the money of account originated from the spontaneous adoption by individuals of a numeraire to denominate their private credits and debits? In my view, the notion that private credit monies are denominated in a chartalist, national, unit of account is far more illuminating. Further, there is a "pyramidal" monetary hierarchy that rules clearing—most private clearing of accounts takes place on the balance sheets of banks, while banks use the central bank for ultimate, or net, clearing. All of this is in terms of the national currency. Finally, the central bank is the ultimate clearer for private-government transactions. While all credit money—even that issued by the treasury and central bank—represents a liability, this does not put all liabilities on an equal playing field. Further, as almost all liabilities in any given sovereign nation are denominated in the national currency, it becomes possible to clear accounts in that currency using liabilities high in the debt pyramid. At the same time, it becomes desirable to *hold* these liabilities for clearing. If such a hierarchy is important, then starting analysis without a treasury or central bank is deficient.

Today only the *sovereign* government can impose liabilities on others. This puts it in a privileged position because it can create a demand for its own liabilities simply by requiring that taxpayers must deliver government liabilities in payment of taxes. It can also enact legal tender laws and legal reserve requirements to try to provide further privilege to treasury and central bank liabilities.

Finally, the modern state is, of course, a very large entity—hence an important purchaser of output and source of income—which makes its liabilities ubiquitous. Still, if the state did not impose tax liabilities in its currency and require ultimate payments to itself in the form of its treasury and central bank liabilities, it is difficult to believe that its sheer size and its legal tender laws alone would be sufficient to guarantee its current spot at the top of the money hierarchy.

Perhaps the more significant and contentious point concerns the implication of the state money approach for government budgetary issues. As Lerner (1943, 1947) recognised, the "money as a creature of the state" approach leads logically to a "functional finance" view of state budgeting. Because the state spends by emitting its own liability, it does not need tax revenue or the proceeds from borrowing in order to spend. Thus, the first principle of functional finance is that the state should increase taxes only if the public's income were too high (threatening inflation).

The second principle is that the state should "borrow" (sell bonds) only if "it is desirable that the public should have less money and more government bonds." We will return to these points later but it is important to note how the state money approach conflicts with the conventional "government budget constraint" (GBC) notion, according to which state spending must be "financed" by tax revenues, borrowing, or "printing money". In reality, the GBC is nothing but an ex post identity that conflates the state's financial situation with that of a household.

In any case, there is certainly nothing within the horizontalist or endogenous money approaches that requires a GBC approach to government finance. Indeed, it is a fundamental proposition of horizontalism that central bank provision of its own liabilities is limited only by demand—it can potentially supply reserves without limit. The state money approach simply extends that to the treasury—so long as state liabilities are demanded, they can be supplied by the state (central bank plus treasury). In the US, the Federal Reserve (Fed) is, like the treasury, ultimately a "creature of Congress", and notwithstanding various claims about the desirability of the independence of the central bank, this is a typical arrangement in most developed nations. Leaving aside the logical impossibility of central bank "independence" from its treasury (since hitting overnight rate targets requires cooperation between treasury and central bank), the law-making body can direct its central bank to accommodate the treasury's spending as necessary. (Indeed, if it did not, treasury checks could "bounce".) While a GBC holds ex post as an accounting identity, it is not an operational constraint on treasury spending.

In practice, once the central bank has met all the demand for bank reserves by crediting reserves as the treasury spends, additional treasury spending places downward pressure on the overnight rate, forcing bond sales (by the central bank and/or the treasury) to drain excess reserves and keep overnight rates on target. While it might appear that the bond sales "finance" the treasury spending, in reality, bond sales logically are made after the spending takes place, and are undertaken to mop up the excess reserves that would push overnight rates below target.

We, thus, return to the second principle of functional finance: bonds should be sold only if the private sector holds more HPM than desired, a situation that is manifested by overnight rates falling below target. Hence, the functional finance approach is ultimately consistent with the endogenous money approach that insists that reserves are non-discretionary, indeed, the second principle of functional finance can be seen as a corollary of horizontalism—that bond sales are undertaken only to drain excess reserves. Thus, bond sales, even by the treasury, are non-discretionary and permit the central bank to exogenously hit interest rate targets.

Finally, note that both Keynesians and Institutionalists insist that *at the aggregate level,* saving does not finance investment, rather, that investment spending creates saving flows. In the expanded model, investment plus government spending *injections* determine aggregate saving plus taxes *leakages*; or investment plus the budget deficit creates an equivalent amount of saving. There is thus a link between endogenous money and the recognition that saving does not finance investment, rather, expansion of loans finances increased spending (of any type).

Just as saving (a leakage) cannot finance investment (an injection), neither can taxes (a leakage) finance government spending (an injection) nor can saving (a leakage) finance a budget deficit (a net injection) because logically the injections must come first to generate the income that is then lost through the leakages. Careful analysis of balance sheets (a record of stocks that accumulate flows) strengthens the argument that taxes cannot provide a prior source of finance of government spending. While both investment and saving can take place on the balance sheets of the private sector, in the form of private credit money, both government spending and taxes must ultimately involve the balance sheets of the government sector (treasury and central bank).

It is not possible for taxpayers and their banks to clear accounts with the government in HPM unless there is a mechanism for advance provision of the HPM to be used in clearing. Government spending is the primary source of HPM, although government (treasury, central bank, or other agents of government) can also lend HPM, purchase assets from the private sector, or provide HPM through transfer payments. Hence, Lerner's functional finance and chartalist approaches (or, money as a creature of the state approach) are consistent with the usual Keynesian and Institutionalist views of the temporal relation between injections and leakages: the state must spend its liabilities into existence before they can be redeemed in taxation.

As Lerner argued, the purpose of government bond sales is not to borrow reserves (the government's own IOU), but to offer an interest-earning alternative to undesired reserves that would otherwise drive the overnight rate towards zero. Note that if the central bank paid interest on excess reserves, the treasury would never need to sell bonds because the overnight interest rate could never fall below the rate paid by the central bank on excess reserves. Note also that in spite of the widespread belief that government deficits push up interest rates, they actually reduce the overnight rate to zero unless the treasury and central bank coordinate efforts to drain the resulting excess reserves. (For many years the overnight interest rate in Japan has been kept at zero, in spite of government deficits that reached 8 per cent of GDP, merely by keeping some excess reserves in the banking system.) On the other hand, budget surpluses drain reserves, causing a shortage that drives up the overnight rate unless the central bank and treasury buy and/or retire government debt. Needless to say, orthodoxy has got the interest rate effects of government budgets exactly backwards.

MODERN MONETARY SYSTEMS IN THE GLOBAL

Domestic monetary systems are today very much alike in all the major countries of the world.

They have three levels:

1. The holders of money (the "public") — individuals, businesses, governmental units;
2. Commercial banks (privately or governmentally owned), which borrow from the public, mainly by taking their deposits, and make loans to individuals, firms, or governments; and
3. Central banks, which have a monopoly on the issue of certain types of money, serve as the bankers for the central government and the commercial banks, and have the power to determine the quantity of money.

The public holds its money as:

- Currency (including coin) and
- Bank deposits.

CONSISTS OF CURRENCY SYSTEM

In most countries the bulk of the currency consists of notes issued by the central bank. In the United Kingdom these are Bank of England notes; in the United States, Federal Reserve notes; and so on. It is hard to say precisely what "issued by the central bank" means. In the United States, for example, the currency bears the words "Federal Reserve Note," but these notes are not obligations of the Federal Reserve Banks in any meaningful sense. The holder who presents them to a Federal Reserve Bank has no right to anything except other pieces of paper adding up to the same face value. The situation is much the same in most other countries.

The other major item of currency held by the public is coin. In almost all countries this is token coin, worth as metal much less than its face value. In countries with a history of high inflation, the public may choose to use foreign currency as a medium of exchange and standard of value. The U.S., dollar is chosen most often. Although the dollar is not the currency with lowest average rate of inflation in the years after World War II, it compensates by having lowest costs of information or recognition. Society agrees on the use of dollars, not by a formal decision but from knowledge that others recognise the dollar and accept it as a means of payment. Estimates suggest that as much as two-thirds of the dollars in circulation are outside the United States. They can be found in Russia, Argentina, and many other Latin American and Asian countries.

Bank Deposits: A Part of the Money Holdings

Bank deposits are counted also as part of the money holdings of the public. In the 19th century most economists regarded only currency and coin, including gold and other metals, as "money." They treated deposits as claims to money. As deposits became more and more widely held, and as a larger fraction of transactions came to be effected by check, economists started to include not the checks, but the deposits they transferred, as money on a par with currency and coin.

The definition of money has been the subject of much dispute. The chief point at issue is which categories of bank deposits to call money and which to regard as near money. Many economists include as money only deposits transferable by check (demand deposits). Others include non-checking deposits, such as "time deposits" in commercial banks. Still others include deposits in other financial institutions, such as savings banks, savings and loan associations, and so on.

The term deposits is highly misleading. It connotes something deposited for safekeeping, like currency in a safe-deposit box. Bank deposits are not like that. When one brings currency to a bank for "deposit," the bank does not put the currency in a vault and keep it there. It may put a small fraction of the currency in the vault as "reserves," but it will lend most of it to someone else or buy an investment—that is, a bond or some other security. As part of the inducement to depositors to lend it money, it provides facilities for transferring demand deposits from one person to another by check.

The deposits of commercial banks are assets of their holders but liabilities of the banks. The assets of the banks consist of "reserves" — currency plus deposits at other banks (including the central bank) — and "earning assets" — loans plus investments in the form of bonds and other securities. The banks' reserves are only a small fraction of the aggregate deposits. Initially, in the history of banking, the amount of reserves held was determined by each bank separately in terms of its judgement of the likely demands for withdrawal of deposits. The growth of deposits enabled the total quantity of money (including deposits) to be larger than the total sum available to be held as reserves. A bank that received, say, \$100 in gold might add (25 per cent) \$25 to its reserves and lend out \$75. But the recipient of the \$75 loan would spend it. Some of those who received gold this way would hold it as gold, but others would deposit it in a bank.

For example, if two-thirds was redeposited, on average, some bank or banks would find \$50 added to deposits and to reserves. The receiving bank would repeat the process, adding (25 per cent) \$12.50 to its reserves and lending out \$37.50.

When this process worked itself out fully, total deposits would have increased by \$200, bank reserves would have increased by \$50, and \$50 of the initial \$100 deposited would have been retained as "currency outside banks." There would be \$150 more money in total than before (deposits up by \$200, currency outside banks down by \$50). Although no individual bank created money, the system as a whole did. This multiple expansion process lies at the heart of the modern monetary system.

History of Credit and Money

The history of money is a story of repeated innovations that changed the ways in which the public transacted. Credit cards, debit cards, and automatic transfers are among the many innovations in the years after World War II. A credit card is not money. It provides an efficient way to obtain credit at a bank or financial institution. It obviates the seller's need to know about the credit standing and repayment habits of the borrower.

For a fee that the merchant pays the bank, the bank that issues the credit card makes a loan to the buyer and pays the merchant promptly. The buyer then has a debt that it settles by making payment to the credit card company. Instead of carrying more money, or making credit arrangements with many merchants, the buyer makes a single money payment for purchases from many merchants, at the end of the month. Or, the buyer can pay a fraction of the total debt with interest on the remaining balance.

Before credit cards existed, a buyer could arrange a loan at a bank. The bank would credit the buyer's deposit account. The buyer could then pay for his or her purchases by writing checks. The merchant would bear more of the costs of collecting payment and the costs of acquiring information about the buyer's credit standing. With credit cards, the credit card company, often a bank, bears many of these costs.

A debit card differs from a credit card in the way the debt is extinguished. The issuing bank deducts the payment from the customer's account at the time of purchase. The loan is paid immediately. The merchant receives payment in the same way as with the use of a credit card. Electronic transmission of information permits the bank to refuse payment if the buyer's deposit balance is insufficient.

Electronic Money in Modern Financial Systems

Items used as money in modern financial systems have some combination of attributes that reduce costs or increase convenience. Units of money are readily divisible, easily transported and transferred, and recognised instantly. Legal tender status guarantees final settlement. Currency protects anonymity, avoids record keeping, and permits lower costs of payment. But currency can be lost, stolen or forged, so it is used most often for relatively small transactions or where anonymity is valued highly.

Information processing reduces costs of transfer, record keeping, and acquiring information. "Electronic money" is the name given to several different ways in which the public and financial and non-financial firms use electronic transfers as part of the payments system. Since most of these transfers do not introduce a new medium of exchange (money), electronic transfer is a more appropriate name than electronic money.

Three very different types of transfer can be distinguished. First, depositors can use electronic transfers to withdraw currency from their accounts using automatic teller machines (ATM). This works like a debit card. Or, they can use the ATM to deposit checks to their accounts or repay bank loans. The ATM machine accepts these transactions on weekends, holidays, and at any time of the day. It makes money more available and more convenient to use, but it does not replace the assets used as money.

Second, "smart cards" contain a computer chip that records the balance on the card and can make and receive payments. Users buy the smart card with currency or deposits and can use the card in place of currency. The issuer holds the balance (float) and thus earns interest that may pay for maintaining the system. Most often, the cards have a single purpose or use such as making telephone calls, paying parking meters, or using urban transit systems.

They retain the anonymity of currency, but they are not "generally accepted" as a means of payment beyond their dedicated purpose. There has been considerable speculation that smart cards will replace currency and bring in the "cashless society," but there are several obstacles. Either users will have to purchase many special purpose cards or producers will have to find a way to record and transfer balances from many users to many payees. Further, maintaining the generalised transfer system is more costly than using the government's currency.

The automated clearinghouse is an alternative means of making deposits and paying bills. These systems transfer existing deposit balances, avoid the use of checks, and speed payments and settlement. Third, many large payments to settle securities or foreign exchange transactions between financial institutions now use electronic transfcr systems that net payments and receipts and transfer central bank reserves or clearinghouse deposits for net settlement. Some transactions between creditors and debtors give rise to claims against commodity or financial assets. These may at first be barter transactions that are not settled promptly by paying conventional money. Such transactions economise on cash balances and increase the velocity, or rate of turnover, of money.

Central Banking System

Modern banking systems hold fractional reserves against deposits. If many depositors choose to withdraw their deposits as currency, the size of the banking system shrinks. A run on the bank — a sudden withdrawal of deposits as currency or, in earlier times, as gold or silver — can cause banks to run out of reserves and be forced to close. Bank panics of this kind occurred many times. After 1866 in Great Britain, but not until 1934 in the United States, government learned to use the central bank, or some other government institution, to prevent bank runs.

The Bank of England was the first modern central bank, serving as the model for many others. It was established as a private bank in 1694 but by the mid 19th century had become largely an agency of the government. In 1945, the U.K., government nationalised the Bank. The Bank of France was established as a governmental institution by Napoleon in 1800. In the United States, the 12 Federal Reserve Banks, together with the Board of Governors in Washington, D.C., constitute the Federal Reserve System. The Reserve Banks are technically owned by their member commercial banks, but this is a pure formality. Member banks get only a fixed annual percentage dividend on their stock and have no real power over the bank's policy decisions. To all intents and purposes, the Federal Reserve is an independent, governmental agency. The notes issued by a central bank (or other governmental agency) plus deposits at the central bank are called monetary base. When held as bank reserves, each dollar or pound or euro becomes the base for several dollars or pounds or euros of commercial bank loans and deposits. Earlier in monetary history, the size of the monetary base was limited by the amount of gold or silver owned. There is no longer a formal limit to the amount of notes and deposits that a central bank may have as liabilities.

The way in which a central bank increases or decreases the monetary base is, typically, by making loans (discounting) or by buying and selling government securities (open-market operations) or foreign assets. If, for example, the Federal Reserve System purchases $1,000,000 of government securities, it pays for these securities by a check on itself, adding $1,000,000 to its assets and $1,000,000 to its liabilities. The seller can take the check to a Federal Reserve Bank, which will exchange it for $1,000,000 in Federal Reserve notes. Or the seller may deposit the check at a commercial bank, and the bank will in turn present it to a Federal Reserve Bank. The latter "pays" the check by making an entry on its books increasing that bank's deposits by $1,000,000. The bank may, in turn, transfer this sum to a borrower, who again will convert it into Federal Reserve notes or deposit it.

The important point is that these bookkeeping operations simply record a process whereby the central bank has created, out of thin air as it were, additional base money — the direct counterpart of printing Federal Reserve notes. Similarly, if the central bank sells government securities, it destroys base money. The total quantity of money at any time depends on the stock of base money and on the preferences of the public as to the relative amounts of money it wishes to hold as currency and as deposits and on the preferences of the banks as to the ratio they wish to maintain between their reserves and their deposits. The reserve ratio is, of course, dominated by legal reserve requirements, where they exist. Banks hold Treasury bills and other short-term assets to provide additional liquidity, but they also hold some reserves in the form of currency to cash checks or pay withdrawals from their automated teller machines (ATM).

It follows that, by controlling the amount of the monetary base and by other, less important means, a central bank can vary the total nominal, quantity of money as it wishes within broad limits. The major problem of modern monetary policy is how the central bank should use this power.

Money has an internal and external price. The internal price is the price level of domestic goods and services. The external price is the nominal exchange rate. The principal responsibility of a modern central bank differs with the choice of monetary standard. If the country has a fixed exchange rate, the central bank buys or sells foreign exchange on demand to maintain stability in the exchange rate.

When sales by the central bank are too brisk, growth of the monetary base, and the quantity of money and credit, slows and interest rates increase. The rise in interest rates attracts foreign investors and deters local investors from investing abroad. Also, the increase in interest rates slows domestic expansion and reduces upward pressure on domestic prices. When the central bank's purchases are too brisk, money growth increases and interest rates fall inducing domestic expansion and stimulating an increase in prices.

If the country has a floating exchange rate, it must choose a policy to go with the floating rate. At times in the past, many countries expected their central bank to pursue several different objectives. Eventually, countries recognised that this was an error because it focussed the central bank on short-term goals at the expense of longer-term price stability. After the high inflation of the 1970s, in Europe and the United States, and the hyper-inflations in Latin America and Israel, many central banks and governments recognised an old truth: the main objective of a central bank under floating rates should be to stabilise the domestic price level, thereby maintaining the internal value of money.

Increased awareness of this primary responsibility led to lower rates of inflation in the 1980s and 1990s, although central banks continued to be concerned about employment and recession in addition to price stability. Several adopted rules or procedures to control money growth by adjusting interest rates in response to both inflation and deviations of output from its long-term growth rate. Following New Zealand and Great Britain, several countries adopted inflation targets, one or two year's ahead, and adjusted current policy to reach the target.

MONETARY THEORY IN ECONOMY

Economic theory distinguishes between real and nominal values, between values stated in current dollars, pounds, or euros and the same quantities adjusted by the price level. The latter is a real value, the (real) quantity of goods, services and assets that money will buy, or the real purchasing power of the money stock. The relation between money and what it will buy has always been a central issue of monetary theory. Economists have generally held that the level of prices is determined mainly by the quantity of money. But precisely how the quantity of money affects the level of prices, and what the effects are of changes in the quantity of money, have been conceptualised in different ways at different times. There are two principal issues. First, what determines the demand for money — the amount of money that the public willingly holds? Second, how do changes in the stock of money affect the price level and other nominal values?

THE DEMAND FOR MONEY IN BANK

The government or its central bank determines the nominal quantity of money that circulates and is held. The public determines money's real value. If the central bank provides more money than the public wants to hold, the public spends the excess on goods, services, or assets. The additional spending cannot reduce the nominal money stock, but the spending bids up the prices of non-money objects; too much money chases the limited stock of goods and assets. The rise in prices lowers the real value of the money stock until the public holds the desired real value. Conversely, if the central bank provides less money than the public desires to hold, spending slows. Prices fall, thereby raising the level of the real stock.

The amount of desired real balances is not a fixed number. It depends on the opportunity cost of holding money, the direct return to holding money, and income or wealth. A short-term, interest rate is the usual measure of the opportunity cost of holding money, but money holders operate on many different markets, so other relative prices may include other relevant opportunity costs. Inflation raises market interest rates and, thus, the opportunity cost of holding money. In countries experiencing rapid inflation, the real value of the money stock shrinks because people choose to hold less of their wealth in this form. Ending inflation causes a jump down in opportunity cost and a jump up in real balances.

Currency pays no interest, and checking deposits typically receives relatively little interest return. Most of the direct return to money balances takes the form of transaction services and convenience. Innovations in the payments system change the demand for money, reducing the amount held, but also increase the service yield of the remaining units. Deflation also raises the return to holding money by giving each nominal unit greater command over goods and assets. Income, wealth, or some measure of transactions volume also influences the amount of money that people willingly hold. As the real value of these measures increase so, too, does the amount of real balances.

Transmission of Monetary Impulses

From the very earliest systematic work on economics, observers have noted a relation between the stock of money and the price level. Often, the relation was one of proportionality; the price level rose in direct proportion to the increase in money. By the middle of the 18th century, systematic observers recognised that changes in money affect output first, but this effect vanishes once prices adjust fully. The quantity theory of money was an early formulation of that insight. Central to this theory is the distinction between the nominal quantity of money and the real quantity of money. The nominal quantity is expressed in whatever units are used to designate money—talents, shekels, pounds, euros, dollars, yen, and so on. The real quantity is expressed in terms of the volume of goods and services that the money will purchase. The quantity theory assumes that what ultimately matters to holders of money is the real rather than the nominal quantity. If this is so, then—whatever factors may determine the nominal quantity of money—it is the holders of money who determine the real quantity and, in the process, the price level.

The following is a hypothetical example. In a certain community the quantity of money in existence is $1,000,000, and the total income of the community is $10,000,000 a year. On the average, each member of the community holds an amount of money equal in value to one-tenth of a year's income, or to 5.2 weeks' income. Put differently, the income velocity of circulation is equal to 10 per year; that is, each $1 on the average is paid out 10 times a year. For the sake of simplicity there are no business enterprises; the members of the community buy and sell services from and to one another.

The quantity of money is somehow then doubled, but in such a way that no one expects the quantity to change again. Each member of the community will regard himself as better off. Each now has 10.4 weeks' income in the form of cash instead of the previous 5.2 weeks'. If everyone were to hold onto the extra cash, nothing further would happen. But people will try to spend it to reduce the amount of wealth held as money. One person's spending, however, is another's receipts. All the people together cannot spend more than all the people receive. The attempt of each to do so is bound to be frustrated. In the attempt to spend more than they receive, people will simultaneously try to buy more of various services from each other and to sell less. To induce others to sell, they will offer higher prices; to induce others not to buy, they will ask higher prices. Whether the quantity sold goes up or down depends on whether the attempt to buy more is stronger or weaker than the attempt to sell less.

But in either case total spending is sure to go up and so are total income and prices paid. When income has doubled, to $20,000,000, the amount of money in existence will again be equal in value to 5.2 weeks' income. The community will have succeeded in reducing its real cash balances to their former level, not by reducing nominal balances but by raising incomes and prices. The process of adjustment may not be smooth; spending may go too far and leave people with real balances that are too small, requiring a subsequent fall in the price level; but the final position will tend towards a doubling of prices, and the previous real flows of services will be resumed with no one any better off than before the new money was distributed.

This simple example embodies most of the basic principles of monetary theory:

- The central distinction between the nominal and the real quantity of money;
- The equally crucial contrast between the alternatives open to the individual and to the community as a whole. To each individual separately (in the hypothetical example and in the real world) it looks as if income is outside personal control, but each individual can determine how much cash to hold. To the community as a whole, the total amount of cash is fixed, but it is able to determine the size of its income in dollars;
- The importance of attempts.

The attempt of people as a whole to spend more than they receive, even though doomed to frustration, has the effect of raising total nominal expenditures and receipts.

Some of the main propositions about the transmission of monetary changes are:

- The rate of growth of the quantity of money is consistently, though not precisely, related to the rate of growth of nominal income. That is, if the quantity of money grows rapidly, so will nominal income, and conversely. The velocity of circulation, though not constant, is reasonably predictable.
- This relation is not obvious, mainly because it takes time for changes in monetary growth to affect income.
- On the average, a change in the rate of monetary growth produces a change in the rate of growth of nominal income six to nine months later. But this is an average.
- If the rate of monetary growth is reduced, then about six to nine months later the rate of growth of nominal income and also of physical output will decline, but the rate of price rise will be affected very little. There will be downward pressure on prices only as a gap emerges between actual and potential output.
- The effect on prices comes on the average about a year after the effect on nominal income and output, so that the total delay between a change in monetary growth and a change in the rate of inflation averages roughly two years.
- The above relationships are variable. There is many a slip between the monetary change and the income change.
- Monetary changes affect output only in the short run—though "short run" may mean three to five years. Over the longer run, the rate of monetary growth affects only prices. What happens to output in the long run depends on such "real" factors as the enterprise, ingenuity, and industry of the people; the extent of thrift; the structure of industry and government, the rule of law; the relations among nations; and so on.
- It follows that inflation — a sustained increase in the rate of price change — cannot occur without a more rapid increase in the quantity of money than in output. There are, of course, many possible reasons for monetary growth —gold discoveries, the manner in which government spending is financed, and even the manner in which private spending is financed. The price level may rise or fall for other reasons, for example changes in productivity. These produce one-time changes, not sustained rates of change.
- Government spending may or may not be inflationary. It will be

inflationary if it is financed by creating money—that is, by printing currency or creating bank deposits—and if the resultant rate of monetary growth exceeds the rate of growth of output. If it is financed by taxes or by borrowing from the public, the main effect is that the government spends the funds instead of someone else.

- One of the most difficult things to explain is the way in which a change in the quantity of money affects income. Generally, the initial effect is not on income at all but on the prices of existing assets (bonds, equities, houses, and other physical capital). An increased rate of monetary growth raises the amount of cash people (or businesses) have relative to other assets. The holders of the excess cash will try to correct this imbalance by buying other assets. But one person's spending is another's receipts. All the people together cannot change the amount of cash all hold—only the monetary authorities can do that. Their attempts will tend, however, to raise the prices of assets and to reduce interest rates. These changes will in turn encourage spending to produce new assets. Thus the initial effect on balance sheets is translated into an effect on income and spending. In this connection many economists emphasize such assets as durable consumer goods and other real property, and they regard market interest rates as only a small part of the whole complex of relevant rates.
- One important feature of this mechanism is that a change in monetary growth affects interest rates in one direction at the outset and in the opposite direction later on. More rapid monetary growth at first tends to lower interest rates. But later on, as it raises spending and stimulates price inflation, it also produces a rise in the demand for loans that will tend to raise nominal interest rates. Taking the opposite case, a slower rate of monetary growth at first raises interest rates, but later on, as it reduces spending and price inflation, it lowers interest rates. This inconsistent relation between the quantity of money and interest rates explains why interest rates are often a misleading guide to monetary policy.
- These propositions clearly imply that monetary policy is important and that what is most important about monetary policy is its effect on the quantity of money, not on bank credit or total credit or interest rates. Wide swings in the rate of change of the quantity of money are evidently destabilising and should be avoided. Beyond this, different economists draw different conclusions. Some conclude that the monetary authorities should make deliberate changes in the rate of monetary growth in order to offset other forces making for instability; these changes should be gradual and small and make allowance for the lags involved. Others

maintain that not enough is known about the relations between changes in the quantity of money and in prices and output to assure that a discretionary monetary policy will do good rather than harm. They believe that a wiser policy would be simply to have the quantity of money grow at a steady rate over time. Most central banks now set a short-term interest rate target and adjust it frequently. Some also set an inflation target to be achieved over several years, and they adjust the interest rate to keep inflation near the target.

- Countries that choose to control domestic prices must allow their exchange rates to float. The central bank or monetary authority cannot control both interest rates and money stock or both money and the exchange rate. It must choose one of the three.
- If the central bank fixes the exchange rate and permits capital to flow in and out freely, it leaves control of money to external forces and must accept the rate of inflation consistent with its exchange rate.

THE ROLE OF THE BANKING SYSTEM IN THE ECONOMY

- *What are the goals of individual banks*: Banks, like any other business, want to make money.
- *How do banks make money*: Besides collecting fees on accounts, the main way banks make money is by issuing loans. The bank takes the money from savings accounts and loans them to other people, businesses or governments. In this course, we will only assume that banks make riskless loans (no one defaults). Throughout our analysis, it may be interesting to think what happens if some people default on their loans.
- *How does bank accounting work*: Pretend you are a bank. If you wanted to make as much money as possible, you would loan as much as possible. Suppose on day 1, I deposited money in the bank. On day 2, the bank loaned all that money. On day 3, I went to get my money out of the bank and it was not there because the bank loaned it out. If I thought this would happen, I probably would not have kept my money in the bank.

For this reason, the government decided that it would require that all banks keep a minimum percentage of the deposits on hand in their vault. That way, if people come in to get some money, their money would be there.

BANK ACCOUNTING

In accounting, total assets must equal total liabilities. Assets for a bank are the amount of money they have in reserves (in their vault and at the Federal Reserve) plus the amount of loans they make. The total liabilities are the deposits that people make in their bank. Total deposits must equal total loans plus total cash in the vault (total reserves) or

$$TD = TL + TR; (1)$$

TD = Total deposits
TL = Total Loans
TR = Total Reserves

If this relationship holds, then the change in total deposits must equal the change in total loans plus the change in total reserves. (The change in assets must equal the change in liabilities):

$$\Delta TD = \Delta TL + \Delta TR \ (2)$$

Equations 1 and 2 are very important to the analysis of the banking system.

A Simple Example of the Banking System

With all the above stuff on the banking system in mind, let us look at how bank accounting works. Suppose that I deposit \$100 into bank A (suppose further that this money was previously NOT in the banking system – it was under my mattress). Also assume that the required reserve ratio set by the government is.2 (the bank has to keep 20 per cent of all liabilities as deposits). The following would be the accounting statement for the bank.

Assets	Liabilities
Change in TR = 20	Change in TD = 100
	Change in TL = 80
Change in Assets = 100	Change in Liabilities = 100

Notice that total assets equal the total liabilities. (Total Assets = 100; Total liabilities equal 100). How do we get the numbers in the above chart? TD is easy. I put 100 into the bank. Total deposits should increase by 100. In other words, $\Delta TD = 100$.

The change in reserves is not difficult. The government requires that the bank keep some of that deposit in the vault. The amount they keep will be the required reserve ratio times the initial deposit.

$$\Delta TR = m^* \Delta TD; \text{ where } m = \text{reserve ratio. } (3).$$

In this example, $\Delta TR = .2^* \ 100$ or 20.

If $\Delta TD = \Delta TL + \Delta TR$ then the change in TL = 80. We are assuming that the bank will lend out all the money that it can. Of the \$100 in new deposits, the bank only has to keep \$20 as required reserves. The remaining \$80 can be loaned out to other economic agents.

Suppose that they lent the \$80 out to you. (\$80 was created by the banking system – consumption was NOT created, but purchasing power was!). Now suppose you bought a bike and the bike shop that you purchased it from put the revenues from the sale of the bike into their bank. (We will assume your bank is the same as mine. This is not necessary, but it is just easier to think about. If it makes you feel better, think of the banking system that we are analysing as being for the banking system as a whole). Let us look at the accounting record for this transaction:

Assets	Liabilities
Change in TR = 16	Change in TD = 18
Change in TL = 64	Change in Assets = 80
Change in Liabilities = 80	

The bike shop puts $80 into their bank. TD increases by $80. The bank has to keep $16 in required reserves. It could loan out the remaining $64 to someone else. Again, the banking system has created $64 of purchasing power by making loans.

From my initial deposit of $100, let us look at the effects on the banking system:

Assets	Liabilities
Change in TR from transaction 1 = 20	Change in TD from transaction 1 = 100
Change in TR from transaction 2 = 16	Change in TD from transaction 2 = 80 Total
Change in TR from both transaction = 36	Total Change in TD from both transaction = 180
Change in TL from transaction 1 = 80	
Change in TL from transaction 2 = 64	
Total change in TL from both transaction = 144	
Total change in Assets = 180	Total change in Liabilities = 180

The two transactions have created $144 in new loans. The banking system has created $144 of money. The last $64 that was loaned from the bank will be re-deposited and the process will continue.

The Role of the Fed and the Money Supply

Why is the money multiplier important? Because the Fed - if it wants to increase the money supply by $X, does not have to buy $X worth of bonds on the open market. If the assumptions we have hold, the Fed only has to buy (m*$X) bonds. Doing so, they can let the money multiplier work.

Remember this as we start to put our model together: the Fed sets the money supply urve!!! If they want the money supply to be $Y - they make it $Y. The Fed is the only one who has real control over the money supply. The Treasury, by printing money, could also have control - printing more money will increase the money supply - but, this will only happen if the Fed lets it. The Fed can simply undo the actions of the Treasury by selling bonds on the open market which will reduce the money supply.

THE ROLE OF HOUSEHOLDS AND MONEY DEMAND

If the Fed controls the money supply, who controls the money demand? Households and firms control money demand. We are talking about the demand for money as opposed to the demand for some other asset. We can choose to hold our savings in many forms - money in the bank - stocks, home equity, etc... We are talking about money in the bank - cash, checking accounts, saving accounts.

What are the Reimbursement of Money

We can transact with it (it is hard to go to Dominick's and buy groceries using equity in your home). We like money because it is liquid - we can buy stuff with it. The cost of money is that it offers a really low return. In terms of cash and checking accounts - it may even earn a zero nominal return (a negative real return). So the cost of holding liquidity (money) is the forgone interest we would lose. With money in our pocket and in most checking accounts, we lose both the real return and the expected inflation return! This is one of the few places in our class where nominal returns matter.

When you think about the demand for money, think about checking accounts and cash in your pocket (this is M1 definition of money for those who like to read the book). We are going to talk about real money demand - the effect of money demand once we account for price changes - think of the example I gave in class as to why prices are important. For a given amount of Y you would like to buy, if the price of Y increases - you need more money. If the price of Y increases by Z per cent, the amount of additional money you would need would increase by Z%. As a result, we are going to talk about the real demand for money.

As seen in class - there are only three things that affect the real demand for money:

1. GDP (Y)
2. Real interest rates (r)
3. Expected inflation.

We draw money demand in real money, real interest rate space {Y,r}. As r increases, for a given Y and expected inflation, nominal interest rates will increase. It is more expensive to hold money. As a result, our demand for money will fall. *This is why the money demand curve slopes down!!!!*

What shifts the money demand curve? Y and expected inflation. Again, the only things that affect the money demand curve are the costs and benefits of holding money - the benefit of holding money is the ability to transact - the cost is the forgone interest of holding money in liquid form which usually earns a zero return.

If Y goes up, that means there are more goods in the economy. The more goods in the economy, the more we need to transact (we have to buy those goods somehow). We need more money. The benefit of money is the transaction demand. That says, when we want to transact more, we want to hold more money. An increase in Y will increase our demand for money at every given real interest rate (holding expected inflation fixed). When expected inflation increases, for a given Y and r, the cost of holding money increases. Why? If r is fixed and expected inflation increases, nominal interest rates will increase. Increasing nominal interest rates will make holding money more expensive - as a result, the demand for money will fall!!!!

Basically, at the end of this lecture, you should realise that the Fed controls M -the nominal money supply. The real money supply = M/P. We will solve for prices in Notes 9. The money demand is a function of Y and expected inflation. Money demand = money supply which will set the interest rates in the economy (actually, the Fed is targeting interest rates and sets money supply accordingly). This interest rate also has to clear investment and savings.

The heterodox economists have been paying attention in three approaches to money: the credit money, state money, and endogenous money approaches. The primary purpose of this article will be to draw out explicitly the links among the three approaches to money. We begin by discussing the nature of money via historical and sociological analysis, contrasting the typical orthodox story that focuses on a natural and largely asocial approach to money with a heterodox, social approach. It will be seen that views on the nature of money are important for understanding differences between orthodox and heterodox approaches to money. We next turn to relatively brief surveys of the three alternative heterodox approaches before discussing a possible integration.

The state money move towards is associated with Knapp, Keynes, and Lerner, while the credit money approach is associated with Schumpeter and more loosely with some of the progenitors of the endogenous money approach—especially with the French-Italian "circuit" approach, and also with Minsky's views. Innes provided an integration of the state money and credit money approaches, but his work was long forgotten. Post Keynesians (and to a lesser extent, Institutionalists) have participated in a modern revival of an endogenous money approach that had been common in the nineteenth century, although most recent writers on the endogenous money approach have not explored links to the credit money and state money approaches.

While this article will not trace the development of the endogenous money approach, nor will it examine recent controversies among the camps of its supporters, it will show how the endogenous money approach relates to the state money and credit money approaches. By intention, what follows is a survey that attempts to find common ground in heterodox approaches, not only contrasting the shared general approach to money with the orthodox approach, but also pointing the direction towards a possible integration acceptable to heterodoxy.

2

Money: Nature Functions and Significance

TROUBLES OF BARTER SYSTEM

The initial level of swap is recognized since barter swap. Under barter economy, the goods are exchanged for goods. This implies that if one wants some commodity, this can be exchanged only through giving some other commodity in swap.

In short, barter economy, signifies the swap of goods by the medium of goods. These days, barter transactions have virtually disappeared. Several difficulties were faced throughout barter transactions. Usually, the largest difficulties faced were since follows.

LACK OF DOUBLE COINCIDENCE OF WANTS

Barter transactions can be possible only when two persons desiring swap of commodities should have such commodities which are mutually needed through each other. For instance, if Ram wants cloth, which Shyma has, then Ram should have such commod-ity which Shyma wants. In the absence of such coincidence of wants, there will be no swap. Though, it is extremely hard to discover such persons where there is coincidence of wants. One had to face such difficulties in barter economy because of which this organization had to be abandoned.

Luck of Division

The second difficulty of barter swap relates to the swap of such commodities which cannot be divided. For instance, a person has a cow and he wants cloth, food granules, and other things of consumption. Under such a term, swap can be possible only when he finds a person, who is in require of a cow and has all such commodities, but it is extremely hard to get such a person. Likewise the second trouble relates to the swap of such commodities which cannot be divided into pieces, because in this type of situation, a large commodity like cow cannot be divided into little pieces for creation payment of the goods of smaller value.

Lack of a General Measure of Value

The major trouble in the barter swap was the lack of general measure of value i.e., there was no such commodity in lieu of which all commodities could be bought and sold. In such a situation, while facilitating the swap of a commodity its value was to be expressed in all commodities, such since one yard cloth is equal to ½ kilogram of potato etc. It was an extremely hard proposition and made swap virtually impossible. Now, with the detection of money, this difficulty has been completely eliminated.

Lack of Store of Value

In a barter economy, the store of value could be done only in the shape of commodities. Though, we all know that commodities are perishable and they cannot be kept for an extensive time in the store. Because of this difficulty, the accumulation of capital or store of value was extremely hard and without the accumulation of capital, economic progress could not be made. It is because of this cause that since extensive since barter organization sustained, important progress was not made in the world anywhere.

DEVELOPMENT AND TYPES OF MONEY

Money, since we know it today, is the result of an extensive procedure. At the beginning, there was no money. People occupied in barter, the swap of merchandise for merchandise, without value equivalence. Then, a person catching more fish than the necessary for himself and his cluster exchanged his excess fish for the surplus of another person who, for example, had planted and harvested more corn that what he would require. This elementary shape of deal prevailed at the beginning of culture, and may be establish today in the middle of people of primitive economies, in areas where hard access creates money scarce and, even in special situations, where people barter things without regard for their equivalence in value. This is the case, for example, of a child who exchanges with his friend an expensive toy for another of lesser value, which it treasures.

Goods used in barter are usually in their natural state, in row with the habitation circumstances and behaviors urbanized through the cluster, corresponding to elementary requires of the cluster's members. This swap, though, is not free from difficulties, as there is not a general measure of value in the middle of the things bartered.

COMMODITY MONEY

Some commodities, for their utility, came to be more sought than others are. Carried through all, they assumed the role of currency, circulating since a unit of swap for other products and used to assess their value. This was the commodity money. Cattle, largely bovine, was one of the mostly used, and had the advantages of moving for itself, reproducing and rendering services, although there was the risk of diseases and death.

Salt was commodity money, hard to obtain, largely in the interior section of continents, also used since a preservative for food. Both cattle and salt left the spots in the Portuguese language of their function since a swap instrument, since we stay by languages such since pecunia (money) and pecúlio (accumulated money) derived from the Latin job pecus (cattle). The word capital (asset) comes from the Latin capita (head). Likewise, the job salário (salary, compensation, normally in money, due through the employer for the services of an employee) originates from the exploit of sal [salt], in Rome, for payment of services rendered.

Brazil used, in the middle of other commodity moneys, cowry – brought through Africans –, Brazil wood, sugar, cocoa, tobacco and cloth, exchanged in Maranhão in the 17 Century due to the approximately complete lack of money, traded in the shape of yarn balls, skeins, and fabrics. Later, commodities became inconvenient for commercial deals, due to changes in their values, the information of being indivisible and easily perishable, so checking the accumulation of wealth.

Metal

Since soon since man exposed metal, it was used to made utensils and weapons previously made of stone. For its advantages, since the possibility of treasuring, divisibility, simple of transportation and beauty, metal became the largest average of value.

It was exchanged under dissimilar shapes. At the beginning, metal was used in its natural state and later under the shape of ingots and, even, transformed into substances, from rings to bracelets. The metal therefore traded required weight assessment and assaying of its purity at each transaction. Later, metal money gained definite shape and weight, getting a spot indicating its value, indicating also the person responsible for its issue. This measure made transactions faster, since it saved the problem of weighing it and enabled prompt identification of the quantity of metal offered for deal.

MONEY IN THE SHAPE OF SUBSTANCES

Metal things came to be extremely valued commodities. Since its manufacture required, in addition to knowledge of melting, knowing where the metal could be establish in nature, the task was not at the reach of everyone. The increased value of these substances led to its exploit since money and the circulation since money of little-level replicas of metal substances. This is the case of the knife and key coins establish in the East and the talent, a copper or bronze coin with the shape of an animal skin that circulated in Greece and Cyprus.

Ancient Coins

In the 7 century B.C. the first coins resembling current ones emerged: they were little metal pieces, with fixed weight and value, and bearing an official seal that is the spot of who has minted them and also a guaranty of their value. Gold and silver coins are minted in Greece, and little oval ingots are used in Lydia, made of gold and silver alloy described electrum. Coins reflect the mentality of a people and their time. One may discover political, economic, technical, and cultural characteristics in coins. By the impressions establish in coins, we are able to know the effigy of personalities who existed centuries ago. Almost certainly, the first historic character to have his effigy registered in a coin was Alexander the Great, of Macedonia, approximately the year 330 B.C. At the beginning, coin pieces were made through hand in an extremely coarse method, had irregular edges, and were not absolutely equal to one another since today's ones.

Gold, Silver and Copper

The first metals used in coinage were gold and silver. Employment of these metals happened for their rarity, beauty, immunity to corrosion, economic value, and for old religious habits. In primeval cultures, Babylonian priests, knowledgeable in relation to the astronomy, taught to people the secure connection flanked by gold and the sun, silver and the moon. This led to a belief in the magic domination of such metals and of substances made with them. Minting of gold and silver coins was general for several centuries, and pieces were guaranteed through their intrinsic value, that is to say, through the deal value of the metal used in their manufacture. Then, a coin made with twenty grams of gold was exchanged for goods of even value. For several centuries, countries minted their mainly highly valued coins in gold, by silver and copper for lesser value coins. This organization was kept up to the end of the last century, when cupronickel, and later other metallic alloys, became used, and coins came to circulate for their extrinsic value, that is to say, for their face value, which is self-governing from their metal content. With the appearance of paper money, minting of metal coins was restricted to lower values, necessary since transform. In this new role, durability became the mainly requested excellence for coins. Big quantities of contemporary alloys emerged, produced to support the high circulation of transform money.

Paper Money

In the transitional Ages, the keeping of values with goldsmiths, persons trading with gold and silver things, was general. The goldsmith, since a guaranty, delivered a receipt. With time, these receipts came to be used to create payments, circulating from hand to hand, giving origin to paper money. In Brazil, the first bank notes, forerunners of the current notes, were issued through

Banco do Brasil in 1810. They had its value written through hand, since we today do with our checks. With time, in the similar shape it happened with coins, the government came to conduct the issue of notes, controlling counterfeits and securing the domination to pay. Currently, all countries have their central bank in charge of issuing coins and notes. Paper money experienced a development concerning the technique used in their printing. Today, the printing of notes exploits especially prepared paper and many printing procedures, which are complementary to each other, assuring to the final product a great periphery of security and durability circumstances.

Dissimilar Forms

Money has greatly changed its physical aspect beside the centuries. Coins had already extremely little sizes, since the stater, which circulated in Aradus, Phenicia, and some reached big sizes, such since the thaler, a 17 century Swedish copper piece. Although today the circular shape is used in approximately the entire world, there had been oval, square, polygonal, and other forms for coins. They were also minted in dissimilar non-metallic materials, such since wood, leather, and even porcelain. Porcelain coins circulated, in this century, in Germany, when the country was under the economic hardships caused through the war. Bank notes were usually of rectangular lengthwise format, although with great diversity of sizes. There are, even, square notes and those with inscriptions written in the vertical. Bank notes depict the civilization of the issuing country, and we may see in them feature and motivating motifs since landscapes, human kinds, fauna and flora, monuments of ancient and modern architecture, political leaders, historical scenes, etc. Bank notes bear, in addition, inscriptions, usually in the country's official language, although many also bear the similar inscriptions in other idioms. The inscriptions, regularly in English, aim at permitting the piece to be read through a superior number of people.

Monetary Organization

The set of coins and bank notes used through a country shape its monetary organization. The organization is regulated through suitable legislation and organized from a monetary element, its foundation value. Currently approximately all countries exploit a monetary organization of centesimal foundation, in which the coinage dividing the element symbolizes one hundredth of its value. Normally, higher values are expressed in notes while smaller values are represented through coins. The current world trend is that daily expenses be paid with coins. Contemporary metallic alloys enable coins to be more durable than notes, creation them more suitable to the intense exploit of money since transform. The countries, by their central banks, manage and guarantee the issue of money. The set of notes and coins in circulation, the therefore described monetary mass, is constantly renewed by the procedure of sanitation, substitution of worn out and torn notes

Checks

Since coins and notes ceased to be convertible into valuable metal, money became more dematerialized and assumed abstract shapes. One of these shapes is the check that, for simplicity of exploit and security offered, is being adopted through a rising number of people in their day-through-day behaviors. This document, through which one orders payment of a sure amount to its bearer or to a person mentioned in it, aims largely at transactions with bank deposits. The significant role played today in the economy through this shape of payment is due to the innumerable advantages offered through it, speeding transactions with big sums, avoiding hoarding and diminishing the require of transform through being a document completed through hand in the necessary amount.

Money, whatever the shape it has, is not precious for itself, but for the goods and services it may purchase. It is a sort of security giving its bearer the faculty of being creditor of community and take advantage, by his or her purchasing domination, of all conquests of contemporary man. Money was not, hence, invented through a stroke of genius, but stemmed from require, and its development reflects, at each time, the willingness of man to harmonize its monetary instrument to the reality of its economy.

WHAT IS MONEY?

Money is any substance or record that is usually carried since payment for goods and services and repayment of debts in a given socio-economic context or country. The largest functions of money are distinguished since: a medium of swap; an element of explanation; a store of value; and, occasionally in the past, an average of deferred payment. Any type of substance or close verifiable record that fulfills these functions can be measured money. Money is historically an emergent market phenomenon establishing commodity money, but almost all modern money organizations are based on fiat money. Fiat money, like any check or note of debt, is without intrinsic exploit value since a physical commodity.

It derives its value through being declared through a government to be legal tender; that is, it necessity be carried since a shape of payment within the boundaries of the country, for "all debts, public and private". Such laws in practice reason fiat money to acquire the value of any of the goods and services that it may be traded for within the nation that issues it. The money supply of a country consists of currency (banknotes and coins) and bank money (the balance held in checking accounts and savings accounts). Bank money, which consists only of records, shapes through distant the main section of the money supply in urbanized nations.

FUNCTIONS

In the past, money was usually measured to have the following four largest functions, which are summed up in a rhyme establish in older economics textbooks: "Money is a matter of functions four, a medium, a measure, an average, a store." That is, money functions since a medium of swap, an element of explanation, an average of deferred payment, and a store of value. Though, contemporary textbooks now list only three functions, that of medium of swap, element of explanation, and store of value, not considering a average of deferred payment since a distinguished function, but rather subsuming it in the others.

There have been several historical disputes concerning the combination of money's functions, some arguing that they require more separation and that a single element is insufficient to trade with them all. One of these arguments is that the role of money since a medium of swap is in clash with its role since a store of value: its role since a store of value needs holding it without spending, whereas its role since a medium of swap needs it to circulate. Others argue that storing of value is presently deferral of the swap, but does not diminish the information that money is a medium of swap that can be transported both crossways space and time.

The condition 'financial capital' is a more common and inclusive condition for all liquid instruments, whether or not they are a consistently established tender.

Medium of Swap

When money is used to intermediate the swap of goods and services, it is performing a function since a medium of swap. It thereby avoids the inefficiencies of a barter organization, such since the 'double coincidence of wants' trouble.

Element of Explanation

An element of explanation is an average numerical element of measurement of the market value of goods, services, and other transactions. Also recognized since a measure or average of comparative worth and deferred payment, an element of explanation is a necessary prerequisite for the formulation of commercial agreements that involve debt. To function since an 'element of explanation', whatever is being used since money necessity be:

- Divisible into smaller elements without loss of value; valuable metals can be coined from bars, or melted down into bars again.
- *Fungible:* That is, one element or piece necessity is perceived since equivalent to any other, which is why diamonds, jobs of art or real estate are not appropriate since money.
- A specific weight, or measure, or size to be verifiably countable. For

example, coins are often milled with redid edge, therefore that any removal of material from the coin (lowering its commodity value) will be simple to detect.

Store of Value

To act since a store of value, a money necessity is able to be reliably saved, stored, and retrieved – and be predictably usable since a medium of swap when it is retrieved. The value of the money necessity also remains stable in excess of time. Some have argued that inflation, through reducing the value of money, diminishes the skill of the money to function since a store of value.

Average of Deferred Payment

While average of deferred payment is distinguished through some texts, particularly older ones, other texts subsume this under other functions. An "average of deferred payment" is a carried method to settle a debt – an element in which debts are denominated, and the status of money since legal tender, in those jurisdictions which have this concept, states that it may function for the discharge of debts. When debts are denominated in money, the real value of debts may transform due to inflation and deflation, and for sovereign and international debts via debasement and devaluation.

Measure of Value

Money acts since an average measure and general denomination of deal. It is therefore a foundation for quoting and bargaining of prices. It is necessary for developing efficient accounting organizations. But its mainly significant usage is since a way for comparing the values of different substances.

MONEY SUPPLY

In economics, money is a broad condition that refers to any financial instrument that can fulfill the functions of money. These financial instruments jointly are collectively referred to since the money supply of an economy. In other languages, the money supply is the amount of financial instruments within a specific economy accessible for purchasing goods or services. As the money supply consists of several financial instruments (generally currency, demand deposits and several other kinds of deposits), the amount of money in an economy is considered through adding jointly these financial instruments creating a *monetary aggregate*.

Contemporary monetary theory distinguishes in the middle of dissimilar ways to measure the money supply, reflected in dissimilar kinds of monetary aggregates, by a categorization organization that focuses on the liquidity of the financial instrument used since money. The mainly commonly used monetary aggregates (or kinds of money) are conventionally designated M1, M2, and M3.

These are successively superior aggregate categories: M1 is currency (coins and bills) plus demand deposits (such since checking accounts); M2 is M1 plus savings accounts and time deposits under $100,000; and M3 is M2 plus superior time deposits and same institutional accounts. M1 comprises only the mainly liquid financial instruments, and M3 relatively illiquid instruments.

Another measure of money, M0, is also used; unlike the other events, it does not symbolize actual purchasing domination through firms and households in the economy. M0 is foundation money, or the amount of money actually issued through the central bank of a country. It is considered since currency plus deposits of banks and other organizations at the central bank. M0 is also the only money that can satisfy the reserve necessities of commercial banks.

MARKET LIQUIDITY

Market liquidity defines how easily a thing can be traded for another thing, or into the general currency within an economy. Money is the mainly liquid asset because it is universally recognized and carried since the general currency. In this method, money provides consumers the freedom to deal goods and services easily without having to barter. Liquid financial instruments are easily tradable and have low transaction costs. There should be no (or minimal) spread flanked by the prices to buy and sell the instrument being used since money.

KINDS OF MONEY

Currently, mainly contemporary monetary organizations are based on fiat money. Though, for mainly of history, approximately all money was commodity money, such since gold and silver coins. Since economies urbanized, commodity money was eventually replaced through representative money, such since the gold average, since traders establish the physical transportation of gold and silver burdensome. Fiat currencies slowly took in excess of in the last hundred years, especially as the breakup of the Bretton Woods organization in the early 1970s.

Commodity Money

Several things have been used since commodity money such since naturally scarce valuable metals, conch shells, barley, drops etc., since well since several other things that are idea of since having value. Commodity money value comes from the commodity out of which it is made. The commodity itself constitutes the money, and the money is the commodity. Examples of commodities that have been used since mediums of swap contain gold, silver, copper, rice, salt, peppercorns, big stones, decorated belts, shells, alcohol, cigarettes, cannabis, candy, etc. These things were sometimes used in a metric of perceived value in conjunction to one another, in several commodity valuation or Price Organization economies. Exploit of commodity money is same to barter, but commodity money gives an easy and automatic element of explanation for the commodity which is being used since money. Although some gold coins such since the Kruger and are measured legal tender, there is no record of their face value on either face of the coin. The rationale for this is that emphasis is laid on their direct link to the prevailing value of their fine gold content. American Eagles are imprinted with their gold content and legal tender face value.

Representative Money

In 1875, the British economist William Stanley Jevons called the money used at the time since "representative money". Representative money is money that consists of token coins, paper money, or other physical tokens such since certificates that can be reliably exchanged for a fixed quantity of a commodity such since gold or silver. The value of representative money stands in direct and fixed relation to the commodity that backs it, while not itself being collected of that commodity.

Fiat Money

Fiat money or fiat currency is money whose value is not derived from any intrinsic value or guarantee that it can be converted into a precious commodity (such since gold). Instead, it has value only through government order (fiat). Generally, the government declares the fiat currency (typically notes and coins from a central bank, such since the Federal Reserve Organization in the U.S.) to be legal tender, creation it unlawful to not accept the fiat currency since a means of repayment for all debts, public and private.

Some bullion coins such since the Australian Gold Nugget and American Eagle are legal tender, though, they deal based on the market price of the metal content since a commodity, rather than their legal tender face value (which is generally only a little fraction of their bullion value).

Fiat money, if physically represented in the shape of currency (paper or coins) can be accidentally damaged or destroyed. Though, fiat money has an advantage in excess of representative or commodity money, in that the similar laws that created the money can also describe rules for its replacement in case of damage or destruction. For instance, the U.S. government will replace mutilated Federal Reserve notes (U.S. fiat money) if at least half of the physical note can be reconstructed, or if it can be otherwise proven to have been destroyed. Through contrast, commodity money which has been lost or destroyed cannot be recovered.

Coinage

These factors led to the shift of the store of value being the metal itself: at first silver, then both silver and gold, at one point there was bronze since well.

Now we have copper coins and other non-valuable metals since coins. Metals were mined, weighed, and stamped into coins. This was to assure the individual taking the coin that he was receiving a sure recognized weight of valuable metal. Coins could be counterfeited, but they also created a new element of explanation, which helped lead to banking. Archimedes' principle provided the after that link: coins could now be easily tested for their fine weight of metal, and therefore the value of a coin could be determined, even if it had been shaved, debased or otherwise tampered with.

In mainly major economies by coinage, copper, silver, and gold shaped three tiers of coins. Gold coins were used for big purchases, payment of the military and backing of state behaviors. Silver coins were used for midsized transactions, and since an element of explanation for taxes, dues, contracts, and fealty, while copper coins represented the coinage of general transaction. This organization had been used in ancient India as the time of the Mahajanapadas. In Europe, this organization worked by the medieval era because there was virtually no new gold, silver or copper introduced by mining or conquest. Therefore the overall ratios of the three coinages remained roughly equivalent.

Paper Money

In pre-modern China, the require for credit and for circulating a medium that was less of a burden than exchanging thousands of copper coins led to the introduction of paper money, commonly recognized today since banknotes. This economic phenomenon was a slow and gradual procedure that took lay from the late Tang Dynasty (618–907) into the Song Dynasty (960–1279). It began since a means for merchants to swap heavy coinage for receipts of deposit issued since promissory notes from shops of wholesalers, notes that were valid for temporary exploit in a little local territory. In the 10th century, the Song Dynasty government began circulating these notes amongst the traders in their monopolized salt industry.

The Song government granted many shops the sole right to issue banknotes, and in the early 12th century the government finally took in excess of these shops to produce state-issued currency. Yet the banknotes issued were still regionally valid and temporary; it was not until the mid 13th century that an average and uniform government issue of paper money was made into an acceptable nationwide currency. The already widespread methods of woodblock printing and then Pi Sheng's movable kind printing through the 11th century was the impetus for the huge manufacture of paper money in pre-modern China.

At approximately the similar time in the medieval Islamic world, a vigorous monetary economy was created throughout the 7th–12th centuries on the foundation of the expanding stages of circulation of a stable high-value currency (the dinar). Innovations introduced through Muslim economists, traders and merchants contain the earliest exploits of credit, cheques, promissory notes, savings accounts, transactional accounts, loaning, trusts, swap rates, the transfer of credit and debt, and banking organizations for loans and deposits.

In Europe, paper money was first introduced in Sweden in 1661. Sweden was rich in copper; therefore, because of copper's low value, remarkably large coins (often weighing many kilograms) had to be made. The advantages of paper currency were numerous: it reduced transport of gold and silver, and therefore lowered the risks; it made loaning gold or silver at interest easier, as the specie (gold or silver) never left the possession of the lender until someone else redeemed the note; and it allowed for a division of currency into credit and specie backed shapes. It enabled the sale of stock in joint stock companies, and the redemption of those shares in paper.

Though, these advantages held within them disadvantages. First, as a note has no intrinsic value, there was nothing to stop issuing authorities from printing more of it than they had specie to back it with. Second, because it increased the money supply, it increased inflationary pressures, information observed through David Hume in the 18th century. The result is that paper money would often lead to an inflationary bubble, which could collapse if people began challenging difficult money, causing the demand for paper notes to fall to zero. The printing of paper money was also associated with wars, and financing of wars, and so regarded since section of maintaining a standing army. For these causes, paper currency was held in suspicion and hostility in Europe and America. It was also addictive, as the speculative profits of deal and capital making were quite big. Major nations recognized mints to print money and mint coins, and branches of their treasury to collect taxes and hold gold and silver stock.

At this time both silver and gold were measured legal tender, and carried through governments for taxes. Though, the instability in the ratio flanked by the two grew in excess of the course of the 19th century, with the augment both in supply of these metals, particularly silver, and of deal. This is described bimetallism and the effort to make a bimetallic average where both gold and silver backed currency remained in circulation engaged the attempts of inflationist's. Governments at this point could exploit currency since an instrument of policy, printing paper currency such since the United States Greenback, to pay for military expenditures. They could also set the conditions at which they would redeem notes for specie, through limiting the amount of purchase, or the minimum amount that could be redeemed.

Through 1900, mainly of the industrializing nations were on some shape of gold average, with paper notes and silver coins constituting the circulating medium. Private banks and governments crossways the world followed Gresham's Law: keeping gold and silver paid, but paying out in notes. This did not occur all approximately the world at the similar time, but occurred sporadically, usually in times of war or financial crisis, beginning in the early section of the 20th century and continuing crossways the world until the late 20th century, when the regime of floating fiat currencies came into force. One of the last countries to break absent from the gold average was the United States in 1971. No country anywhere in the world today has an enforceable gold average or silver average currency organization.

Commercial Bank Money

Commercial bank money or demand deposits are claims against financial organizations that can be used for the purchase of goods and services. A demand deposit explanation is an explanation from which finances can be withdrawn at any time through check or cash withdrawal without giving the bank or financial organization any prior notice. Banks have the legal obligation to return finances held in demand deposits immediately upon demand (or 'at call'). Demand deposit withdrawals can be performed in person, via checks or bank drafts, by automatic teller machines (ATMs), or by online banking.

Commercial bank money is created by fractional-reserve banking, the banking practice where banks stay only a fraction of their deposits in reserve (since cash and other highly liquid assets) and lend out the remainder, while maintaining the simultaneous obligation to redeem all these deposits upon demand. Commercial bank money differs from commodity and fiat money in two ways, firstly it is non-physical, since its subsistence is only reflected in the explanation ledgers of banks and other financial organizations, and secondly, there is some unit of risk that the claim will not be fulfilled if the financial organization becomes insolvent. The procedure of fractional-reserve banking has a cumulative effect of money making through commercial banks, since it expands money supply (cash and demand deposits) beyond what it would otherwise be. Because of the prevalence of fractional reserve banking, the broad money supply of mainly countries is a multiple superior than the amount of foundation money created through the country's central bank. That multiple (described the money multiplier) is determined through the reserve requirement or other financial ratio necessities imposed through financial regulators.

The money supply of a country is generally held to be the total amount of currency in circulation plus the total amount of checking and savings deposits in the commercial banks in the country. In contemporary economies, relatively small of the money supply is in physical currency. For instance, in December 2010 in the U.S., of the $8853.4 billion in broad money supply (M2), only $915.7 billion (in relation to the 10%) consisted of physical coins and paper money.

Digital Money

Digital currencies gained momentum in before the 2000 tech bubble. Flooz and Beenz were particularly advertised since an alternative shape of money.

While the tech bubble caused them to be short existed, several new digital currencies have reached some, albeit usually little user bases.

Mainly digital currencies are basically fiat currencies parleyed crossways a digital medium. Though, protocols like Bitcoin allow money to only exist in cyberspace which allows for some classic limitations to be lifted. Never before has the sending of money crossways a geographical divide not required the trust of a third party which of course then is susceptible to regulatory capture. New shapes of currency coming to fruition this extremely days allow for the free swap of wealth crossways distances.

DEMAND FOR AND SUPPLY OF MONEY

In the marketability of the several commodities and services there prevail considerable variations. There are goods for which it is not hard to discover applicants ready to disburse the highest recompense which, under the given state of affairs, can perhaps be obtained, *or* recompense only slightly smaller. There are other goods for which it is extremely difficult to discover a customer quickly, even if the vendor is ready to be content with compensation much smaller than he could reap if he could discover another aspirant whose demand is more intense.

It is these variations in the marketability of the several commodities and services which created indirect swap. A man who at the instant cannot acquire what he wants to get for the conduct of his own household or business, or who does not yet know what type of goods he will require in the uncertain future, comes nearer to his ultimate goal if he exchanges a less marketable good he wants to deal against a more marketable one. It may also occur that the physical properties of the merchandise he wants to provide absent (since, for example, its perish ability or the costs incurred through its storage or same conditions) impel him not to wait longer. Sometimes he may be prompted to hurry in giving absent the good concerned because he is afraid of a deterioration of its market value. In all such cases he improves his own situation in acquiring a more marketable good, even if this good is not appropriate to satisfy directly any of his own requires.

A medium of swap is a good which people acquire neither for their own consumption nor for employment in their own manufacture behaviors, but with the intention of exchanging it at a later date against those goods which they want to exploit either for consumption or for manufacture.

Money is a medium of swap. It is the mainly marketable good which people acquire because they want to offer it in later acts of interpersonal swap. Money is the thing which serves since the usually carried and commonly used medium of swap. This is its only function. All the other functions which people ascribe to money are merely scrupulous characteristics of its primary and sole function, that of a medium of swap.

Media of swap are economic goods. They are scarce; there is a demand for them. There are on the market people who desire to acquire them and are ready to swap goods and services against them. Media of swap have value in swap. People create sacrifices for their acquisition; they pay "prices" for them. The peculiarity of these prices lies merely in the information that they cannot be expressed in conditions of money. In reference to the vendible goods and services we speak of prices or of money prices. In reference to money we speak of its purchasing domination with regard to several vendible goods.

There exists a demand for media of swap because people want to stay a store of them. Every member of a market community wants to have a definite amount of money in his pocket or box, a cash holding or cash balance of a definite height. Sometimes he wants to stay a superior cash holding, sometimes a smaller; in exceptional cases he may even renounce any cash holding. At any rate, the immense majority of people aim not only to own several vendible goods; they want no less to hold money. Their cash holding is not merely a residuum, an unspent periphery of their wealth. It is not an unintentional remainder left in excess of after all intentional acts of buying and selling has been consummated. Its amount is determined through a deliberate demand for cash. And since with all other goods it is the changes in the relation flanked by demand for and supply of money that bring in relation to the changes in the swap ratio flanked by money and the vendible goods.

Every piece of money is owned through one of the members of the market economy. The transfer of money from manages of one actor into that of another is temporally immediate and continuous. There is no fraction of time in flanked by in which the money is not a section of an individual's or a firm's cash holding, but presently in "circulation." It is unsound to distinguish flanked by circulating and idle money. It is no less faulty to distinguish flanked by circulating money and hoarded money. What is described hoarding is a height of cash holding which — just as to the personal opinion of an observer — exceeds what is deemed normal and adequate. Though, hoarding is cash holding. Hoarded money is still money and it serves in the hoards the similar purposes which it serves in cash holdings described normal. He who hoards money considers that some special circumstances create it expedient to accumulate a cash holding which exceeds the amount he himself would stay under dissimilar circumstances, or other people stay, or an economist censuring his action believes suitable. That he acts in this method powers the configuration of the demand for money in the similar method in which every "normal" demand powers it.

Several economists avoid applying the conditions demand and supply in the sense of demand for and supply of money for cash holding because they fear confusion with the current terminology since used through the bankers. It is, in information, customary to call demand for money the demand for short-condition loans and supply of money the supply of such loans. Accordingly one calls the market for short-condition loans the money market. One says money is scarce if there prevails a tendency toward a rise in the rate of interest for short-condition loans, and one says money is plentiful if the rate of interest for such loans is decreasing. These manners of speech are therefore firmly entrenched that it is out of the question to venture to discard them. But they have favored the spread of fateful errors. They made people confound the notions of *money* and of capital and consider that rising the quantity of money could lower the rate of interest lastingly. But it is precisely the crassness of these errors which creates it unlikely that the terminology suggested could make any misunderstanding. It is difficult to assume that economists could err with regard to such fundamental issues.

Others maintained that one should not speak of the demand for and supply of money because the aims of those challenging money differ from the aims of those challenging vendible commodities. Commodities, they say, are demanded ultimately for consumption, while money is demanded in order to be given absent in further acts of swap. This objection is no less invalid. The exploit which people create of a medium of swap consists eventually in its being given absent. But first of all they are eager to accumulate a sure amount of it in order to be ready for the moment in which a purchase may be accomplished. Precisely because people do not want to give for their own requires right at the instant at which they provide absent the goods and services they themselves bring to the market, precisely because they want to wait or are forced to wait until propitious circumstances for buying seem, they barter not directly but indirectly by the interposition of a medium of swap. The information that money is not worn out through the exploit one creates of it and that it can render its services practically for an unlimited length of time is a significant factor in the configuration of its supply. But it does not alter the information that the appraisement of money is to be explained in the similar method since the appraisement of all other goods: through the demand on the section of those who are eager to acquire a definite quantity of it.

Economists have tried to enumerate the factors which within the entire economic organization may augment or decrease the demand for money. Such factors are: the population figure; the extent to which the individual households give for their own requires through autarkic manufacture and the extent to which they produce for other people's requires, selling their products and buying for their own consumption on the market; the sharing of business action and the resolution of payments in excess of the several seasons of the year; organizations for the resolution of claims and counterclaims through mutual cancellation, such since clearinghouses. All these factors indeed power the demand for money and the height of the several individuals' and firms' cash holding. But they power them only indirectly through the role they play in the thoughts of people regarding the determination of the amount of cash balances they deem suitable. What decide the matter are always the value judgments of the men concerned. The several actors create up their minds in relation to they consider the adequate height of their cash holding should be. They carry out their settlement through renouncing the purchase of commodities, securities, and interest-bearing claims, and through selling such assets or conversely through rising their purchases. With money, things are not dissimilar from what they are with regard to all other goods and services. The demand for money is determined through the conduct of people intent upon acquiring it for their cash holding.

Another objection raised against the notion of the demand for money was this: The marginal utility of the money element decreases much more gradually than that of the other commodities; in information its decrease is therefore slow that it can be practically ignored. With regard to money nobody ever says that his demand is satisfied, and nobody ever forsakes an opportunity to acquire more money provided the sacrifice required is not too great. It is so impermissible to believe the demand for money since limited. The extremely notion of an unlimited demand is, though, contradictory. This popular reasoning is entirely fallacious. It confounds the demand for money for cash holding with the desire for more wealth since expressed in conditions of money. He, who says that his thirst for more money can never be quenched, does not mean to say that his cash holding can never be too big. What he really means is that he can never be rich sufficient. If additional money flows into his hands, he will not exploit it for an augment of his cash balance or he will exploit only a section of it for this purpose. He will expend the surplus either for instantaneous consumption or for investment. Nobody ever keeps more money than he wants to have since cash holding.

The insight that the swap ratio flanked by money on the one hand and the vendible commodities and services on the other is determined, in the similar method since the mutual swap ratios flanked by the several vendible goods, through demand and supply was the essence of the *quantity theory of money.* This theory is essentially an application of the common theory of supply and demand to the special example of money. Its merit was the endeavor to explain the determination of money's purchasing domination through resorting to the similar reasoning which is employed for the account of all other swap ratios. Its shortcoming was that it resorted to a holistic interpretation. It looked at the total supply of money in the Volkswirtschaft and not at the actions of the individual men and firms. An outgrowth of this erroneous point of view was the thought that there prevails a proportionality in the changes of the — total — quantity of money and of money prices. But the older critics failed in their efforts to explode the errors inherent in the quantity theory and to substitute a more satisfactory theory for it. They did not fight what was wrong in the quantity theory; they attacked, on the contrary, its nucleus of truth. They were intent upon denying that there is a causal relation flanked by the movements of prices and those of the quantity of money. This denial led them into a labyrinth of errors, contradictions, and nonsense. Contemporary monetary theory takes up the thread of the traditional quantity theory since distant since it starts from the cognition that changes in the purchasing domination of money necessity be dealt with just as to the principles applied to all other market phenomena and that there exists a relationship flanked by the changes in the demand for and supply of money on the one hand and those of purchasing domination on the other. In this sense one may call the contemporary theory of money an improved diversity of the quantity theory.

MONEY AND PRICES

QUANTITY THEORY OF MONEY

In monetary economics, the quantity theory of money is the theory that money supply has a direct, proportional connection with the price stage. For instance, if the currency in circulation increased, there would be a proportional augment in the price of goods.

The theory was challenged through Keynesian economics, but updated and reinvigorated through the monetarist school of economics. While mainstream economists agree that the quantity theory holds true in the extensive run, there is still conflict in relation to the its applicability in the short run. Critics of the theory argue that money velocity is not stable and, in the short-run, prices are sticky, therefore the direct connection flanked by money supply and price stage does not hold. Alternative theories contain the real bills doctrine and the more recent fiscal theory of the price stage.

Origins and Growth of the Quantity Theory

The quantity theory descends from Copernicus, followers of the School of Salamanca, Jean Bodin, and several others who noted the augment in prices following the import of gold and silver, used in the coinage of money, from the New World. The "equation of swap" relating the supply of money to the value of money transactions was stated through John Stuart Mill who expanded on the thoughts of David Hume. The quantity theory was urbanized through Simon Newcomb, Alfred de Foville, Irving Fisher, and Ludwig von Mises in the latter 19th and early 20th century, while it had been argued against through Karl Marx. The theory was influentially restated through Milton Friedman in response to Keynesianism.

For example, Bieda argues that Copernicus's observation amounts to a report of the theory, while other economic historians date the detection later, to figures such since Jean Bodin, David Hume, and John Stuart Mill. Historically, the largest rival of the quantity theory was the real bills doctrine, which says that the issue of money does not raise prices, since extensive since the new money is issued in swap for assets of enough value.

Equation of Swap

In its contemporary shape, the quantity theory builds upon the following definitional connection.

$$M \bullet V_T = \sum_i (p_i \cdot q_i) = p^T q$$

where

- M is the total amount of money in circulation on standard in an economy throughout the era, say a year.
- V_T is the transactions velocity of money, that is the standard frequency crossways all transactions with which an element of money is spent. This reflects availability of financial organizations, economic variables, and choices made since to how fast people turn in excess of their money.
- p_i and q_i are the price and quantity of the transaction.
- P is a column vector of the p_i, and the superscript is the transpose operator.
- q is a column vector of the q_i.

Mainstream economics accepts a simplification, the equation of swap:

$$M \cdot V_T = P_T \cdot T$$

where

- P_T is the price stage associated with transactions for the economy throughout the era
- T is an index of the real value of aggregate transactions.

The equation presents the difficulty that the associated data are not accessible for all transactions. With the growth of national income and product accounts, emphasis shifted to national-income or final-product transactions, rather than gross transactions.

Economists may so job with the shape

$$M \cdot V = P \cdot Q$$

where

- V is the velocity of money in final expenditures.
- Q is an index of the real value of final expenditures.

Since an instance, M might symbolize currency plus deposits in checking and savings accounts held through the public, Q real output (which equals real expenditure in macroeconomic equilibrium) with P the corresponding price stage, and $P \bullet Q$ the nominal (money) value of output. In one empirical formulation, velocity was taken to be "the ratio of net national product in current prices to the money stock".

Therefore distant, the theory is not particularly controversial, since the equation of swap is an identity. A theory needs that assumptions be made in relation to the causal relationships in the middle of the four variables in this one equation. There are debates in relation to the extent to which each of these variables is dependent upon the others. Without further restrictions, the equation does not need that a transform in the money supply would transform the value of any or all of P, Q, or $P \bullet Q$. For instance, a 10% augment in M could be accompanied through a 10% decrease in V, leaving $P \bullet Q$ unchanged. The quantity theory postulates that the primary causal effect is an effect of M on P.

A Rudimentary Adaptation of the Quantity Theory

The equation of swap can be used to shape a rudimentary adaptation of the quantity theory of the effect of monetary development on inflation.

$$P = \frac{M \cdot V}{Q}.$$

If V and Q were consistent, then:

$$\frac{dP}{P} = \frac{dM}{M}$$

and therefore

$$\frac{dP/P}{dt} = \frac{dM/M}{dt}$$

where

t is time.

That is to say that, if V and Q were consistent, then the inflation rate (the rate of development $\frac{dP/P}{dt}$ of the price stage) would exactly equal the development rate $\frac{dM/M}{dt}$ of the money supply. In short, the inflation rate is a function of the monetary development rate.

Less restrictively, with time-varying V and Q, we have the identity,

$$\frac{dP/P}{dt} = \frac{dM/M}{dt} + \frac{dV/V}{dt} - \frac{dQ/Q}{dt}$$

which says that the inflation rate equals the monetary development rate plus the development rate of the velocity of money minus the development rate of real expenditure? If one creates the quantity theory assumptions that, at least in the extensive run:

- The monetary development rate is controlled through the central bank,
- The development rate of velocity is purely determined through the development of payments mechanisms, and

- The development rate of real expenditure is determined through the rate of technical progress plus the rate of labor force development, then while the inflation rate requires not *equal* the monetary development rate, an x percentage point rise in the monetary development rate will result in an x percentage point rise in the inflation rate.

Cambridge Style

Economists Alfred Marshall, A.C. Pigou, and John Maynard Keynes (before he urbanized his own, eponymous school of idea) associated with Cambridge University, took a slightly dissimilar style to the quantity theory, focusing on money demand instead of money supply. They argued that a sure portion of the money supply will not be used for transactions; instead, it will be held for the convenience and security of having cash on hand. This portion of cash is commonly represented since k, a portion of nominal income (P•Y). The Cambridge economists also idea wealth would play a role, but wealth is often omitted for simplicity. The Cambridge equation is therefore:

- $M^d = k \cdot P \cdot Y$

Assuming that the economy is at equilibrium ($M^d = M$), Y is exogenous, and k is fixed in the short run, the Cambridge equation is equivalent to the equation of swap with velocity equal to the inverse of k:

$$M \cdot \frac{1}{k} = P \cdot Y$$

The Cambridge adaptation of the quantity theory led to both Keynes's attack on the quantity theory and the Monetarist revival of the theory.

Quantity Theory and Proof

Since restated through Milton Friedman, the quantity theory emphasizes the following connection of the nominal value of expenditures PQ and the price stage P to the quantity of money M:

$$PQ = f\left(\overset{+}{M}\right)$$

$$P = g\left(\overset{+}{M}\right)$$

The plus signs indicate that a transform in the money supply is hypothesized to transform nominal expenditures and the price stage in the similar direction. Friedman called the empirical regularity of substantial changes in the quantity of money and in the stage of prices since possibly the mainly-evidenced economic phenomenon on record. Empirical studies have establish dealings constant with the models above and with causation running from money to prices. The short-run relation of a transform in the money supply in the past has been relatively more associated with a transform in real output Q than the price stage P in (1) but with much difference in the precision, timing, and size of the relation. For the *extensive*-run, there has been stronger support for (1) and (2) and no systematic association of Q and M.

Principles

The theory is based on the following hypotheses:

- The source of inflation is fundamentally derived from the development rate of the money supply.
- The supply of money is exogenous.
- The demand for money, since reflected in its velocity, is a stable function of nominal income, interest rates, and therefore forth.
- The mechanism for injecting money into the economy is not that significant in the extensive run.
- The real interest rate is determined through non-monetary factors: (productivity of capital, time preference).

Decline of Money-supply Targeting

An application of the quantity-theory style aimed at removing monetary policy since a source of macroeconomic instability was to target a consistent, low development rate of the money supply. Even, practical identification of the relevant money supply, including measurement, was always somewhat controversial and hard. Since financial intermediation grew in complexity and sophistication in the 1980s and 1990s, it became more therefore. Since a result, some central banks, including the U.S. Federal Reserve, which had targeted the money supply, reverted to targeting interest rates. But monetary aggregates remain a leading economic indicator. with "some proof that the linkages flanked by money and economic action are robust even at relatively short-run frequencies."

Criticisms

John Maynard Keynes criticized the quantity theory of money in The Common Theory of Employment, Interest, and Money. Keynes had originally been a proponent of the theory, but he presented an alternative in the Common Theory. Keynes argued that price stage was not strictly determined through money supply.

Changes in the money supply could have effects on real variables like output. Ludwig von Mises agreed that there was a core of truth in the Quantity Theory, but criticized its focus on the supply of money without adequately explaining the demand for money. He said the theory "fails to explain the mechanism of differences in the value of money".

KEYNES' THEORY OF MONEY AND PRICES

The traditional quantity theory of money and the quantity equations do not illustrate how a transform in the quantity of money reacts upon the price stage. Keynes tries to tackle this aspect of the trouble in his Common Theory through a restatement of the quantity theory. In doing therefore, he tried to integrate the theory of money with the theory of employment. To Keynes, the effect of changes in the quantity of money on the price stage (in turn, the value of money) should be visualized by the inter-related effect on the wage rate, income, investment, employment, etc.

Therefore, an augment in the quantity of money will have no affect whatsoever on prices, therefore extensive since there is any unemployment, and that employment will augment in exact proportion to any augment in effective demand brought in relation to the through the augment in the quantity of money. While, since soon since full employment is reached, wage rate and price will augment in exact proportion to the augment in effective demand. Hence, Keynes enunciated the quantity theory of money since follows: "Therefore extensive since there is unemployment, employment will transform in the similar proportion since the quantity of money." To elucidate this point, Keynes first believes the effect of changes in the quantity of money on the quantum of effective demand; the augment in effective demand is supposed to be spent partly in rising the quantity of employment and partly in raising the stage of prices. Therefore, Keynes conceived a term where prices rise slowly since employment increases, instead of prices growing in proportion to the quantity of money, which is true in a term of full employment, since assumed through the classical theorists.

Keynes stressed that there is no direct link flanked by money supply and price stage, but there is a series of causal links flanked by the two. Changes in the quantity of money first affect the rate of interest, which in turn, affects the investment function and the stage of effective demand and consequently the volume of employment and output.

Say, if money supply increases with a given demand for money, the rate of interest will fall. Given the marginal efficiency of capital, a fall in interest rate will induce an augment in investment. With an augment in investment expenditure the stage of effective demand will go up. Increased investment leads to an augment in the stage of employment, output, and income. There is a multiplier effect involved in the procedure of income propagation, based on the phenomenon of marginal propensity to consume and consequent changes in the flow of consumption expenditure.

Therefore extensive since there is sufficient of unemployed labour and capital possessions, an augment in the quantity of money would, in this method, lead to augment in real income or output (that is, T in conditions of Fisher's equation of swap) rather than price stage. In short, the common stage of prices will not rise since output increases on explanation of augment in money supply, therefore extensive since there are efficient unemployed possessions of every kind accessible. But, since output increases, a series of bottlenecks will be successively reached, where the supply of scrupulous commodities ceases to be elastic and their prices tend to rise sharply. After a full employment level is reached, an augment in the quantity of money spends itself entirely in raising the price stage because, an augment in effective stage caused through the increased quantity of money would not be to augment the volume of employment and output.

Hence, its full effect will be on raising the stage of prices. Therefore, every augment in the quantity of money is associated with an exactly proportionate augment in the price stage and vice versa under full employment circumstances. Keynes further stressed that Fisher's quantity theory of money, in conditions of the equation of swap (MV = PT), holds well only in a state of full employment. Keynes' restatement of the quantity theory spots a great improvement in excess of the Fisherian adaptation, in the sense that he views the role of money in the causal procedure via consumption, investment, liquidity preference, and the rate of interest. Through formulating the quantity theory of money, he maintains that there is an extreme complexity of the connection flanked by prices and the quantity of money, in contrast to the easy immediate connection discovered in the quantity equations given through Fisher and through the Cambridge economists. Keynes holds the old fallacy that prices are determined directly through the quantity of money. He illustrates that prices are determined directly through the quantity of money and are convinced indirectly by the effect of changes in the quantity of money upon the rate of interest, which is one of the three strategic variables determining the stage of output and employment. (The original efficiency of capital and the propensity to consume are the other two variables).

Keynes, in short, viewed that changes in P do not affect M directly but they do therefore indirectly by a host of strategic factors, such since the rate of interest, stage of investment, employment, income and output. Just as to Keynes, the quantity theory of money would be valid if the elasticity of money prices is unity. Though, no such direct connection could exist flanked by the quantity of money and the price stage, except in a full-employment phenomenon. Therefore extensive since there is unemployment, employment will transform in the similar proportion since the quantity of money; when there is full employment, prices will transform in the similar proportion since the quantity of money. That means, therefore extensive since there is any unemployment, an enough augment in M can always bring in relation to the full employment; a further augment in M will be reflected in the rise of P. This is illustrated. M rises from zero to OM, real output rises up to OF, at full employment stage of the given possessions. A further rise in M leads to a proportionate rise in P since depicted through FP the price curve. However a price rise is measured a post full-employment phenomenon, throughout the transition era, though, before full employment is reached, with an augment in M, P may rise, however not proportionately due to the following causes:

- Increased bargaining domination of workers leading to a rise in wages and a high cost of manufacture;
- Operation of the law of diminishing returns, causing rising costs;
- Bottlenecks in manufacture, such since shortage of raw materials, domination cuts, lack of adequate transport, and immobility of factors; and
- Heterogeneity of factors, especially labour elements which differ in ability and efficiency.

In this reformulation, Keynes' great merit lies in integrating the theory of money with the theory of value. He showed that prices rise because of a rise in the cost of manufacture, and the cost of manufacture rises due to the inelasticity of supply of output and employment in the short era. Again, Keynes successfully integrated the theory of money with the theory of output. He pointed out that, in information, the theories of value and money are juxtaposed, by the theory of output or employment. This happens because changes in the quantity of money, by reacting on the effective demand for investment, via the changes in the rate of interest, transform the stage of employment and output and, by reacting on the cost of manufacture, affect the prices or the value of money. Therefore, Keynes, in his restatement of the theory, provided the missing link in the old quantity theory of money. The traditional theory missed the point that the quantity of money exerts a power on the rate of interest, which, in turn, reacts upon output and employment.

They viewed a direct connection flanked by the quantity of money and the price stage with the omission of a factor, such since the rate of interest. Keynes has, through reformulating the quantity theory, corrected this grave error of the traditional quantity theorists. In short, Keynes' theory of money and prices has the merit of providing the procedure of causation and identifying factors determining the price stage or the value of money, giving due respect to the role played through the rate of interest which was neglected through the traditional economists.

He integrates the theory of money with the theory of value, which were wrongly separated through traditional theorists. We may conclude that Keynes formulated quantity theory is at once larger and a bigger guide to practical policies than the old theory. For it stresses the truth that an augment in money supply is inflationary only after full employment is reached; therefore, inflation should not be feared at all under circumstances of big-level unemployment since is generally establish throughout a depression. The theory suggests cheap money policy to be followed to overcome a depression. Though, Keynes' reformulation of the quantity theory is not without its imperfections. Its largest shortcomings are:

- It fails to give a complete account of a price rise before full employment is reached through the economy. In scrupulous, inflationary tendencies in undeveloped countries, such since India, cannot be well explained through the theory.
- The theory has therefore several qualifications that its usefulness since a leading proposition of monetary theory has become doubtful.
- Keynes' theory of money and prices is too common. It fails to analyze the sectional price behaviour of interrelationship flanked by money supply and prices.

Nevertheless, it should be admitted that Keynes' theory of money and prices is definitely larger to the old quantity theory as it recognizes the real phenomenon of unemployment equilibrium in the economy.

INFLATION

In economics, inflation is a rise in the common stage of prices of goods and services in an economy in excess of an era of time. When the common price stage rises, each element of currency buys fewer goods and services. Consequently, inflation also reflects erosion in the purchasing domination of money – a loss of real value in the internal medium of swap and element of explanation in the economy. A chief measure of price inflation is the inflation rate, the annualized percentage transform in a common price index (normally the Consumer Price Index) in excess of time.

Inflation's effects on an economy are several and can be simultaneously positive and negative. Negative effects of inflation contain an augment in the opportunity cost of holding money, uncertainty in excess of future inflation which may discourage investment and savings, and if inflation is rapid sufficient, shortages of goods since consumers begin hoarding out of concern that prices will augment in the future. Positive effects contain ensuring that central banks can adjust real interest rates (designed to mitigate recessions), and encouraging investment in non-monetary capital projects.

Economists usually agree that high rates of inflation and hyperinflation are caused through an excessive development of the money supply. Views on which factors determine low to moderate rates of inflation are more varied. Low or moderate inflation may be attributed to fluctuations in real demand for goods and services, or changes in accessible supplies such since throughout scarcities, since well since to development in the money supply. Though, the consensus view is that an extensive continued era of inflation is caused through money supply rising faster than the rate of economic development.

Today, mainly economists favor a low and steady rate of inflation. Low (since opposed to zero or negative) inflation reduces the severity of economic recessions through enabling the labor market to adjust more quickly in a downturn, and reduces the risk that a liquidity trap prevents monetary policy from stabilizing the economy. The task of keeping the rate of inflation low and stable is generally given to monetary authorities. Usually, these monetary authorities are the central banks that manage monetary policy by the setting of interest rates, by open market operations, and by the setting of banking reserve necessities.

KINDS OF INFLATION

There are two primary kinds of inflation: demand-pull and cost-push. Understanding which kind of inflation is occurring at any given point in time is significant if policymakers want to respond appropriately. The two kinds of inflation are not mutually exclusive, therefore it is possible for both to happen simultaneously. Left untreated, inflation can reason a wage-price spiral or even hyperinflation.

Demand-Pull Inflation

Demand-pull inflation occurs when spending on goods and services drives up prices. Demand-pull inflation is fueled through income, therefore attempts to stop it involve reducing consumer's income or giving consumers more stimuli to save than to spend. Demand-pull inflation persists if the public or foreign sector reinforces it. Low taxes and profligate government spending exacerbate demand-pull inflation. A failure of the central bank to reign in the money supply also creates the demand-pull inflation worse.

Demand-pull inflation can spread crossways borders since well. China and India's economic development not only puts pressure on prices in these countries but also on prices worldwide since the demand for imports augment. If government spending is financed through printing currency or through the central bank monetizing the debt, demand-pull inflation can become hyperinflation.

Hyperinflation is defined since annual inflation of 100% or greater. All cases of hyperinflation have been accompanied through the government or central bank issuing too much money.

Cost-Push Inflation

Cost-push inflation occurs when the price of inputs increases. Businesses necessity acquires raw materials, labor, power, and capital to operate. If the price of these were to rise, it would reduce the skill of producers to generate output because their element cost of manufacture had increased. If these increases in manufacture cost are relatively big and pervasive, the effect is to simultaneously make higher inflation, reduce real GDP, and augment the unemployment rate.

You might recognize this combination through another name, stagflation. In the 1970s, OPEC cut oil manufacture, which led to much higher power prices beside with double-digit inflation and unemployment. Because producers faced higher operating costs, they reduced output. Comparative to the demand for their products, the supply decreased, which resulted in cost-push inflation.

If cost-push inflation has a bright face, it is the information that it is self-limiting. Cost-push inflation is associated with decreases in GDP. The decreased GDP and resulting high unemployment helps to bring producer prices back down. The trick to combating cost-push inflation is realizing that it is not demand-pull. The policy prescription for each is dissimilar, and applying the wrong prescription can make more troubles than it solves. It is the unemployment issue that generally spurs policymakers to action.

If they respond to the increased unemployment through rising spending, the inflation trouble is made worse. A wage-price spiral can result if the policy responses make more demand for goods and services at the similar time that element costs are growing. Through method of analogy, the prescription for a grease fire is dissimilar from that of a forest fire. Grease fires are put out through removing the source of oxygen, while a forest fire is extinguished with water. If you pour water on a grease fire, then things only get worse. This is what happened in the 1970s. Instead of letting cost-push inflation run its natural course, the Fed poured money on it, and inflation worsened.

EVENTS

Inflation is generally estimated through calculating the inflation rate of a price index, generally the Consumer Price Index. The Consumer Price Index events prices of a selection of goods and services purchased through a "typical consumer". The inflation rate is the percentage rate of transform of a price index in excess of time. The Retail Prices Index is also a measure of inflation that is commonly used in the United Kingdom. It is broader than the CPI and includes a superior basket of goods and services. To show the way of calculation, in January 2007, the U.S. Consumer Price Index was 202.416, and in January 2008 it was 211.080. The formula for calculating the annual percentage rate inflation in the CPI in excess of the course of 2007 is

$$\left(\frac{211.080-202.416}{202.416}\right)\times 100\% = 4.28\%$$

The resulting inflation rate for the CPI in this one year era is 4.28%, meaning the common stage of prices for typical U.S. consumers rose through almost four percent in 2007. Other widely used price indices for calculating price inflation contain the following:

- Producer price indices (PPIs) which events standard changes in prices received through domestic producers for their output. This differs from the CPI in that price subsidization, profits, and taxes may reason the amount received through the producer to differ from what the consumer paid. There is also typically a delay flanked by an augment in the PPI and any eventual augment in the CPI. Producer price index events the pressure being put on producers through the costs of their raw materials. This could be "passed on" to consumers, or it could be absorbed through profits, or offset through rising productivity. In India and the United States, an earlier adaptation of the PPI was described the Wholesale Price Index.

- Commodity price indices, which measure the price of a selection of commodities. In the present commodity price indices are weighted through the comparative importance of the components to the "all in" cost of an employee.
- Core price indices: because food and oil prices can transform quickly due to changes in supply and demand circumstances in the food and oil markets, it can be hard to detect the extensive run trend in price stages when those prices are incorporated. So mainly statistical agencies also statement a measure of 'core inflation', which removes the mainly volatile components (such since food and oil) from a broad price index like the CPI. Because core inflation is less affected through short run supply and demand circumstances in specific markets, central banks rely on it to bigger measure the inflationary impact of current monetary policy.

Other general events of inflation are:

- GDP deflator is a measure of the price of all the goods and services incorporated in gross domestic product (GDP). The US Commerce Department publishes a deflator series for US GDP, defined since its nominal GDP measure divided through its real GDP measure.
- Local inflation The Bureau of Labor Statistics breaks down CPI-U calculations down to dissimilar areas of the US.
- Historical inflation Before collecting constant econometric data became average for governments, and for the purpose of comparing absolute, rather than comparative standards of livelihood, several economists have calculated imputed inflation figures. Mainly inflation data before the early 20th century is imputed based on the recognized costs of goods, rather than compiled at the time. It is also used to adjust for the variations in real average of livelihood for the attendance of technology.
- Asset price inflation is an undue augment in the prices of real or financial assets, such since stock (equity), and real estate. While there is no widely carried index of this kind, some central bankers have suggested that it would be bigger to aim at stabilizing a wider common

price stage inflation measure that comprises some asset prices, instead of stabilizing CPI or core inflation only. The cause is that through raising interest rates when stock prices or real estate prices rise, and lowering them when these asset prices fall, central banks might be more successful in avoiding bubbles and crashes in asset prices.

Issues in Measuring

Measuring inflation in an economy needs objective means of differentiating changes in nominal prices on a general set of goods and services, and distinguishing them from those price shifts resulting from changes in value such since volume, excellence, or performance. For instance, if the price of a 10 oz. can of corn changes from $0.90 to $1.00 in excess of the course of a year, with no transform in excellence, then this price variation symbolizes inflation. This single price transform would not, though, symbolize common inflation in an overall economy.

To measure overall inflation, the price transform of a big "basket" of representative goods and services is considered. This is the purpose of a price index, which is the combined price of a "basket" of several goods and services. The combined price is the sum of the weighted prices of things in the "basket". A weighted price is calculated through multiplying the element price of a thing through the number of that thing the standard consumer purchases. Weighted pricing is a necessary means to measuring the impact of individual element price changes on the economy's overall inflation. The Consumer Price Index, for instance, exploits data composed through surveying households to determine what proportion of the typical consumer's overall spending is spent on specific goods and services, and weights the standard prices of those things accordingly. Those weighted standard prices are combined to calculate the overall price. To bigger relate price changes in excess of time, indexes typically choose a "foundation year" price and assign it a value of 100. Index prices in subsequent years are then expressed in relation to the foundation year price. While comparing inflation events for several eras one has to take into consideration the foundation effect since well.

Inflation events are often customized in excess of time, either for the comparative weight of goods in the basket, or in the method in which goods and services from the present are compared with goods and services from the past. In excess of time, adjustments are made to the kind of goods and services selected in order to reflect changes in the sorts of goods and services purchased through 'typical consumers'. New products may be introduced, older products disappear, the excellence of existing products may transform, and consumer preferences can shift. Both the sorts of goods and services which are incorporated in the "basket" and the weighted price used in inflation events will be changed in excess of time in order to stay pace with the changing marketplace. Inflation numbers are often seasonally adjusted in order to differentiate expected cyclical cost shifts. For instance, house heating costs are expected to rise in colder months, and seasonal adjustments are often used when measuring for inflation to compensate for cyclical spikes in power or fuel demand. Inflation numbers may be averaged or otherwise subjected to statistical techniques in order to remove statistical noise and volatility of individual prices.

When looking at inflation, economic organizations may focus only on sure types of prices, or special indices, such since the core inflation index which is used through central banks to formulate monetary policy. Mainly inflation indices are calculated from weighted averages of selected price changes. This necessarily introduces distortion, and can lead to legitimate disputes in relation to the the true inflation rate is. This trouble can be overcome through including all accessible price changes in the calculation, and then choosing the median value.

EFFECTS

Common

An augment in the common stage of prices implies a decrease in the purchasing domination of the currency. That is, when the common stage of prices rises, each monetary element buys fewer goods and services. The effect of inflation is not distributed evenly in the economy, and since a consequence there are hidden costs to some and benefits to others from this decrease in the purchasing domination of money. For instance, with inflation, lenders or depositors who are paid a fixed rate of interest on loans or deposits will lose purchasing domination from their interest earnings, while their borrowers benefit. Individuals or organizations with cash assets will experience a decline in the purchasing domination of their holdings. Increases in payments to workers and pensioners often lag behind inflation, especially for those with fixed payments. Increases in the price stage (inflation) erode the real value of money (the functional currency) and other things with an underlying monetary nature.

Debtors who have debts with a fixed nominal rate of interest will see a reduction in the "real" interest rate since the inflation rate rises. The real interest on a loan is the nominal rate minus the inflation rate. The formula R = N-I approximates the correct answer since extensive since both the nominal interest rate and the inflation rate are little. The correct equation is r = n/i where r, n and i are expressed since ratios (e.g. 1.2 for +20%, 0.8 for "20%). Since an instance, when the inflation rate is 3%, a loan with a nominal interest rate of 5% would have a real interest rate of almost 2%. Any unexpected augment in the inflation rate would decrease the real interest rate. Banks and other lenders adjust for this inflation risk either through including an inflation risk premium to fixed interest rate loans, or lending at an adjustable rate.

Negative

High or unpredictable inflation rates are regarded since harmful to an overall economy. They add inefficiencies in the market, and create it hard for companies to budget or plan extensive-condition. Inflation can act since a drag on productivity since companies are forced to shift possessions absent from products and services in order to focus on profit and losses from currency inflation. Uncertainty in relation to the future purchasing domination of money discourages investment and saving. And inflation can impose hidden tax increases, since inflated earnings push taxpayers into higher income tax rates unless the tax brackets are indexed to inflation.

With high inflation, purchasing domination is redistributed from those on fixed nominal incomes, such since some pensioners whose pensions are not indexed to the price stage, towards those with variable incomes whose earnings may bigger stay pace with the inflation. This redistribution of purchasing domination will also happen flanked by international trading partners. Where fixed swap rates are imposed, higher inflation in one economy than another will reason the first economy's exports to become more expensive and affect the balance of deal. There can also be negative impacts to deal from an increased instability in currency swap prices caused through unpredictable inflation.

- *Cost-push inflation:* High inflation can prompt employees to demand rapid wage increases, to stay up with consumer prices. In the cost-push theory of inflation, growing wages in turn can help fuel inflation. In the case of communal bargaining, wage development will be set since a function of inflationary expectations, which will be higher when inflation is high. This can reason a wage spiral. In a sense, inflation begets further inflationary expectations, which beget further inflation.
- *Hoarding:* People buy durable and/or non-perishable commodities and other goods since stores of wealth, to avoid the losses expected from the declining purchasing domination of money, creating shortages of the hoarded goods.
- *Social unrest and revolts:* Inflation can lead to huge demonstrations and revolutions. For instance, inflation and in scrupulous food inflation is measured since one of the largest causes that caused the 2010–2011 Tunisian revolution and the 2011 Egyptian revolution, just as to several observators including Robert Zoellick, president of the World Bank. Tunisian president Zine El Abidine Ben Ali was ousted, Egyptian President Hosni Mubarak was also ousted after only 18 days of demonstrations, and protests soon spread in several countries of North Africa and Transitional East.

- *Hyperinflation:* If inflation gets completely out of manage (in the upward direction), it can grossly interfere with the normal workings of the economy, hurting its skill to supply goods. Hyperinflation can lead to the abandonment of the exploit of the country's currency, leading to the inefficiencies of barter.
- *Allocative efficiency:* A transform in the supply or demand for a good will normally reason its comparative price to transform, signaling to buyers and sellers that they should re-allocate possessions in response to the new market circumstances. But when prices are constantly changing due to inflation, price changes due to genuine comparative price signals are hard to distinguish from price changes duc to common inflation, therefore mediators are slow to respond to them. The result is a loss of allocative efficiency.
- *Shoe leather cost:* High inflation increases the opportunity cost of holding cash balances and can induce people to hold a greater portion of their assets in interest paying accounts. Though, as cash is still needed in order to carry out transactions this means that more "trips to the bank" are necessary in order to create withdrawals, proverbially wearing out the "shoe leather" with each trip.
- *Menu costs:* With high inflation, firm's necessity transforms their prices often in order to stay up with economy-wide changes. But often changing prices is itself a costly action whether explicitly, since with require to print new menus, or implicitly.
- *Business cycles:* Just as to the Austrian Business Cycle Theory, inflation sets off the business cycle. Austrian economists hold this to be the mainly damaging effect of inflation. Just as to Austrian theory, artificially low interest rates and the associated augment in the money supply lead to reckless, speculative borrowing, resulting in groups of mal investments, which eventually have to be liquidated since they become unsustainable.

Positive

- *Labor-market adjustments:* Nominal wages are slow to adjust downwards. This can lead to prolonged disequilibrium and high unemployment in the labor market. As inflation allows real wages to fall even if nominal wages are kept consistent, moderate inflation enables labor markets to reach equilibrium faster.
- *Room to maneuver:* The primary apparatus for controlling the money supply are the skill to set the discount rate, the rate at which banks can borrow from the central bank, and open market operations, which are the central bank's interventions into the bonds market with the aim of affecting the nominal interest rate. If an economy discovers

itself in a recession with already low, or even zero, nominal interest rates, then the bank cannot cut these rates further (as negative nominal interest rates are impossible) in order to stimulate the economy – this situation is recognized since a liquidity trap. A moderate stage of inflation tends to ensure that nominal interest rates keep sufficiently above zero therefore that if the require arises the bank can cut the nominal interest rate.

- *Mundell–Tobin effect:* The Nobel laureate Robert Mundell noted that moderate inflation would induce savers to substitute lending for some money holding since a means to fund future spending. That substitution would reason market clearing real interest rates to fall. The lower real rate of interest would induce more borrowing to fund investment. In a same vein, Nobel laureate James Tobin noted that such inflation would reason businesses to substitute investment in physical capital (plant, equipment, and inventories) for money balances in their asset portfolios. That substitution would mean choosing the creation of investments with lower rates of real return. (The rates of return are lower because the investments with higher rates of return were already being made before.) The two related effects are recognized since the Mundell–Tobin effect. Unless the economy is already over investing just as to models of economic development theory, that extra investment resulting from the effect would be seen since positive.
- *Instability with Deflation:* Economist S.C. Tsaing noted that once substantial deflation is expected, two significant effects will seem; both a result of money holding substituting for lending since a vehicle for saving. The first was that continually falling prices and the resulting stimulus to hoard money will reason instability resulting from the likely rising fear, while money hoards grow in value, that the value of those hoards are at risk, since people realize that a movement to deal those money hoards for real goods and assets will quickly drive those prices up. Any movement to spend those hoards "once started would become a tremendous avalanche, which could rampage for an extensive time before it would spend itself." Therefore, a regime of extensive-condition deflation is likely to be interrupted through periodic spikes of rapid inflation and consequent real economic disruptions. Moderate and stable inflation would avoid such a seesawing of price movements.
- *Financial Market Inefficiency with Deflation:* The second effect noted through Tsaing is that when savers have substituted money holding for lending on financial markets, the role of those markets in channeling savings into investment is undermined. With nominal

interest rates driven to zero, or close to zero, from the competition with a high return money asset, there would be no price mechanism in whatever is left of those markets. With financial markets effectively euthanized, the remaining goods and physical asset prices would move in perverse directions. For instance, an increased desire to save could not push interest rates further down (and thereby stimulate investment) but would instead reason additional money hoarding, driving consumer prices further down and creation investment in consumer goods manufacture thereby less attractive. Moderate inflation, once its expectation is included into nominal interest rates, would provide those interest rates room to go both up and down in response to shifting investment opportunities, or savers' preferences, and therefore allow financial markets to function in a more normal fashion.

REASONS

Historically, a great trade of economic literature was concerned with the question of what reasons inflation and what effect it has. There were dissimilar schools of idea since to the reasons of inflation. The excellence theory of inflation rests on the expectation of a seller accepting currency to be able to swap that currency at a later time for goods that are desirable since a buyer. The quantity theory of inflation rests on the quantity equation of money that relates the money supply, its velocity, and the nominal value of exchanges. Adam Smith and David Hume proposed a quantity theory of inflation for money, and an excellence theory of inflation for manufacture. Currently, the quantity theory of money is widely carried since an accurate model of inflation in the extensive run. Consequently, there is now broad agreement in the middle of economists that in the extensive run, the inflation rate is essentially dependent on the development rate of money supply comparative to the development of the economy. Though, in the short and medium condition inflation may be affected through supply and demand pressures in the economy, and convinced through the comparative elasticity of wages, prices, and interest rates. The question of whether the short-condition effects last extensive sufficient to be significant is the central topic of debate flanked by monetarist and Keynesian economists. In monetarism prices and wages adjust quickly sufficient to create other factors merely marginal behavior on a common trend-row. In the Keynesian view, prices and wages adjust at dissimilar rates, and these variations have sufficient effects on real output to be "extensive condition" in the view of people in an economy.

Keynesian View

Keynesian economic theory proposes that changes in money supply do not directly affect prices, and that visible inflation is the result of pressures in the economy expressing themselves in prices. There are three major kinds of inflation, since section of what Robert J. Gordon calls the "triangle model":

- *Demand-pull inflation* is caused through increases in aggregate demand due to increased private and government spending, etc. Demand inflation is constructive to a faster rate of economic development as the excess demand and favorable market circumstances will stimulate investment and expansion.
- *Cost-push inflation*, also described "supply shock inflation," is caused through a drop in aggregate supply (potential output). This may be due to natural disasters, or increased prices of inputs. For instance, a sudden decrease in the supply of oil, leading to increased oil prices, can reason cost-push inflation. Producers for whom oil is a section of their costs could then pass this on to consumers in the shape of increased prices. Another instance stems from unexpectedly high Insured Losses, either legitimate (catastrophes) or fraudulent (which might be particularly prevalent in times of recession).
- Built-in inflation is induced through adaptive expectations, and is often connected to the "price/wage spiral". It involves workers trying to stay their wages up with prices (above the rate of inflation), and firms passing these higher labor costs on to their customers since higher prices, leading to a 'vicious circle'. Built-in inflation reflects measures in the past, and therefore might be seen since hangover inflation.

Demand-pull theory states that the rate of inflation accelerates whenever aggregate demand is increased beyond the skill of the economy to produce (its potential output). Hence, any factor that increases aggregate demand can reason inflation. Though, in the extensive run, aggregate demand can be held above productive capability only through rising the quantity of money in circulation faster than the real development rate of the economy. Another (although much less general) reason can be a rapid decline in the *demand* for money, since happened in Europe throughout the Black Death, or in the Japanese engaged territories presently before the defeat of Japan in 1945.

The effect of money on inflation is mainly obvious when governments fund spending in a crisis, such since a civil war, through printing money excessively. This sometimes leads to hyperinflation, a term where prices can double in a month or less.

Money supply is also idea to play a major role in determining moderate stages of inflation, although there are variations of opinion on how significant it is. For instance, Monetarist economists consider that the link is extremely strong; Keynesian economists, through contrast, typically emphasize the role of aggregate demand in the economy rather than the money supply in determining inflation. That is, for Keynesians, the money supply is only one determinant of aggregate demand.

Some Keynesian economists also disagree with the notion that central banks fully manage the money supply, arguing that central banks have small manage, as the money supply adapts to the demand for bank credit issued through commercial banks. This is recognized since the theory of endogenous money, and has been advocated strongly through post-Keynesians since distant back since the 1960s. It has today become a central focus of Taylor rule advocates. This location is not universally carried – banks make money through creation loans, but the aggregate volume of these loans diminishes since real interest rates augment. Therefore, central banks can power the money supply through creation money cheaper or more expensive, therefore rising or decreasing its manufacture.

A fundamental concept in inflation analysis is the connection flanked by inflation and unemployment, described the Phillips curve. This model suggests that there is a deal-off flanked by price continuity and employment. So, some stage of inflation could be measured desirable in order to minimize unemployment. The Phillips curve model called the U.S. experience well in the 1960s but failed to define the combination of growing inflation and economic stagnation (sometimes referred to since *stagflation*) experienced in the 1970s.

Therefore, contemporary macroeconomics defines inflation by a Phillips curve that *shifts* (therefore the deal-off flanked by inflation and unemployment changes) because of such matters since supply shocks and inflation becoming built into the normal workings of the economy. The former refers to such measures since the oil shocks of the 1970s, while the latter refers to the price/wage spiral and inflationary expectations implying that the economy "normally" suffers from inflation. Therefore, the Phillips curve symbolizes only the demand-pull component of the triangle model.

Another concept of note is the potential output (sometimes described the "natural gross domestic product"), a stage of GDP, where the economy is at its optimal stage of manufacture given institutional and natural constraints. (This stage of output corresponds to the Non-Accelerating Inflation Rate of Unemployment, NAIRU, or the "natural" rate of unemployment or the full-employment unemployment rate.) If GDP exceeds its potential (and unemployment is below the NAIRU), the theory says that inflation will *accelerate* since suppliers augment their prices and built-in inflation worsens. If GDP falls below its potential stage (and unemployment is above the NAIRU), inflation will *decelerate* since suppliers effort to fill excess capability, cutting prices and undermining built-in inflation.

Though, one trouble with this theory for policy-creation purposes is that the exact stage of potential output (and of the NAIRU) is usually strange and tends to transform in excess of time. Inflation also looks to act in an asymmetric method, growing more quickly than it falls. Worse, it can transform because of policy: for instance, high unemployment under British Prime Minister Margaret

Thatcher might have led to a rise in the NAIRU (and a fall in potential) because several of the unemployed establish themselves since structurally unemployed, unable to discover occupations that fit their skills. A rise in structural unemployment implies that a smaller percentage of the labor force can discover occupations at the NAIRU, where the economy avoids crossing the threshold into the realm of accelerating inflation.

Monetarist View

Monetarists consider the mainly important factor influencing inflation or deflation is how fast the money supply grows or shrinks. They believe fiscal policy, or government spending and taxation, since ineffective in controlling inflation. Just as to the well-known monetarist economist Milton Friedman, "Inflation is always and everywhere a monetary phenomenon." Some monetarists, though, will qualify this through creation an exception for extremely short-condition conditions.

Monetarists assert that the empirical revise of monetary history illustrates that inflation has always been a monetary phenomenon. The quantity theory of money, basically stated, says that any transform in the amount of money in an organization will transform the price stage. This theory begins with the equation of swap:

$$MV = PQ$$

where

- M is the nominal quantity of money.
- V is the velocity of money in final expenditures;
- P is the common price stage;
- Q is an index of the real value of final expenditures;

In this formula, the common price stage is related to the stage of real economic action (Q), the quantity of money (M) and the velocity of money (V). The formula is an identity because the velocity of money (V) is defined to be the ratio of final nominal expenditure (PQ) to the quantity of money (M).

Monetarists assume that the velocity of money is unaffected through monetary policy (at least in the extensive run), and the real value of output is determined in the extensive run through the productive capability of the economy. Under these assumptions, the primary driver of the transform in the common price stage is changes in the quantity of money. With exogenous velocity (that is, velocity being determined externally and not being convinced through monetary policy), the money supply determines the value of nominal output (which equals final expenditure) in the short run. In practice, velocity is not exogenous in the short run, and therefore the formula does not necessarily imply a stable short-run connection flanked by the money supply and nominal output. Though, in the extensive run, changes in velocity are assumed to be determined through the development of the payments mechanism. If velocity is relatively unaffected through monetary policy, the extensive-run rate of augment in prices (the inflation rate) is equal to the extensive run development rate of the money supply plus the exogenous extensive-run rate of velocity development minus the extensive run development rate of real output.

Unemployment

A relationship flanked by inflation and unemployment has been drawn as the emergence of big level unemployment in the 19th century, and connections continue to be drawn today. In Marxian economics, the unemployed serve since a reserve army of labour, which restrain wage inflation. In the 20th century, same concepts in Keynesian economics contain the NAIRU (Non-Accelerating Inflation Rate of Unemployment) and the Phillips curve.

Rational Expectations Theory

Rational expectations theory holds that economic actors seem rationally into the future when trying to maximize their well-being, and do not respond solely to immediate opportunity costs and pressures. In this view, while usually grounded in monetarism, future expectations and strategies are significant for inflation since well.

A core assertion of rational expectations theory is that actors will seek to "head off" central-bank decisions through acting in ways that fulfill predictions of higher inflation. This means that central banks necessity set up their credibility in fighting inflation, or economic actors will create bets that the central bank will expand the money supply rapidly sufficient to prevent recession, even at the expense of exacerbating inflation. Therefore, if a central bank has a reputation since being "soft" on inflation, when it announces a new policy of fighting inflation with restrictive monetary development economic mediators will not consider that the policy will persist; their inflationary expectations will remain high, and therefore will inflation. On the other hand, if the central bank has a reputation of being "tough" on inflation, then such a policy announcement will be whispered and inflationary expectations will approach down rapidly, therefore allowing inflation itself to approach down rapidly with minimal economic disruption.

Austrian View

The Austrian School asserts that inflation is an augment in the money supply, growing prices are merely consequences, and this semantic variation is significant in defining inflation. Austrians stress that inflation affects prices in several degree, i.e. that prices rise more sharply in some sectors than in other sectors of the economy. The cause for the disparity is that excess money will be concentrated to sure sectors, such since housing, stocks, or health care. Because of this disparity, Austrians argue that the aggregate price stage can be extremely misleading when observing the effects of inflation. Austrian economist's measure inflation through calculating the development of new elements of money that is accessible for immediate exploit in swap that has been created in excess of time.

Critics of the Austrian view point out that their preferred alternative to fiat currency designed to prevent inflation, commodity-backed money, is likely to grow in supply at a dissimilar rate than economic development. Therefore it has proven to be highly deflationary and destabilizing, including in instances where it has caused and prolonged depressions.

Real Bills Doctrine

Within the context of a fixed specie foundation for money, one significant controversy was flanked by the quantity theory of money and the real bills doctrine (RBD). Within this context, quantity theory applies to the stage of fractional reserve accounting allowed against specie, usually gold, held through a bank. Currency and banking schools of economics argue the RBD that banks should also be able to issue currency against bills of trading, which is "real bills" that they buy from merchants. This theory was significant in the 19th century in debates flanked by "Banking" and "Currency" schools of monetary soundness, and in the formation of the Federal Reserve. In the wake of the collapse of the international gold average post 1913, and the move towards deficit financing of government, RBD has remained a minor topic, primarily of interest in limited contexts, such since currency boards. It is usually held in ill repute today, with Frederic Mishkin, a governor of the Federal Reserve going therefore distant since to say it had been "totally discredited."

The debate flanked by currency, or quantity theory, and banking schools in Britain throughout the 19th century prefigures current questions in relation to the credibility of money in the present. In the 19th century the banking school had greater power in policy in the United States and Great Britain, while the currency school had more power "on the continent", that is in non-British countries, particularly in the Latin Monetary Union and the earlier Scandinavia monetary union.

Anti-classical or Backing Theory

Another issue associated with classical political economy is the anti-classical hypothesis of money, or "backing theory". The backing theory argues that the value of money is determined through the assets and liabilities of the issuing agency. Unlike the Quantity Theory of classical political economy, the backing theory argues that issuing authorities can issue money without causing inflation therefore extensive since the money issuer has enough assets to cover redemptions. There are extremely few backing theorists, creation quantity theory the dominant theory explaining inflation.

CONTROLLING INFLATION

Stimulating Economic Development

If economic development matches the development of the money supply, inflation should not happen when all else is equal. A big diversity of factors can affect the rate of both. For instance, investment in market manufacture, infrastructure, education, and preventative health care can all grow an economy in greater amounts than the investment spending.

Monetary Policy

Today the primary tool for controlling inflation is monetary policy. Mainly central banks are tasked with keeping their inter-bank lending rates at low stages, normally to a target rate approximately 2% to 3% per annum, and within a targeted low inflation range, somewhere from in relation to the 2% to 6% per annum. A low positive inflation is generally targeted, since deflationary circumstances are seen since dangerous for the health of the economy.

There are a number of methods that have been suggested to manage inflation. Central banks such since the U.S. Federal Reserve can affect inflation to an important extent by setting interest rates and by other operations. High interest rates and slow development of the money supply are the traditional ways by which central banks fight or prevent inflation, however they have dissimilar approaches. For example, some follow a symmetrical inflation target while others only manage inflation when it rises above a target, whether express or implied.

Monetarists emphasize keeping the development rate of money steady, and by monetary policy to manage inflation (rising interest rates, slowing the rise in the money supply). Keynesians emphasize reducing aggregate demand throughout economic expansions and rising demand throughout recessions to stay inflation stable. Manage of aggregate demand can be achieved by both monetary policy and fiscal policy (increased taxation or reduced government spending to reduce demand).

Fixed Swap Rates

Under a fixed swap rate currency regime, a country's currency is tied in value to another single currency or to a basket of other currencies (or sometimes to another measure of value, such since gold). A fixed swap rate is generally used to stabilize the value of a currency, vis-à-vis the currency it is pegged to. It can also be used since a means to manage inflation. Though, since the value of the reference currency rises and falls, therefore does the currency pegged to it. This essentially means that the inflation rate in the fixed swap rate country is determined through the inflation rate of the country the currency is pegged to. In addition, a fixed swap rate prevents a government from by domestic monetary policy in order to achieve macroeconomic continuity. Under the Bretton Woods agreement, mainly countries approximately the world had currencies that were fixed to the US dollar. This limited inflation in those countries, but also discovered them to the danger of speculative attacks. After the Bretton Woods agreement broke down in the early 1970s, countries slowly turned to floating swap rates. Though, in the later section of the 20th century, some countries reverted to a fixed swap rate since section of an effort to manage inflation. This policy of by a fixed swap rate to manage inflation was used in several countries in South America in the later section of the 20th century (e.g. Argentina (1991–2002), Bolivia, Brazil, and Chile).

Gold Average

The gold average is a monetary organization in which an area's general media of swap are paper notes that are normally freely convertible into pre-set, fixed quantities of gold. The average identifies how the gold backing would be implemented, including the amount of specie per currency element. The currency itself has no innate value, but is carried through traders because it can be redeemed for the equivalent specie. A U.S. silver certificate, for instance, could be redeemed for an actual piece of silver.

The gold average was partially abandoned via the international adoption of the Bretton Woods Organization. Under this organization all other major currencies were tied at fixed rates to the dollar, which itself was tied to gold at the rate of $35 per ounce. The Bretton Woods organization broke down in 1971, causing mainly countries to switch to fiat money – money backed only through the laws of the country.

Just as to Lawrence H. White, an F. A. Hayek Professor of Economic History "who values the Austrian custom", economies based on the gold average rarely experience inflation above 2 percent annually. Though, historically, the U.S. saw inflation in excess of 2% many times and a higher peak of inflation under the gold average when compared to inflation after the gold average. Under a gold average, the extensive condition rate of inflation (or deflation) would be determined through the development rate of the supply of gold comparative to total output. Critics argue that this will reason arbitrary fluctuations in the inflation rate, and that monetary policy would essentially be determined through gold mining.

Wage and Price Dominates

Another way attempted in the past has been wage and price dominates ("incomes policies"). Wage and price dominates have been successful in wartime environments in combination with rationing. Though, their exploit in other contexts is distant more mixed. Notable failures of their exploit contain the 1972 imposition of wage and price dominates through Richard Nixon. More successful examples contain the Prices and Incomes Accord in Australia and the Wassenaar Agreement in the Netherlands.

In common wage and price dominates are regarded since a temporary and exceptional measure, only effective when coupled with policies intended to reduce the underlying reasons of inflation throughout the wage and price manage regime, for instance, winning the war being fought. They often have perverse effects, due to the distorted signals they send to the market. Artificially low prices often reason rationing and shortages and discourage future investment, resulting in yet further shortages. The usual economic analysis is that any product or service that is under-priced is over consumed. For instance, if the official price of bread is too low, there will be too small bread at official prices, and too small investment in bread creation through the market to satisfy future requires, thereby exacerbating the trouble in the extensive condition.

Temporary dominates may complement a recession since a method to fight inflation: dominates create the recession more efficient since a method to fight inflation (reducing require to augment unemployment), while the recession prevents the types of distortions that dominates reason when demand is high. Though, in common the advice of economists is not to impose price dominates but to liberalize prices through assuming that the economy will adjust and abandon unprofitable economic action. The lower action will lay fewer demands on whatever commodities were driving inflation, whether labor or possessions, and inflation will fall with total economic output. This often produces a severe recession, since productive capability is reallocated and is therefore often extremely unpopular with the people whose livelihoods are destroyed.

Cost-of-livelihood Allowance

The real purchasing-domination of fixed payments is eroded through inflation unless they are inflation-adjusted to stay their real values consistent. In several countries, employment contracts, pension benefits, and government entitlements (such since social security) are tied to a cost-of-livelihood index, typically to the consumer price index. A cost-of-livelihood allowance (COLA) adjusts salaries based on changes in a cost-of-livelihood index. Salaries are typically adjusted annually in low inflation economies. Throughout hyperinflation they are adjusted more often. They may also be tied to a cost-of-livelihood index that varies through geographic site if the employee moves.

Annual escalation clauses in employment contracts can specify retroactive or future percentage increases in worker pay which are not tied to any index. These negotiated increases in pay are colloquially referred to since cost-of-livelihood adjustments ("COLAs") or cost-of-livelihood increases because of their parallel to increases tied to externally determined indexes.

3

Global Integration of Indian Money Market

Financial openness exists when residents of one country are able to trade assets with residents of another country, *i.e.*, when financial assets are traded goods. A weak definition of complete financial openness, which one might refer to as financial integration, can be given as a situation in which the law of one price holds for financial assets- *i.e.*, domestic and foreign residents trade identical assets at the same price. A strong definition would add to this the restriction that identically defined assets, *e.g.*, a six-month Treasury bill, issued in different political jurisdictions and denominated in different currencies are perfect substitutes in all private portfolios.

The degree of financial integration has important macroeconomic implications in terms of the effectiveness of fiscal and monetary policy in influencing aggregate demand as well as the scope for promoting investment in an economy. The free and unrestricted flow of capital in and out of countries and the ever increasing integration of world capital markets can be attributed to the process of Globalisation.

The benefits of such integration are liquidity enhancement on one hand and risk diversification on the other, both of which are instrumental in making markets more efficient and also facilitate smooth transfers of funds between lenders and borrowers. India began a very gradual and selective opening of the domestic capital markets to foreign residents, including non-resident Indians (NRIs), in the eighties.

The capital market opening picked up pace during the nineties. In this paper we try and estimate the degree of financial integration between India and the rest of the World, by focussing on the degree of integration of the Indian money market with global markets. Frenkel (1992) in his review of Capital Mobility measurement outlined four different definitions of perfect capital mobility that are in widespread use, of which three are of relevance to the current paper.

These are real interest parity, uncovered interest parity and covered interest parity.

- Real interest parity hypothesis states that international capital flows equalise real interest rates across countries.

- Uncovered interest parity states that capital flows equalise expected rates of return on countries' bonds regardless of exposure to exchange risk.
- Covered interest parity states that capital flows equalise interest rates across countries when contracted in the same currency. Frenkel (1992) shows that these three definitions are in ascending order of specificity in the following sense. Only definition
  - That the covered interest differential is zero is an unalloyed criterion for "capital mobility" in the sense of the degree of financial market integration across national boundaries. Condition
  - That the uncovered interest differential is zero requires that
  - Hold and that there be zero exchange risk premium. Condition.
    i. That the real interest differential be zero requires condition
    ii. And in addition that expected real depreciation is zero.

The uncovered interest parity (UIP) theory states that differences between interest rates across countries can be explained by expected changes in currencies. Empirically, the UIP theory is usually rejected assuming rational expectations, and explanations for this rejection include that expectations are irrational. In a survey of 75 published estimates, Froot and Thaler (1990) report few cases where the sign of the coefficient on interest rate differentials in exchange rate prediction equations is consistent with the un-biased-ness hypothesis and not a single case where it exceeds the theoretical value of unity.

This resounding unanimity on the failure of the predictive power of interest differentials is virtually unique in the empirical literature in economics. A third explanation was provided by McCallum (1994a), who observes that regressing the change in spot exchange rates on the forward premium, one typically finds a negative regression parameter of -4 to -3 contrary to the expected parameter of +1. McCallum argues, however, that this finding may be consistent with the UIP theory, if one introduces policy behaviour.

Assuming policymakers adjust interest rates in order to keep exchange rates stable, and that they are interested in smoothing interest rate movements, McCallum derives a reduced form equation for the spot exchange rate under rational expectations. In fact, this results in a negative theoretical relationship between the change in the spot exchange rate and the forward premium consistent with his empirical findings. Christensen, M. (2000) extend the data set used by McCallum to include the recent 8 years and find that \$/DM, \$/£ and \$/Yen for the period 1978.01m to 1999.03m behave amasingly well according to the modified UIP theory developed by McCallum.

However, when he estimates the policy reaction function, its structural parameters are inconsistent with the UIP relationships estimated. Nevertheless, there appears to be overwhelming empirical evidence against UIRP, at least at frequencies less than one year. Fama (1984) focuses on statistical properties of this relation. He finds that from the end of August 1973 to the end of 1982, the variance of the exchange risk premium has been large, exceeding the variance of expected future spot rates changes of the dollar against each of ten other major currencies (over monthly intervals).

On the other hand Frankel and Froot (1987), among others, propose an explanation of UIP deviations based on the existence of asymmetries between currencies. Using survey data to approximate the exchange rates' behaviour, they show that agents were expecting a 10 per cent depreciation of the Dollar against the Mark over 1981-85 whereas the differential in corresponding interest rates was only around 4 per cent. Given that this empirical evidence has not stopped theorists from relying on UIRP, it is fortunate that recent evidence is more favourable.

Bekaert and Hodrick (2001) and Baillie and Bollerslev (2000) argue that doubtful statistical inference may have contributed to the strong rejections of UIRP at higher frequencies. Chinn and Meredith (2001) marshal evidence that UIRP holds much better at long horizons. They test this hypothesis using interest rates on longer-maturity bonds for the U.S., Germany, Japan and Canada. The results of these long horizon regressions are much more positive — the coefficients on interest differentials are of the correct sign, and most are closer to the predicted value of unity than to zero.

Ravi Bansal and Magnus Dahlquist (2000) conclude that the often found negative correlation between the expected currency depreciation and interest rate differential is, contrary to popular belief, not a pervasive phenomenon. It is confined to developed economies, and here only to states where the U.S., interest rate exceeds foreign interest rates.

The covered interest parity (CIP) postulates that interest rates denominated in different currencies are equal once you cover yourself against foreign exchange risk. Unlike the UIP, there is empirical evidence supporting CIP hypothesis. Empirical studies such as Frenkel and Levich, Frankel (1989), among others, find that the CIP holds in most cases on the Eurocurrency market (where remunerated assets have similar default and political risk characteristics) since the collapse of the Bretton Woods regime in early 1970's.

Lewis shows that risk premia do not vary significantly and often switch sign, contrary to what the observed stability of the countries' global creditor or debtor status would predict. However she explains that not only the conditional variance of exchange rate is not significant enough to account for risk premia movements, but also that risk premia examined in the short run should concern capital flows and investors with similar temporal horizons, such as currency traders, hedge funds and mutual funds managers. Frankel (1991) reports mean covered interest differentials (CIDs) for the period 1982 to 1987 for a selection of developed and developing economies using monthly observations of the 3-month local money market rate against the equivalent Eurodollar rate.

Focusing on the East Asian economies in the sample – Japan, Hong Kong, Malaysia and Singapore – the null of a zero differential is rejected for the first three economies, though only marginally in that the CIDs are very low. Chinn and Frankel (1992) found that the CIDs were small for Japan, Hong Kong and Singapore, but large for Malaysia. In the Indian context, Varma (1997) has undertaken an analysis of the covered interest parity. His posits a structural break in the money market in India in September 1995, with CIP become effective from that point on for the first time in the Indian money market.

The structural break itself is attributed to interplay between the money market and the foreign exchange market. The period after 1995 is however witness to several deviations from the CIP. Varma has used rates on Treasury bills, certificates of deposit and commercial paper and call money rate to analyse the Indian money market. For the foreign rate he has calculated an implicit euro-rupee rate for six, three and overnight maturity.

Thus he uses a mix of actual and constructed rates of different maturity. A rigourous test requires use of interest rates on identical instruments (*e.g.*, maturity, risk) and a consistent forward rate (period of forwards should be identical to that of instruments). This is perhaps the first time that such a test is being carried out for India.

MODEL AND ESTIMATION

Estimating Equations

One of the key implications of international financial integration is on the degree of movement/co-movement of interest rates in countries over time and their comparison in terms of convergence or having a common trend. The relationship between two countries' interest rates is termed as interest rate parity.

The interest rate theory proposes that given perfect capital mobility, perfect capital market and fixed exchange rates the interest on identical assets (identical in terms of maturity etc) would be equal across countries. However, in the real world 5 with capital controls, flexible exchange rates and imperfect capital markets divergence between interest rate is frequently observed and persist over long periods.

Given the reality of non-frictionless capital markets and flexible exchange rates the recent versions of the interest parity theorem attribute this divergence to the expectation about exchange rate movements.

Based on the preference individuals have for risk there are two versions of this basic relation:

- *Uncovered Interest Rate Parity*- Assume that individuals are risk neutral. With no capital controls and perfect capital markets the interest differential between two countries is equal to change in exchange rate: it – it* = St+1-St where it is domestic interest rate it*/ is foreign interest rate on similar asset (identical in all respects except for yield and currency denomination) St is the spot exchange rate. A risk neutral person would replace St+1 by his expectation about future exchange rate. So we get it – it* = E (St+1) – St Any deviation from UIP can be attributed to currency associated risks in the absence of hedging agreements- namely currency premium and expectation bias.

- *Covered Interest Parity*- Assume that individuals are risk averse. Such an individual would like to cover himself for any unexpected currency fluctuation during the tenure of the deal. Given the forward contract market, he would purchase a forward contract and use the exchange rate mentioned in the contract. Then any difference in interest rate should be equated to forward premium.

This is called CIP: it – it* = Ft- St or it – it* = ft where Ft is forward rate and ft is forward premium. Any deviation from CIP would suggest that the markets are inefficient, regulations like capital controls exist and costs like sovereign risk, individual borrowing constraints are not accounted for.

Econometrics

The problem with using Ordinary Least Square as an estimation technique relates to the issue of non-stationarity of the time series involved in the equation. In case of non-stationary times series the estimate would be spurious and biased. However if we can show that the two variables in question are cointegrated than the OLS estimates are super consistent and would converge to their true value faster. Thus before drawing inferences based on the results of ordinary least squares it is imperative to check the variables namely F (3-month forward premium) and IDIFF (3-month TB auction rate differential between India and U.S). In case the two series are integrated of the same order we can then test for cointegartion between the two non-stationary variables. Under the null hypothesis the above statistic follows a t-distribution with n-2 degrees of freedom.

Stationarity and Co-Integration

Since we are using high frequency time series data it is necessary to test for stationarity of the variables involved in above regressions. In case of non-stationarity, we need to show that the variables of same order of integration are cointegrated.

The next step is to test for Co-integration between IDIFF and F using Johansen's procedures. Both the maximum and trace eigen value statistics strongly reject the null hypothesis that there is no cointegration between the variables (*i.e.*, r = 0), but do not reject the hypothesis that there is one cointegrating relation between the variables (*i.e.*, r = 1). Hence using least squares would yield super-consistent estimators. Note that DCALL is stationary and thus can be included as an exogenous policy variable in the interest parity equation.

The calculated absolute value of t for the hypothesis test is 1.09, which is less than the critical value 2. So we can accept the Ho at 5 per cent level of significance and conclude that CIP holds for the period under consideration. This shows that short-term money markets (3-month) in India are getting integrated with global (US) money markets even though the integration is far from perfect. We would have liked to test the hypothesis for 1-month, 6-month and 1 year treasury bills, but a completely consistent data set is not available. In our view hybrid data sets do not provide a rigourous test (*e.g.*, using 6 month forwards to test integration between one year securities).

Un-covered Interest Parity

The interest rate parity hypothesis postulates that with flexible exchange rates and non-frictionless capital markets the difference between the yield on identical assets in two countries could be explained by expected change in the exchange rate. Assuming perfect foresight we can test for uncovered interest rate parity by regressing change in spot exchange rate on interest rate differential and testing for the coefficient of interest rate differential being equal to 1. Given that CIP has been shown to hold during the same time period, this implies that the exchange risk premium for the Indian rupee is not zero (*i.e.*, it is positive). There have been a number of recognised external shocks during the nineties, such as the Mexican crisis and the Asian crises that lead to heightened external uncertainty and increased foreign exchange risk perception. These were also situations in which the Central bank (RBI) intervened in the financial markets.

Exchange Risk and RBI Intervention

As per the declared policy of the Reserve Bank of India (RBI), RBI intervenes to smooth out short term fluctuations in demand-supply balances arising from lumpy demand for foreign exchange (*e.g.*, large repayment of debt) that it thinks will lead to excessive volatility given the thinness of the market.

This intervention is commonly done through sale/purchase of foreign exchange. If the behaviour of the RBI is completely symmetric with zero sterilisation, we would expect symmetric effects on call markets (increased/reduced liquidity) and on forward rates (higher/lower reserves). The higher the degree of sterilisation the less the effect of foreign inflow on liquidity and more asymmetric the relationship between call rates and forward rates (*i.e.*, rising call rates have larger co-efficient than falling ones).

The RBI also intervenes to counter sharp adverse changes in expectations, like those arising from domestic and global political developments (*e.g.*, post

Pokharan sanctions, Kargil war) and external crisis such as the Mexican and Asian crisis. This intervention is commonly done through short-term instruments (overnight and 7-day repos, bank rate/moral suasion of banks), and translates into sharp upward movement in the inter-bank call money market rates. These in turn are reflected in a rise in foreign exchange forward rates. It is only at the time of the next auction, however, that these developments get reflected in the T-bill auction rates. Such tightening is generally followed in due course by a loosening to the starting position, but forwards may not revert to the original level given the residual uncertainty.

The estimated coefficient of the interest differential has now fallen from 0.65 to 0.58. However, to see whether it is statistically different from 1 we would perform the t- test for the restriction again. External shocks and RBI exchange market stabilisation efforts through the short-term money market seem to loosen the link between the domestic and foreign money markets.

The paper shows that the short-term (up to 3 month) money markets in India are getting progressively integrated with those in the USA even though the degree of integration is far from perfect. Covered interest parity is found to hold for while uncovered interest parity fails to hold.

The difference between the two can be attributed to the existence of an exchange risk premium over and above the expected depreciation of the currency. Analysis of RBI interventions in response to foreign exchange shocks suggests that these may play a role in the deviations from interest parity. Further work needs to be done however on this as well as on instruments of other maturity such as 1 month and 6 month (for which consistent data was not available).

INDIA MONEY MARKET

The money market is a mechanism that deals with the lending and borrowing of short term funds. The India Money Market has come of age in the past two decades. In order to study the money market of India in detail, we at first need to understand the parameters around which the money market in India revolves. The performance of the Indian Money Market is heavily dependent on real interest rate that is the interest rate that is inflation adjusted.

Though the money market is free from interest rate ceilings, structural barriers and other institutional factors can be held responsible for creating distortions in India Money Market. Apart from the call market rates, the other interest rates in the Indian Money Market usually do not change in the short run. It is due to this disparity between the opposite forces that is prevalent in the money market in India that a well defined income path cannot be traced. Owing to the deregulation of the interest rate in the early nineties following the economic reforms laid down by the then finance minister Dr. Manmohan Singh, studies concerning the behaviour of interest rate were restricted.

However the liquidity of the market makes its a good subject for empirical research. The Indian Money Market involves a wide range of instruments. Here, maturities range from one day to a year, issued by banks and corporates of various sizes. The money market is also closely linked with the Foreign Exchange Market through the process of covered interest arbitrage in which the forward premium acts as a bridge between domestic and foreign interest rates.

To analyse the interest rates that characterise the Indian Money Market, the following elements need to be covered:

- The term structure of interest rate.
- The difference between domestic and international interest rates
- The market structure differences between the auction markets that clear continuously and the customer markets.
- The credit speed between instruments involving similar maturity but diverse risk factor. Such is the distortion in the Indian Money Market.

INDIA MARKET SIZE

In order to estimate the size of the Indian Market, we need to understand the scope of the Indian Market. India Market Size is huge probably bigger in comparison to its geographical extent. The Size of the Indian Market owes much of its credit to the fact that it is the second most populated country in the world. The Indian Market can be classified in a number of ways. The Indian Market can be broadly classified under the following heads:

- Commodity Market
- Money Market
- Labour Market
- Capital Market

The commodity market in India deals with the exchange of goods, the cost of which is estimated in terms of domestic currency. It can be subdivided into the following two categories:

- Wholesale Market
- Retail Market

The money market of India involves all monetary transactions. It be further divided under the following two categories.

- Currency Market
- Bond Market

The labour market as the name suggests, consists of the entire working population of the nation. It involves the services provided by the people of India in the primary, secondary and tertiary sectors. The services of the individuals are assessed in terms of the wages they get for their services. The Capital Market deals with all those assets which are responsible for production both directly and indirectly. Let us now take a look at what the present scenario of each of the above markets is like. The traditional wholesale market in India dealt with whole sellers who bought goods from the farmers and manufacturers and then sold them to the retailers after making a profit in the process. It was the retailers who finally sold the goods to the consumers. With the passage of time the importance of whole sellers began to fade out for the following reasons:

- The whole sellers in most situations, acted as mere parasites who did not add any value to the product but raised its price which was eventually faced by the consumers.
- The improvement in transport facilities made the retailers directly interact with the producers and hence the need for whole sellers was not felt.

In recent years, the extent of the retail market (both organised and unorganised) has evolved in leaps and bounds. Considering the present growth rate, the total valuation of the Indian Retail Market is estimated to cross ₹. 10,000 billion by the year 2010. Similar scenario can be observed in other markets as well. Demand for commodities is likely to become four times by 2010 than what it presently is. The money market is also expected to experience a similar increase with the encouragement of Foreign Direct Investment (FDI) by the central government. Thus the ever increasing extent of the Indian Market is complementing the growth of the economy in a big way.

THE ART MARKET IN INDIA

For an uninitiated Westerner, making your way to one of this city's new art galleries can be a disorienting study in contrasts. In the crowded streets behind the Taj Mahal Palace and Tower, where the air is heavy with the smell of gasoline and flowers, you are approached by women begging for money and food. Men shout invitations to enter their carpet shops or purchase wares like watches, magazines, leather jackets and cigarettes. Then, from a narrow thoroughfare, you enter a courtyard where an old man sits wearing a black security uniform. He speaks no English but, when asked for directions, points towards a flight of wood stairs so worn they are bowed in the middle. At the top, a door is opened by a barefoot woman in a scarlet sari. Behind her is an art gallery as white and sleek as any space in Chelsea. These contradictions do not arise from any calculated exoticism. This is simply the new India. "It isn't as if we are not aware of what is happening in New York or Berlin or in China," the dealer Usha Mirchandani said in an interview at the gallery. "It is just that we find ourselves in a new position, and we must find our own way.

TODAY IN ASIA – PACIFIC

"We are an old civilization. We have untold treasures. But what has happened here in the last year and a half has changed things, with the economy booming and so much art being sold and the prices just going off the graph."

The Indian art world has more than changed. It has exploded. Prices have increased tenfold since 2002. In the last two years alone, they have nearly doubled. Works by India's top-selling contemporary artists - Atul Dodiya and Subodh Gupta are the names most often cited - can fetch hundreds of thousands of dollars. The auction price of paintings by the older generation of great Indian modernists, like M.F. Husain or F.N. Souza, can easily pass a million dollars, hardly uncommon for leading Western artists but staggering in a country where the average income among the 1.1 billion residents is about $820 a year. Although the usual metaphors are marched out to describe the new art scene - a Wild West, a gold rush - there are signs that speculators have begun to pull back since the government imposed new capital gains taxes on art sales. Still, the global art world is enthralled.

The abiding fascination with China's modish new art has now spread to its southwestern neighbour, with international dealers and curators flocking in to discover talent. In the next few weeks alone, at least seven large-scale exhibitions of contemporary Indian art will open in Italy, Switzerland and the United States. Given the attention and fistfuls of money being thrown at Indian art, more and more galleries are opening or refashioning themselves.

Some spaces are being retrofitted or built from scratch to accommodate bigger art and the more complex video or multimedia installations that are fresh additions to artistic practice in India. In New Delhi, Gallery Espace, Vadehra Art Gallery and Talwar Gallery are three elegant examples. A fourth is Nature Morte, considered by many to be the pre-eminent gallery of contemporary art in India. It recently opened a second space in Delhi to house artists' projects and a third space in Calcutta with its New York partner, the gallery Bose Pacia.

Similar energy is gathering in Mumbai, where Galerie Mirchandani + Steinruecke, Bodhi Art (which has other spaces in New York, Delhi and Singapore), Sakshi Gallery, Project 88 and Chatterjee and Lal have all opened or moved and expanded during the market's rise. Shilpa Gupta, a 31-year-old artist based in New Delhi whose videos and installations are exhibited in Asia, Europe and the United States, echoes the breathlessness of the moment. "It doesn't matter who's a star now," she said. "It's so beautiful. You can hang out, chill out. We all know each other, and everyone is doing very well, and it's fantastic."

Yet paradoxes surface in even the briefest conversations with artists, dealers, collectors and writers here. Money pouring into the art world from non-resident Indians who have made their fortunes in the United States and Europe, along with the racing engine of India's $4 trillion economy, has enabled artists to travel abroad far more often than they did before. But with this change has come the slow unraveling of the tight-knit community that Gupta idealises and that now gathers mostly at far-flung exhibition openings, hardly the forum for intense discussions of issues and artwork. And for all its recent plenty, as the art consultant Jai Danani pointed out, the money has yet to bring its Midas touch to the Indian art world as a whole, that is, to generate the largess needed to create art schools, studios and museums for contemporary art. Nikhil Chopra, a young performance artist in Mumbai, said: "I can't believe we're a country of a billion people that doesn't have more than a couple of decent art schools, no contemporary art museum, no real funding, no group of trained curators fluent in contemporary art, no art criticism in the newspapers, just one serious art magazine, Art India, and only a few major collectors of contemporary work. In other words, no real infrastructure at all." But there are signs that the situation is improving. A modern art museum is being planned for Calcutta. A leading collector, Anupam Poddar, will soon open the Devi Art Foundation's new headquarters in New Delhi to house his collection, organise exhibitions and hold lectures and talks. Jawaharlal Nehru University in New Delhi now has a School of Arts and Aesthetics, a fairly sophisticated programme of art history and cultural studies.

Yet there is no doubt, as Peter Nagy, the owner of Nature Morte, put it, that the Indian art scene is in its "pimply, adolescent phase." It is an art community in upheaval, straining to reinvent itself for the 21st century. The artists themselves, exposed firsthand to European and American art and artists as never before, with the Internet allowing them to sample whatever they care to see, find themselves in a fluid global arena of influence and identity. Their art is no longer confined to Indianness in subject or style, and the topic comes up without prompting in every conversation. Gayatri Sinha, a critic and curator in New Delhi, suggests that more than any other source of influence, it is the politics of the subcontinent that mold the context in which Indian art is created today. Husain, generally considered the country's most distinguished painter, just spent his 92nd birthday in exile, forced out by threats from Hindu groups enraged by his paintings of nude gods and goddesses. The filmmaker Amar Kanwar, who recently showed "The Lightning Testimonies," his video installation about sexual violence to Indian women, at Documenta 12 in Kassel, Germany, said that artists in India are "challenged ideologically every step of the way." "And yet this friction can be a source of great creativity," he added. "This is an extremely intolerant society, an extremely racist society," he said in an interview at his office in a middle-class neighbourhood in New Delhi. "You will run into censorship, but you can make a place to work here."

"Indian artists are showing all over the world," he said, "and each day they have to decide how they will confront their society and themselves. They will be critical, or they will just make work for the market." A note of defiance entered his voice, a note often heard in reply to questions on this issue: Why do Westerners assume that globalisation only runs one way, from West to East? The dealer Deepak Talwar, with galleries in New York and New Delhi, said: "The real history of modernism hasn't been written yet. It is all about Europe and New York. But that's hardly the whole of modernism. A hundred years from now, people will laugh at these narrow histories."

4

Modern Technology in Plastic Money

PLAST MONEY: CREDIT AND DEBIT CARD

CREDIT CARD

A credit card is a small plastic card issued to users as a system of payment. It allows its holder to buy goods and services based on the holder's promise to pay for these goods and services. The issuer of the card grants a line of credit to the consumer from which the user can borrow money for payment to a merchant or as a cash advance to the user. Usage of the term "credit card" to imply a credit card account is a metonym.

A credit card is different from a charge card: a charge card requires the balance to be paid in full each month. In contrast, credit cards allow the consumers a continuing balance of debt, subject to interest being charged. Most credit cards are issued by banks or credit unions, and are the shape and size specified by the ISO/IEC 7810 standard as ID-1. This is defined as 85.60 × 53.98 mm in size.

How Credit Cards Work

Credit cards are issued after an account has been approved by the credit provider, after which cardholders can use it to make purchases at merchants accepting that card.

When a purchase is made, the credit card user agrees to pay the card issuer. The cardholder indicates consent to pay by signing a receipt with a record of the card details and indicating the amount to be paid or by entering a personal identification number. Also, many merchants now accept verbal authorizations via telephone and electronic authorization using the Internet, known as a 'Card/Cardholder Not Present' transaction.

Electronic verification systems allow merchants to verify in a few seconds that the card is valid and the credit card customer has sufficient credit to cover the purchase, allowing the verification to happen at time of purchase. The verification is performed using a credit card payment terminal or Point of Sale system with a communications link to the merchant's acquiring bank. Data from the card is obtained from a magnetic stripe or chip on the card; the latter system is called Chip and PIN in the United Kingdom and Ireland, and is implemented as an EMV card.

For transactions at which the buyer is not present and the card not shown, merchants additionally verify that the customer is in physical possession of the card and is the authorised user by asking for additional information such as the security code printed on the back of the card, date of expiry, and billing address.

Each month, the credit card user is sent a statement indicating the purchases undertaken with the card, any outstanding fees, and the total amount owed. After receiving the statement, the cardholder may dispute any charges that he or she thinks are incorrect. Otherwise, the cardholder must pay a defined minimum proportion of the bill by a due date, or may choose to pay a higher amount up to the entire amount owed. The credit issuer charges interest on the amount owed if the balance is not paid in full.

Some financial institutions can arrange for automatic payments to be deducted from the user's bank accounts, thus avoiding late payment altogether as long as the cardholder has sufficient funds.

Advertising, Solicitation, Application and Approval

Credit card advertising regulations include the Schumer box disclosure requirements. A large fraction of junk mail consists of credit card offers created from lists provided by the major credit reporting agencies. In the United States, the three major US credit bureaus allow consumers to opt out from related credit card solicitation offers via its Opt Out Pre Screen programme.

Interest Charges

Credit card issuers usually waive interest charges if the balance is paid in full each month, but typically will charge full interest on the entire outstanding balance from the date of each purchase if the total balance is not paid. For example, if a user had a $1,000 transaction and repaid it in full within this grace period, there would be no interest charged. If, however, even $1.00 of the total amount remained unpaid, interest would be charged on the $1,000 from the date of purchase until the payment is received.

The precise manner in which interest is charged is usually detailed in a cardholder agreement which may be summarized on the back of the monthly statement. The general calculation formula most financial institutions use to determine the amount of interest to be charged is APR/100 x ADB/365 x number of days revolved. Take the Annual percentage rate and divide by 100 then multiply to the amount of the average daily balance divided by 365 and then take this total and multiply by the total number of days the amount revolved before payment was made on the account.

Financial institutions refer to interest charged back to the original time of the transaction and up to the time a payment was made, if not in full, as RRFC or residual retail finance charge. Thus after an amount has revolved and a payment has been made, the user of the card will still receive interest charges on their statement after paying the next statement in full.

The credit card may simply serve as a form of revolving credit, or it may become a complicated financial instrument with multiple balance segments each at a different interest rate, possibly with a single umbrella credit limit, or with separate credit limits applicable to the various balance segments. Usually this compartmentalization is the result of special incentive offers from the issuing bank, to encourage balance transfers from cards of other issuers.

In the event that several interest rates apply to various balance segments, payment allocation is generally at the discretion of the issuing bank, and payments will therefore usually be allocated towards the lowest rate balances until paid in full before any money is paid towards higher rate balances. Interest rates can vary considerably from card to card, and the interest rate on a particular card may jump dramatically if the card user is late with a payment on that card or any other credit instrument, or even if the issuing bank decides to raise its revenue.

Benefits to Customers

The main benefit to each customer is convenience. Compared to debit cards and checks, a credit card allows small short-term loans to be quickly made to a customer who need not calculate a balance remaining before every transaction, provided the total charges do not exceed the maximum credit line for the card.

Credit cards also provide more fraud protection than debit cards. In the UK for example, the bank is jointly liable with the merchant for purchases of defective products over £100. Many credit cards offer rewards and benefits packages, such as offering enhanced product warranties at no cost, free loss/damage coverage on new purchases, and points which may be redeemed for cash, products, or airline tickets. Additionally, carrying a credit card may be a convenience to some customers as it eliminates the need to carry any cash for most purposes.

Detriments to Customers

High interest and Bankruptcy

Low introductory credit card rates are limited to a fixed term, usually between 6 and 12 months, after which a higher rate is charged. As all credit cards charge fees and interest, some customers become so indebted to their credit card provider that they are driven to bankruptcy. Some credit cards often levy a rate of 20 to 30 per cent after a payment is missed; in other cases a fixed charge is levied without change to the interest rate.

In some cases universal default may apply: the high default rate is applied to a card in good standing by missing a payment on an unrelated account from the same provider. This can lead to a snowball effect in which the consumer is drowned by unexpectedly high interest rates. Further most card holder agreements enable the issuer to arbitrarily raise the interest rate for any reason they see fit.

Inflated Pricing for all Consumers

Merchants that accept credit cards must pay interchange fees and discount fees on all credit-card transactions. In some cases merchants are barred by their credit agreements from passing these fees directly to credit card customers, or from setting a minimum transaction amount.

The result, at least in the United States, is that merchants may charge all customers higher prices to cover the fees on credit card transactions.

In the United States in 2008 credit card companies collected a total of $48 billion in interchange fees, or an average of $427 per family, with an average fee rate of about 2% per transaction.

Grace Period

A credit card's grace period is the time the customer has to pay the balance before interest is assessed on the outstanding balance. Grace periods vary, but usually range from 20 to 50 days depending on the type of credit card and the issuing bank. Some policies allow for reinstatement after certain conditions are met.

Usually, if a customer is late paying the balance, finance charges will be calculated and the grace period does not apply. Finance charges incurred depend on the grace period and balance; with most credit cards there is no grace period if there is any outstanding balance from the previous billing cycle or statement.

However, there are some credit cards that will only apply finance charge on the previous or old balance, excluding new transactions.

Benefits to Merchants

For merchants, a credit card transaction is often more secure than other forms of payment, such as checks, because the issuing bank commits to pay the merchant the moment the transaction is authorized, regardless of whether the consumer defaults on the credit card payment. In most cases, cards are even more secure than cash, because they discourage theft by the merchant's employees and reduce the amount of cash on the premises.

Prior to credit cards, each merchant had to evaluate each customer's credit history before extending credit. That task is now performed by the banks which assume the credit risk. Credit cards can also aid in securing a sale, especially if the customer does not have enough cash on his or her person or checking account.

Extra turnover is generated by the fact that the customer can purchase goods and/or services immediately and is less inhibited by the amount of cash in his or her pocket and the immediate state of his or her bank balance. Much of merchants' marketing is based on this immediacy. For each purchase, the bank charges the merchant a commission for this service and there may be a certain delay before the agreed payment is received by the merchant. The commission is often a percentage of the transaction amount, plus a fixed fee.

In addition, a merchant may be penalized or have their ability to receive payment using that credit card restricted if there are too many cancellations or reversals of charges as a result of disputes. Some small merchants require credit purchases to have a minimum amount to compensate for the transaction costs.

In some countries, for example the Nordic countries, banks guarantee payment on stolen cards only if an ID card is checked and the ID card number/civic registration number is written down on the receipt together with the signature. In these countries merchants therefore usually ask for ID.

Non-Nordic citizens, who are unlikely to possess a Nordic ID card or driving license, will instead have to show their passport, and the passport number will be written down on the receipt, sometimes together with other information. Some shops use the card's PIN for identification, and in that case showing an ID card is not necessary.

Costs to Merchants

Merchants are charged several fees for the privilege of accepting credit cards. The merchant is usually charged a commission of 1%-3%+ of the value of each transaction paid for by credit card.

The merchant may also pay a variable charge, called an interchange rate, for each transaction. In some instances of very low-value transactions, use of credit cards will significantly reduce the profit margin or cause the merchant to lose money on the transaction.

Merchants must accept these transactions as part of their costs to retain the right to accept credit card transactions. Merchants with very low average transaction prices or very high average transaction prices are more averse to accepting credit cards. In some cases merchants may charge users a "credit card supplement", either a fixed amount or a percentage, for payment by credit card. In certain countries, merchants are required to pay the acquiring banks a monthly terminal rental fee if the terminals are provided by the acquiring banks. Merchants can apply to the acquiring banks for waivers of the fees, which the banks usually agree to for merchants with a high volume of sales, but not for smaller ones.

Parties Involved

- *Cardholder*: The holder of the card used to make a purchase; the consumer.
- *Card-issuing bank*: The financial institution or other organization that issued the credit card to the cardholder. This bank bills the consumer for repayment and bears the risk that the card is used fraudulently. American Express and Discover were previously the only card-issuing banks for their respective brands, but as of 2007, this is no longer the case. Cards issued by banks to cardholders in a different country are known as offshore credit cards.
- *Merchant*: The individual or business accepting credit card payments for products or services sold to the cardholder.
- *Acquiring bank*: The financial institution accepting payment for the products or services on behalf of the merchant.
- *Independent sales organization*: Resellers of the services of the acquiring bank.
- *Merchant account*: This could refer to the acquiring bank or the independent sales organization, but in general is the organization that the merchant deals with.
- *Credit Card association*: An association of card-issuing banks such as Visa, MasterCard, Discover, American Express, etc. that set transaction terms for merchants, card-issuing banks, and acquiring banks.
- *Transaction network*: The system that implements the mechanics of the electronic transactions. May be operated by an independent company, and one company may operate multiple networks.
- *Affinity partner*: Some institutions lend their names to an issuer to attract customers that have a strong relationship with that institution, and get paid a fee or a percentage of the balance for each card issued using their name. Examples of typical affinity partners are sports teams, universities, charities, professional organizations, and major retailers.

The flow of information and money between these parties — always through the card associations — is known as the interchange, and it consists of a few steps.

Transaction Steps

- *Authorization*: The cardholder pays for the purchase and the merchant submits the transaction to the acquirer. The acquirer verifies the credit card number, the transaction type and the amount with the issuer and reserves that amount of the cardholder's credit limit for the merchant. An authorization will generate an approval code, which the merchant stores with the transaction.

- *Batching*: Authorized transactions are stored in "batches", which are sent to the acquirer. Batches are typically submitted once per day at the end of the business day. If a transaction is not submitted in the batch, the authorization will stay valid for a period determined by the issuer, after which the held amount will be returned back to the cardholder's available credit. Some transactions may be submitted in the batch without prior authorizations; these are either transactions falling under the merchant's floor limit or ones where the authorization was unsuccessful but the merchant still attempts to force the transaction through.
- *Clearing and Settlement*: The acquirer sends the batch transactions through the credit card association, which debits the issuers for payment and credits the acquirer. Essentially, the issuer pays the acquirer for the transaction.
- *Funding*: Once the acquirer has been paid, the acquirer pays the merchant. The merchant receives the amount totaling the funds in the batch minus either the "discount rate," "mid-qualified rate", or "non-qualified rate" which are tiers of fees the merchant pays the acquirer for processing the transactions.
- *Chargebacks*: A chargeback is an event in which money in a merchant account is held due to a dispute relating to the transaction. Chargebacks are typically initiated by the cardholder. In the event of a chargeback, the issuer returns the transaction to the acquirer for resolution. The acquirer then forwards the chargeback to the merchant, who must either accept the chargeback or contest it. A merchant is responsible for the chargeback only if she has violated the card acceptance procedures as per the merchant agreement with card acquirers.

Secured Credit Cards

A secured credit card is a type of credit card secured by a deposit account owned by the cardholder. Typically, the cardholder must deposit between 100% and 200% of the total amount of credit desired. Thus if the cardholder puts down $1000, they will be given credit in the range of $500–$1000. In some cases, credit card issuers will offer incentives even on their secured card portfolios.

In these cases, the deposit required may be significantly less than the required credit limit, and can be as low as 10% of the desired credit limit. This deposit is held in a special savings account. Credit card issuers offer this because they have noticed that delinquencies were notably reduced when the customer perceives something to lose if the balance is not repaid. The cardholder of a secured credit card is still expected to make regular payments, as with a regular credit card, but should they default on a payment, the card issuer has the option of recovering the cost of the purchases paid to the merchants out of the deposit. The advantage of the secured card for an individual with negative or no credit history is that most companies report regularly to the major credit bureaus. This allows for building of positive credit history.

Although the deposit is in the hands of the credit card issuer as security in the event of default by the consumer, the deposit will not be debited simply for missing one or two payments. Usually the deposit is only used as an offset when the account is closed, either at the request of the customer or due to severe delinquency.

This means that an account which is less than 150 days delinquent will continue to accrue interest and fees, and could result in a balance which is much higher than the actual credit limit on the card. In these cases the total debt may far exceed the original deposit and the cardholder not only forfeits their deposit but is left with an additional debt.

Most of these conditions are usually described in a cardholder agreement which the cardholder signs when their account is opened. Secured credit cards are an option to allow a person with a poor credit history or no credit history to have a credit card which might not otherwise be available.

They are often offered as a means of rebuilding one's credit. Fees and service charges for secured credit cards often exceed those charged for ordinary non-secured credit cards, however, for people in certain situations, secured cards can often be less expensive in total cost than unsecured credit cards, even including the security deposit. Sometimes a credit card will be secured by the equity in the borrower's home.

Prepaid "Credit" Cards

A prepaid credit card is not a true credit card, since no credit is offered by the card issuer: the card-holder spends money which has been "stored" via a prior deposit by the card-holder or someone else, such as a parent or employer. However, it carries a credit-card brand and can be used in similar ways just as though it were a regular credit card. Unlike debit cards, prepaid credit cards do not require a PIN. After purchasing the card, the cardholder loads the account with any amount of money, up to the predetermined card limit and then uses the card to make purchases the same way as a typical credit card. Prepaid cards can be issued to minors since there is no credit line involved.

The main advantage over secured credit cards is that you are not required to come up with $500 or more to open an account. With prepaid credit cards you are not charged any interest but you are often charged a purchasing fee plus monthly fees after an arbitrary time period. Many other fees also usually apply to a prepaid card. Prepaid credit cards are sometimes marketed to teenagers for shopping online without having their parents complete the transaction. Because of the many fees that apply to obtaining and using credit-card-branded prepaid cards, the Financial Consumer Agency of Canada describes them as "an expensive way to spend your own money". The agency publishes a booklet, "Pre-paid cards", which explains the advantages and disadvantages of this type of prepaid card.

Features

As well as convenient, accessible credit, credit cards offer consumers an easy way to track expenses, which is necessary for both monitoring personal expenditures and the tracking of work-related expenses for taxation and reimbursement purposes. Credit cards are accepted worldwide, and are available with a large variety of credit limits, repayment arrangement, and other perks. Some countries, such as the United States, the United Kingdom, and France, limit the amount for which a consumer can be held liable due to fraudulent transactions as a result of a consumer's credit card being lost or stolen.

KINDS OF PLASTIC MONEY

There has been a growth on electronic payment due to the shift in technology, growing access to internet among the customers and convenient modes of delivery and payment. Plastic money also known as Plastic cards acts as a vital tool for every day transaction of people today.

The various Plastic cards include ATM cards,Debit Card,ATM cum Debit Card,Credit Cards, Smart Card, Charge Cards, Co-branded cards, add on cards and so on.

ATM CARDS

Automated Teller machine (ATM) cards is capable of doing variety of functions.It can perform both cash and non-cash transactions in secured environment.

- ATM Cash Transactions includes deposits and withdrawals
- Non cash transactions incude
  - Providing Mini Statement of last five transactions.In some banks upto last ten transactions
  - Balance enquiry
  - Stop Payment instructions
  - Transfer of funds between acounts
  - Requisition of Cheque books,drafts etc.
  - Bill payments

DEBIT CARD

The bank issues debit card only if the person has an account in the bank.This card is useful to make payment from Member Establishments who have arrangements with the card issuing bank or agency. They check the balance and deduct the amount from the bank balance online. When a debit card is issued to make the payment,the total amount charged is instantly reduced from the bank balance of the account holder.

All credit and debit cards are affiliated to two major issuers-VISA and Master Card.Master Card and VISA are global non-profit organizations who promote the growth of the card business throughout the world.They have built vast network of Member Establishments so that customers can use the cards worldwide for their debit and credit purchases.

DEBIT CUM ATM CARD

This is most common nowadays.The same debit card can be used to draw cash from the ATM and also make payment to the shops for purchases.This is two in one card.

CREDIT CARDS

This card enables the client to obtain goods or services from the various shops having arrangement with the issuing agency even if there is no balance in his/her savings or current account.The bank assumes that the loan will be repaid by the customers at later date.

The credit card holder has to make payment for the dues before the due date. Otherwise late payment fee is levied in the next billing statement. Normally,a limit of the credit will be fixed by the bank for the amount of purchases to be made by the customer based on the net worth of the customer.

CHARGE CARDS

A Charge card has all features of credit card.But, after using the charge card the entire payments of the bills has to be made by the due date.If it is failed to be done,then the client is likely to be considered as a defaulter and he has to pay a steep late payment charges. But in case of Credit cards, the client is not declared as a defaulter if he misses to pay by due date..In such case,a late fee is levied in the next billing statements of the credit card holder.

AMEX and Diners Club card are well known branded charge cards.They have their own merchant establishments and tie ups and does not depend on the network of Master card or VISA. These care are typically meant for the high income group categories and companies. These cards are not acceptable at many outlets. But wide variety of special privileges are enjoyed by the AMEX card holders and Diners Club Cardholders.

SMART CARDS

A smart Card contains an electronic chip which is used to store Cash. This is most useful to pay for small purchases for example in Fairs,coffee shops etc. No identification, signature or payment authorization is required for using this card. The exact amount of purchase is deducted from smart card during payment.Currently, this product is available in very developed countries like US.

AFFINITY CARD

The card issuer has a tie up with popular organizations and institutions which are often non-profit organizations like Stanchart Cricket Cards or City WWF card.When a card is used, a certain percentage is contributed to the organization or institution by the card issuer.

PHOTO CARD

When a Photo is imprinted on the card,it helps to identify the user of the credit card and is considered to be safer. In many cases,Photo card can also be used as identity card.

GLOBAL CARD

Global cards can be used as credit cards instead of cash and traveller cheques while traveling abroad to foreign countries for business or personal reasons.

ADD ON CARDS

It is a privilege offered to the spouse, parents, Children or other family members of the original card holder.Normally, an issuing bank permits two add on cards per credit card. All expenses incurred on add on card are billed to the primary card holder.

PETRO CARD

Some Petroleum companies allow customers to pay for the fuel through electronic medium.It offers a scheme of gifting the points to the customers,when they pay for the fuel using petro card.It is convenient, secured and speedy mode of transaction. Co-branded credit cards like IOC-Citi bank and HPCL-ICICI bank are the co-branded petro cards avaiable in the market.

Today,the Indian mode of payment has shifted from currency to electronic mode.This is due to the high money valued transactions and more risk involvement.The new electronic payment and settlement should follow the strict norms for banks and merchants to make secure payments and prevent money laundering as the transactions through plastic money will be increasing and increasing in the near future..

SECURITY PROBLEMS AND SOLUTIONS IN CREDIT AND DEBIT CARD

Credit card security relies on the physical security of the plastic card as well as the privacy of the credit card number. Therefore, whenever a person other than the card owner has access to the card or its number, security is potentially compromised. Once, merchants would often accept credit card numbers without additional verification for mail order purchases. It's now common practice to only ship to confirmed addresses as a security measure to minimise fraudulent purchases.

Some merchants will accept a credit card number for in-store purchases, whereupon access to the number allows easy fraud, but many require the card itself to be present, and require a signature. A lost or stolen card can be cancelled, and if this is done quickly, will greatly limit the fraud that can take place in this way.

For internet purchases, there is sometimes the same level of security as for mail order hence requiring only that the fraudster take care about collecting the goods, but often there are additional measures. European banks can require a cardholder's security PIN be entered for in-person purchases with the card.

The PCI DSS is the security standard issued by The PCI SSC. This data security standard is used by acquiring banks to impose cardholder data security measures upon their merchants. The low security of the credit card system presents countless opportunities for fraud. This opportunity has created a huge [specify] black market in stolen credit card numbers, which are generally used quickly before the cards are reported stolen.

The goal of the credit card companies is not to eliminate fraud, but to "reduce it to manageable levels". This implies that high-cost low-return fraud prevention measures will not be used if their cost exceeds the potential gains from fraud reduction - as would be expected from organisations whose goal is profit maximisation.

Internet fraud may be by claiming a chargeback which is not justified, or carried out by the use of credit card information which can be stolen in many ways, the simplest being copying information from retailers, either online or offline. Despite efforts to improve security for remote purchases using credit cards, security breaches are usually the result of poor practice by merchants. For example, a website that safely uses SSL to encrypt card data from a client may then email the data, unencrypted, from the webserver to the merchant; or the merchant may store unencrypted details in a way that allows them to be accessed over the Internet or by a rogue employee; unencrypted card details are always a security risk. Even encryption data may be cracked.

Controlled Payment Numbers which are used by various banks such as Citibank, Discover (Secure Online Account Numbers, Bank of America (Shop Safe), 5 banks using eCarte Bleue and CMB's Virtualis in France, and Swedbank of Sweden's eKort product are another option for protecting against credit card fraud.

These are generally one-time use numbers that front one's actual account (debit/credit) number, and are generated as one shops on-line. They can be valid for a relatively short time, for the actual amount of the purchase, or for a price limit set by the user. Their use can be limited to one merchant. If the number given to the merchant is compromised, it will be rejected if an attempt is made to use it again.

A similar system of controls can be used on physical cards. For example if a consumer has a Chip and PIN enabled card the card can be limited so that it be used only at point of sale locations and only in a given territory. This technology provides the option for banks to support many other controls too that can be turned on and off and varied by the credit card owner in real time as circumstances change.

Apart from the obvious benefits of such controls: from a security perspective this means that a customer can have a Chip and PIN card secured for the real world, and limited for use in the home country.

In this eventuality a thief stealing the details will be prevented from using these overseas in non chip and pin countries. Similarly the real card can be restricted from use on-line so that stolen details will be declined if this tried. Then when card users shop online they can use virtual account numbers. In both circumstances an alert system can be built in notifying a user that a fraudulent attempt has been made which breaches their parameters, and can provide data on this in real time. This is the optimal method of security for credit cards, as it provides very high levels of security, control and awareness in the real and virtual world. Furthermore it requires no changes for merchants at all and is attractive to users, merchants and banks, as it not only detects fraud but prevents it.

Additionally, there are security features present on the physical card itself in order to prevent counterfeiting. For example, most modern credit cards have a watermark that will fluoresce under ultraviolet light.

A Visa card has a letter V superimposed over the regular Visa logo and a Mastercard has the letters MC across the front of the card. Older Visa cards have a bald eagle or dove across the front. In the aforementioned cases, the security features are only visible under ultraviolet light and are invisible in normal light. Similar security features are present in paper currency and certain ID cards in the United States, as well.

The Federal Bureau of Investigation and U.S. Postal Inspection Service are responsible for prosecuting criminals who engage in credit card fraud in the United States, but they do not have the resources to pursue all criminals. In general, federal officials only prosecute cases exceeding US$5,000.

Three improvements to card security have been introduced to the more common credit card networks but none has proven to help reduce credit card fraud so far. First, the on-line verification system used by merchants is being enhanced to require a 4 digit Personal Identification Number known only to the card holder.

Second, the cards themselves are being replaced with similar-looking tamper-resistant smart cards which are intended to make forgery more difficult. The majority of smart card based credit cards comply with the EMV standard. Third, an additional 3 or 4 digit Card Security Code is now present on the back of most cards, for use in "card not present" transactions.

Stakeholders at all levels in electronic payment have recognized the need to develop consistent global standards for security that account for and integrate both current and emerging security technologies. They have begun to address these needs through organizations such as PCI DSS and the Secure POS Vendor Alliance.

Code 10

Code 10 calls are made when merchants are suspicious about accepting a credit card. The phrase "Code 10 authorization" is used to avoid alerting the customer to the fact that the merchant is suspicious of their card.

The operator then asks the merchant a series of YES or NO questions to find out whether the merchant is suspicious of the card or the cardholder. The merchant may be asked to retain the card if it is safe to do so.

Credit History

The way credit card owners pay off their balances has a tremendous effect on their credit history. Two of the most important factors reported to a credit bureau are the timeliness of the debt payments and the amount of debt to credit limit.

Lenders want to see payments made as agreed, usually on a monthly basis, and a credit balance of around one-third the credit limit. The credit information stays on the credit report generally for 7 years. However, there are a few jurisdictions and situations where the timeframe might differ.

Profits and Losses

In recent times, credit card portfolios have been very profitable for banks, largely due to the booming economy of the late nineties.

However, in the case of credit cards, such high returns go hand in hand with risk, since the business is essentially one of making unsecured loans, and thus dependent on borrowers not to default in large numbers.

Costs

Interest Expenses

Banks generally borrow the money they then lend to their customers. As they receive very low-interest loans from other firms, they may borrow as much as their customers require, while lending their capital to other borrowers at higher rates. If the card issuer charges 15% on money lent to users, and it costs 5% to borrow the money to lend, and the balance sits with the cardholder for a year, the issuer earns 10% on the loan. This 10% difference is the "net interest spread" and the 5% is the "interest expense".

Operating Costs

This is the cost of running the credit card portfolio, including everything from paying the executives who run the company to printing the plastics, to mailing the statements, to running the computers that keep track of every cardholder's balance, to taking the many phone calls which cardholders place to their issuer, to protecting the customers from fraud rings. Depending on the issuer, marketing programmes are also a significant portion of expenses.

Charge Offs

When a consumer becomes severely delinquent on a debt, the creditor may declare the debt to be a charge-off. It will then be listed as such on the debtor's credit bureau reports. The item will include relevant dates, and the amount of the bad debt.

A charge-off is considered to be "written off as uncollectable." To banks, bad debts and even fraud are simply part of the cost of doing business. However, the debt is still legally valid, and the creditor can attempt to collect the full amount for the time periods permitted under state law, which is usually 3 to 7 years. This includes contacts from internal collections staff, or more likely, an outside collection agency. If the amount is large, there is the possibility of a lawsuit or arbitration.

In the United States, as the charge off number climbs or becomes erratic, officials from the Federal Reserve take a close look at the finances of the bank and may impose various operating strictures on the bank, and in the most extreme cases, may close the bank entirely.

Rewards

Many credit card customers receive rewards, such as frequent flyer points, gift certificates, or cash back as an incentive to use the card. Rewards are generally tied to purchasing an item or service on the card, which may or may not include balance transfers, cash advances, or other special uses.

Depending on the type of card, rewards will generally cost the issuer between 0.25% and 2.0% of the spread. Networks such as Visa or MasterCard have increased their fees to allow issuers to fund their rewards system. Some issuers discourage redemption by forcing the cardholder to call customer service for rewards.

On their servicing website, redeeming awards is usually a feature that is very well hidden by the issuers. Others encourage redemption for lower cost merchandise; instead of an airline ticket, which is very expensive to an issuer, the cardholder may be encouraged to redeem for a gift certificate instead.

With a fractured and competitive environment, rewards points cut dramatically into an issuer's bottom line, and rewards points and related incentives must be carefully managed to ensure a profitable portfolio. Unlike unused gift cards, in whose case the breakage in certain US states goes to the state's treasury, unredeemed credit card points are retained by the issuer.

Fraud

In relative numbers the values lost in bank card fraud are minor, calculated in 2006 at 7 cents per 100 dollars worth of transactions. In 2004, in the UK, the cost of fraud was over £500 million.

When a card is stolen, or an unauthorized duplicate made, most card issuers will refund some or all of the charges that the customer has received for things they did not buy. These refunds will, in some cases, be at the expense of the merchant, especially in mail order cases where the merchant cannot claim sight of the card. In several countries, merchants will lose the money if no ID card was asked for, therefore merchants usually require ID card in these countries. Credit card companies generally guarantee the merchant will be paid on legitimate transactions regardless of whether the consumer pays their credit card bill. Most banking services have their own credit card services that handle fraud cases and monitor for any possible attempt at fraud. Employees that are specialized in doing fraud monitoring and investigation are often placed in Risk Management, Fraud and Authorization, or Cards and Unsecured Business.

Fraud monitoring emphasizes minimizing fraud losses while making an attempt to track down those responsible and contain the situation. Credit card fraud is a major white collar crime that has been around for many decades, even with the advent of the chip based card that was put into practice in some countries to prevent cases such as these. Even with the implementation of such measures, credit card fraud continues to be a problem.

Promotion

Promotional purchase is any purchase on which separate terms and conditions are set on each individual transaction unlike a standard purchase where the terms are set on the cardholder's account record and their pricing strategy. All promotional purchases that post to a particular account will be carrying its own balance called as Promotional Balance.

Revenues

Interchange Fee

In addition to fees paid by the card holder, merchants must also pay interchange fees to the card-issuing bank and the card association. For a typical credit card issuer, interchange fee revenues may represent about a quarter of total revenues. These fees are typically from 1 to 6 per cent of each sale, but will vary not only from merchant to merchant, but also from card to card, with business cards and rewards cards generally costing the merchants more to process. The interchange fee that applies to a particular transaction is also affected by many other variables including: the type of merchant, the merchant's total card sales volume, the merchant's average transaction amount, whether the cards were physically present, how the information required for the transaction was received, the specific type of card, when the transaction was settled, and the authorized and settled transaction amounts.

In some cases, merchants add a surcharge to the credit cards to cover the interchange fee, encouraging their customers to instead use cash, debit cards, or even cheques.

Interest on Outstanding Balances

The major fees are for:

- Late payments or overdue payments
- Charges that result in exceeding the credit limit on the card, called overlimit fees
- Returned cheque fees or payment processing fees
- Cash advances and convenience cheques
- Transactions in a foreign currency. A few financial institutions do not charge a fee for this.
- Membership fees, sometimes a percentage of the credit limit.
- Exchange rate loading fees. The variation of exchange rates applied by different credit cards can be very substantial, as much as 10% according to a Lonely Planet report in 2009.

Controversy

Credit card debt has increased steadily. Since the late 1990s, lawmakers, consumer advocacy groups, college officials and other higher education affiliates have become increasingly concerned about the rising use of credit cards among college students.

The major credit card companies have been accused of targeting a younger audience, in particular college students, many of whom are already in debt with college tuition fees and college loans and who typically are less experienced at managing their own finances. Credit card debt may also negatively affect their grades as they are likely to work more both part and full time positions.

Another controversial area is the universal default feature of many North American credit card contracts. When a cardholder is late paying a particular credit card issuer, that card's interest rate can be raised, often considerably. With universal default, a customer's other credit cards, for which the customer may be current on payments, may also have their rates and/or credit limit changed. The universal default feature allows creditors to periodically check cardholders' credit portfolios to view trade, allowing these other institutions to decrease the credit limit and/or increase rates on cardholders who may be late with another credit card issuer. Being late on one credit card will potentially affect all the cardholder's credit cards.

Citibank voluntarily stopped this practice in March 2007 and Chase stopped the practice in November 2007. The fact that credit card companies can change the interest rate on debts that were incurred when a different rate of interest was in place is similar to adjustable rate mortgages where interest rates on current debt may rise.

However, in both cases this is agreed to in advance, and is a trade off that allows a lower initial rate as well as the possibility of an even lower rate or perpetually keeping a below-market rate. It should be noted that the Universal Default practice was actually encouraged by Federal Regulators, particularly those at the Office of the Comptroller of the Currency as a means of managing the changing risk profiles of cardholders.

Another controversial area is the trailing interest issue. Trailing interest is the practice of charging interest on the entire bill no matter what percentage of it is paid. U.S Senator Carl Levin raised the issue of millions of Americans affected by hidden fees, compounding interest and cryptic terms. Their woes were heard in a Senate Permanent Subcommittee on Investigations hearing which was chaired by Senator Levin, who said that he intends to keep the spotlight on credit card companies and that legislative action may be necessary to purge the industry. In 2009, the C.A.R.D. Act was signed into law, enacting protections for many of the issues Levin had raised.

In the United States, some have called for Congress to enact additional regulations on the industry; to expand the disclosure box clearly disclosing rate hikes, use plain language, incorporate balance payoff disclosures, and also to outlaw universal default. At a congress hearing around March 1, 2007, Citibank announced it would no longer practice this, effective immediately.

Opponents of such regulation argue that customers must become more proactive and self-responsible in evaluating and negotiating terms with credit providers. Some of the nation's influential top credit card issuers, who are among the top fifty corporate contributors to political campaigns, successfully opposed it.

Hidden Costs

In the United Kingdom, merchants won the right through The Credit Cards Order 1990 to charge customers different prices according to the payment method. As of 2007, the United Kingdom was one of the world's most credit-card-intensive countries, with 2.4 credit cards per consumer, according to the

UK Payments Administration Ltd. In the United States, until 1984 federal law prohibited surcharges on card transactions. Although the federal Truth in Lending Act provisions that prohibited surcharges expired that year, a number of states have since enacted laws that continue to outlaw the practice; California, Colorado, Connecticut, Florida, Kansas, Massachusetts, Maine, New York, Oklahoma, and Texas have laws against surcharges.

As of 2006, the United States probably had one of the world's if not the top ratio of credit cards per capita, with 984 million bank-issued Visa and MasterCard credit card and debit card accounts alone for an adult population of roughly 220 million people. The credit card per US capita ratio was nearly 4:1 as of 2003 and as high as 5:1 as of 2006.

Credit Card Numbering

The numbers found on credit cards have a certain amount of internal structure, and share a common numbering scheme.

The card number's prefix, called the Bank Identification Number, is the sequence of digits at the beginning of the number that determine the bank to which a credit card number belongs. This is the first six digits for MasterCard and Visa cards. The next nine digits are the individual account number, and the final digit is a validity check code.

In addition to the main credit card number, credit cards also carry issue and expiration dates, as well as extra codes such as issue numbers and security codes. Not all credit cards have the same sets of extra codes nor do they use the same number of digits.

CREDIT CARDS IN ATMS

Many credit cards can also be used in an ATM to withdraw money against the credit limit extended to the card, but many card issuers charge interest on cash advances before they do so on purchases. The interest on cash advances is commonly charged from the date the withdrawal is made, rather than the monthly billing date.

Many card issuers levy a commission for cash withdrawals, even if the ATM belongs to the same bank as the card issuer. Merchants do not offer cashback on credit card transactions because they would pay a percentage commission of the additional cash amount to their bank or merchant services provider, thereby making it uneconomical.

Many credit card companies will also, when applying payments to a card, do so at the end of a billing cycle, and apply those payments to everything before cash advances. For this reason, many consumers have large cash balances, which have no grace period and incur interest at a rate that is higher than the purchase rate, and will carry those balance for years, even if they pay off their statement balance each month.

Credit Cards as Funding for Entrepreneurs

Credit cards are a risky way for entrepreneurs to acquire capital for their start ups when more conventional financing is unavailable. It's widely reported that Len Bosack and Sandy Lerner used personal credit cards to start Cisco Systems. It is rumoured that Larry Page and Sergey Brin's start up of Google was financed by credit cards to buy the necessary computers and office equipment, more specifically "a terabyte of hard disks".

Similarly, filmmaker Robert Townsend financed part of Hollywood Shuffle using credit cards. Director Kevin Smith funded Clerks in part by maxing out several credit cards. Actor Richard Hatch also financed his production of Battlestar Galactica: The Second Coming partly through his credit cards. Famed hedge fund manager Bruce Kovner began his career in financial markets by borrowing from his credit card. UK entrepreneur James Caan financed his first business using several credit cards.

DEBIT CARD

A debit card is a plastic card that provides an alternative payment method to cash when making purchases. Functionally, it can be called an electronic cheque, as the funds are withdrawn directly from either the bank account, or from the remaining balance on the card. In some cases, the cards are designed exclusively for use on the Internet, and so there is no physical card.

In many countries the use of debit cards has become so widespread that their volume of use has overtaken the cheque and, in some instances, cash transactions. Like credit cards, debit cards are used widely for telephone and Internet purchases and, unlike credit cards, the funds are transferred immediately from the bearer's bank account instead of having the bearer pay back the money at a later date.

Debit cards may also allow for instant withdrawal of cash, acting as the ATM card for withdrawing cash and as a cheque guarantee card. Merchants may also offer cashback facilities to customers, where a customer can withdraw cash along with their purchase.

Types of Debit Card Systems

There are currently three ways that debit card transactions are processed: online debit, offline debit and the Electronic Purse Card System. It should be noted that one physical card can include the functions of an online debit card, an offline debit card and an electronic purse card.

Although many debit cards are of the Visa or MasterCard brand, there are many other types of debit card, each accepted only within a particular country or region, for example Switch and Solo in the United Kingdom, Interac in Canada, Carte Bleue in France, Laser in Ireland, "EC electronic cash" in Germany and

EFTPOS cards in Australia and New Zealand. The need for cross-border compatibility and the advent of the euro recently led to many of these card networks being re-branded with the internationally recognised Maestro logo, which is part of the MasterCard brand. Some debit cards are dual branded with the logo of the national card as well as Maestro.

The use of a debit card system allows operators to package their product more effectively while monitoring customer spending. An example of one of these systems is ECS by Embed International.

Online Debit System

Online debit cards require electronic authorization of every transaction and the debits are reflected in the user's account immediately. The transaction may be additionally secured with the personal identification number authentication system and some online cards require such authentication for every transaction, essentially becoming enhanced automatic teller machine cards. One difficulty in using online debit cards is the necessity of an electronic authorization device at the point of sale and sometimes also a separate PINpad to enter the PIN, although this is becoming commonplace for all card transactions in many countries. Overall, the online debit card is generally viewed as superior to the offline debit card because of its more secure authentication system and live status, which alleviates problems with processing lag on transactions that may only issue online debit cards.

Offline Debit System

Offline debit cards have the logos of major credit cards or major debit cards and are used at the point of sale like a credit card. This type of debit card may be subject to a daily limit, and/or a maximum limit equal to the current/checking account balance from which it draws funds. Transactions conducted with offline debit cards require 2–3 days to be reflected on users' account balances.

In some countries and with some banks and merchant service organizations, a "credit" or offline debit transaction is without cost to the purchaser beyond the face value of the transaction, while a small fee may be charged for a "debit" or online debit transaction. Other differences are that online debit purchasers may opt to withdraw cash in addition to the amount of the debit purchase; also, from the merchant's standpoint, the merchant pays lower fees on online debit transaction as compared to "credit" debit transaction.

Electronic Purse Card System

Smart-card-based electronic purse systems are in use throughout Europe since the mid-1990s, most notably in Germany, Austria, the Netherlands, Belgium and Switzerland. In Austria and Germany, all current bank cards now include electronic purses.

Prepaid Debit Card

Prepaid debit cards, also called reloadable debit cards or reloadable prepaid cards, are often used for recurring payments. The payer loads funds to the cardholder's card account. Prepaid debit cards use either the offline debit system or the online debit system to access these funds. Particularly for companies with a large number of payment recipients abroad, prepaid debit cards allow the delivery of international payments without the delays and fees associated with international checks and bank transfers.

Providers include Caxton FX prepaid cards, Escape prepaid cards and Travelex prepaid cards. Whereas, web-based services such as stock photography websites, outsourced services, and affiliate networks have all started offering prepaid debit cards for their contributors/freelancers/vendors.

Advantages and Disadvantages

Debit and check cards, as they have become widespread, have revealed numerous advantages and disadvantages to the consumer and retailer alike.

The following allegations seem to be based only on the current situation within the U.S.A.

Advantages are as follows:

- A consumer who is not credit worthy and may find it difficult or impossible to obtain a credit card can more easily obtain a debit card, allowing him/her to make plastic transactions.
- For most transactions, a check card can be used to avoid check writing altogether. Check cards debit funds from the user's account on the spot, thereby finalizing the transaction at the time of purchase, and bypassing the requirement to pay a credit card bill at a later date, or to write an insecure check containing the account holder's personal information.
- Like credit cards, debit cards are accepted by merchants with less identification and scrutiny than personal checks, thereby making transactions quicker and less intrusive. Unlike personal checks, merchants generally do not believe that a payment via a debit card may be later dishonoured.
- Unlike a credit card, which charges higher fees and interest rates when a cash advance is obtained, a debit card may be used to obtain cash from an ATM or a PIN-based transaction at no extra charge, other than a foreign ATM fee.

The Debit card has many disadvantages as opposed to cash or credit:

- Use of a debit card is not usually limited to the existing funds in the account to which it is linked, most banks allow a certain threshold over the available bank balance which can cause overdraft fees if the customer does not depend on their own records of spending.

- Many banks are now charging over-limit fees or non-sufficient funds fees based upon pre-authorizations, and even attempted but refused transactions by the merchant.
- Many merchants mistakenly believe that amounts owed can be "taken" from a customer's account after a debit card has been presented, without agreement as to date, payee name, amount and currency, thus causing penalty fees for overdrafts, over-the-limit, amounts not available causing further rejections or overdrafts, and rejected transactions by some banks.
- In some countries debit cards offer lower levels of security protection than credit cards. Theft of the users PIN using skimming devices can be accomplished much easier with a PIN input than with a signature-based credit transaction. However, theft of users' PIN codes using skimming devices can be equally easily accomplished with a debit transaction PIN input, as with a credit transaction PIN input, and theft using a signature-based credit transaction is equally easy as theft using a signature-based debit transaction.
- In many places, laws protect the consumer from fraud much less than with a credit card. While the holder of a credit card is legally responsible for only a minimal amount of a fraudulent transaction made with a credit card, which is often waived by the bank, the consumer may be held liable for hundreds of dollars, or even the entire value of fraudulent debit transactions. The consumer also has a shorter time to report such fraud to the bank in order to be eligible for such a waiver with a debit card, whereas with a credit card, this time may be up to 60 days. A thief who obtains or clones a debit card along with its PIN may be able to clean out the consumer's bank account, and the consumer will have no recourse.

Table. Federally Imposed Maximum Liability for Unauthorized Card Use (United States)

Reported	**Maximum Card Holder Liability**	
Credit Card	**Debit Card**	
Before Use	$0	$0
Within 2 business days	$50	$50
After 2 but before 60 business days	$50	$500
After 60 business days	Unlimited	Unlimited

- In the UK and Ireland, among other countries, a consumer who purchases goods or services with a credit card can pursue the credit card issuer if the goods or services are not delivered or are unmerchantable. While they must generally exhaust the process provided by the retailer first, this is not necessary if the retailer has gone out of business. This protection is not provided by legislation when using a debit card but may be offered to a limited extent as a benefit provided by the card network, e.g. Visa debit cards.

- When a transaction is made using a credit card, the bank's money is being spent, and therefore, the bank has a vested interest in claiming its money where there is fraud or a dispute. The bank may fight to void the charges of a consumer who is dissatisfied with a purchase, or who has otherwise been treated unfairly by the merchant. But when a debit purchase is made, the consumer has spent his/her own money, and the bank has little if any motivation to collect the funds.
- In some countries, and for certain types of purchases, such as gasoline, lodging, or car rental, the bank may place a hold on funds much greater than the actual purchase for a fixed period of time. However, this isn't the case in other countries, such as Sweden. Until the hold is released, any other transactions presented to the account, including checks, may be dishonoured, or may be paid at the expense of an overdraft fee if the account lacks any additional funds to pay those items.
- While debit cards bearing the logo of a major credit card are accepted for virtually all transactions where an equivalent credit card is taken, a major exception in some countries is at car rental facilities. In some countries car rental agencies require an actual credit card to be used, or at the very least, will verify the creditworthiness of the renter using a debit card. In these unspecified countries, these companies will deny a rental to anyone who does not fit the requirements, and such a credit check may actually hurt one's credit score, as long as there is such a thing as a credit score in the country of purchase and/or the country of residence of the customer.

Consumer Protection

Consumer protections vary, depending on the network used. Visa and MasterCard, for instance, prohibit minimum and maximum purchase sizes, surcharges, and arbitrary security procedures on the part of merchants. Merchants are usually charged higher transaction fees for credit transactions, since debit network transactions are less likely to be fraudulent.

This may lead them to "steer" customers to debit transactions. Consumers disputing charges may find it easier to do so with a credit card, since the money will not immediately leave their control.

Fraudulent charges on a debit card can also cause problems with a checking account because the money is withdrawn immediately and may thus result in an overdraft or bounced checks. In some cases debit card-issuing banks will promptly refund any disputed charges until the matter can be settled, and in some jurisdictions the consumer liability for unauthorized charges is the same for both debit and credit cards. In some countries, like India and Sweden, the consumer protection is the same regardless of the network used. Some banks set minimum and maximum purchase sizes, mostly for online-only cards.

However, this has nothing to do with the card networks, but rather with the bank's judgement of the person's age and credit records. Any fees that the customers have to pay to the bank are the same regardless of whether the transaction is conducted as a credit or as a debit transaction, so there is no advantage for the customers to choose one transaction mode over another.

Shops may add surcharges to the price of the goods or services in accordance with laws allowing them to do so. Banks consider the purchases as having been made at the moment when the card was swiped, regardless of when the purchase settlement was made.

Regardless of which transaction type was used, the purchase may result in an overdraft because the money is considered to have left the account at the moment of the card swiping.

Financial Access

Debit cards and secured credit cards are popular among college students who have not yet established a credit history. Debit cards may also be used by expatriated workers to send money home to their families holding an affiliated debit card.

Issues With Deferred Posting of Offline Debit

To the consumer, a debit transaction is perceived as occurring in real-time; *i.e.* the money is withdrawn from their account immediately following the authorization request from the merchant, which in many countries, is the case when making an online debit purchase. However, when a purchase is made using the "credit" option, the transaction merely places an authorization hold on the customer's account; funds are not actually withdrawn until the transaction is reconciled and hard-posted to the customer's account, usually a few days later. However, the previous sentence applies to all kinds of transaction types, at least when using a card issued by a European bank.

This is in contrast to a typical credit card transaction; though it can also have a lag time of a few days before the transaction is posted to the account, it can be many days to a month or more before the consumer makes repayment with actual money.

Because of this, in the case of a benign or malicious error by the merchant or bank, a debit transaction may cause more serious problems than in the case of a credit card transaction. This is especially true in the United States, where cheque fraud is a crime in every state, but exceeding your credit limit is not.

Internet Purchases

Debit cards may also be used on the Internet. Internet transactions may be conducted in either online or offline mode, although shops accepting online-only cards are rare in some countries, while they are common in other countries. For a comparison, PayPal offers the customer to use an online-only Maestro card if the customer enters a Dutch address of residence, but not if the same customer enters a Swedish address of residence.

Internet purchases may be conducted in either online or offline mode, and just as in the case where you use your card in a shop, it is impossible to tell whether the transaction was conducted in online or offline mode, since the mode isn't mentioned on any receipt or similar.

Internet purchases use neither a PIN code nor a signature for identification. Transactions may be conducted in either credit or debit mode, and this has nothing to do with whether the transaction was conducted on online or offline mode, since both credit and debit transactions may be conducted in both modes.

Overdraft Fees

On banks' lucrative debit card overdraft fees - pointed out that debit card issuers could notify customers electronically, allowing them to avoid overdraft fees. Nessa Feddis, banking industry spokesperson and lobbyist, contended that "current technology makes real-time notification of overdrafts cost-prohibitive."

The contended that "financial institutions don't want to change the status quo because they make good and easy money off their own customers' mistakes and irresponsibility."

PLASTIC MONEY: DEBIT CARDS AROUND THE WORLD

In some countries, banks tend to levy a small fee for each debit card transaction. In some countries the merchants bear all the costs and customers are not charged. There are many people who routinely use debit cards for all transactions, no matter how small.

Some retailers refuse to accept debit cards for small transactions, where paying the transaction fee would absorb the profit margin on the sale, making the transaction uneconomic for the retailer.

Australia

Debit cards in Australia are called different names depending on the issuing bank: Commonwealth Bank of Australia: Keycard; Westpac Banking Corporation: Handycard; National Australia Bank: FlexiCard; ANZ Bank: Access card; Bendigo Bank: Cashcard.

EFTPOS is very popular in Australia and has been operating there since the 1980s. EFTPOS-enabled cards are accepted at almost all swipe terminals able to accept credit cards, regardless of the bank that issued the card, including

Maestro cards issued by foreign banks, with most businesses accepting them, with 450,000 Point Of Sale terminals. EFTPOS cards can also be used to deposit and withdraw cash over the counter at Australia Post outlets participating in giroPost, just as if the transaction was conducted at a bank branch, even if the bank branch is closed. Electronic transactions in Australia are generally processed via the Telstra Argent and Optus Transact Plus network - which has recently superseded the old Transcend network in the last few years. Most early keycards were only usable for EFTPOS and at ATM or bank branches, whilst the new debit card system works in the same ways a credit card, except it will only use funds in the specified bank account. This means that, among other advantages, the new system is suitable for electronic purchases without a delay of 2 to 4 days for bank-to-bank money transfers.

Australia operates both electronic credit card transaction authorization and traditional EFTPOS debit card authorization systems, the difference between the two being that EFTPOS transactions are authorized by a personal identification number while credit card transactions are usually authorized by the printing and signing of a receipt. If the user fails to enter the correct pin 3 times, the consequences range from the card being locked out and requiring a phone call or trip to the branch to reactivate with a new PIN, the card being cut up by the merchant, or in the case of an ATM, being kept inside the machine, both of which require a new card to be ordered.

Generally credit card transaction costs are borne by the merchant with no fee applied to the end user while EFTPOS transactions cost the consumer an applicable withdrawal fee charged by their bank. The introduction of Visa and MasterCard debit cards along with regulation in the settlement fees charged by the operators of both EFTPOS and credit cards by the Reserve Bank has seen a continuation in the increasing ubiquity of credit card use among Australians and a general decline in the profile of EFTPOS. However, the regulation of settlement fees also removed the ability of banks, who typically provide merchant services to retailers on behalf of Visa, MasterCard or Bankcard, from stopping those retailers charging extra fees to take payment by credit card instead of cash or EFTPOS. Though only a few operators with strong market power have done so, the passing on of fees charged for credit card transactions may result in an increased use of EFTPOS.

Brazil

In Brazil debit cards are called cartão de débito and are getting increasingly popular as a replacement of cheques, that are still uncommonly popular in the country.

Canada

Canada has a nation-wide EFTPOS system, called Interac Direct Payment. Since being introduced in 1994, IDP has become the most popular payment method in the country. Previously, debit cards have been in use for ABM usage since the early 1980s.

In the early 1990s, pilot projects were conducted among Canada's six largest banks to gauge security, accuracy and feasibility of the Interac system. Slowly in the later half of the 1990s, it was estimated that approximately 50% of retailers offered Interac as a source of payment. Retailers, many small transaction retailers like coffee shops, resisted offering IDP to promote faster service. In 2009, 99% of retailers offer IDP as an alternative payment form.

In Canada, the debit card is sometimes referred to as a "bank card". It is a client card issued by a bank that provides access to funds and other bank account transactions, such as transferring funds, checking balances, paying bills, etc., as well as point of purchase transactions connected on the Interac network.

Since its national launch in 1994, Interac Direct Payment has become so widespread that, as of 2001, more transactions in Canada were completed using debit cards than cash. This popularity may be partially attributable to two main factors: the convenience of not having to carry cash, and the availability of automated bank machines and Direct Payment merchants on the network.

Canadians, in fact, rank as the undisputed world leaders in debit card use, making 71.7 debit transactions per person in 2001, which is significantly more than consumers in the next closest country. The average value of a debit transaction in Canada was the lowest in an 11-country comparison, with Japan and Switzerland markedly standing out.93 Thus, compared to consumers in other countries, Canadians appear to be using their debit cards more often, even for frequent low-cost transactions. Debit cards may be considered similar to stored-value cards in that they represent a finite amount of money owed by the card issuer to the holder. They are different in that stored-value cards are generally anonymous and are only usable at the issuer, while debit cards are generally associated with an individual's bank account and can be used anywhere on the Interac network.

In Canada, the bank cards can be used at POS and ABMs. Interac Online has also been introduced in recent years allowing clients of most major Canadian banks to use their debit cards for online payment with certain merchants as well. Certain financial institutions also allow their clients to use their debit cards in the United States on the NYCE network.

Consumer Protection in Canada

Consumers in Canada are protected under a voluntary code* entered into by all providers of debit card services, The Canadian Code of Practice for Consumer Debit Card Services. Adherence to the Code is overseen by the Financial Consumer Agency of Canada, which investigates consumer complaints.

The FCAC website, revisions to the Code that came into effect in 2005 put the onus on the financial institution to prove that a consumer was responsible for a disputed transaction, and also place a limit on the number of days that an account can be frozen during the financial institution's investigation of a transaction.

Chile

Chile has an EFTPOS system called Redcompra which is currently used in at least 23,000 establishments throughout the country. Goods may be purchased using this system at most supermarkets, retail stores, pubs and restaurants in major urban centres.

Colombia

Colombia has a system called Redeban-Multicolour and Credibanco Visa which are currently used in at least 23,000 establishments throughout the country. Goods may be purchased using this system at most supermarkets, retail stores, pubs and restaurants in major urban centres. Colombian debit cards are Maestro, Visa Electron, Visa Debit and MasterCard-Debit.

Denmark

The Danish debit card Dankort was introduced on 1 September 1983, and despite the initial transactions being paper-based, the Dankort quickly won widespread acceptance in Denmark. By 1985 the first EFTPOS terminals were introduced, and 1985 was also the year when the number of Dankort transactions first exceeded 1 million. It is not uncommon that Dankort is the only card accepted at smaller stores, thus making it harder for tourists to travel without cash.

Miscellaneous Facts and Numbers

- In 2007 PBS, the Danish operator of the Dankort system, processed a total of 737 million Dankort transactions. Of these, 4.5 million just on a single day, 21 December. This remains the current record.
- At the end of 2007, there were 3.9 million Dankort in existence.
- More than 80,000 Danish shops have a Dankort terminal. Another 11,000 internet shops also accept the Dankort.

France

Carte Bancaire, the national payment scheme, in 2008, had 57,5 milion carts carrying its logo and 7,76 billion transactions were processed through the e-rsb network. Most CB cards are debit cards, either debit or deferred debit. Less than 10% of CB cards were credit cards. Banks in France charge annual fees for debit cards, yet they do not charge personal customers for checkbooks or processing checks. This imbalance most probably dates from the unilateral introduction in France of Chip and PIN debit cards in the early 1990s, when the cost of this technology was much higher than it is now. Credit cards of the type found in the United Kingdom and United States are unusual in France and the closest equivalent is the deferred debit card, which operates like a normal debit card, except that all purchase transactions are postponed until the end of the month, thereby giving the customer between 1 and 31 days of interest-free credit.

The annual fee for a deferred debit card is around □10 more than for one with immediate debit. Most France debit cards are branded with the Carte Bleue logo, which assures acceptance throughout France. Most card holders choose to pay around □5 more in their annual fee to additionally have a Visa or a MasterCard logo on their Carte Bleue, so that the card is accepted internationally.

A Carte Bleue without a Visa or a MasterCard logo is often known as a "Carte Bleue Nationale" and a Carte Bleue with a Visa or a MasterCard logo is known as a "Carte Bleue Internationale", or more frequently, simply called a "Visa" or "MasterCard". Many smaller merchants in France refuse to accept debit cards for transactions under a certain amount because of the minimum fee charged by merchants' banks per transaction. But more and more merchants accept debit cards for small amounts, due to the massive daily use of debit card nowadays. Merchants in France do not differentiate between debit and credit cards, and so both have equal acceptance. This is legal in France to set a minimum amount to transactions but the merchants must display it clearly.

Germany

Debit cards have enjoyed wide acceptance in Germany for years. Facilities already existed before EFTPOS became popular with the Eurocheque card, an authorization system initially developed for paper checks where, in addition to signing the actual check, customers also needed to show the card alongside the check as a security measure. Those cards could also be used at ATM Terminals and for card-based electronic funds transfer. These are now the only functions of such cards: the Eurocheque system was abandoned in 2002 during the transition from the Deutsche Mark to the euro. As of 2005, most stores and petrol outlets have EFTPOS facilities. Processing fees are paid by the businesses, which leads to some business owners refusing debit card payments for sales totalling less than a certain amount, usually 5 or 10 euro.

To avoid the processing fees, many businesses resorted to using direct debit, which is then called electronic direct debit. The point-of-sale terminal reads the name and account number from the card but instead of handling the transaction through the ec network it simply prints a form, which the customer signs to authorise the debit note.

However, this method also avoids any verification or payment guarantee provided by the network. Further, customers can return debit notes by notifying their bank without giving a reason. This means that the beneficiary bears the risk of fraud and illiquidity. Some business mitigate the risk by consulting a proprietary blacklist or by switching to electronic cash for higher transaction amounts.

Around 2000, an Electronic Purse Card was introduced, dubbed Geldkarte. It makes use of the smart card chip on the front of the standard issue debit card. This chip can be charged with up to 200 euro, and is advertised as a means of making medium to very small payments, even down to several euros or cent payments. The key factor here is that no processing fees are deducted by banks. It did not gain the popularity its inventors had hoped for. However, this could change as this chip is now used as means of age verification at cigarette vending machines, which has been mandatory since January 2007. Furthermore, some payment discounts are being offered when paying with "Geldkarte". The "Geldkarte" payment lacks all security measures, since it does not require the user to enter a PIN or sign a sales slip: the loss of a "Geldkarte" is similar to the loss of a wallet or purse - anyone who finds it can then use their find to pay for their own purchases.

Hong Kong

One popular payment method that is widely used in Hong Kong which is similar to the debit card is called EPS. EPS is a payment method that lets customers use their ATM Card like a debit card. Most of the big banks in Hong Kong provide the customer with an ATM card with EPS.

Hungary

In Hungary debit cards are far more common and popular than credit cards. Many Hungarians even refer to their debit card mistakenly using the word for credit card.

India

The debit card has limited popularity in India as the merchant is charged for each transaction. The debit card therefore is mostly used for ATM transactions. Most of the banks issue VISA debit cards, while some banks issue Maestro cards.

The debit card transactions are routed through the VISA or MasterCard networks rather than directly via the issuing bank The National Payments Corporation of India is introducing a payment network and debit card dubbed 'india card'.

The Reserve Bank of India is expecting this system will gradualy replace the overseas run networks from Visa and MaterCard for Indian ATM, debit and credit card services.

Italy

Debit cards are quite popular in Italy. There are both classic and prepaid cards. The main classic debit card in Italy is PagoBancomat: this kind of card is issued by Italian banks, often with a credit card. It allows access to the owner's bank account funds and it is widely accepted in most shops, although on the Internet it is allowed only the credit card mode.

The major debit prepaid card is issued by Poste Italiane S.p.A., is called Postepay and runs on the Visa Electron circuit. It can be used on Poste Italiane's ATMs and on Visa Electron-compatible bank ATMs all over the world. It has no fees when used on the Internet and in POS-based transactions. Other cards are issued by other companies, such as Vodafone CashCard, Banca di Milano's Carta Jeans and Carta Moneta Online.

Japan

In Japan people usually use their cash cards, originally intended only for use with cash machines, as debit cards. The debit functionality of these cards is usually referred to as J-Debitand only cash cards from certain banks can be used. A cash card has the same size as a VISA/MasterCard. As identification, the user will have to enter his or her four-digit PIN when paying. J-Debit was started in Japan on March 6, 2000.

Kuwait

In Kuwait, all banks provide a debit card to their account holders. This card is branded as KNET, which is the central switch in Kuwait. KNET card transactions are free for both customer and the merchant and therefore KNET debit cards are used for low valued transactions as well.

KNET cards are mostly co-branded as Maestro or Visa Electron which makes it possible to use the same card outside Kuwait on any terminal supporting these payment schemes.

The Netherlands

In the Netherlands using EFTPOS is known as pinnen, a term derived from the use of a Personal Identification Number. PINs are also used for ATM transactions, and the term is used interchangeably by many people, although it was introduced as a marketing brand for EFTPOS. The system was launched in 1987, and in 2006 there were 166,375 terminals throughout the country, including mobile terminals used by delivery services and on markets. All banks offer a debit card suitable for EFTPOS with current accounts.

PIN transactions are usually free to the customer, but the retailer is charged per-transaction and monthly fees. Equens, an association with all major banks as its members, runs the system, and until August 2005 also charged for it. Responding to allegations of monopoly abuse, it has handed over contractual responsibilities to its member banks, who now offer competing contracts. Interpay, a legal predecessor of Equens, was fined EUR 47 million in 2004, but the fine was later dropped, and a related fine for banks was lowered from EUR 17 to 14 million. Per-transaction fees are between 5-10 eurocents, depending on volume.

Credit cards use in the Netherlands is very low, and most credit cards cannot be used with EFTPOS, or charge very high fees to the customer. Debit cards can often, though not always, be used in the entire EU for EFTPOS. Most debit cards are Maestro cards. Electronic Purse Cards were introduced in 1996, but have never become very popular.

New Zealand

The EFTPOS system is highly popular in New Zealand, with more debit card terminals per head of population than any other country, and being used for about 60% of all retail transactions.

The largest EFTPOS network provider, "New Zealanders use EFTPOS twice as much as any other country." It is not unusual for a New Zealander to have more than one EFTPOS card and for banks to offer fixed monthly fees for unlimited EFTPOS transactions during that month. EFTPOS systems are capable of handling huge volumes of transactions during busy periods such as Christmas. The networks are highly sophisticated and have a number of safeguards in place to ensure security and to minimise the risk of disruption even during peak transaction periods.

Virtually all retail outlets have EFTPOS terminals, particularly supermarkets, "dairies", service stations, and bars. Increasingly Taxi operators, businesses operating from stands at events and even pizza delivery people have mobile EFTPOS terminals.

New Zealanders use EFTPOS for both small and large transactions. It would not be unusual for a New Zealander to use an EFTPOS card to pay for an amount as small as 50 cents NZD. Because EFTPOS is such an integral part of spending in New Zealand, rare network failures cause tremendous delays, inconvenience and lost income to businesses who must resort to manual "zip-zap" swipe machines to process EFTPOS transactions until the network returns to service. Typically New Zealand merchants do not pay a fee per transaction as is the case in Australia and other countries.

Transaction fees are typically borne by the customer, and retailers pay a fixed monthly equipment rental fee. As bank accounts for students and children under 18 years old typically attract low or no electronic transaction fees, the use of EFTPOS by the younger generations has become virtually ubiquitous. In recent times, major banks have started to offer accounts with no EFTPOS transaction fees. The Bank of New Zealand introduced EFTPOS to New Zealand in 1985 through a pilot scheme with petrol stations. EFTPOS is operated through two primary networks. One, EFTPOS NZ, owned by ANZ, and a second operated by Paymark Limited which is owned by ASB Bank, Westpac, and the Bank of New Zealand.

The Paymark network processes approximately 75% of all EFTPOS transactions in New Zealand on their Paymark EFTPOS network and has over 73,000 points of sale. During July 2006 the five billionth EFTPOS payment flowed across the ETSL/Paymark EFTPOS network since the electronic form of payment was introduced in New Zealand in 1989. On 9 May 2007, Payment Express was certified as the first IP/broadband certified terminal allowing EFTPOS transactions to be transmitted securely over the Internet.

However security issues regarding EFTPOS payments over the public Internet and the costs associated with legacy terminal replacement has hampered the growth of the IP medium in New Zealand. One company, Merchant IP Services offers an alternative IP-POS solution allowing for the secure IP connection of most legacy terminals without the need for terminal replacement.

The PCI compliant and Paymark certified MIPS IP-POS system consists of a MIPS WebNAC connected to the legacy EFTPOS terminal converting dial up transaction data to IP before transporting the payment securely to the bank switch.

In March 2008 Paymark partnered with virtual wallet payment system pago to create New Zealands first debit or "stored value" system for online shopping. The New Zealand eftpos system was one of the first in the world to be designed and its success and popularity have ironically meant that little has been done to incorporate it with systems from other countries as they were developed.

Cards can only be used within New Zealand and only when physically at a merchant terminal. In response most banks started issuing eftpos cards co-branded as maestro so they could be used overseas. In 2009 a number of banks started introducing eftpos cards that, as well as having New Zealand eftpos facility also incorporated the Visa Debit system so that clients could use them on-line as well as overseas.

Philippines

In the Philippines, all three national ATM network consortia offer proprietary PIN debit. This was first offered by Express Payment System in 1987, followed by Megalink with Paylink in 1993 then BancNet with the Point-of-Sale in 1994. Express Payment System or EPS was the pioneer provider, having launched the service in 1987 on behalf of the Bank of the Philippine Islands.

The EPS service has subsequently been extended in late 2005 to include the other Expressnet members: Banco de Oro and Land Bank of the Philippines. They currently operate 10,000 terminals for their cardholders. Megalink launched Paylink EFTPOS system in 1993. Terminal services are provided by Equitable Card Network on behalf of the consortium. Service is available in 2,000 terminals, mostly in Metro Manila.

BancNet introduced their Point of sale System in 1994 as the first consortium-operated EFTPOS service in the country. The service is available in over 1,400 locations throughout the Philippines, including second and third-class municipalities. In 2005, BancNet signed a Memorandum of Agreement to serve as the local gateway for China UnionPay, the sole ATM switch in the People's Republic of China. This will allow the estimated 1.0 billion Chinese ATM cardholders to use the BancNet ATMs and the EFTPOS in all SM Supermalls. Visa debit cards are issued by Union Bank of the Philippines, Chinatrust, Equicom Savings Bank, Banco De Oro, HSBC, HSBC Savings Bank and Sterling Bank of Asia. Union Bank of the Philippines cards, Equicom Savings Bank and Sterling Bank of Asia EMV cards which can also be used for internet purchases.

Sterling Bank of Asia has released its first line of prepaid and debit Visa cards with EMV chip. MasterCard debit cards are issued by Banco de Oro, Security Bank and Smart Communications tied up with Banco De Oro. MasterCard Electronic cards are issued by BPI and Security Bank. All VISA and MasterCard based debit cards in the Philippines are non-embossed and are marked either for "Electronic Use Only" or "Valid only where MasterCard Electronic is Accepted"

Poland

In Poland, local debit cards, such as PolCard, have become largely substituted with international ones, such as Visa, MasterCard, or the unembossed Visa Electron or Maestro. Most banks in Poland block Internet and MOTO transactions with unembossed cards, requiring the customer to buy an embossed card or a card for Internet/MOTO transactions only. The number of banks which do not block MOTO transactions on unembossed cards has recently started to increase.

Russia

In addition to VISA and Master Card, there are some local payment system based in general on Smart Card technology:

- *Sbercard*: This payment system was created by Sberbank around 1995–1996. It uses BGS Smartcard Systems AG smart card technology *i.e.* DUET. Sberbank was a single retail bank in USSR before 1990. De facto this is a payment system of the SberBank.
- *Zolotaya Korona*: This card brand was created in 1994. Zolotaya Korona is based on CFT technology.
- *STB Card*: This card uses the classic magnetic stripe technology. It almost fully collapsed after 1998 with STB bank failure.

- *Union Card*: The card also uses the classic magnetic stripe technology. This card brand is on the decline. These accounts are being reissued as Visa or MasterCard accounts.

Nearly every transaction, regardless of brand or system, is processed as an immediate debit transaction. Non-debit transactions within these systems have spending limits that are strictly limited when compared with typical Visa or MasterCard accounts.

Saudi Arabia

In Saudi Arabia, all debit card transactions are routed trough Saudi Payments Network, the only electronic payment system in the Kingdom and all banks are required by the Saudi Arabian Monetary Agency to issue cards fully compatible with the network.

It connects all point of sale terminals throughout the country to a central payment switch which in turn re-routes the financial transactions to the card issuer, local bank, VISA, AMEX or MasterCard. As well as its use for debit cards, the network is also used for ATM and credit card transactions.

Singapore

Singapore's debit service is managed by Network for Electronic Transfers, founded by Singapore's leading banks, DBS, Keppel Bank, OCBC, OUB, POSB, Tat Lee Bank and UOB in 1985 as a result of a need for a centralised e-Payment operator.It will deduct money from your bank directly when you buy things using debit cards.

United Kingdom

In the UK debit cards are an established part of the retail market and are widely accepted both by bricks and mortar stores and by internet stores. The term EFTPOS is not widely used by the public, debit card is the generic term used. Cards commonly in circulation include Maestro, Solo, Visa Debit and Visa Electron. Banks do not charge customers for EFTPOS transactions in the UK, but some retailers make small charges, particularly where the transaction amount in question is small. The UK has converted all debit cards in circulation to Chip and PIN, based on the EMV standard, to increase transaction security; however, PINs are not required for internet transactions.

In the United Kingdom, banks started to issue debit cards in the mid 1980s in a bid to reduce the number of cheques being used at the point of sale, which are costly for the banks to process; the first bank to do so was Barclays with the Barclays Connect card. As in most countries, fees paid by merchants in the United Kingdom to accept credit cards are a percentage of the transaction amount, which funds card holders' interest-free credit periods as well as incentive schemes such as points, airmiles or cashback.

Debit cards do not usually have these characteristics, and so the fee for merchants to accept debit cards is a low fixed amount, regardless of transaction amount. For very small amounts, this means it is cheaper for a merchant to accept a credit card than a debit card. Although merchants won the right through The Credit Cards Order 1990 to charge customers different prices according to the payment method, few merchants in the UK charge less for payment by debit card than by credit card, the most notable exceptions being budget airlines, travel agents and IKEA.

Debit cards in the UK lack the advantages offered to holders of UK-issued credit cards, such as free incentives, interest-free credit and protection against defaulting merchants under Section 75 of the Consumer Credit Act 1974. Almost all establishments in the United Kingdom that accept credit cards also accept debit cards but a minority of merchants, for cost reasons, accept debit cards and not credit cards.

United States

In the U.S., EFTPOS is universally referred to simply as debit. The same interbank networks that operate the ATM network also operate the POS network. Most interbank networks, such as Pulse, NYCE, MAC, Tyme, SHAZAM, STAR, etc. are regional and do not overlap, however, most ATM/POS networks have agreements to accept each other's cards. This means that cards issued by one network will typically work anywhere they accept ATM/POS cards for payment.

For example, a NYCE card will work at a Pulse POS terminal or ATM, and vice versa. Many debit cards in the United States are issued with a Visa or MasterCard logo allowing use of their signature-based networks.

The liability of a U.S. debit card user in case of loss or theft is up to 50 USD if the loss or theft is reported to the issuing bank in two business days after the customer notices the loss. The fees charged to merchants on offline debit purchases—and the lack of fees charged merchants for processing online debit purchases and paper checks—have prompted some major merchants in the U.S. to file lawsuits against debit-card transaction processors such as Visa and MasterCard. In 2003, Visa and MasterCard agreed to settle the largest of these lawsuits and agreed to settlements of billions of dollars.

Some consumers prefer "credit" transactions because of the lack of a fee charged to the consumer/purchaser; also, a few debit cards in the U.S. offer rewards for using "credit". However, since "credit" costs more for merchants, many terminals at PIN-accepting merchant locations now make the "credit" function more difficult to access.

For example, if you swipe a debit card at Wal-Mart in the U.S., you are immediately presented with the PIN screen for online debit; to use offline debit you must press "cancel" to exit the PIN screen, then press "credit" on the next screen. One additional problem surrounding the use of debit cards is their use at a self-service gas pump like those common in the U.S. The customer might want to purchase fuel on their debit card, but the pump's computer does not know how much fuel the customer wants. The pump is activated by the customer presenting their card to a card reader and possibly entering a PIN. At this point the pump will dispense fuel, though no sales transaction has completed. The pump has no way of knowing how much fuel will be sold, nor how much money is available in the customer's debit account. In a typical sale transaction, trying to spend more money than is available in your account will result in a "no-sale" alert to the merchant, and the sale does not occur. At a self-serve fuel pump, the fuel is already in the customer's tank by the time the bank knows the final sale price.

Several solutions to this problem are in place, such as denying $1 pre-authorizations when an account holds less than $10 while still allowing transactions for specific amounts, but the concept of delivering the merchandise before the sales transaction plagues the debit card system.

The commission is sometimes so high that the gas station sometimes actually loses money when someone pays for gas with credit. When pay at the pump started in the 1980s, many gas stations offered a discount for paying with cash. Most of them stopped doing that because the discount did not significantly increase their cash sales.

2009-07-08: Minimum and Maximum Charges for Visa in USA The Merchants Agreement for Visa states:

Always honour valid Visa cards in your acceptance category, regardless of the dollar amount of the purchase. Imposing minimum or maximum purchase amounts in order to accept a Visa card transaction is a violation of the Visa rules.

FSA, HRA, and HSA Debit Cards

In the U.S.A, a FSA debit card only allows medical expenses. It is used by some banks for withdrawals from their FSAs, MSAs, and HSAs as well. They have Visa or MasterCard logos, but cannot be used as "debit cards", only as "credit cards"", and they are not accepted by all merchants that accept debit and credit cards, but only by those that accept FSA debit cards.

Merchant codes and product codes are used at the point of sale to restrict sales if they do not qualify. Because of the extra checking and documenting that goes on, later, the statement can be used to substantiate these purchases for tax deductions.

In the occasional instance that a qualifying purchase is rejected, another form of payment must be used. In the more likely case that non-qualifying items are accepted, the consumer is technically still responsible, and the discrepancy could be revealed during an audit.

A small but growing segment of the debit card business in the U.S. involves access to tax-favoured spending accounts such as flexible spending accounts, health reimbursement accounts, and health savings accounts. Most of these debit cards are for medical expenses, though a few are also issued for dependent care and transportation expenses.

Traditionally, FSAs were accessed only through claims for reimbursement after incurring, and often paying, an out-of-pocket expense; this often happens after the funds have already been deducted from the employee's paycheck. The only method permitted by the Internal Revenue Service to avoid this "double-dipping" for medical FSAs and HRAs is through accurate and auditable reporting on the tax return.

Statements on the debit card that say "for medical uses only" are invalid for several reasons:

- The merchant and issuing banks have no way of quickly determining whether the entire purchase qualifies for the customer's type of tax benefit;
- The customer also has no quick way of knowing; often has mixed purchases by necessity or convenience; and can easily make mistakes;
- Extra contractual clauses between the customer and issuing bank would cross-over into the payment processing standards, creating additional confusion.

Therefore, using the card exclusively for qualifying purchases may be convenient for the customer, but it has nothing to do with how the card can actually be used. If the bank rejects a transaction, for instance, because it is not at a recognized drug store, then it would be causing harm and confusion to the cardholder.

In the United States, not all medical service or supply stores are capable of providing the correct information so an FSA debit card issuer can honour every transaction-if rejected or documentation is not deemed enough to satisfy regulations, cardholders may have to send in forms manually.

PARTICULAR ISSUES OF PROS AND CONS

Pros and cons are arguments for or against a particular issue. Pros are arguments which aim to promote the issue, while cons suggest points against it. The term has been in use since the 16th century and is a shortening of a Latin phrase, *pro et contra*, which means "for and against." Considering the pros and cons of an issue is a very useful way to weigh the issue thoughtfully and reach an informed decision.

Many people find themselves considering pros and cons in daily life, although they may not be aware of it. For example, someone shopping at a supermarket might weigh the cost of an item and the quality to decide whether or not to purchase it. People making larger decisions, like purchasing a new car or home, often spend a great deal of time thinking about the pros and cons of the purchase so that they can be sure that the right choice will be made.

In addition to being useful in daily life, pros and cons can also strengthen academic papers and debates. By weighing the pros and cons beforehand, someone can consider potential objections to a point, as well as ways to dismiss a counter-argument.

Skilled authors will often include pros and cons in a paper to indicate that they have considered all sides of an issue and are confident that their feelings are correct. They can also be used to identify weaknesses in an argument: if you notice a lack of discussion of the cons of an issue, for example, it is probably too good to be true.

Many politicians have highly refined the art of examining pros and cons, especially when it comes to major issues. Campaign and staff advisers are kept on staff to thoroughly and carefully research issues and ultimately provide a list of pros and cons.

This list can be used to build solid, well thought out persuasive arguments that can be used on the campaign trail, in political debates, on the floor of a legislative body, or to counter statements made by opponents. When using pros and cons to reach a difficult decision, many people find it helpful to divide a piece of paper into two columns, writing the pros in one column and the cons in another.

Sometimes providing a clear visual guide allows the decision to become obvious, as one side may overwhelmingly outweigh the other. If nothing else, weighing the pros and cons will allow someone to consider every aspect of a situation.

5

The Time Value of Money

The time value of money (TVM) is the basic mathematics of investing and is the basis of all financial calculations. Most importantly, it explains the concept of compound returns, which causes investments to grow exponentially over time. An understanding of the time value of money is crucial to understanding the expected and actual returns on investments and analyzing past returns on investments. It's something every investor should know well, and being armed with a good financial calculator will help. Financial calculators are indispensable to investors when it comes to doing anything that involves the time value of money.

Return can be the interest earned on a bond, the rate of return realized on a stock or mutual fund over its holding period, the rate of return a corporation earns on invested capital and more. In finance, the letter r is used to represent the rate of return. In some references you will find the letter k is used instead of r. Unfortunately, no one told the calculator manufacturers about this. You'll usually find that i is used instead of r on financial calculators. In the interest of continuity and because r is a more logical representation of return than k, I have used r.

The basic time value of money formula, which applies the concept of compound return, is:

$FV_n = PV(1 + r)^n$

Where:

FV = Future Value after n periods

PV = Present Value

r = Periodic rate of return

n = Number of compounding periods

This formula computes the future value (FV) of a current amount (PV) earning a compound rate of return r for n periods. Compounding can also be continuous, but that requires a formula that is derived by solving an infinite series. You'll find that formula farther down this page.

Although we tend to think of returns as being annual returns, the compounding period can be any fixed duration, such as days, weeks, months or years. For instance, you've probably noticed that the APR of monthly credit card interest is greater than 12 times the monthly rate. That's explained by the fact that the compounding period is monthly. If the monthly rate is 1.5 per cent, then the APR will be 19.56 per cent which is greater than 12 x 1.5 per cent = 18.00 per cent.

$$(1 + 0.015)^{12} - 1 = 0.1956 = 19.56\%$$

The 1 in the formula represents the beginning value, thus it must be subtracted to find the compound return, which in this case is the credit card company's return.

This formula can be used to compare investment opportunities. Suppose you have the option of investing in one of two mutual funds which are identical in every respect except the management fees they charge. Both funds have a ten year historical rate of return of 12 per cent and they also have identical standard deviations (risk). However, fund B charges an annual management fee of 1.25 per cent but fund A only charges 0.75 per cent. (Of course, the usual disclaimer applies: Past performance is not necessarily indicative of future results.) As the two funds are equal in every way except the management fee and management fees must be deducted from performance to determine return, you will obviously choose fund A. So lets see how much better you'll do over the years with fund A assuming your initial investment is $10,000, that the funds' future performance is equivalent to their past performance and all distributions are reinvested.

Yeae	Fund A	Fund B	Difference	Difference
0	$10,000	$10,000	$0	0%
5	$17,041	$16,662	$380	2.3%
10	$29,040	$27,761	$1,279	4.6%
15	%49,488	$46,255	$3,233	7.0%
20	$84,334	$77,068	$7,265	9.4%
25	$143,714	$128,408	$15,306	11.9%

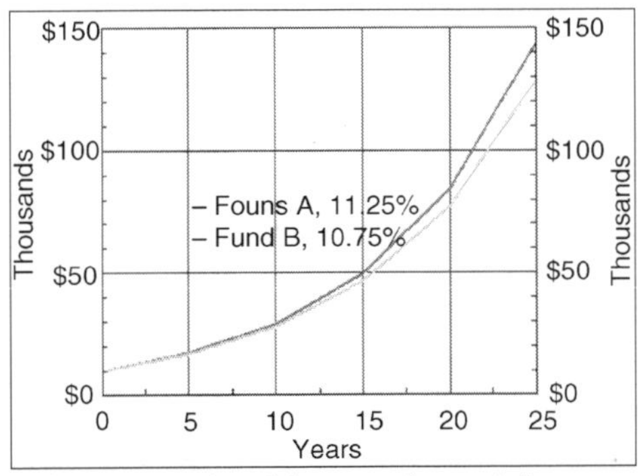

There are a few things you should note about this example:

- Both curves are upward-sweeping, *i.e.*, they are exponential curves.
- In both cases, the value of your investment increases at an increasing

rate, which is expected given the basic time value of money formula for compound return.

- The 0.50 per cent difference in management fees results in an 11.9 per cent difference in the value of the investments after 25 years.
- The 11.25 per cent compound rate of return causes fund A to grow to \$143,714 in 25 years, which is a total return of \$133,714 or 1337 per cent, compared to 1184 per cent for fund B.

Here's how the total return on fund A looks in the compound return formula, where ROI = return on investment:

Fund A has an 11.25 per cent annual ROI for 25 years.

$$FV_n = PV(1 + r)^n = \$10,000(1 + 0.1125)^{25}$$

$$= \$10,000 \times 14.37 = \$143,714$$

$$\$143,714 - \$10,000 = \$133,714 \text{ Total ROI}$$

$$\$133,714 \div \$10,000 = 13.37$$

$$13.37 \times 100 \text{ per cent} = 1337\% \text{ Total ROI}$$

That, ladies and gentlemen, is the power of compounding. With time, compounding will turn a modest investment into a tidy sum and a small difference in the rate of return can become a significant gap. I can't overemphasize the importance of these two points to you as investors. The following chart shows how the value of the SandP 500 index has grown exponentially since 1950.

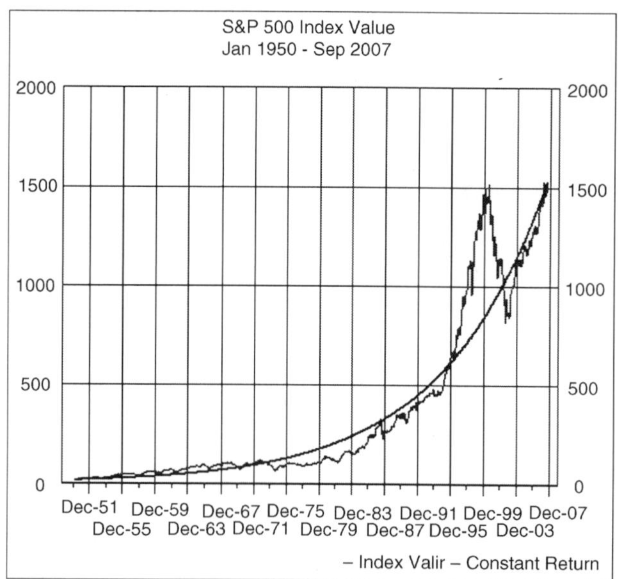

The red line was plotted from the actual values of the S&P 500 index at the end of each month. The blue line is what the index would have been if the rate of return had been constant over the period January 1950 through September 2007 and reflects a compound annual rate of return of 8.13 per cent computed from monthly returns. The average annual return for the period was 8.84 per cent, also computed from monthly returns. (The difference in these two numbers is explained in the subsection on mutual fund returns.) In 57 years and nine months, the S&P 500 grew from a value of 16.71 to 1526.75, which is an excellent example of the power of compounding. The dividend yield would add approximately 2 per cent to each of these returns, thus making the compound growth of an investment in the index even greater than growth of the index itself.

You should note that the compound return formula works in reverse.

$$(FV \div PV)^{1/n} - 1 = r$$

$$(14.3714)^{1/25} = 1.1125$$

$$(\$143{,}714 \div \$10{,}000)^{1/25} = (14.3714)^{1/25} = 1.1125$$

1 represents the original investment, so it must be subtracted to determine the rate of return:

$$1.1125 - 1 = 0.1125$$

$$0.1125 \text{ x } 100\% = 11.25\%$$

You'll need either a financial or scientific calculator, or a spreadsheet, to perform calculations involving the time value of money. All of them should have the functions used in the formulas above.

Continuous compounding falls under the heading of the time value of money. The formula for continuous compounding is:

$FV_n = PV(e^{r\,n})$

Where:

FV = Future Value after n periods

PV = Present Value

r = Periodic rate of return

n = Number of compounding periods

e is the base of natural logarithms,2.71828

Continuous compounding was big in the early 1980s when the T-Bill rate was as high as 17 per cent. At that time, inflation was so high that it was extremely important to keep your cash someplace where it would earn a reasonable rate of interest. Many banks offered continuous compounding on their interest-bearing checking accounts in an attempt to lure new customers, and it worked because people wanted to get the very highest rate of return possible in an attempt to keep up with inflation. The formula for the present value of a future amount is derived by simply rearranging the terms of the future value formula:

$$PV = FV_n \div (1 + r)^n$$

The other time value of money formulas also are based on the principle of compound return. You need to know how to use the preceding formulas because they are used for much more than just computing present and future value. However, you shouldn't ever have to use these additional formulas, as there are calculator and spreadsheet functions and tables that can be used for all calculations involving the time value of money. Some of them are used in the valuation of bonds and also in some stock valuation models. Those used in bond valuation are included in the bond functions in financial calculators, but it's good to know how those functions work. The other formulas are as follows:

Future Value of an Ordinary Annuity

(Payments due end of period.)

$FVA_n = PMT[((1 + r)^n - 1) \div r]$

Where:

FVA = Future Value of Annuity

PMT = Amount of periodic payment

n = number of payments

The period between payments can be any *constant* lengthof time.

This formula computes the FVA at the time the nth payment is made.

Future Value of an Annuity Due

(Payments due at beginning of period.)

$FVN_n = PMT[((1 + r)^n - 1) \div r](1 + r)$

The period between payments can be any *constant* length of time.

This formula computes the FVA at the time the nth payment is made.

Present Value of an Ordinary Annuity

(Payments due at end of period.)

$PVA_n = (1 - (1 + r)^{-n}) \div r$

Where PVA = Present Value of an Annuity

Present Value of an Annuity Due

(Payments due at beginning of period.)

$PVA_n = [(1 - (1 + r)^{-n}) \div r](1 + r)$

The value of a bond is the sum of the present value of an ordinary annuity (the coupon payments) and the present value of a future amount (the return of your principal). Like many things in finance, bond calculations involve computing a missing piece of the puzzle with the rest of the pieces. If you know the time to maturity, coupon payment, face value and current market interest rate, you can compute the current value of the bond. It's all based on the time value of money.

Perpetuities are an interesting but archaic instrument involving the time value of money. They make a constant periodic payment forever. Say you sell 1000 acres of your farm to the state fish and game commission and they pay you with a perpetuity, which will provide income to your heirs forever. The value of the perpetuity is the payment you and your heirs will receive divided by the opportunity rate of return, *i.e.*, the rate of return you could make on investments if the state paid you a lump sum rather than a perpetuity. The payment might look good now, but in 50 years it will be peanuts. Why? Plug a future value, r = the current rate for intermediate bonds and n = 50 into the formula for the present value of a future amount and see what happens to that payment 50 years hence. Which brings us to the final point.

Corporations commonly use net present value for evaluating investments or estimating the value of their assets. But present value analysis is only valid in the short term, as you should know if you tried what I suggested in the prior paragraph. If a company owns assets like forest land that is harvested on a 30 year rotation, harvests 30 years in the future don't appear to be worth much and harvests 60 years in the future have almost no value by present value analysis, which is counterintuitive when one considers the basic concept of the time value of money.

Many analysts picked up on this in the 1980s and found some real gems, like railroads that had tens of thousands of acres that they carried on their books at their 19th century acquisition costs. And there are undoubtedly more to be found. Also in the 1980s, a lot of timber land was sold to developers by forest products companies that used present value to assess the value of their holdings. So beware of companies making such suboptimal decisions and keep an eye out for those undiscovered gems. This is an example of the inappropriate use of the time value of money.

VALUE OF MONEY

What gives money value? We know that intrinsically, a dollar bill is just worthless paper and ink. However, the purchasing power of a dollar bill is much greater than that of another piece of paper of similar size. From where does this power originate?

Like most things in economics, there is a market for money. The supply of money in the money market comes from the Fed. The Fed has the power to adjust the money supply by increasing or decreasing the number of bills in circulation. Nobody else can make this policy decision. The demand for money in the money market comes from consumers.

The determinants of money demand are infinite. In general, consumers need money to purchase goods and services. If there is an ATM nearby or if credit cards are plentiful, consumers may demand less money at a given time than they would if cash were difficult to obtain. The most important variable in determining money demand is the average price level within the economy. If the average price level is high and goods and services tend to cost a significant amount of money, consumers will demand more money. If, on the other hand, the average price level is low and goods and services tend to cost little money, consumers will demand less money.

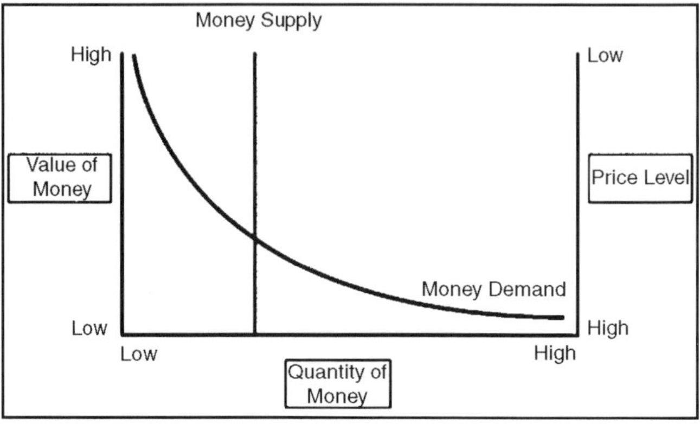

Fig. Sample Money Market

The value of money is ultimately determined by the intersection of the money supply, as controlled by the Fed, and money demand, as created by consumers. Figure depicts the money market in a sample economy. The money supply curve is vertical because the Fed sets the amount of money available without consideration for the value of money. The money demand curve slopes downward because as the value of money decreases, consumers are forced to carry more money to make purchases because goods and services cost more money. Similarly, when the value of money is high, consumers demand little money because goods and services can be purchased for low prices. The intersection of the money supply curve and the money demand curve shows both the equilibrium value of money as well as the equilibrium price level.

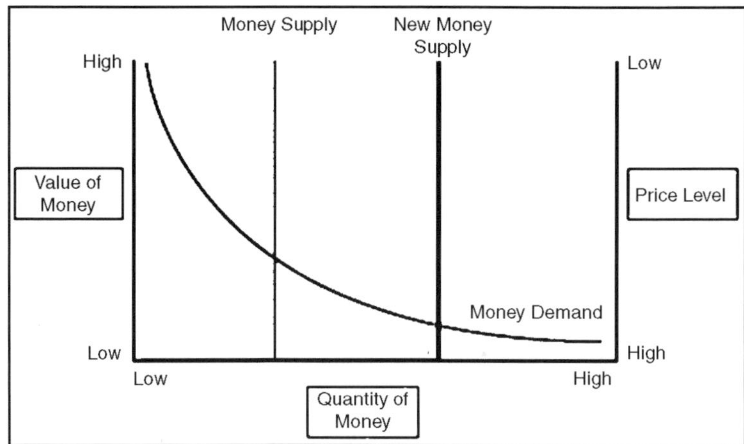

Fig. Sample Shift in the Money Market

The value of money, as revealed by the money market, is variable. A change in money demand or a change in the money supply will yield a change in the value of money and in the price level. Notice that the change in the value of money and the change in the price level are of the same magnitude but in opposite directions. An increase in the money supply is depicted in Figure.

Notice that the new intersection of the money supply curve and the money demand curve is at a lower value of money but a higher price level. This happens because more money is in circulation, so each bill becomes worth less. It takes more bills to purchase goods and services, and thus the price level increases accordingly.

The quantity theory of money is based directly on the changes brought about by an increase in the money supply. The quantity theory of money states that the value of money is based on the amount of money in the economy. Thus, according to the quantity theory of money, when the Fed increases the money supply, the value of money falls and the price level increases. In the SparkNote on inflation we learned that inflation is defined as an increase in the price level. Based on this definition, the quantity theory of money also states that growth in the money supply is the primary cause of inflation.

Velocity

While the relationship between money supply, money demand, the price level, and the value of money presented above is accurate, it is a bit simplistic. In the real world economy, these factors are not connected as neatly as the quantity theory of money and the basic money market diagram present. Rather, a number of variables mediate the effects of changes in the money supply and money demand on the value of money and the price level.

The most important variable that mediates the effects of changes in the money supply is the velocity of money. Imagine that you purchase a hamburger. The waiter then takes the money that you spent and uses it to pay for his dry cleaning. The dry cleaner then takes that money and pays to have his car washed. This process continues until the bill is eventually taken out of circulation. In many cases, bills are not removed from circulation until many decades of service. In the end, a single bill will have facilitated many times its face value in purchases.

Velocity of money is defined simply as the rate at which money changes hands. If velocity is high, money is changing hands quickly, and a relatively small money supply can fund a relatively large amount of purchases. On the other hand, if velocity is low, then money is changing hands slowly, and it takes a much larger money supply to fund the same number of purchases.

As you might expect, the velocity of money is not constant. Instead, velocity changes as consumers' preferences change. It also changes as the value of money and the price level change. If the value of money is low, then the price level is high, and a larger number of bills must be used to fund purchases. Given a constant money supply, the velocity of money must increase to fund all of these purchases. Similarly, when the money supply shifts due to Fed policy, velocity can change. This change makes the value of money and the price level remain constant.

The relationship between velocity, the money supply, the price level, and output is represented by the equation M * V = P * Y where M is the money supply, V is the velocity, P is the price level, and Y is the quantity of output. P * Y, the price level multiplied by the quantity of output, gives the nominal GDP. This equation can thus be rearranged as V = (nominal GDP)/ M. Conceptually, this equation means that for a given level of nominal GDP, a smaller money supply will result in money needing to change hands more quickly to facilitate the total purchases, which causes increased velocity.

The equation for the velocity of money, while useful in its original form, can be converted to a percentage change formula for easier calculations. In this case, the equation becomes (percent change in the money supply) + (percent change in velocity) = (percent change in the price level) + (percent change in output). The percentage change formula aids calculations that involve this equation by ensuring that all variables are in common units.

The velocity equation can be used to find the effects that changes in velocity, price level, or money supply have on each other. When making these calculations, remember that in the short run, output (Y), is fixed, as time is required for the quantity of output to change.

Let's try an example. What is the effect of a 3 per cent increase in the money supply on the price level, given that output and velocity remain relatively constant? The equation used to solve this problem is (percent change in the money supply) + (percent change in velocity) = (percent change in the price level) + (percent change in output). Substituting in the values from the problem we get 3 per cent + 0 per cent = x per cent + 0 per cent. In this case, a 3 per cent increase in the money supple results in a 3 per cent increase in the price level. Remember that a 3 per cent increase in the price level means that inflation was 3 per cent. In the long run, the equation for velocity becomes even more useful. In fact, the equation shows that increases in the money supply by the Fed tend to cause increases in the price level and therefore inflation, even though the effects of the Fed's policy is slightly dampened by changes in velocity. This results a number of factors. First, in the long run, velocity, V, is relatively constant because people's spending habits are not quick to change. Similarly, the quantity of output, Y, is not affected by the actions of the Fed since it is based on the amount of production, not the value of the stuff produced. This means that the percent change in the money supply equals the percent change in the price level since the percent change in velocity and percent change in output are both equal to zero. Thus, we see how an increase in the money supply by the Fed causes inflation.

Let's try another example. What is the effect of a 5 per cent increase in the money supply on inflation? Again, we being by using the equation (percent change in the money supply) + (percent change in velocity) = (percent change in the price level) + (percent change in output). Remember that in the long run, output not affected by the Fed's actions and velocity remains relatively constant. Thus, the equation becomes 5 per cent + 0 per cent = x per cent + 0 per cent. In this case, a 5 per cent increase in the money supply results in a 5 per cent increase in inflation.

The velocity of money equation represents the heart of the quantity theory of money. By understanding how velocity mitigates the actions of the Fed in the long run and in the short run, we can gain a thorough understanding of the value of money and inflation.

MEAN AND STANDARD DEVIATION ANALYZING INVESTMENT RETURNS

The arithmetic mean and standard deviation are the first and most simple of the basic statistical concepts used in investing. The mean and standard deviation of investment returns provide the basic profile of any security with respect to risk and return.

The mean, in statistics, is merely the arithmetic average. For example, if you have average returns for 10 years, you simply add them together and divide by 10 to find the mean. The term "mean" usually refers to the arithmetic mean but there's also a geometric mean, which will be discussed in the section on comparing mutual funds with key statistics ("Compare Funds" on the menu bar).

The mean is used as an estimate of expected future returns of mutual funds because it's the best estimate we can make solely from past data.

Analysts have many resources at their disposal to help them project the future returns of securities and they have the time required to put those resources to work. However, most of us don't have the time and resources to do detailed securities analysis and, as the focus of this site is mutual fund investing, it's really not relevant to us. For all intents and purposes, predicting future mutual fund performance from historical data is appropriate as long as any trends are noted and taken into consideration. So we use the mean to project the future and always deliver the obligatory caveat that past returns are not necessarily indicative of future returns.

The standard deviation is a measure of variability which is used as the standard measure of the total risk of individual assets and portfolios of assets. There are two variants of standard deviation: population and sample. The sample standard deviation is used when working with historical returns, as they are deemed to be samples unless 100 per cent of the data points are used in the calculation.

The population standard deviation is only used when working with 100 per cent of the data points. Daily NAVs from a fund's inception through the most recent trading day would be considered to be a population. Monthly returns for the past ten years is a sample.

In plain English, the standard deviation is the absolute value of the average deviation of the data points from the mean. In mathematical terms the it is the square root of the sample variance and the sample variance is the sum of the squared deviations divided by the number of data points less one, (n - 1). To compute the population variance, you would simply divide by n instead of (n - 1) and the population standard deviation would be the square root of the population variance.

The arithmetic mean is computed as follows:

$r_{Avg} = [Sum(r_i)] \div n$

Where:

n= the number of data points and i = 1 through n.

When r_{Avg} is used as an estimate of future returns it is referred to as the expected value of r, E(r).

The population standard deviation is computed as follows:

Population Variance = V = $[Sum(r_i - r_{Avg})^2] \div n$

Population Standard Deviation = S = $V^{1/2}$

Where $V^{1/2}$ is equivalent to the square root of V.

The sample standard deviation is computed as follows:

Sample Variance = V = $[Sum(r_i - r_{Avg})^2] \div (n - 1)$

Sample Standard Deviation = S = $V^{1/2}$

Where $V^{1/2}$ is equivalent to the square root of V.

Here's an example calculation of the mean and standard deviation of of investment returns for a sample:

Table. A Large-Cap Mutual Fund's Retums

Year	Retum%	Deviation from Mean	Deviation Squared
1997	47.5	34.1	1162.8
1998	33.6	20.2	408
1999	33.4	20.0	400
2000	-7.6	-21.0	441
2001	-17.6	-31.0	961
2002	-24.4	-37.8	1428.8
2003	30.8	17.4	302.8
2004	15.1	1.7	2.9
2005	15.9	2.5	6.3
2006	7.5	-5.9	34.8
Sum	134.2	Sum	5148.4
n	10.0	n-1	9
Mean	13.4	Variance	572.0
		Std Dev	23.9

In the Interest Rates subsection I introduced the risk-free rate of return, r*, as being the basis from which securities are priced. As the T-Bill rate is used as a proxy for r*, the basis can vary quite a bit over time.

Indeed, the T-Bill rate was above 17 per cent in 1981 and as low as 0.01 per cent in 2009. Therefore, the proper way to evaluate returns is with *excess* returns, which is the actual return less the average T-Bill rate for the period over which the returns were computed. In the example above, the period was yearly, so the average T-Bill rate for each year should have been deducted from each year's return.

However, you won't find this in most published data, so you should do it yourself. If the T-Bill rate was relatively stable over the period being analyzed, then it's not terribly important, as you'll be comparing everything on a relative basis. But if you compare raw returns for 2009 to 1981, you'll not be comparing apples to apples. If your only means of projecting future returns is by using historic returns, then you definitely should work with excess returns.

Security returns have been found to be approximately normally distributed, which means it's relatively safe to use the normal distribution to make some general inferences of what can be expected if the past is repeated in the future. This is a pretty good assumption for the variability of returns but not the returns themselves. But, as mentioned above, that's all most of us have so that's what we use, thus the standard disclaimer that past returns are not necessarily indicative of future returns.

STANDARD DEVIATION RULES OF THUMB

Here are some rules of thumb regarding the standard normal distribution. (The probabilities have been rounded, as these are just rules of thumb.): 68 per cent of the probability lies within one standard deviation of the mean, and as the distribution is symmetric, that 68 per cent can be interpreted as being centered on the mean. What's that mean, you say? It means that the actual return for any given year could have been expected to be within one standard deviation of the mean 68 per cent of the time. In the example above, there's a 68 per cent probability that the return in any year selected at random from the 10-year sample would be between -10.5 per cent (13.4 - 23.9) and +37.3 per cent (13.4 + 23.9). As the distribution is symmetric, this can be refined to a 34 per cent probability that the return would be between 13.4 per cent and -10.5 per cent and a 34 per cent probability that it would be between 13.4 per cent and 37.3 per cent. But that only covers 68 per cent of the probability.

There's nearly a 96 per cent probability that the return for any given year was within two standard deviations of the mean and nearly a 100 per cent probability that it was within three. Again, this is centered on the mean, so it can be interpreted as +/- 2 SD and +/- 3 SD respectively.

Standard Deviation Rules of Thumb

Span	Probability
+/- 1 SD	68%
+/- 2 SD	96%
+/- 3 SD	100%

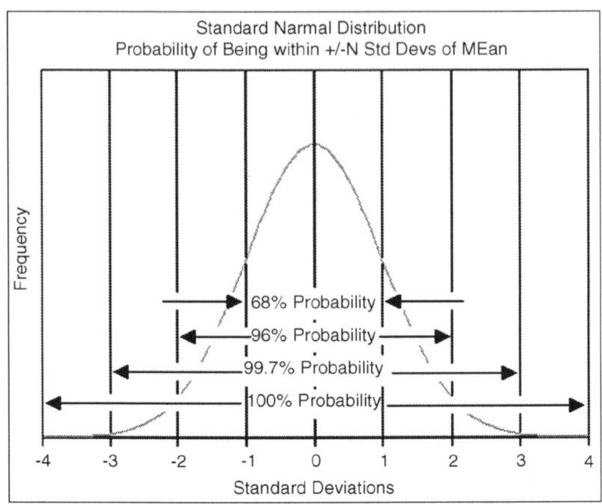

The mean splits the total probability of normally distributed data. Thus there is a 50 per cent probability that the return for any year would be less than the mean and a 50 per cent probability that it would be greater than the mean. Taking this a step farther, we can look at the upside and downside potential on a cumulative basis. This is shown in the following table and charts:

Table. Cumulative Probabilities of the Standard Normal Distribution

Number of Standard Deviations from the Mean, X	-4	-3	-2	-1	0	+1	+2	+3	+4
Probability of being X Standard Deviations from the Mean	>0.49999	0.4987	0.4772	0.3413	-	0.3413	0.4772	0.4987	>0.49999
Cumulative Probability, Left to Right	<0.00001	0.0013	0.0228	0.1587	0.50000	0.8413	0.9772	0.0.9987	<0.99999
Cumulative Probability, Right to Left	>0.99999	0.9987	0.9972	0.8413	0.50000	0.1587	0.0228	0.0013	<0.00001

The first row of probabilities are the probabilities that the actual return will be X standard deviations (SD) from the mean. For example, there is a 34.13 per cent probability that the return will be between the mean and one SD greater than the mean. Also, the probability of being between -1 SD and +1 SD is 68.26 per cent. The second row of probabilities is the pessimistic view. This tells us that there is a 2.28 per cent probability that the return will be greater than two SD below the mean and a 15.87 per cent probability that it will be greater than one SD below the mean. In the example above, these would be losses of 34.4 per cent and 10.5 per cent, respectively.

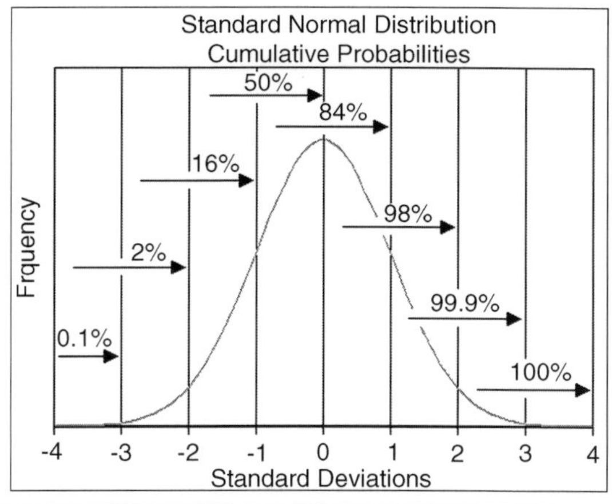

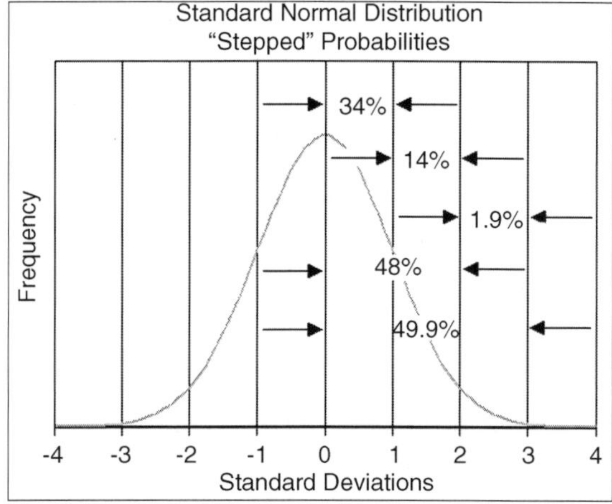

The third row of probabilities is the optimistic view. This tells us that there is a 97.72 per cent probability that the return will be greater than two SD below the mean and an 84.13 per cent probability that it will be greater than one SD below the mean.

This is how risk is viewed in the world of investing and why understanding standard deviation is so important. If you can assemble a portfolio that has a standard deviation equal to its expected return you will only have a 16 per cent probability of losing money in any one year, (100 per cent - 84 per cent = 16 per cent).

In the example above, there is a 34 per cent probability that a portfolio comprised solely of the large-cap growth fund could lose as much as 10.5 per cent in any year based on annual return data from 1997 through 2006. More specifically, using the probability tables for the standard normal distribution, there is a 12.9 per cent probability that the portfolio's return will be between 0.0 per cent and -10.5 per cent and a 15.9 per cent probability that a loss greater than 10.5 per cent will be suffered, and the total probability of a loss is 12.9 per cent + 15.9 per cent = 28.8 per cent. Diversifying that portfolio would reduce its standard deviation. Good diversification can be achieved by assembling a portfolio whose constituent securities have a low degree of correlation with each other.

STANDARDS OF VALUE MONEY

When money consisted primarily of coins, silver and gold coins circulated simultaneously. As governments came increasingly to take over the coinage, and especially as fiduciary money was introduced, they specified their nominal monetary units in terms of fixed weights of either silver or gold. Some adopted a national bimetallic standard, with fixed weights for both gold and silver based on their relative values on a given date. As the prices changed, Gresham's law assured that the bimetallic standard degenerated into a monometallic standard: if the quantity of silver designated as the monetary equivalent of one ounce of gold (15 to 1) was less than the quantity that could be purchased in the market for one ounce of gold, (say 16 to 1), no one would bring gold to be coined. Holders of gold found it was better to buy silver in the market, receiving 16 ounces for each ounce of gold, then take 15 ounces of silver to the mint to be coined and accept payment in gold.

Continuing this profitable exchange drains the gold from the mint, and leaves the mint with silver coinage. Silver, the cheaper metal in the market, "drove out" gold and became the standard. This happened in most of the countries of Europe, so that by the early 19th century all were effectively on a silver standard. In Britain, on the other hand, the ratio established in the 18th century, on the advice of Sir Isaac Newton then serving as master of the mint, overvalued gold and therefore led to an effective gold standard. In the United States a ratio of 15 ounces of silver to one ounce of gold was set in 1792. This ratio overvalued silver, so silver became the standard. In 1834 the ratio was altered to 16 to one, which overvalued gold, so gold became the standard.

THE GOLD STANDARD

The great gold discoveries in California and Australia in the 1840s and 50s produced a temporary decline in the value of gold in terms of silver. This price change, plus the dominance of Britain in international finance, led to a widespread shift from a silver standard to a gold standard. Germany adopted gold in 1871-73, the Latin Monetary Union (France, Italy, Belgium, Switzerland) in 1873-74, the Scandinavian Union (Denmark, Norway, and Sweden) and The Netherlands in 1875-76. By the final decades of the century, silver remained dominant only in the Far East (China, in particular). Elsewhere the gold standard reigned.

The early 20th century was the great era of the international gold standard. Gold coins circulated in most of the world; paper money, whether issued by private banks or by government, was convertible on demand into gold coins or gold bullion at an official price (with perhaps the addition of a small fee); and bank deposits were convertible into either gold coin or paper currency that was itself convertible into gold.

In a few countries, a minor variant prevailed — the so-called gold-exchange standard, under which a country's reserves included not only gold but also currencies of other countries that were convertible into gold. Currencies were exchanged at a fixed price into the currency of another country (usually the British pound sterling) that was itself convertible into gold.

There was, in effect, a single world money called by different names in different countries. A U.S., dollar, for example, was defined as 23.22 grains of pure gold (25.8 grains of gold 9/10ths fine). A British pound sterling was defined as 113.00 grains of pure gold (123.274 grains of gold 11/12ths fine). Accordingly, one British pound equaled 4.8665 U.S., dollars (113.00/23.22) at the official parity.

The actual exchange rate could deviate from this value only by an amount that corresponded to the cost of shipping gold. If the price of the pound sterling in terms of dollars rose to a considerably higher value than this in the foreign exchange market, someone in New York City who had a debt to pay in London might find that, rather than buy the needed pounds on the market, it was cheaper to get gold for dollars at a bank or at the U.S., subtreasury, ship the gold to London, and get pounds for the gold from the Bank of England. This set an upper limit to the exchange rate. Similarly, the cost of shipping gold from Britain to the United States set a lower limit. These limits were known as the gold points.

Under such an international gold standard, the quantity of money in each country was determined by this mechanism, known as the price-specie-flow adjustment mechanism and analysed by 19th-century economists. If, for whatever reason, the quantity of money in a country rose unduly, this would tend to raise prices in that country relative to prices in other countries; the rise in prices would have the effect of discouraging exports and encouraging imports. The decreased supply of foreign currency from the sale of exports plus the increased demand for foreign currency to pay for imports would tend to raise the price of foreign currency in terms of domestic currency.

As soon as this price hit the upper gold point, gold would be shipped out of the country to other countries. The decline in the amount of gold would produce in turn a reduction in the total amount of money—because banks and government institutions, seeing their gold reserves decline, would want to protect themselves against further demands by reducing the claims against gold that were outstanding. This would tend to lower prices at home. The influx of gold abroad would have the opposite effect, increasing the quantity of money there and raising prices. These adjustments would continue until the gold flow ceased or was reversed.

Precisely the same mechanism that operates within a unified currency area. That mechanism determines how much money there is in Illinois compared to how much there is in other states or how much there is in Wales compared to how much there is in other parts of the United Kingdom. In the early 20th century, most of the commercial world was a unified currency area, so the gold standard functioned throughout the world. Its great advantage was that—if permitted to operate—it would greatly limit the power of any national government to engage in irresponsible monetary expansion. This was also its great disadvantage. In an era of big government and of full-employment policies, a real gold standard would tie the hands of governments in one of the most important areas of policy.

The Decline of Gold

World War I ended the real international gold standard. Most belligerents suspended the free convertibility of gold. The United States, even after its entry into the war, maintained convertibility but embargoed gold exports. For a few years after the end of the war, most nations had inconvertible national paper standards—inconvertible in that paper money was not convertible into gold or silver. The exchange rate between any two currencies was a market rate that fluctuated from time to time.

At the time, this was regarded as a temporary phenomenon, like the British suspension of gold payments during the Napoleonic era, and the U.S., suspension during the Civil War greenback period. The great aim was a restoration of the prewar gold standard. Since price levels had increased in all countries during the war, countries had to choose deflation or devaluation to restore the gold standard. This effort dominated monetary developments during the 1920s. Britain, still a major financial power, chose deflation.

Winston Churchill, Chancellor of the Exchequer in 1925, decided to follow prevailing financial opinion and adopt the prewar parity (*i.e.*, to define a pound sterling once again as equal to 123.274 grains of gold 11/12ths fine). This produced exchange rates that, at the existing prices in sterling, overvalued the pound and so tended to produce gold outflows, especially after France chose devaluation and returned to gold in 1928 at a parity that undervalued the franc. By 1929 the important currencies of the world, and most of the less important ones, were again linked to gold.

The gold standard that was restored, however, was a far cry from the prewar gold standard. The establishment of the Federal Reserve System in the United States in 1913 introduced an additional link in the international specie-flow mechanism. That mechanism no longer operated automatically. It operated only if the Federal Reserve chose to let it do so, and the Federal Reserve did not so choose; to prevent domestic prices from rising, it offset the effect on the quantity of money of an increase in gold. (It "sterilised" the monetary effect.) France made a similar choice. With the franc undervalued, gold flowed to France. The French government sold the foreign exchange for gold, draining gold from Britain and other gold standard countries. The two countries receiving gold, the United States and France did not permit gold inflows to raise their price levels. Countries that lost gold had to deflate. Thus, the gold exchange standard forced deflation and unemployment on much of the world economy. By the summer of 1929, Canada had left the gold standard and recessions were underway in Great Britain and Germany. In August, the United States joined the recession that became the Great Depression.

In 1931, Great Britain left the gold standard followed by the Scandinavian countries and many of the countries in the British Empire. The United States followed in 1933, restoring a fixed—but higher—dollar price for gold in January 1934, at $35 an ounce but barring U.S., citizens from owning gold. France, Switzerland and members of the Latin Union left the gold standard in 1936. Although not clear at the time, that was the end of the gold standard.

The Bretton Woods Organisation

During World War II, Great Britain and the United States planned the postwar monetary system. Their plan, approved by more than 40 countries at Bretton Woods, New Hampshire in July 1944, aimed to correct the perceived deficiencies of the gold exchange standard. These included the volatility of floating exchange rates, the inflexibility of fixed exchange rates and reliance on an adjustment mechanism for countries with payment surpluses or deficits that often required recessions and deflation in deficit countries and expansion and inflation in surplus countries.

Countries joined an International Monetary Fund, paid a subscription to start the Fund, and agreed to a system of fixed but adjustable exchange rates. Countries with payments deficits could borrow from the Fund, and countries with surpluses would lend. If deficits or surpluses persisted, the agreement provided for changes in exchange rates. The dollar price of gold was fixed at $35 an ounce. The U.S., agreed to maintain that price by buying or selling gold. Postwar recovery, low inflation, growth of trade and payments and the build up of international reserves in industrial countries permitted the new system to come into full operation at the end of 1958. Although a vestigial tie to gold remained and the gold price stayed at $35 an ounce, in practice the Bretton Woods system put the market economies of the world on a dollar standard. The U.S., dollar served as the world's principal currency, and countries held most of their reserves in interest bearing dollar securities.

The dollar was the most widely used currency in international trade, even in trade between countries other than the United States. It was the unit in terms of which countries expressed their exchange rate. Countries maintained their "official" exchange rates by buying and selling U.S., dollars and held dollars as their primary reserve currency for that purpose. The existence of a dollar standard did not mean that other countries could not change their exchange rates, just as the gold standard did not mean that they could not "devalue" or "appreciate" in terms of gold. Many countries devalued or revalued including major countries, Great Britain in 1967 and Germany and France in 1969, as the System neared its end. In practice, however, the United States was not free to determine its own exchange rate or its balance of payments position.

Monetary expansion in the United States provided reserves for other countries; monetary contraction absorbed reserves. Central banks could convert dollars into gold, and they did, especially in the early years. As the stock of dollars held by central banks outside the United States rose and the U.S., gold stock dwindled, the United States could not honour its commitment to pay gold for dollars. The Bretton Woods System of fixed exchange rates appeared doomed. Governments and central banks tried for years to find a way to extend its life, but they could not agree. The end came on August 15, 1971, when President Nixon announced that the United States would no longer sell gold.

After Bretton Woods

The breakdown of the fixed exchange rate system ended countries' obligation to maintain a fixed price of their currency against gold or other currencies by buying when the exchange rate fell and selling when it rose. National currencies floated; the exchange rate rose or fell with market demand. If the exchange rate appreciated, buyers received fewer units in exchange for a unit of their own currency.

Purchasers of local (home) goods and assets faced higher prices. Conversely, if the currency depreciated, home goods and assets became cheaper for foreigners. Countries heavily dependent on foreign trade disliked the frequent changes in price and costs under floating rates. Governments or their central banks often intervened to slow nominal (market) exchange rate changes. These interventions have been effective only against temporary changes.

In the long-run, a country's exchange rate depends on such fundamental factors as relative productivity growth, opportunities for investment, the public's willingness to save, and monetary and fiscal policies. These fundamental factors are at work whether the country has a fixed or a floating exchange rate and whether the authorities intervene to adjust the exchange rate or slow its changes. As long as markets for goods, services, assets and foreign exchange remain open, the country must adjust. The principal difference between adjustment under fixed and floating exchange rates is how the country adjusts. With fixed exchange rates, adjustment occurs mainly by changing costs and prices of the myriad commodities that a country produces and consumes. Under floating exchange rates, the adjustment occurs mainly by changing the nominal exchange rate. For example, if Brazil's monetary policy increases Brazilian inflation, domestic prices of shoes, cocoa and most everything else rise. With a fixed exchange rate, the price rise deters exports and purchases by foreigners. Demand shifts from Brazil to other countries, lowering demand and reducing payments for its products that lower Brazil's money stock. The reduction in money, and the fall in demand, slow the Brazilian economy and reduce Brazilian prices. With a floating exchange rate, the adjustment comes about by reducing the demand for Brazilian currency, depreciating the exchange rate, thereby reducing the prices paid by foreigners.

Adjustment comes in many other ways. Brazilians may decide to invest more abroad, or foreigners may decide to invest less in Brazil. The long-run outcome will be the same. The reason is very basic: buyers and sellers do not care about the nominal exchange rate. What matters is the so-called real exchange rate — the nominal exchange rate adjusted by prices at home and abroad. The buyer of Brazilian shoes in England cares about the local cost in U.K., pounds. The Brazilian price of shoes is multiplied by the exchange rate to get the U.K., price. Under floating exchange rates, the exchange rate adjusts to keep a country's commodities competitive.

Most countries allowed their currencies to float in 1971, but that soon changed. Generally, small countries with relatively large trade sectors disliked floating rates. They wanted to avoid the often transitory, but sometimes large, changes in prices and costs arising in the foreign exchange market. Many of the smaller Asian countries, and countries in Central America and the Caribbean, fixed their exchange rates to the U.S., dollar. Countries like the Netherlands and Austria, with much West German trade, soon fixed their exchange rates to the German mark. These countries gave up independent central bank policy. When West Germany's central bank, or the U.S., central bank, changed interest rates, countries that fixed their exchange rate changed their interest rates also.

A country on a fixed exchange rate sacrifices independent monetary policy. But, a small country that is open to external trade has little scope for independent monetary policy. It cannot influence most of the prices at which its citizens buy and sell. If it inflates, its currency depreciates to bring its home prices back to equivalent world market prices. Even a large country cannot maintain an independent monetary policy if its exchange rate is fixed and its capital market remains open to inflows and outflows. With reduced reliance on capital controls, in the 1980s, many countries abandoned fixed exchange rates to preserve some control over domestic monetary policy.

Large economies such as the United States, Japan, and Great Britain continue to float. Switzerland and Canada are relatively small economies that prefer to retain some influence over domestic monetary conditions, so they too float. Hong Kong made the opposite choice. Although it was a British colony at the time and, later, a part of China, it chose to fix its exchange rate to the U.S., dollar. The method it revived is a nineteenth century system known as a currency board. There is no central bank. The exchange rate is fixed. Local banks increase the number of Hong Kong dollars only when they receive additional U.S., dollars, and they must reduce the stock of Hong Kong dollars, when U.S., dollar holdings decline. Hong Kong's experience with its currency board encouraged a few other, mainly small, countries to follow its lead.

Some countries went a further step away from autonomous policy by adopting the U.S., dollar as their domestic currency. The most notable change of this general type is the decision by principal European countries to surrender their local currencies in exchange for a new common currency, the Euro.

The Euro Trade

Western European countries have a considerable share of their trade with each other. Soon after the breakdown of the Bretton Woods System, some of these countries experimented with fixed exchange rates for their group. Before 1997, all such attempts failed within a few years.

European economic integration continued, however. After the founding of the European Union, committed to free exchange of goods, labour, and finance, fifteen governments agreed in 1991 to the Maastricht Treaty calling for a decade of adjustment to a single currency for member countries. Exchange rates were fixed "permanently and irrevocably" for twelve participating countries.

On January 1, 1999 the system began operation. The European Central Bank, in Frankfurt Germany, received a mandate from member governments to maintain price stability. The governments named the new currency the euro. At first, values of debts, assets, and prices of goods and services were expressed in euros, usually with the local currency price given also. During this transition, the Euro was a unit of account but not a medium of exchange. After three years, in January 2002, euro notes and coins circulated, replacing individual country currencies such as French francs, German marks or Italian lira. The treaty did not provide for countries' withdrawal from the system. The euro floated against all non-member currencies.

Member countries receive a seat on the board of the European Central Bank. For small countries such as Holland, Belgium, and Austria, the new arrangements provided increased opportunity to determine policy. Germany sacrificed its dominant role in European monetary policy. Three of the fifteen member states of the European Union, — Denmark, Sweden, and the United Kingdom — decided either to remain outside or delay entry into monetary union.

6

Indian Banking

INTRODUCTION

In simple words, Banking can be defined as the business activity of accepting and safeguarding money owned by other individuals and entities, and then lending out this money in order to earn a profit. However, with the passage of time, the activities covered by banking business have widened and now various other services are also offered by banks. The banking services these days include issuance of debit and credit cards, providing safe custody of valuable items, lockers, ATM services and online transfer of funds across the country/ world.

It is well said that banking plays a silent, yet crucial part in our day-to-day lives. The banks perform financial intermediation by pooling savings and channelising them into investments through maturity and risk transformations, thereby keeping the economy's growth engine revving.

Banking business has done wonders for the world economy. The simple looking method of accepting money deposits from savers and then lending the same money to borrowers, banking activity encourages the flow of money to productive use and investments. This in turn allows the economy to grow.

In the absence of banking business, savings would sit idle in our homes, the entrepreneurs would not be in a position to raise the money, ordinary people dreaming for a new car or house would not be able to purchase cars or houses.

WHAT IS A BANK DEFINE A BANK

In simple words, we can say that Bank is a financial institution that undertakes the banking activity ie.it accepts deposits and then lends the same to earn certain profit.

What is a Banking Company

Any company, which transacts the business of banking defined above is termed as Banking company

What is Banking System

Banking systems can be defined as a mechanism through which the money supply of the country is created and controlled.

Which are the Oldest Banks in India

In 1839, some Indian merchants in Calcutta established India's first bank known as "Union Bank", but it could not survive for long and failed in 1848 due to economic crisis of 1848-49. Similarly, in 1863, "Bank of Upper India" was formed but it failed in 1913. In 1865, "Allahabad Bank" was established as a joint stock bank. This bank has survived till date and is now considered as the oldest surviving bank in India.

BANKING IN INDIA

Banking has been known in India since time immemorial. It was initially only a system of money lending in which rates varied not according to the nature of the transaction, but in relation to the particular caste to which the borrower belonged. Deposit banking was practically unknown then. By the time the Europeans arrived, Indian banking houses had become more organized. Many among them had transregional connections across the subcontinent through an extensive network of Kothis or agencies. They financed other bankers, landlords, traders and princes and maintained close with the rulers of the princely states.

The British, who introduced a joint stock banking with limited liability in India, first set up through a charter the Bank of Bengal (after a brief period of infancy of three years at the Bank of Calcutta) in 1809 and followed it up by establishing the Bank of Bombay in 1840 and the Bank of Madras three years later. These three banks, which formed the highest tier of the apex banking system in British India, principally, finance internal trade and assisted the Company's Governments in the three presidencies to raise loans from time to time. They were also government bankers within the concerned presidencies. The position remained unaltered even for the Imperial Bank of India, which was created in 1921 by amalgamating the three presidency banks of Bengal, Bombay and Madras. Until the creation of the Reserve Bank of India in 1935, the Imperial Bank combined the functions of a commercial bank and a central bank. The Bank, thereafter, became a purely commercial bank and acquired a pre-eminent status in the Indian banking industry.

Innumerable private joint-stock banks under both European and Indian control also emerged during the 19th century, mainly to cater to the credit needs of the vast hinterland of the subcontinent. While some amongst them, like the Agra and United Services Bank and the Alliance Bank of Simla under European control, eventually collapsed owing to financial irregularities, there were many others under Indian management, especially in Bombay and Punjab, which succumbed during the banking crisis of 1913 and later in the 1930s and 1940s. It was these failures, which paved the way for the passing of the Banking Companies Act (later renamed as the Banking Regulation Act), in 1949. Quite a few of these private joint-stock banks, however survived and grew over the years, including the Allahabad Bank (1865) and the Punjab National Bank (1895) in the north, the Canara Bank (1906) and the Indian Bank (1907) in the south and the Bank of India (1906) and the Central Bank of India (1911) in the west.

The 19th century also witnessed the arrival of several exchange banks in India for financing the subcontinent's burgeoning foreign trade, which the three presidency banks and the Imperial Bank (until the establishment of the Reserve Bank), were rigorously excluded from engaging in. Such banks either chartered by the British Parliament or incorporated in Europe included the Chartered Bank of India, Australia and China, the Chartered Mercantile Bank of India, London and China, the Hongkong and Shanghai Banking Corporation, the Compote d' Escompte de Paris and so on.

Besides the above constituents of the formal sector of Indian banking, cooperative credit societies were also set up in the beginning of the 20th century and vested with the task of meeting the credit needs of the Indian peasantry. The progress in this regard was unfortunately sluggish, particularly outside the Bombay, Madras and Punjab provinces.

By the end of 1947, there were 654 scheduled, non-scheduled and exchange banks operating in the country with a network of 5009 offices and deposits and advances of ₹ 1153.45 crore and ₹ 520.299 crore respectively. The average population per bank office, though sharply reduced from about 8.5 lakh in 1916 to less than 70,000 in 1947, was still considerably high by international standards.

The almost total absence of banking facilities outside large towns or centres of trade, however, sadly left the vast majority of the rural masses in the clutches of the private creditor – the professional moneylender, the agriculturist moneylender and the trader. The committee of Direction of the All India Rural Credit Survey (AIRCS) constituted by the Reserve Bank to formulate a long-term policy for rural credit brought to focus the awful inadequacy of the banking system in providing rural credit, the Government's failure to strengthen the cooperative sector and the stranglehold of the moneylenders over the rural sector. The findings of the Committee revealed that the private creditor reigned 'supreme in the field of rural credit' accounting for more than 70 per cent of the total borrowings. The government, cooperatives and commercial banks together accounted for only 7.3 per cent. Perhaps more disturbing was the revelation that of this very little, the major part went to the bigger cultivators and only a minor fraction percolated down to the smaller cultivator.

Realizing that banks in India could not in the foreseeable future respond to the emergent needs of economic regeneration of rural areas, the Government decided to extend the concept of the state partnership to the important sector of commercial banking. On the recommendations of the AIRCS, the country's large commercial bank, the Imperial Bank, was nationalized for extending banking facilities, particularly to the rural and semi-urban areas in order to increase the flow of credit for both agriculture and small-scale industries and mobilize rural savings.

With the creation of the State Bank of India by an Act of Parliament on 1st July 1955, more than a quarter of the resources of the Indian banking system passed under the direct control of the state. Four years, later, the State Bank of India (Subsidiary Banks) Act was passed, enabling the State Bank to take over eight former State-associated banks as its subsidiaries.

The concept of banking underwent a sea change with the advent of the State Bank. A distinct shift in focus was evident – from security – oriented to need-based lending, from urban to rural banking, from class to mass banking and from activities that contributed essentially to the bank's commercial objectives to also those that largely served a social purpose. This transition from a primarily profit-seeking commercial bank to a great national institution with public responsibilities was however by no means an easy task. It became necessary for the Bank to reshape its organization and reset its tradition to make them sufficiently dynamically to suit the altered conditions. It also involved a re-orientation of the Bank's policies, a modification of its business methods and practices and a change of outlook on the part of its staff engaged at every level.

From its inception, the State Bank played a dual role with due 'regard being had to the public interest'. As a commercial bank, it continued to provide, as hitherto, finance to industry and trade. As a nationalized institution, it undertook several promotional and developmental activities by way of opening branches all over the country, including the remotest corners, evolving and implementing a special scheme for financing small-scale industries, extending financial accommodation to marketing and processing cooperative societies and fostering India's foreign trade.

The Bank succeeded in aligning itself with the planned economic development of the country and allocated credit according to the needs of the economy. Even before the Government had initiated measures under the scheme of social control in 1968, the State Bank had evolved schemes for all agricultural operations until the marketing of agricultural produce as also for mechanization and modernization of farms, provision of irrigation facilities and development of land. Innovative and well-planned strategies were also evolved as the bank's response to the main thrust of the Government on removing poverty and creating employment opportunities through accelerated economic development of the rural sector, with special emphasis on agricultural production, cottage industries, small industries, arts and crafts. Financial assistance to rural poor apart, an integrated view of the composite needs of the rural people covering economic, social and cultural areas was also evolved. Besides setting up the State Bank of India, new institutions like the Industrial Finance Corporation of India (IFCI) (1948), the Agricultural Refinance Corporation (ARC) (1963), the Industrial Development Bank of India (IDBI) (1964) and the State Financial Corporations were also established for providing long-term finance to industry and agriculture.

Growing emphasis on agricultural, cottage and small-scale industrial development in the meantime, made it even more necessary that all the banks gear themselves to a more meaningful credit operation in India's hinterland. The Government thus initiated several measures under the scheme of social control in 1968 to secure a better alignment of banking policy with the needs of economic planning. Born out of persistent complaints of the deficiencies in the banking system, the basic postulate was 'to ensure that particular clients or groups of clients [were] not favoured in the matter of distribution of credit and whatever the character of the shareholding, its influence was neutralized in the constitution of the board of directors and in the actual credit decision taken at different levels of bank management'.

The National Credit Council set up in February 1968, to coordinate credit planning with economic planning and ensure allocation of credit to priority sectors, became the cornerstone of the social control scheme. From the position of mere purveyors of credit, especially to big industry and trading concerns, banks were hereafter encouraged to extend credit to agriculture and small-scale industries in a much larger measure as a matter of national responsibility. The same year, the Parliament also passed the banking Laws (Amendment) Bill seeking to reorient banking as a specialized profession. The amendment aimed, inter alia, at reconstituting the boards of directors of Indian commercial banks, appointing professional bankers and financial experts as full-time Chairmen and prohibiting loans and advances to directors and their concerns.

Soon after this, in February 1969, the Government appointed a banking commission under R.G. Saraiya, Chairman, Bombay State Cooperative Bank, to recommend, based on a comprehensive enquiry, changes in the structure, procedure and policy of the Indian banking system. Although the Commission made several recommendations relating to restructuring of commercial and cooperative banks, measures for widening their functional coverage, improving their operational efficiency, legislative reforms an area for further research and study, nothing much was done to implement them.

An event of far-reaching significance in the sphere of banking occurred in July 1969 when the Government of India promulgated an ordinance to nationalize major Indian scheduled banks with deposits of ₹ 50 crore and above, thereby ushering in a new phase of financial development. In a broadcast to the nation, Prime Minister Indira Gandhi observed-

"An institution such as the banking system, which touches – and should touch – the lives of millions, has necessarily to be inspired by a larger social purpose and has to subserve national priorities and objectives. That is why there has been widespread demand that the major banks should be not only socially controlled but also publicly owned."

The broad aims of nationalization as stated in the Preamble to the Act were ' to control the heights of the economy and to meet progressively and serve better the needs of development of the economy in conformity with national policy and objectives'. Nationalized banks were to ensure that the needs of productive efforts irrespective of the size and social status of the borrower and, in particular, those of farmers, small-scale industries and self-employed professional groups, were increasingly met. They were also to actively foster the growth of new and progressive entrepreneurs and create fresh opportunities for backward areas in different parts of the country. Besides widening the network of branches, particularly in the rural and semi-urban areas, banks were also to mobilize savings. Under the Lead Bank Scheme formulated thereafter, they were to act as pacesetters in providing integrated banking facilities at the districts allotted to them. Banks were also to be closely associated with credit linked poverty alleviation programmes (IRDP, SEPUP SEEUY, etc.) initiated from time to time.

In 1980, six more private banks with deposits of not less than ₹ 200 crore were nationalized. It was aimed 'to further control the heights of the economy, tom meet progressively and serve better the needs of the development of the economy, and to promote the welfare of the people in conformity with the policy of the State'. With this, the number of public sector banks increased to 28 including the State Bank and its seven associates, accounting at all for about 91 per cent of the total deposits and advances of commercial banks in the country. Banks in the private sector continued to exist, though only in the periphery of the industry.

Indian banking underwent a major structural transformation after the nationalization of banks. A phenomenal expansion of the branch network occurred, particularly in the hitherto under-banked rural areas. The Reserve Bank geared its branch licensing policy to the objectives of ensuring an expansion of offices both in unbanked centres and in under-banked states as well as in the urban and metropolitan centres. While the total number of commercial bank offices rose from 8,262 to as much as 60,294 between June 1969 and March 1990, the number of rural branches increased from 1,833 to 34,940 accounting for more than 57 per cent of the total compared with barely 22 per cent in 1969. The average population served by each bank office declined from 65,000 to about 12,000 during the same period.

There was also a massive qualitative change in the operations of the banking system as banks assumed a variety of new responsibilities in the area of social banking for which 'no procedures or guidelines in the history of modern banking existed elsewhere in the world'. The ratio of priority sector advances to net bank credit rose from 14 per cent by March 1990.

The phenomenal growth and development of the banking system during the 1970s and 1980s however rendered the system unwieldy. A complex structure of interest rates arising from economic and social concerns of providing concessional credit to certain sectors not only distorted the interest rate mechanism, but also adversely affected the viability and profitability of banks. Inability to gauge the importance of transparency, accountability and prudential norms in the operations of the banking system resulted in an increasing burden of non-performing assets (NPAs). Low operational efficiency, unhealthy balance sheets and unsatisfactory customer service further threatened the very stability of the financial system.

With the country facing a serious economic crisis partially due to a critical balance of payments situation, the Government in 1991 decided to initiate measures to stabilize the economy and simultaneously introduce structural reforms. The scheme of structural reforms was aimed at enhancing the productivity and efficiency of the economy as a whole and increasing global competitiveness. As a part of this, reforms based on the recommendations of the Narasimham Committee were also initiated in two phases in the financial sector to imbue it with operational flexibility and functional autonomy. Substantial reduction in pre-emptions in the form of reserve requirements, dismantling administered structure of interest rates, introduction of internationally accepted prudential norms relating to income recognition, asset classification, provisioning for bad debts and capital adequacy, granting licenses to new private sector banks, allowing a more liberal entry for foreign banks and permitting nationalized banks access to capital markets were some of the policy measures initiated in the first phase.

The second phase of reforms, aimed to strengthen the foundations of the banking system, saw guidelines being put in place for risk management systems in banks, initiation of risk-based supervision, etc., besides further strengthening prudential norms. A new framework for capital adequacy according to Basel II norms is now awaiting adoption by banks. New norms have also been evolved for recognizing the income of banks. All these measures have led to the strengthening of the Indian banking system making it one of the strongest in the region today.

The impact of the first phase of the financial sector reforms was felt within a few years. A marked improvement in the financial health of commercial banks was evident by the rise in operating and net profits and a decreasing tended in the percentage of NPAs. Most of the banks also succeeded in meeting the minimum capital adequacy ratio. The ongoing deregulation and liberalization of the financial markets have thrown up some challenges for banks in India.

The most exciting among them has been the emergence of an increasingly competitive environment in the banking industry with the arrival of new domestic and foreign private players. Starting with the advantage of strong capitalisation, modern technology, lear network, and more importantly without any accumulated problems of the past, the new domestic entrants in particular were ambitious in their business targets and keen to expand their activities all over the county. Empowered with a model that ensures networking of branches with connection to a central processing centre for back office operations like account opening, loan maintenance, etc. and equipped with the ability to employ the best workforce in the market by offering attractive compensation packages, the new generation banks soon began to pose a stiff competition to public sector banks (PSBs).

In the face of this unprecedented onslaught, PSBs realized that in times to come, they would need to convert challenges into opportunities. The success obtained by private players through the networked model of banking prompted PSBs to embrace the same design. Today, not only are all PSBs fully computerized, some among them are also fully networked, while others are not far from accomplishing it. The seven Associate Banks of the State Bank Group are in fact the first PSBs to be fully networked in India.

In addition to computerization and networking, another major innovation that competition as encouraged in the banking industry is the popularization of alternative delivery channels like Automated Teller Machines (ATMs) and Internet Banking. These channels provide customers access to basic banking facilities round the clock and also help reduce operating costs of banks. Banks are also investing substantially in Information Technology to improve efficiency in their operations as also provide top class customer service.

The post-reform era has also witnessed a rapid growth of retail finance, which till recently was perhaps somewhat neglected as banks concentrated mostly in financing the manufacturing and agricultural sectors. With large manufacturing companies finding alternative and cheaper sources for funding their needs, banks have now turned to consumer finance in a big way. Retail finance today forms about a quarter of bank credit. The ready availability of bank credit has contributed in no small measure to the consumer boom that the economy has been witnessing of late including an upsurge in the housing and automobile sectors giving in turn a fillip to the real economy.

While the opening up of the Indian financial markets has provided enormous opportunities for banks to tap new areas of business, it has also posed an enormous challenge for the smaller banks to compete with the new entrants in terms of funds, base, technology and new products. With the further opening up of the Indian banking sector to foreign investors under the WTO agreement in April 2009, the smaller PSBs may well not be able to withstand the pressures on profitability for long. In order to overcome this, these banks would perhaps need to consolidate through amalgamations, as it the global phenomenon today. Notwithstanding India's expanding economy and the phenomenal growth of bank credit in recent times, it is however lamentable that in India's countryside, about 58 per cent of farming households and 70 per cent of non-farming households still lack access to basic banking services. Banking penetration is in fact so low in India that bank deposits represent only 60 per cent of the GDP as compared to 190 per cent in China or 142 per cent in Japan. Despite the boom in the economy, economic disparities thus continue to grow in India with the rich becoming richer and the poor poorer. It is therefore imperative that a balance is struck between the demands of a market economy and the urgent needs of financial inclusion.

Drawing on Prof. C. K. Prahalad's much-publicized theory that 'the world's most exciting, fastest-growing new market is where you least expect it: at the bottom of the pyramid', Indian banks have increasingly begun to look for business among the rural poor. They are now working towards providing basic financial services to the villagers through a network of e-kiosks and agents – a business model that has been successfully tried in other developing economics. The day when a bouquet of financial services will be available to six lac Indian villages is perhaps not too far away.

The saga of Indian banking like most others has seen its vicissitudes. Its genre has not, however, changed much since the colonial days. Thanks to the booming global economy, expanding technology and changing mindsets, banking is now set to be transformed. Age-old processes and systems are about to be discarded as fresh rules are being framed. The age of 'disruptive technology' has already made its tentative foray. There is excitement in the air all around.

BANKING IN THE PRE-REFORM PERIOD

It is useful to briefly recall the nature of the Indian banking sector at the time of initiation of financial sector reform in India in the early 1990s. This would facilitate a greater clarity of the rationale and basis of reforms. The Indian financial system in the pre-reform period, *i.e.*, upto the end of 1980s, essentially catered to the needs of planned development in a mixed economy framework where the government sector had a domineering role in economic activity. The strategy of planned economic development required huge development expenditures, which was met thorough the dominance of government ownership of banks, automatic monetisation of fiscal deficit and subjecting the banking sector to large pre-emptions – both in terms of the statutory holding of Government securities (statutory liquidity ratio, or SLR) and administrative direction of credit to preferred sectors. Furthermore, a complex structure of administered interest rates prevailed, guided more by social priorities, necessitating cross-subsidisation to sustain commercial viability of institutions. These not only distorted the interest rate mechanism but also adversely affected financial market development. All the signs of `financial repression' were found in the system. There is perhaps an element of commonality in terms of such a 'repressed' regime in the financial sector of many emerging market economies at that time. The decline of the Bretton Woods system in the 1970s provided a trigger for financial liberalisation in both advanced and emerging markets. Several countries adopted a 'big bang' approach to liberalisation, while others pursued a more cautious or 'gradualist' approach. The East Asian crises in the late 1990s provided graphic testimony as to how faulty sequencing and inadequate attention to institutional strengthening could significantly derail the growth process, even for countries with otherwise sound macroeconomic fundamentals.

India, in this context, has pursued a relatively more 'gradualist' approach to liberalisation. The bar was gradually raised. Each year the Central Bank slowly, in a manner of speaking, tightened the screws. Nevertheless, the transition to a regime of prudential norms and free interest rates had its own traumatic effect. It must be said to the credit of our financial system that these changes were absorbed and the system has emerged stronger for this reason.

CONTOURS OF REFORMS

Financial sector reforms encompassed broadly institutions especially banking, development of financial markets, monetary fiscal and external sector management and legal and institutional infrastructure.

Reform measures in India were sequenced to create an enabling environment for banks to overcome the external constraints and operate with greater flexibility. Such measures related to dismantling of administered structure of interest rates, removal of several pre-emptions in the form of reserve requirements and credit allocation to certain sectors. Interest rate deregulation was in stages and allowed build up of sufficient resilience in the system. This is an important component of the reform process which has imparted greater efficiency in resource allocation.

Parallel strengthening of prudential regulation, improved market behaviour, gradual financial opening and, above all, the underlying improvements in macroeconomic management helped the liberalisation process to run smooth. The interest rates have now been largely deregulated except for certain specific classes, these are: savings deposit accounts, non-resident Indian (NRI) deposits, small loans up to ₹.2 lakh and export credit. Without the dismantling of the administered interest rate structure, the rest of the financial sector reforms could not have meant much.

As regards the policy environment on public ownership, the major share of financial intermediation has been on account of public sector during the pre-reform period. As a part of the reforms programme, initially there was infusion of capital by Government in public sector banks, which was subsequently followed by expanding the capital base with equity participation by private investors up to a limit of 49 per cent. The share of the public sector banks in total banking assets has come down from 90 per cent in 1991 to around 75 per cent in 2006: a decline of about one percentage point every year over a fifteen-year period. Diversification of ownership, while retaining public sector character of these banks has led to greater market accountability and improved efficiency without loss of public confidence and safety. It is significant that the infusion of funds by government since the initiation of reforms into the public sector banks amounted to less than 1 per cent of India's GDP, a figure much lower than that for many other countries.

Another major objective of banking sector reforms has been to enhance efficiency and productivity through increased competition. Establishment of new banks was allowed in the private sector and foreign banks were also permitted more liberal entry. Nine new private banks are in operation at present, accounting for around 10-12 per cent of commercial banking assets. Yet another step towards enhancing competition was allowing foreign direct investment in private sector banks up to 74 per cent from all sources. Beginning 2009, foreign banks would be allowed banking presence in India either through establishment of subsidiaries incorporated in India or through branches.

Impressive institutional reforms have also helped in reshaping the financial marketplace. A high-powered Board for Financial Supervision (BFS), constituted in 1994, exercise the powers of supervision and inspection in relation to the banking companies, financial institutions and non-banking companies, creating an arms-length relationship between regulation and supervision. On similar lines, a Board for Regulation and Supervision of Payment and Settlement Systems (BPSS) prescribes policies relating to the regulation and supervision of all types of payment and settlement systems, set standards for existing and future systems, authorise the payment and settlement systems and determine criteria for membership to these systems.

The system has also progressed with the transparency and disclosure standards as prescribed under international best practices in a phased manner. Disclosure requirements on capital adequacy, NPLs, profitability ratios and details of provisions and contingencies have been expanded to include several areas such as foreign currency assets and liabilities, movements in NPLs and lending to sensitive sectors. The range of disclosures has gradually been increased. In view of the increased focus on undertaking consolidated supervision of bank groups, preparation of consolidated financial statements (CFS) has been mandated by the Reserve Bank for all groups where the controlling entity is a bank.

The legal environment for conducting banking business has also been strengthened. Debt recovery tribunals were part of the early reforms process for adjudication of delinquent loans. More recently, the Securitisation Act was enacted in 2003 to enhance protection of creditor rights. To combat the abuse of financial system for crime-related activities, the Prevention of Money Laundering Act was enacted in 2003 to provide the enabling legal framework. The Negotiable Instruments (Amendments and Miscellaneous Provisions) Act 2002 expands the erstwhile definition of 'cheque' by introducing the concept of 'electronic money' and 'cheque truncation'. The Credit Information Companies (Regulation) Bill 2004 has been enacted by the Parliament which is expected to enhance the quality of credit decisions and facilitate faster credit delivery.

Improvements in the regulatory and supervisory framework encompassed a greater degree of compliance with Basel Core Principles. Some recent initiatives in this regard include consolidated accounting for banks along with a system of Risk-Based Supervision (RBS) for intensified monitoring of vulnerabilities.

The structural break in the wake of financial sector reforms and opening up of the economy necessitated changes in the monetary policy framework. The relationship between the central bank and the Government witnessed a salutary development in September 1994 in terms of supplemental agreements limiting initially the net issuance of *ad hoc* treasury Bills. This initiative culminated in the abolition of the *ad hoc* Treasury Bills effective April 1997 replaced by a limited ways and means advances. The phasing out of automatic monetisation of budget deficit has, thus, strengthened monetary authority by imparting flexibility and operational autonomy. With the passage of the Fiscal Responsibility and Budget Management Act in 2003, from April 1, 2006 the Reserve Bank has withdrawn from participating in the primary issues of Central Government securities

Reforms in the Government securities market were aimed at imparting liquidity and depth by broadening the investor base and ensuring market-related interest rate mechanism. The important initiatives introduced included a market-related government borrowing and consequently, a phased elimination of automatic monetisation of Central Government budget deficits. This, in turn, provided a fillip to switch from direct to indirect tools of monetary regulation, activating open market operations and enabled the development of an active secondary market. The gamut of changes in market development included introduction of newer instruments, establishment of new institutions and technological developments, along with concomitant improvements in transparency and the legal framework.

Processes of Reform

What are the unique features of our reform process? First, financial sector reform was undertaken early in the reform cycle in India. Second, the banking sector reforms were not driven by any immediate crisis as has often been the case in several emerging economies. Third, the design and detail of the reform were evolved by domestic expertise, while taking on board the international experience in this regard. Fourth, enough space was created for the growth and healthy competition among public and private sectors as well as foreign and domestic sectors.

How useful has been the financial liberalisation process in India towards improving the functioning of institutions and markets? Prudential regulation and supervision has improved; the combination of regulation, supervision and safety nets has limited the impact of unforeseen shocks on the financial system. In addition, the role of market forces in enabling price discovery has enhanced. The dismantling of the erstwhile administered interest rate structure has permitted financial intermediaries to pursue lending and deposit taking based on commercial considerations and their asset-liability profiles. The financial liberalisation process has also enabled to reduce the overhang of non-performing loans: this entailed both a 'stock' (restoration of net worth) solution as well as a 'flow' (improving future profitability) solution.

Financial entities have become increasingly conscious about risk management practices and have instituted risk management models based on their product profiles, business philosophy and customer orientation. Additionally, access to credit has improved, through newly established domestic banks, foreign banks and bank-like intermediaries. Government debt markets have developed, enabling greater operational independence in monetary policy making. The growth of government debt markets has also provided a benchmark for private debt markets to develop.

There have also been significant improvements in the information infrastructure. The accounting and auditing of intermediaries has improved. Information on small borrowers has improved and information sharing through operationalisation of credit information bureaus has helped to reduce information asymmetry. The technological infrastructure has developed in tandem with modern-day requirements in information technology and communications networking.

The improvements in the performance of the financial system over the decade-and-a-half of reforms are also reflected in the improvement in a number of indicators. Capital adequacy of the banking sector recorded a marked improvement and stood at 12.3 per cent at end-March 2006. This is a far cry from the situation that prevailed in early 1990s.

On the asset quality front, notwithstanding the gradual tightening of prudential norms, non-performing loans (NPL) to total loans of commercial banks which was at a high of 15.7 per cent at end-March 1997 declined to 3.3 per cent at end-March 2006. Net NPLs also witnessed a significant decline and stood at 1.2 per cent of net advances at end-March 2006, driven by the improvements in loan loss provisioning, which comprises over half of the total provisions and contingencies. The proportion of net NPA to net worth, sometimes called the solvency ratio of public sector banks has dropped from 57.9 per cent in 1998-99 to 11.7 per cent in 2006-07.

Operating expenses of banks in India are also much more aligned to those prevailing internationally, hovering around 2.1 per cent during 2004-05 and 2005-06. These numbers are comparable to those obtaining for leading developed countries which were range-bound between 1.4-3.3 per cent in 2005.

Bank profitability levels in India have also trended upwards and gross profits stood at 2.0 per cent during 2005-06 (2.2 per cent during 2004-05) and net profits trending at around 1 per cent of assets. Available information suggests that for developed countries, at end-2005, gross profit ratios were of the order of 2.1 per cent for the US and 0.6 per cent for France.

The extent of penetration of our banking system in our country as measured by the proportion of bank assets to GDP has increased from 50 per cent in the second half of nineties to over 80 per cent a decade later.

Way Ahead

While we have made a significant progress, let me highlight a few issues that we believe would need significant attention in the near term. The first is the issue of consolidation. The emergence of titans has been one of the noticeable trends in the banking industry at the global level. These banking entities are expected to drive the growth and volume of business in the global segment. In the Indian banking sector also, consolidation is likely to gain prominence in the near future. Despite the liberalisation process, state-owned banks dominate the industry, accounting for three-quarter of bank assets. The consolidation process in recent years has primarily been confined to a few mergers in the private sector segment, although some recent consolidation in the state-owned segment is evident as well. These mergers have been based on the need to attain a meaningful balance sheet size and market share in the face of increased competition, driven largely by synergies and locational and business-specific complementarities. Efforts have been initiated to iron out the legal impediments inherent in the consolidation process.

As the bottom lines of domestic banks come under increasing pressure and the options for organic growth exhaust themselves, banks in India will need to explore ways for inorganic expansion. This, in turn, is likely to unleash the forces of consolidation in Indian banking. However, there are two caveats. First, any process of consolidation must come out of a felt need for merger rather than as an imposition from outside. The synergic benefits must be felt by the entities themselves. The process of consolidation that is driven by fiat is much less likely to be successful, particularly if the decision by fiat is accompanied by restrictions on the normal avenues for reducing costs in the merged entity.

Thus, any meaningful consolidation among the public sector banks must be driven by commercial motivation by individual banks, with the government and the regulator playing at best a facilitating role. Second, the process of consolidation does not mean that small or medium sized banks will have no future. Many of the Indian banks are of appropriate size in relation to the Indian situation. Actual experience shows that small and medium sized banks even in advanced countries have been able to survive and remain profitable. These banks have survived along with very large financial conglomerates. Small banks may be the more natural lenders to small businesses.

The second issue is related to capital adequacy. Basel I standards have been successfully implemented in India and the authorities are presently moving towards adoption of Basel II tailored to country's specific considerations. Adoption of Base II norms will enhance the required capital. Besides, banks' assets will grow or will have to grow in tandem with the growth of the real sectors of the economy. The public sector banks' ability to meet the growing needs will be inhibited, unless the government is willing to bring in more capital. At present, the share of the government in the public sector banks cannot go below 51 per cent. While there is some scope for expanding capital through various modalities, tier-I capital, that is equity, is still critical.

While this constraint may not be binding immediately, sooner or later it will be. If growth is modest, retained earnings may form an adequate source of supply. However, when growth is rapid which is likely to be the case, there is need for injection of equity, enlarging the shareholding. In this situation, the government will have to make up its mind either to bring in additional capital or move towards reducing its share from 51 per cent through appropriate statutory changes. A third alternative could, however, be to include in the definition of government such entities as the Life Insurance Corporation that are quasi-government in nature and are likely to remain to be fully owned or an integral part of the government system in the future. However, even to do this an amendment is needed in the statute.

The third aspect concerns risk management. The most important facet of risk in India or for that matter in most developing countries markets remains the credit risk. Management of credit risks is an area which has received considerable attention in recent years. The new Basle accord rests on the assumption that an internal assessment of risks by a financial institution will be a better measure than an externally imposed formula.

The economic structure is undergoing a change. The service sector has emerged as major sector. Assessing credit risk in lending to service sectors needs a methodology different from assessing risks while lending to manufacturing. There are other areas of lending such as housing and consumer credit which will need new approaches. Equally important will be the area of management of exchange risk. Besides enabling customers to adopt appropriate exchange cover, banks themselves will have to ensure that their exposure is within acceptable limits and is properly hedged. The entire area of risk management encompassing all aspects of risk including credit risk, market risk and operational risk will have to receive prime attention.

The fourth and final concern I want to refer to is improvement in customer service. Banks exist to provide service to customers. With the introduction of technology, there has been a significant change in the way banks operate. This is a far cry from the situation that existed even 15 years ago. The induction of technology has enabled several transactions to be processed in a shorter period of time. Transmission of funds to customers takes less time now. ATMs provide easy access to cash. Nevertheless, it is not very clear whether the customers as depositors and users of other banking services are fully satisfied with the services provided when they come to a bank. This is an area, which must receive continuous attention. The interface with the customers needs to improve.

Provision of credit is a basic function of banks. The effective discharge of this function is part of the intermediation process. The sectoral deployment of credit must keep pace with the changes in the structure of the economy. The banking industry in India must equip itself to be able to assess and meet the credit needs of the emerging segments of the economy. In this context, two aspects require special attention.

First, as the Indian economy gets increasingly integrated with the rest of the world, the demands of the corporate sector for banking services will change not only in size but also in composition and quality. The growing foreign trade in goods and services will have to be financed. Apart from production credit, financing capital requirements from the cheapest sources will become necessary. Provision of credit in foreign currency will require in turn a management of foreign exchange risk. Thus, the provision of a whole gamut of services related to integration with the rest of the world will be a challenge.

Foreign banks operating in India will be the competitors to Indian banks in this regard. The foreign banks have access to much larger resources and have presence in many parts of the world. Therefore, Indian banks will have to evolve appropriate strategies in enabling Indian firms to accessing funds at competitive rates. Another aspect of global financial strategy relates to the presence of Indian banks in foreign countries. Indian banks will have to be selective in this regard. Here again the focus may be on how to help Indian firms acquire funds at internationally competitive rates and how to promote trade and investment between India and other countries.

We must recognise that in foreign lands, Indian banks will be relatively smaller players. The motivation to build up an international presence must be guided by the route Indian entities take in the global business.

Second, despite the faster rate of growth of manufacturing and service sectors, bulk of the population still depends on agriculture and allied activities for its livelihood. In this background, one cannot over-emphasize the need for expanding credit to agricultural and allied activities. While banks have achieved a higher growth in provision of credit to agriculture and allied activities last year, this momentum has to be carried further. In this context, it has to be noted that credit for agriculture is not a single market.

Provision of credit for high-tech agriculture is no different from providing credit to industry. Provision of credit to farmers with a surplus is also of similar nature. Commercial banks in particular must have no hesitation in providing credit to these segments where the normal calculation of risk and return applies. It is only with respect to provision of credit to small and marginal farmers, special attention is required. They constitute a bulk of the farmers and accounting for a significant proportion of the total output.

The National Sample Survey Organisation has recently released a Report entitled, "Indebtedness of Farmer Households". This Report contains a wealth of data relating to the extent and nature of indebtedness. As per NSSO data 51.4 per cent of the total farm households did not have access to credit. Another fact that emerges is that there is a substantial difference between marginal and sub-marginal farmers on the one hand and the rest of the farmer households on the other regarding the purpose for which loans are obtained and the sources of credit. For all farmer households taken together, at the all-India level, institutional sources were responsible for providing 57.5 per cent of the total credit.

But as far as farmer households owning one hectare and less, this proportion is only 39.6 per cent. For all farmer households, the proportion of loan going for production purposes is 65.1 per cent as against 40.2 per cent for marginal and sub-marginal farmer households. Thus, for sub-marginal and marginal farmers, the proportion of production loan is lower than for all farmers. Similarly, the proportion of institutional credit is lower for sub-marginal and marginal farmers than for all farmers. This, in fact, is true of every state of the country. Thus, a critical issue is how to meet the credit requirements of marginal and sub-marginal farmers.

What changes do we need to introduce so that credit can flow to this class of farmer households? Can the banking system through its present mode of distribution of credit meet this challenge? Should we think in terms of banks supporting other institutions who are in a better position to lend to marginal and sub-marginal farmers? Banks need to think hard on how to effectively use the `facilitator and correspondent' models. These models have great potential to reach out to small borrowers and depositors. In any case, a re-look at the organisational structure of our rural branches is called for. Banks need to think deeply on how to meet this challenge of meeting the credit needs of marginal farmers. Financial inclusion is no longer an option; it is a compulsion. The task to be fulfilled by the Indian banks is truly formidable. At one end we expect banks to be able to lend billions of rupees to large borrowers. At the same time we want them to be able to deliver extremely small loans to meet the requirements of the small borrowers. We must reflect on the kind of organisational structure and human talent that we need in order to achieve these twin goals which are at the two extreme ends of the spectrum of lending.

The first phase of banking sector reform has come to a close and we are moving on to the second phase. In the years to come, the Indian financial system will grow not only in size but also in complexity as the forces of competition gain further momentum and as financial markets get more and more integrated. As globalisation accelerates, the Indian financial system will also get integrated with the rest of the world.

As the task of the banking system expands, there is need to focus on the organisational effectiveness of banks. To achieve improvements in productivity and profitability, corporate planning combined with organisational restructuring become necessary. Issues relating to consolidation, competition and risk management will remain critical. Equally, governance and financial inclusion will emerge as key issues for India at this stage of socio-economic development.

POST-REFORM TRANSFORMATION AND FUTURE CHALLENGES

The banking sector plays a crucial role in the economic development of a nation. A sound, efficient, effective vibrant and innovative banking system stimulates economic growth by mobilizing savings on a massive scale and efficiently allocating resources for productive purposes and also for consumption which too is a driver or growth. Indian banking which remained weak, inefficient and ineffective and over the years developed many ills and maladies witnessed a remarkable transformation in post-reform era, consequent on the implementation of banking reforms based on the recommendation of Narsimham Committee.

The reform measures implemented on the basis of recommendations of Narsimham Committee included progressive reduction of statutory liquidity ratio and cash reserve ratio, prescription of uniform accounting norms with regard to classification of assets recognition income and provisioning enactment of an Act of Parliament providing for setting up of tribunals for expeditious adjudication and recovery of bank loans establishment of separate board for financial supervision of banks, permission for the entry of new private banks to inject an element of competition between public and private sector banks rationalization and deregulation of interest rates, enactment of SARFAESI Act implementation of capital adequacy norms and re-capitalisation of banks, revision of balance sheet format to ensure increased transparency, permission to banks to access capital market for mobilizing additional equity, introduction of Prime Lending Rate (PLR), New branch licensing and New bank licensing policy, banking ombudsman scheme, etc.

CLASSIFICATION OF REFORMS

Reform measures can be classified into six categories namely a) measures meant for promotion of competition(b) measures meant for strengthening role of the market (c) prudential measures (d) legal measures (e) measures meant for strengthening supervision or supervisory measures and (f) measures relating technology.

Some of the reform measures were meant for strengthening of competition. They included grant of some operational autonomy to public sector banks, reduction of government stake to51 per cent of the total equity and permission to mobilize equity to the extent of 49 per cent from the market, adoption of transparent norms for the entry of private sector, foreign and joint venture banks, permission for foreign investment in the financial sector in the form of FDI as well as port-folio investment, permission to public sector banks to diversify product port-folio and business activities, road map for presence of foreign banks and guidelines for mergers and amalgamation of private sector banks and NBFCs with banks, issue of guidelines on ownership and governance in private sector banks, etc.

Reform measures initiated to strengthen the role of market forces included progressive reduction in SLR and CRR, market determined pricing of government securities, deregulation of interest rates with a few exceptions and increased transparency and disclosure standards to facilitate market discipline introduction of pure call money market, auction based repo-reverse repos for short term liquidity requirement, introduction of improved payment and settlement systems, etc. Prudential measures which have been implemented, covered, fulfillment of capital adequacy norms, new accounting, income recognition, provisioning and exposure norms. Measures initiated to strengthen risk weights to different categories of assets, norms on connected lending, credit concentration norms, application of market-to-market principle for investment port-folio and fixation of limits for deployment of funds in sensitive sectors and activities.

In addition, KYC guidelines, anti-money laundering standards, introduction of capital charge for market risk, higher graded provisioning for NPAs etc. were adopted for implementation. Institutional and legal measures introduced by way of supportives to banks to improve their performance in the area of recovery and asset quality up-gradation included setting up of Lok Adalats, debt recovery tribunal's asset reconstruction companies, settlement advisory committees, corporate debt restructuring mechanism, etc.

Enactment of SARFAESI At was another important measure initiated by the government. Setting up of CIBIL for the purpose of sharing credit information and establishment of clearing corporation of India (CCIL) to act as central counter party for facilitating payments and settlements systems relating to fixed income securities and money market instruments were also supportives extended to banks. Certain supervisory measures were also initiated in the reform period. They were establishment of separate Board for Financial Supervision in RBI introduction of CAMELS supervisory rating system, recasting of the role of statutory auditors and increased internal control through strengthening of internal audit, strengthening of corporate governance etc. The technology related measures implemented were setting up of INFINET as the communication back bone for the financial sector introduction of negotiated dealing system for screen based trading in government securities and Real Time Gross Settlement System (RTGS).

CHANGES GALORE

Reforms have made significant impact on banks and their functioning. The following are the details of the banking transformation that took place as a result of impact of reforms:

Risk based management: There are various types of risk such as interest rate risk, credit risk, liquidity risk, market risk, operational risk, etc. Banks have started to give attention to all types of risks in their risk management strategies. The RBI has also shifted its focus to risk based supervision. Banks have adopted comprehensive risk management systems. Risk management systems spells out internationally accepted methods of risk measurement for various charge required for meeting prescribed capital charge required for meeting prescribed capital adequacy ratio. Banks have set up separate risk management departments charged with the task of risk management.

Risk management involves many challenges. These challenges include compliance with risk adjusted capital and capital ratios, as a key regulatory and supervisory tool, ensuring risk assessment by line of business, product or even individual customer for making risk profile comprehensive adoption of risk adjusted return on capital and return on risk adjusted capital for efficient portfolio management arranging for adequate IT initiatives for enabling comprehensive MIS and better risk based decision – support, adoption and implementation of better and prudent ALM system that would conform to the dictums of risk based supervisory system.

Acute competition: In post-reform era, competition between banks is constantly on the increase. The market for bank services and products has now became a buyers' market in respect of some products and services and the same will become a completely and universally buyers' market in the years to come. Competition has become acute consequent on the birth of new generation private sector banks. Because of competition now there is need to lay greater focus on product innovation backed by IT advancement and thrust on customization process of such products.

There is also need for greater focus on R&D initiatives and efforts. There is now increased focus on customer-orientation in all activities of banks. Because of competition banks are now giving greater attention to marketing of various products and services. Increase in competition may bring about further change in marketing strategy of banks, involving simulative analysis for clients, products and market segments with the help of sophisticated quantitative tools.

Change in Efficiency Parameters: In post-reform period, we find a complete change in efficiency parameters. To-day, what is important is strength of Balance Sheet. Return on assets, return on risk adjusted capital net interest margin, quality of assets, NPA percentage per employee business, per employee productivity proportion of low cost deposits are considered important to-day. Because of change inefficiency parameters there is now added emphasis on professionalism on the part of bank officers and staff and also on good corporate governance to increase customer satisfaction and enhance shareholder value. Banks will have to assume still tougher posture to recover NPAs and further reduce NPA percentage.

Universal Banking: As a result of reforms, the trend has been clearly towards universal banking. Now banks market credit cards, insurance products, mutual funds and even provide demat accounts and trading platform. There is no takers for narrow banking.

MERGERS AND ACQUISITIONS

In post-reform era, we have seen many mergers and acquisitions. New Bank of India, a nationalized bank and Negungadi Bank Ltd were merged with Punjab National Bank. Kashinath Seth Bank was merged with SBI in 1995-96. Barelley Corp bank and South Gujarat Local Area Bank were merged with Bank of Baroda. Times Bank and Centurion Bank of Punjab have been merged with HDFC Bank. Bank of Madura, ICICI Ltd and Sangli Bank have been merged with ICICI Bank. Sikkim Bank was merged with Union Bank of India in 1999-2000. Global Trust Bank was merged with Oriental Bank of Commerce; United Western Bank was merged with IDBI Bank. Ganesh Bank of Kuruvalwad was merged with Federal Bank in 2006. Lord Krishna Bank and Bank of Muscat SAOG were merged with Centurion Bank of Punjab.

Government of India encourages mergers as there is need for mergers to create larger and stronger banks and to bring about a new banking order. Mergers may be synergy-based mergers to derive economies of scale, market-driven mergers and mergers between banks and financial institutions including NBFCs in the interests of furthering universal banking. Mergers of public sector banks can also be done to create global banking institutions. Through the process of mergers, it is better to create 4 to 5 global banks, 10 to 15 national level players and remaining banks can be institutions, having regional character. We have seen even mergers of RRBs. State-wise and sponsor-bank wise mergers have brought about reduction in the number of RRBs from 196 to 98. Merger of South Gujarat Local Area Bank with Bank of Baroda has taken place in 2004.

IT INITIATIVES

In a post - reform era, there have been significant IT initiatives. In every bank, there has been stress on increased IT application and efforts are on to absorb latest technology is respect of all branches for greater customer conveniences right sizing manpower better MIS and internal control improved risk management, better ALM etc. Banks are striving hard to expand CBS to branches in a phased manner. Strategic alliance among banks in areas like, ATM sharing and funds transfer, etc. has been new developments in post-reform eta. Computerization of all branches including rural branches establishment of rural ATMs, etc. are expected in the days to come.

Focus on Concerns: Another development in post-reform period has been a shift in focus from size related issues to concerns in respect of productivity, efficiency profitability return on capital net interest margin return on assets etc. In the days to come, there will be greater stress on these concerns. This will result in adoption of still better and more prudent risk management system, better and more effective management of spreads and net interest margin through cost cutting product innovation, product-wise and business-line-wise cost, income and profitability analysis steps at an augmentation of fee-based income etc.

Towards Partial Privatisation: Moving towards partial privatization was a trend observed in port-reform period. Government stake in public sector bank stands reduced by 51 per cent from the original 100 per cent. It is possible that any new government coming to power in future may reduce stake to 33 per cent if there is adequate support for the same. When BIP led government was in power there was such a move, but the same was given up because of opposition from the left.

HRD Initiatives: In the post - reform era, there has been lot of human resource development initiatives. There is stress on objective manpower planning, adoption of scientific methods for evaluating the contributions of staff, etc. outsourcing of certain items of work is also a development in the post - reform period. Fresh recruitment of staff, including specialists is taking place in all banks. The performance linked reward system may also be implemented in public sector banks in the years ahead. Average age of staff in some public sector banks is high and this must be reduced by shedding of excessive inefficient staff aged beyond 50 and younger boys and girls with good educational background and IT skills must be recruited in their place.

There should be special courses for preparing bankers for tomorrow. National Institute of Bank Management (NIBM) has launched a post graduate programme in banking. This is meant for preparing bank officers. NIBM alone cannot meet the requirements of such trained officers in all banks. Hence, all management institutes may also start suitably designed post graduate programmers for preparing bank officers for tomorrow. MBA (finance) candidates coming out from management institutes have to be given training by banks in job specific skills. If management institutes have to be given training by banks in job specific skills. If management institutes launch programmers on the lines of the programme launched by NIBM, banks can recruit them and straight away put them on the job. This will save lot of time taken in providing job-specific training in banks.

Increased strength: On account of banking reforms, Indian banks have become relatively much stronger vis-à-vis their counterparts in other Asian countries in terms of range of loan products and services, range of deposit products, capital adequacy ratio, quality of assets, profitability and productivity and overall balance sheet strength. But, the banking sector will have to encounter new challenges particularly in the context Basel II norms that are being implemented and the creation of global brands, anti-money laundering standards and entry of foreign and new players. Standard and poor's analysis have shown that

Indian banking is ahead of China. Indonesia, Philippines and Vietnam. But, the banking sectors of Australia, New Zealand, Singapore, Hongkong, Japan, South Korea and Thailand are ahead of Indian banks. The study undertaken by Moody's Investor Service has revealed that Indian banking is qualitatively better than its counterparts even in developed countries like, Japan, Singapore and Australia. Indian banks have posted the highest return on equity compared to their Asian counter parts during the last four years. There has been a distinctly discernible improvement in the performance of Indian banks on various fronts.

But, the acquisition of a globally competitive size for Indian banks is a major challenge. Banks in other Asian countries, particularly in China are large in size compared to Indian banks. There will be a severe strain on capital on account of implementation of Basel II norms. The RBI has recently issued guidelines to banks on Pillar 2 of Basel II Framework. Pillar 2 deals with supervisory review process the objective of which is to ensure that banks have adequate capital to support all risks and also to encourage them to develop and use better risk management techniques for monitoring and managing their risks.

The RBI guidelines listed some risks that banks are generally exposed to, but which are not fully captured in the regulatory Capital to Risk Asset Ratio (CRAR), such as interest rate risk, credit concentration risk, liquidity risk, settlement risk and reputational risk among others. The RBI has asked banks to develop an Internal Capital Adequacy Assessment Process (ICAAP) commensurate with their size, level of complexity, risk profile an scope of operations. This would be in addition to calculation of regulatory capital requirement under Pillar I. The implementation of new norms and guidelines involves a new challenge for banks.

Acquisition of competitive advantage: The vision for a strong vibrant and globally competitive banking sector in India is based on achievement of competitive advantage the acquisition of which is possible only through stress on efficiency increase in productivity and improvement in profitability, up scaling of technological up gradation and continued improvement of overall balance sheet strength of banks. This would also require adoption of globally recognized best practices on the part of banks.

Facing the challenge of change in terms of range of products, delivery channels, process, culture, structure and overall capabilities would require key structural changes such as consolidation full implementation of real time gross settlement system at all branches, greater efficiency and higher productivity most effective risk management practices better credit management techniques to ensure improved credit quality good corporate governance better technology effective customer relationship management, focus on non-interest income improvement in human resource capabilities and increase in professionalism at all levels. Concentrated attention on these vital aspects can alone fetch competitive advantage.

PRODUCTIVITY

Business per employee of Indian banks increased from ₹ 5-4 million in 1992 to ₹ 163 million in 2004 and profit per employee rose from ₹ 20,000/- to ₹ 1,50,000/- in the same period. Also, business per branch increased from ₹109.9 million to ₹254.5 million in the above period. Measures of profitability *i.e.* return on assets and operating profit ratio and efficiency measures of net interest margin, operating profit to staff expense, operating cost ratio and staff expense ratio have to be improved. There is therefore need to increase business volumes by leveraging technology and down-sizing of staff strength to reduce cost of intermediation. All controllable costs must be reduced by banks.

RETAIL BANKING

This must continue to be an area of focus. Core banking solution must be expanded by all banks to cover all of their branches. Measuring and managing risk across a range of diverse business activities through integrated risk management requires devising a comprehensive integrated risk management framework. This requires urgent attention by all banks.

Banks to-day find it difficult to maintain the minimum required controls expected of them in a new complex and increasingly regulated business environment. The traditional audit and inspection provide assurance that control systems are adequate and function satisfactorily. But, audit and inspections are in fact, a post-mortem and the findings emerging there-from are only after the transactions may not cover all transactions are over. Also audit and inspections may not cover all transactions and many go un-noticed.

They are rarely able to check all transactions in a detailed manner for controls compliance. Therefore, there is a risk of even frauds remaining undetected. To assist in the efficient capture and evaluation of data sophisticated software tools need to be used for evaluation of disclosure controls and procedures and internal controls and supervision over financial reporting.

CORPORATE GOVERNANCE

Corporate governance is of crucial importance for banks. The corporate governance philosophy of banks has to be based on the pursuit of sound business ethics and strong professionalism that aligns the interests of all stakeholders and the society at large. It is therefore necessary to constantly strengthen the corporate governance mechanism in all banks.

Disclosure of reliable information facilitates market discipline, strengthens confidence and reduces the chances for rumours and creation of atmosphere of suspicion and misleading information that may bring about market instability. Indian accounting standards still lag behind global practices in many respects. This has to be addressed effectively at the earliest.

INNOVATIVE BUSINESS MODEL

The introduction of innovative business models and financial technologies the world over has received an impetus through slashing operating cost through higher labour productivity, innovation and business process re-engineering, further reduction of NPAs, micro planning, branch-centric profit planning, effective implementation of plans and monitoring of results CBS and market centric HRM policies and manpower planning. Very high average age of staff, requirement of new skills and talents, working in a computerized environment, foray into new and emerging areas require recruitment of new staff and specialists, extensive training, etc. Although 86 per cent of PSBs are fully computerized only 44 per cent are actually functioning under CBS platform. Covering all branches of all banks under CBS will be a challenge for banks.

Increased customer-orientation and customer focus, product innovation, greater use of multiple channels like ATMs internet and mobile banking, etc. efficient credit delivery besides building up sound financial are vital for banks for facing emerging challenges and obstacles.

Camping of Human Resource Management: Staff at banks irrespective of their functional domain needs to add value to acquire an extra cutting edge. Human resources policies and Human resource management should be revamped so as to convert human resource management from a support function to a strategic partner to the banking business. This must happen in all banks. It is, therefore, necessary to develop a proper recruitment strategy and ensure that it dovetails with identified objectives of banks and helps attract and retain talent through flexible compensation packages and an institutional mechanism of recognition and reward.

FINANCIAL INCLUSION:

There are abundant opportunities for intermediation and mobilisation of savings and extension of bank credit at the bottom of the pyramid. About 60 to 70 per cent of enterprises and individuals do not have access to basic financial services such as savings and credit. Hence, increased financial inclusion of all those who presently stand excluded is of paramount importance. Bank linkage with SHGs, financing of SMEs, rural artisans, rural non-farm activities, etc will be great business opportunities for banks. Emphasis on volume-led growth in competitive balance sheet size, shift of focus from interest income to non-interest income and from capital adequacy to capital efficiency, etc. are vital from the point of view of maintaining benchmarks of return on assets, return on owning funds, net NPAs, capital adequacy, cost to income ratio, net interest margin and intermediation cost.

In bracing for tomorrow a paradigm shift in bank financing through innovative mechanism such as, templates for assessing customer risk and pricing products and services credit scoring, ensuring availability and use of information etc are absolutely essential. Retail banking requires product development and differentiation innovation and business process re-engineering, micro-planning marketing prudent pricing customization technology upgradation home, electronic and mobile banking cost-reduction and cross selling. All these must be given adequate attention. Banking success requires imaginative strategic planning organizational restructuring streamlining and revamping of human resources management, etc.

Developing Immunity: Banks have to adopt and implement strategies to ensure immunity of their balance sheets from interest rate fluctuations by paying greater attention to non-interest income. Growing services sector and financial markets have created new avenues for fee based income. Merchant banking international trade, funds transfer, payment and settlements, consultancy services financial derivatives utility service etc opened up new income sources for banks. But, what is required is a total transition from branch banking to virtual banking, market segmentation to customer-profitability and these are real challenges for banks. Many new challenges may also crop up in the years ahead.

Areas of continues challenge: The areas of continued challenge for banks would be risk management, full implementation of Basel II norms, achievement of full and meaningful financial inclusion an availment of rural business opportunities and opportunities at the bottom of the pyramid, rural credit delivery system, enhancing customer satisfaction, technology upgradation on a continual basis, expansion of CBS platform to all branches including rural branches, further reduction of NPAs reducing intermediation cost increasing non-interest income and fee based income for improving profitability staff involvement in all bank functions, revamping of human resource management

– increasing volumes of business despite competition from other banks and other dis-in-termedition sources and participative and strategic planning.

As all the existing and future challenges have to be faced through staff banks have to give top priority to revamping of human resources management and development of human resources. Development of human resources through training, inducing participation and full involvement of all staff in bank functions and activities etc are very vital. Streamlining of audit and inspection, strict internal control and house-keeping, improved risk management, increasing capital efficiency and mobiisation of fresh equity from time to time, asset-liability management and balance sheet management are real challenges, requiring utmost attention.

Ensuring optimum performance: Developing concern for results and performance on the part of entire personnel in banks is a vital requirement. This too will be a challenge. Future of banks will depend on their alertness, operational and capital efficiency, customer orientation and standard of service creation of larger and larger volumes of performing assets, attainment of optimum levels of productivity profitability and overall performance.

Future of banks hinges on these and also on their ability to build up large volumes of quality assets with lesser capital charge thereon that perform on an enduring basis. Ensuring optimum performance of each manager, officer and staff will be crucial. Only those banks which are pro-active and which respond quickly to changing customer needs and changing environment and which give adequate attention to the above issues alone can successfully face the future challenges, perform well and grow as strong, vibrant, efficient and sound financial institutions.

TRANSFORMING IN INDIAN BANKING

The significant transformation of the banking industry in India is clearly evident from the changes that have occurred in the financial markets, institutions and products. While deregulation has opened up new vistas for banks to augment revenues, it has entailed greater competition and consequently greater risks. Cross-border flows and entry of new products, particularly derivative instruments, have impacted significantly on the domestic banking sector, forcing banks to adjust the product mix, as also to effect rapid changes in their processes and operations in order to remain competitive to the globalised environment. These developments have facilitated greater choice for consumers, who have become more discerning and demanding compelling banks to offer a broader range of products through diverse distribution channels. The traditional face of banks as mere financial intermediaries has since altered and risk management has emerged as their defining attribute.

- Report on Trend and Progress of Banking in India 2001-02, Reserve Bank of India

It gives me great pleasure to deliver the valedictory address at the Bank Eonomists' Conference (BECON) 2002. We would like to thank the Corporation Bank and the Indian Banks' Association for giving me this opportunity. Over the years, the BECON has evolved as an important forum for intensive discussions on both contemporary and futuristic issues facing the Indian banking industry. This forum has served as an important platform for structured information-sharing among bankers, research analysts, credit rating agencies and other financial sector bodies. Currently, the most important factor shaping the world is globalisation. The benefits of globalisation have been well documented and are being increasingly recognised. Integration of domestic markets with international financial markets has been facilitated by tremendous advancement in information and communications technology. But, such an environment has also meant that a problem in one country can sometimes adversely impact one or more countries instantaneously, even if they are fundamentally strong.

There is a growing realisation that the ability of countries to conduct business across national borders and the ability to cope with the possible downside risks would depend, *inter alia*, on the soundness of the financial system. This has consequently meant the adoption of a strong and transparent, prudential, regulatory, supervisory, technological and institutional framework in the financial sector on par w®ith international best practices.

All this necessitates a transformation: a transformation in the mindset, a transformation in the business processes and finally, a transformation in knowledge management. This process is not a one shot affair; it needs to be appropriately phased in the least disruptive manner. The subject of the Conference is, therefore, very timely and appropriate and we would like to take this opportunity to congratulate the organisers for this theme.

As you would all appreciate, the banking and financial crises in recent years in emerging economies have demonstrated that, when things go wrong with the financial system, they can result in a severe economic downturn. Furthermore, banking crises often impose substantial costs on the exchequer, the incidence of which is ultimately borne by the taxpayer. The World Bank Annual Report (2002) has observed that the loss of US $1 trillion in banking crises in the 1980s and 1990s is equal to the total flow of official development assistance to developing countries from the 1950s to the present date. As a consequence, the focus of financial market reform in many emerging economies has been towards increasing efficiency while at the same time ensuring stability in financial markets.

From this perspective, financial sector reforms are essential in order to avoid such costs. It is, therefore, not surprising that financial market reform is at the forefront of public policy debate in recent years. The burgeoning literature on endogenous growth theory has come to recognise the crucial role of sound financial markets in promoting rapid economic growth and ensuring financial stability. Indeed, it is by now widely documented that the structure of financial markets helps explain why some countries remain poor, while others grow richer. Financial sector reform, through the development of an efficient financial system, is thus perceived as a key element in raising countries out of their 'low level equilibrium trap'. As the World Bank Annual Report (2002) observes, 'a robust financial system is a precondition for a sound investment climate, growth and reduction of poverty'.

Financial sector reforms were initiated in India a decade ago with a view to improving efficiency in the process of financial intermediation, enhancing the effectiveness in the conduct of monetary policy and creating conditions for integration of the domestic financial sector with the global system. The first phase of reforms was guided by the recommendations of Narasimham Committee I.

The approach was to ensure that 'the financial services industry operates on the basis of operational flexibility and functional autonomy with a view to enhancing efficiency, productivity and profitability'. The second phase, guided by Narasimham Committee II, focused on strengthening the foundations of the banking system and bringing about structural improvements. While there may be some concern over the pace and sequencing of reforms in the financial sector vis-à-vis the real sector, you will agree with me when I say that we have traversed a considerable distance since 1991. Reforms in the financial sector and their beneficial impact have been well documented and I will not attempt to repeat them here. The text of the Governor's inaugural address also covers at length important issues such as ownership, corporate governance, regulatory and supervisory issues and the like. I also see from the schedule that you have held intensive discussions on important issues related to corporate governance, reform of the capital structure (in the context of Basel II norms), retail banking, risk management technology, and human resources development, among others.

INTEREST RATE SCENARIO

The first important issue that I would like to highlight relates to interest rates. As a result of interest rate deregulation, the interest rate structure of banks is competitively determined in the market, barring a few exceptions. A major factor that has influenced the trend in interest rates is the sustained decline in the inflation rate in the recent period. Notwithstanding year-to-year fluctuations, there has been a distinct downward drift in the inflation rate during the second half of the 1990s, which is now at around half the level as compared with the first half of the 1990s. Both the popular measures of inflation - the Wholesale Price Index (WPI) and the Consumer Price Index (CPI) – have shown a definite fall in the recent period.

For example, the WPI on an average basis has declined from an average of about 10.5 per cent per annum between 1990-91 to 1995-96 to about 5 per cent per annum over the last 5 years. A similar trend can be observed with regard to the Consumer Price Index for industrial workers. In the current year so far, inflation as measured by variations in WPI, has remained benign around 3 per cent despite the adverse effect of drought and uncertainty on account of oil prices. As the inflation rate has decelerated, it has also had a positive impact on inflationary expectations. This is clearly reflected in the downward trend in nominal interest rates.

For instance, the overnight call money rate has fallen sharply from about 13 per cent in August 2000 to the current levels of 5.5 per cent. Similarly, the 91-day Treasury Bill rate declined from 10.5 per cent to 5.4 per cent and the 364-day Treasury Bill rate from 10.9 per cent to 5.6 per cent over the same period.

The long-term interest rates too have declined. The yield on 10-Year government securities has declined from 11.5 per cent in August 2000 to the current levels of about 6.3 per cent. Similarly, interest rates on corporate paper have fallen significantly. For example, the interest rate on 5-Year AAA rated corporate paper has declined from 12 per cent in August 2000 to about 6.7 per cent currently.

The banks have also reduced their deposit rates. The term deposit rates of public sector banks over one year maturity have declined from a range of 8-10 per cent in August 2000 to 6-8 per cent now. This fall in the interest rates in the recent period has been in consonance with the monetary policy stance of a soft and a flexible interest rate regime. Despite the fall in deposit rates, depositors have received positive real interest rates of close to 2 per cent in the second half of the 1990s, which is much higher than the real return on deposits during the first half of the 1990s.

On the other hand, lending rates of banks have not come down as much. While banks have reduced their prime lending rates (PLRs) to some extent and are also extending sub-PLR loans, effective lending rates continue to remain high. It is estimated that the average lending rate of scheduled commercial banks has declined from a peak of about 17 per cent in 1995-96 to about 14 per cent by 2001-02. Hence, while nominal interest rates have come down, they have not fallen as much as the inflation rate. Consequently, the effective real lending rate continues to remain high. This development has adverse systemic implications, especially in a country like India where interest cost as a proportion of sales of corporates are much higher as compared to many emerging economies.

A cross country comparison of interest rate trends during the 1990s provides some interesting insights. The average inflation rate in all these countries has come down during the second half of that decade (1997-2001) as compared to the first half. In line with this, the average money market interest rates and government securities yields have also come down in real terms in most of these countries. On the lending side, however, prime rates in some countries have not shown similar falls in real interest rates (UK, Germany, Japan, Thailand and Hungary). Thus, the Indian experience of sticky real lending rates is not unique. But, preliminary estimates do show a high correlation between government securities yields and real lending rate in Japan, India and Germany during the 1990s as a whole. Hence, the downward rigidity in lending rates in India as compared with the government securities rates during the second half of the 1990s does seem more surprising in this context. It would seem that changes in inflationary expectations take a little longer to adjust than inflation rates themselves. It would be rational for interest rates to be related to inflationary expectations, and in particular long-term interest rates. Therefore, bank economists have an important role of informing the management of appropriate inflationary expectations so that interest rates can be adjusted more systematically.

Understandably, there are certain rigidities in the overall interest rate structure in the economy that constrain banks from reducing their lending rates. These have been well documented in the earlier monetary and credit policy statements of the Reserve Bank. Subsequently, interest rates on small savings have also moved down and there is a commitment from the Government to link these rates with market related rates. The recovery environment has also improved. A related issue pertains to transparency in lending rates. Especially after the introduction of sub-PLR lending by banks, the spreads between the minimum and maximum lending rates seem to have widened. The Reserve Bank is making efforts to publish on its web site bank-wise information on the minimum and maximum lending rates. Our own internal exercises reveal that the concept of PLR may need to be reviewed in the current context. Perhaps, bank economists may like to study the international experience and come out with suggestions.

Lending to Small and Medium Enterprises

The problem arising out of high lending rates gets accentuated due to segmentation in the credit market. The large corporates are able to negotiate fine rates with banks and are able to bring down their overall interest costs. In addition, the large corporates have the option of accessing the international capital markets for funds. The burden of adjustment has, therefore, fallen on small and medium enterprises (SMEs), which have limited access to funds. The high interest rates paid by SMEs may not always be in accordance with their risk profile.

It is clear that at present the Indian banking system is not fully equipped to promote small-scale enterprises around the country. The key issue is that banking institutions must be enabled to improve their credit assessment capabilities with regard to small-scale enterprises so that they can distinguish adequately between good and bad credit. Small-scale must not be equated with high risk. If the inflation rate is as low as 3 per cent and the interest rates charged to SMEs are much higher than normal good credit risk to large-sized industries, there is an implicit adverse selection in the credit appraisal process. Bank economists need to give focused attention to risk assessment to this sector so that there are no errors of high interest rate to low risk borrowers in the SME sector and vice-versa.

The provision for Credit Information Bureaus and better exchange of information on credit risk between banks and financial institutions is also necessary to enable these institutions to recognise higher risk without excessive costs. Furthermore, the cost of credit assessment of small and medium enterprises can be reduced by a focused recognition of clusters of like small-scale industries that exist around the country.

Such financial assistance programmes also need to be devised to provide assistance to those industries that are in the reserved list to enable them to expand and upgrade technology. This should be done both at the individual and group level. The focus of many such activities can be on the basis of industrial clusters so that economies of scale can be achieved both in financial assistance and in technology upgradation.

Very significant changes are also taking place in the agricultural sector. We can see the beginning of a much closer connection between primary producers, trade intermediaries, food processing entities, and eventual marketing of value added products. With the share of unprocessed foods falling, the real growth area in the agricultural sector is in value added food products such as meat, poultry, fish, vegetables, fruits and the like. There is an accelerating move of consumers to basic processed foods. These trends need to be studied carefully so that supporting policy changes and investments can be made. Banks should explore the feasibility of expanding substantially lending to these activities.

Apart from adequate quantum of credit at an affordable price, there are issues relating to provision of high processing costs and the attendant cumbersome paper work. There are lessons to be learnt from the experience of the Kisan Credit Card (KCC) Schemes and the Laghu Udhyami Credit Card Schemes to the agricultural and small entrepreneur borrowers. Surely, there is some scope for extending the benefits of hassle free credit facilities through similar innovative methods to other borrowers requiring credit limits of over ₹.2 lakh also.

It needs to be recognised that the SME sector has tremendous growth potential and accordingly pricing of loans to this sector should be at commensurate rates. Thus, there is need for realignment of interest rates among various segments of the financial market. As the financial market develops, ideally the interest rates on all types of debt instruments, both in the government and private sectors, and in the credit market should align in a relatively narrow band, reflecting realistic risk premia.

There have been some signals of industrial pick up during the last few months. For the four months from July to October 2002, on a point to point basis, the rise in index of industrial production (IIP) has been above 6 per cent. A major contribution to the high growth rates has been from the manufacturing sector. In use-based classification also, the capital goods sector has registered impressive growth rates of over 15 per cent and 12 per cent in September and October 2002 respectively. Most (14 out of 17) industry groups in the index have shown positive growth rates. The increase in non-food credit of scheduled commercial banks during the current financial year also appears to be commensurate with the IIP performance.

Nevertheless, banks have shown a marked preference for investments in government securities instead of pursuing their core activity of lending to commercial sector. At an aggregate level, the SLR holdings of banks are close to 39 per cent as compared to the regulatory prescription of 25 per cent. Even strong commercial banks seem to be voluntarily adopting 'narrow banking' in a bid to minimise credit risk while increasing profitability.

Such large investments in government securities well beyond the statutory requirement reflect dissipation of banking knowledge capital with regard to credit appraisals. The interest rate risk on investments in gilts need hardly be over emphasised. Further, the current focus of banks is bound to exact some heavy costs in terms of efficiency and credit availability. There is a danger of the link between liquidity, credit, money and economic activity being severed in the long run as a result of continued over-investment in government securities as a substitute for bank financing to the commercial sector.

At a time when the industry is showing signs of pick up, banks should make efforts to increase commercial lending. The need of the hour is revival of the manufacturing sector and financing of the new slew of activities allied to agricultural lending. Of course, this would require focused attention through specialised branches, sound credit appraisals, adoption of sophisticated risk management techniques, and better information sharing. The legal environment has also improved with the passing of the new act to regulate securitisation and reconstruction of financial assets and enforcement of security interest.

Revitalisation of Long-Term Financing

The development finance institutions (DFIs) were set up in the 1950s to provide medium and long-term finance to the private sector. Many of these institutions were sponsored by the Government. DFIs were expected to resolve long-term credit shortages and to acquire and disseminate skills necessary to assess projects and banks creditworthiness. DFIs were traditionally dependent on concessional sources of financing, guaranteed by Government.

On the asset side, they were predominantly engaged in term lending with banks financing working capital requirements. The post-reform period has altered the domain of the operations of DFIs both on the liabilities and assets sides. While DFIs started competing for funds at market rates of interest, their asset profile also shortened. On the other hand, banks have entered the domain of term lending. The current trend is of DFIs converting themselves into banks. In this context, the future of long-term lending acquires great importance. Finance theory suggests that banks can play an important role in corporate financing, especially in situations of asymmetric information, principal-agent problems, design of incentive compatible contracts and corporate governance issues. In their early stages of development, corporates are likely to rely on bank finance for working capital requirements. Bank financing is also likely to be predominant in an economy having a less-sophisticated legal framework. Considerations of lower transactions costs, efficient risk diversification, cost effective assessment, monitoring and renegotiation, etc., are likely to make firms more reliant on bank finance than on market based debt instruments.

International evidence on industrialised countries indicates that since the early 1970s, banks have played an important role in corporate financing. The benefits of a bank-based financial system vis-à-vis a market-based system were clearly noticeable particularly in the case of Japan, France and Italy. During this period, bank financing was equally important in other industrialised and developing countries, although equity finance has gained momentum in recent years.

This is a challenging area as financing of long-term projects involves commitment of large funds over long periods with the concomitant asset liability mismatches. The shift from a fixed to a floating interest rate regime, development of corporate debt market, introduction of derivatives instruments and further enabling changes in the regulatory and legal environment are likely to increase long-term financing by banks. Banks would need to think in terms of setting up special wings for term lending, development of consortia and syndication, and cooperation in assessment of projects. These are areas for further exploration by bank economists.

Non-Performing Possessions

One of the main constraints to the above issues that we have raised is the level of non-performing assets. As of March 31, 2002, the gross NPAs of scheduled commercial banks stood at ₹.71,000 crore, of which the NPAs of public sector banks constituted ₹.57,000 crore. The absolute amount of NPAs continues to be a major drag on the performance of banks. The large volume of NPAs reflects both an overhang of past dues and on-going problem of fresh accretion.

As we move towards the international norm of 90 days for recognition of loan impairment, there may be a temporary increase in crystalisation of NPAs in the banking sector.

There is, therefore, a need to bring about improvements in credit administration and management of credit risk. The Credit Information Bureau (CIB) should help in improving credit decisions by providing institutional mechanism for sharing of credit information on borrowers and potential borrowers among banks and financial institutions. The Reserve Bank modified the guidelines for compromise settlements of NPAs of the small sector to provide a simplified, non-discretionary and non-discriminatory mechanism. Banks should work out processes for settlement procedures and expedite quick recovery of NPAs.

The Securitisation and Reconstruction of Financial Assets and Enforcement of Security Interest Act, 2002 should help in cleansing the balance sheet of banks by facilitating foreclosure. The constitution of an Asset Reconstruction Company (ARC) is another channel to remove NPAs from the balance sheets of banks through the processes of securitisation of assets. The Reserve Bank has recently posted on its web site the draft of the directions on prudential norms proposed to be issued by it to securitisation companies/reconstruction companies. I hope despite the Christmas spirit and the Conference mood, experts would have studied the RBI proposals and sent their comments.

Risk Management in Interest

In the current interest rate environment, banks are finding it more profitable to invest in government securities. In 2001-02, trading profits of public sector banks more than doubled to ₹.5,999 crore from ₹.2,250 crore in 2000-01. The net profits of these banks during these two years were ₹.4,317 crore and ₹.8,301 crore respectively and this includes an additional ₹.1,365 crore and ₹.1,547 crore from forex operations. The Reserve Bank has been encouraging banks to be proactive in risk management. In this context, with a view to building up adequate reserves to guard against any possible reversal of interest rate environment in future, banks have been directed to maintain a certain level of Investment Fluctuation Reserve (IFR). The Reserve Bank is also taking a number of steps to develop further the derivatives market. As announced in the Mid-term review of monetary policy for 2002-03, a Working Group has been set up with representatives from the market to enlarge the avenues of managing interest rate risks for banks and other financial intermediaries as well as corporates in the rupee derivatives market.

Recently, the Reserve Bank has issued a guidance note on market risk management. The guidance note delineates the minimum requirements for a bank including approval levels and requirements for any exceptions, deviations or waivers. The note illustratively covers the responsibilities of risk management with regard to market risk management, the responsibilities of risk taking unit, the responsibilities of market risk manager, risk identification, risk monitoring, funding and liquidity, models of risk analysis, and risk reporting.

In a rapidly changing business environment, no business can afford to remain static. It is well understood that risk-taking is an integral part of any business enterprise. It is important that each bank needs to have in place the technical systems and management processes necessary to not only identify the risks associated with its activities, but also to effectively measure, monitor and control them. If Indian banks are to compete globally, the time is opportune for them to institute sound and robust risk management practices.

7

Commercial Banking

The Commercial Bank of India, also known as Exchange Bank was a bank which was established in Bombay Presidency (nowMumbai), in 1845 of the British Raj period. The bank failed in the crash of 1866, after successfully operating for 20 years.

The bank had eight branches, exclusive of the head office at Bombay, viz: London, Calcutta, Hong Kong, Foochow, Shangai, Hankow,Yokohama and Singapore, with an agency for the purchase of bullion at San Francisco. Commercial Bank of India then was winded up as directed by the Master of the Rolls, under the corresponding section of the Companies Act of England, where the company was registered under the Indian law and was not registered in England, but was carrying on business in England.

CHANGING SCENARIO OF COMMERCIAL BANKS

Liberalization and deregulation have heightened competition among banks, which will only intensify with liberalization under the WTO regime and banks in India will have to benchmark themselves against world class banks. In this context, the way to boost profitability and stay ahead is by developing sophisticated and reaching out to customers in diversified and distant markets by leveraging technology. In line with this, our banks have to make all our efforts to adopt state-of-the art technology with for reaching consequences for efficiency and profitability.

It is truly a beginning has already been made in the direction of modernization involving increasing use of information technology. Virtual banking which is associated with the banks have to redouble efforts to adapt to the advances in technology which are changing the contours of financial intermediation world-wide. Unless we catch up, the technology lag could widen with adverse implications on efficiency and costs.

The popularity which virtual banking services have won among customers, owing to the speed, convenience and round-the-clock access they offer, is likely to increase in future. The banks are recognizing the need to embrace technology in the area of products and service to compete successfully in the years ahead. In fact, the commercial banks, the world over, are among the largest consumers of information technology. The banks perceive the future of the financial services industry as heavily dependent on electronic delivery mechanism and are working towards bringing banking right into their customer's hoes. There has been a noticeable tilt towards technology-driven products and services.

The convergence of technologies has enabled Indian banking to service their customers efficiently on a real-time basis. Computers and communication technology has not only increased the competition among the commercial banks but have also opened new vista for them to innovate themselves and come up with new products and services.

The information technology has a direct impact on vital aspects of Banks. All the major components of a bank, viz, its organizational structure, the customers, personnel and data evolve under the impact of the technology and react to the changes.

TRENDS IN THE BANKING SYSTEMS

1. Electronics and information technology are changing rapidly day by day. It has led to development of more user friendly banking services. The technology offers the financial institution an alternate and better delivery channel. Electronic Banking, Any Branch Banking, Tele banking, Enterprise Resource Management, Call centres, Credit Cards, Smart Cards and Automated Teller Machines have ensured that banking products and services can be provided to consumers with complete ease and maximum efficiency. Now a bank need not be limited by its physical establishments and can have an on-line presence to reach out to more customers. Online banking and electronic payment systems are new and development and diffusion of these technologies by FIs is expected to result in more efficient banking system.
2. A tremendous change has taken place in Networks and Communications; the transfer of information is the basis of office automation. Advances in communication technology, have made possible much of the progress in the field. Networks and Communication systems designed to convey or exchange information from a point of origin to a point of destination.
3. Regulations and artificial barriers are being brought down. Institutions, that have traditionally been operating in one specific segment, are now aggressively looking at the other segments of financial services such as insurance sector.
4. Most Banks focused on delivering treasury management services because customers are used to receiving and working on these services electronically. We are moving beyond treasury management

into areas such as Institutional trust and credit all of which is being delivered through a Jawa based software.

5. The Cash management system is another technology breakthroughs and the system helps in faster payments and fast collection, with browser based easy access by customers to view their accounts without the use of paper.
6. Treasury execution Information Systems and 'gateways to market' which provide line market quote and news through the web as per the preference of each user.
7. The Banks should be ready for implementation of the forthcoming system like Structured Financial Messaging System (SFMS), Centralised Funds Management System (CFMS), Real Time Gross Settlement System (RTGS), Securities Settlement System (SSS), Negotiated Dealing System (NDS) etc.
8. Banks are tapping new sources and finding ways to differentiate themselves from other banks and non-banks and are increasingly venturing into the fee-based services like the: *Marketing of insurance and annuity sales, *Mutual funds, *Financial Planning, and *Trust Services.

IMPACT OF IT ON BANKS

Under the impact of technology, the organization structure of the banks, the role of various functionaries and the approach of banks to customer needs undergo a perceptible change. The technology has helped the banks to strategically look at customer needs to offer newer and efficient banking services, at the same time gearing its staff to cope with the stresses of technology. Here we discuss, the impact of Information Technology in the following components of banking.

Changes in Organisational Structure

Information technology is a means of increasing organisational productivity. IT, in fact, is much more than a series of new machines for organisational efficiency since it brings about a new concept of self-regulating systems and principles in the organization.

Some of the usual changes brought about under the impact of IT relating to organisational structure and orientation of the banking sector are as follows:

- The need for faster information and better control has a direct impact on reducing the hierarchical tier systems in the banks. This has resulted in establishing a direct liaison between top management and the field functionaries.
- As the technology helps in collection, processing, interpretation and transmission of information, the need for middle tiers of management

vanishes and more of self managing groups with autonomy and access to information emerge strongly.

- Managerial attitudes also undergo a change under the impact of IT. This is reflected in the way; the top executives look at IT as a functional requirement and apply it to improving organisational efficiency and effectiveness. IT help in engineering a change mechanism in the overall orientation of the management.
- The organisational change can facilitate the increase involvement of information systems in the mainstream product offerings in the banking and financial sector. In addition to these technical and organisational changes, a psychological repositioning of the information technology function takes place.

Impact on Service Quality

The most visible impact of technology is reflected in the way the banks respond strategically for making its effective use for efficient service delivery. This impact on service quality can be summed up as follows:

- Small and relatively new banks with limited network of branches, become better placed to compete with established banks, by integrating IT in their operations.
- The technology has helped in commoditizing some of the financial services. The technology forces the banks to develop a strategy for an online delivery system to broaden the customer relationship, and to retain customer loyalty.
- The depersonalization can have a negative effect on relationship banking. The advent of home banking, fast changes the banks into shopping malls. This greatly reduces the personal element in the services. It is an established fact that the human interface is the most vital aspect of any service industry, irrespective of how advances the adopted technology is.
- The advent of IT democratizes the information in the sense that bank customers, particularly the corporate customers have access to the same real-time information over which the banks earlier had control. This results in greater competition for the banks.
- In banks the technology pushes the delivery of services out of bank and the focus shifts from cost reduction to maintain market position. However, when properly adopted, the technology helps in accelerating the service delivery to customers providing control over account relationships.

Changes in Customer Aspirations

Today the customers are demanding fast, accurate and reliable services. The absorption of technology, therefore, becomes inevitable for the banks to enable them to respond to customers' needs at all times and at competitive prices. In the changes socio-economic conditions the customers, individual or corporate, no longer want to be restrained by the physical place where their funds and information are stored and wish the banking facility to come to their home/business place rather than in branches of banks. This has given rise to the concept of the Anywhere Banking facility which offers access to banking services at a place and time convenient to the customers. The use of improved telecommunication-technology has made unhindered information flows possible in real-time, online and industry wide.

However, as the facilities provided by the banks increase, so is an increase in the demands of the customers. The business compulsions steered by telecommunications breakthroughs are putting tremendous pressures on individual banks to continuously evolve new techniques for making business transactions better, faster and more efficient than others.

Impact on Human Resources

Information Technology has resulted in improved efficiency, innovating products and effective delivery system for the banks to help them succeed in the marketplace. The technology has also brought about a visible impact, as discussed below, on the human resources which is the most vital component in the banking business.

- The foremost impact of technology on the existing manpower is manifested in the resistance to the new systems. The fear of change gives rise to anxieties, inhibitions and skepticism, which can be overcome only with spread of awareness at all levels. These fears may be described as follows:
  - Job content: Fears such as whether the technology will mean losing one's' expertise or the personal skills will be adequate to meet the challenges of the new-job.
  - Job security: Fears whether the change will mean a loss of job itself, or whether it would be possible to retain oneself in the new scheme of things, or whether the new computer literate employees will have better job profiles or whether it would mean a hindrance in the career growth.
- Technology when introduced in a planned manner, results in enhanced productivity with better placement of employees. With the increased use of IT, there is an even increased demand of the specialised personal in the fields of IT management.
- Another impact of IT on human resources is the high turnover rate of computer-skilled manpower. In nutshell, the application of IT affects the functional responsibility of every individual involved in the organization and proper trainings help in preparing them for this transition.

ROLE TRANSITION

It is a self-regulating system and its log entails a redefinition of work which manifests itself in the following areas:

- With the application of IT, the job profiles and role definitions undergo a complete transformation.
- With the shift of decision-making powers to the point of information, there is also a visible change in the responsibility structure in banks and
- The increased competition stemmed by the use of IT in banks has underlined the need for technically literate and managerially competent persons to help the line management understand their own needs and built their own systems.

IMPACT ON PRIVACY AND CONFIDENTIALITY OF DATA

The concern for misuse of the stored data becomes more profound when the stored data pertain to financial transactions of individuals. Customers feel threatened about the inadequacy of privacy being maintained by the banks with regard to their transactions and look at computerized systems with suspicion.

Whereas inadvertent disclosure may occur when a system rashes and the contents of a user's files get publicly displayed on terminal the serious problem is that of unauthorized disclosures when a person having access rights uses the data for unintended purposes.

Therefore, data privacy assumes two significant dimensions, *viz.*: * the authority to access data, and * the authority to use data only for specified purposes.

The Following principles are broadly common in privacy laws.

- The data about individuals which is held for processing must have been obtained fairly for a specific lawful purpose only.
- The data must be accurate, up-to-date and kept no longer than necessary.
- The data collection of some individual attributes like racial origin, political philosophy, religious views, etc., should be prohibited.
- Special measures over and above the normal computer security procedures should be taken to preserve the privacy personal data.
- Data must be used only for the specific purpose and may be disclosed in accordance with the specific purpose only.

With the adoption of information technology by the banks, the issue of data privacy becomes more relevant particularly in the context of transactions carried through the Electronic Funds Transfer Systems and settlement taking place through RTGS system.

FUNCTIONS OF COMMERCIAL BANKS

PRIMARY FUNCTION

Accepting Deposits

It is the most important function of commercial banks. They accept deposits in several forms according to requirements of different sections of the society. The main kinds of deposits are:

Current Account Deposits or Demand Deposits: These deposits refer to those deposits which are repayable by the banks on demand:

- Such deposits are generally maintained by businessmen with the intention of making transactions with such deposits.
- They can be drawn upon by a cheque without any restriction.
- Banks do not pay any interest on these accounts. Rather, banks impose service charges for running these accounts.

Fixed Deposits or Time Deposits: Fixed deposits refer to those deposits, in which the amount is deposited with the bank for a fixed period of time.

- Such deposits do not enjoy cheque-able facility.
- These deposits carry a high rate of interest.

Basis	Demand Deposits	Fixed Deposits
Cheque facility	They are chequeable deposits.	They are non-chequeable deposits.
Interest payments	They do not carry any interest.	They carry interest which varies directly with the period of time.
Number of transactions	The depositor can make any number of transactions for deposit or with drawl of money.	Depositor generally makes only two transactions: (i) Deposit of Money in the beginning;(ii) Withdrawal of money on maturity.

Saving Deposits: These deposits combine features of both current account deposits and fixed deposits:

- The depositors are given cheque facility to withdraw money from their account. But, some restrictions are imposed on number and amount of withdrawals, in order to discourage frequent use of saving deposits.
- They carry a rate of interest which is less than interest rate on fixed deposits. It must be noted that Current Account deposits and saving deposits are chequable deposits, whereas, fixed deposit is a non-chequable deposit.

ADVANCING OF LOANS

The deposits received by banks are not allowed to remain idle. So, after keeping certain cash reserves, the balance is given to needy borrowers and interest is charged from them, which is the main source of income for these banks. Different types of loans and advances made by Commercial banks are:

Cash Credit

Cash credit refers to a loan given to the borrower against his current assets like shares, stocks, bonds, etc. A credit limit is sanctioned and the amount is credited in his account. The borrower may withdraw any amount within his credit limit and interest is charged on the amount actually withdrawn.

Demand Loans

Demand loans refer to those loans which can be recalled on demand by the bank at any time. The entire sum of demand loan is credited to the account and interest is payable on the entire sum.

Short-term Loans

They are given as personal loans against some collateral security. The money is credited to the account of borrower and the borrower can withdraw money from his account and interest is payable on the entire sum of loan granted.

SECONDARY FUNCTIONS

Overdraft Facility

It refers to a facility in which a customer is allowed to overdraw his current account upto an agreed limit. This facility is generally given to respectable and reliable customers for a short period.

Customers have to pay interest to the bank on the amount overdrawn by them.

Discounting Bills of Exchange

It refers to a facility in which holder of a bill of exchange can get the bill discounted with bank before the maturity. After deducting the commission, bank pays the balance to the holder. On maturity, bank gets its payment from the party which had accepted the bill.

Agency Functions

Commercial banks also perform certain agency functions for their customers. For these services, banks charge some commission from their clients.

Some of the agency functions are:

Transfer of Funds

Banks provide the facility of economical and easy remittance of funds from place-to-place with the help of instruments like demand drafts, mail transfers, etc.

Collection and Payment of Various Items

Commercial banks collect cheques, bills,' interest, dividends, subscriptions, rents and other periodical receipts on behalf of their customers and also make payments of taxes, insurance premium, etc. on standing instructions of their clients.

Purchase and Sale of Foreign Exchange

Some commercial banks are authorized by the central bank to deal in foreign exchange. They buy and sell foreign exchange on behalf of their customers and help in promoting international trade.

Purchase and Sale of Securities

Commercial banks buy and sell stocks and shares of private companies as well as government securities on behalf of their customers.

Income Tax Consultancy

They also give advice to their customers on matters relating to income tax and even prepare their income tax returns.

Trustee and Executor

Commercial banks preserve the wills of their customers as trustees and execute them after their death as executors.

Letters of Reference

They give information about the economic position of their customers to traders and provide the similar information about other traders to their customers.

GENERAL UTILITY FUNCTIONS

Commercial banks render some general utility services like:

Locker Facility

Commercial banks provide facility of safety vaults or lockers to keep valuable articles of customers in safe custody.

Traveller's Cheques

Commercial banks issue traveler's cheques to their customers to avoid risk of taking cash during their journey.

Letter of Credit

They also issue letters of credit to their customers to certify their creditworthiness.

Underwriting Securities

Commercial banks also undertake the task of underwriting securities. As public has full faith in the creditworthiness of banks, public do not hesitate in buying the securities underwritten by banks.

Collection of Statistics

Banks collect and publish statistics relating to trade, commerce and industry. Hence, they advice customers on financial matters. Commercial banks receive deposits from the public and use these deposits to give loans. However, loans offered are many times more than the deposits received by banks. This function of banks is known as 'Money Creation'.

DEFINITIONS OF COMMERCIAL BANKS

INTRODUCTION TO BANKS

Banks have developed around 200 years ago. The natures of banks have changed as the time has changed. The term bank is related to financial transactions. It is a financial establishment which uses, money deposited by customers for investment, pays it out when required, makes loans at interest exchanges currency etc. however to understand the concept in detail we need to see some of its definitions. Many economists have tried to give different meanings of the term bank.

NATURE OF COMMERCIAL BANKS

Commercial banks are an organisation which normally performs certain financial transactions. It performs the twin task of accepting deposits from members of public and make advances to needy and worthy people form the society. When banks accept deposits its liabilities increase and it becomes a debtor, but when it makes advances its assets increases and it becomes a creditor. Banking transactions are socially and legally approved. It is responsible in maintaining the deposits of its account holders.

DEFINITIONS OF COMMERCIAL BANKS

While defining the term banks it is taken into account that what type of task is performed by the banks. Some of the famous definitions are given below:

According to Prof. Sayers, "A bank is an institution whose debts are widely accepted in settlement of other people's debts to each other." In this definition Sayers has emphasized the transactions from debts which are raised by a financial institution.

According to the Indian Banking Company Act 1949, "A banking company means any company which transacts the business of banking. Banking means accepting for the purpose of lending of investment of deposits of money from the public, payable on demand or other wise and withdraw able by cheque, draft or otherwise."

FUNCTIONS OF COMMERCIAL BANKS

Commercial bank being the financial institution performs diverse types of functions. It satisfies the financial needs of the sectors such as agriculture, industry, trade, communication, etc. That means they play very significant role in a process of economic social needs. The functions performed by banks are changing according to change in time and recently they are becoming customer centric and widening their functions. Generally the functions of commercial banks are divided into two categories *viz.* primary functions and the secondary functions. The following chart simplifies the functions of banks.

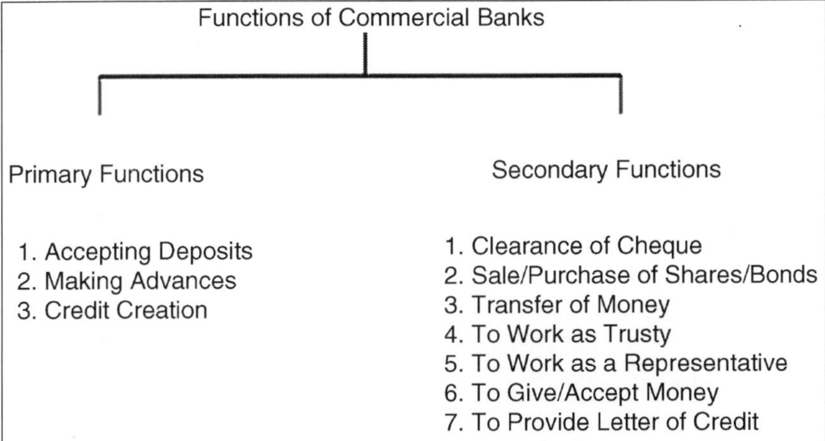

PRIMARY FUNCTIONS OF COMMERCIAL BANKS

Commercial Banks performs various primary functions some of them are given below

Accepting Deposits: Commercial bank accepts various types of deposits from public especially from its clients. It includes saving account deposits, recurring account deposits, fixed deposits, etc. These deposits are payable after a certain time period.

Making Advances: The commercial banks provide loans and advances of various forms. It includes an over draft facility, cash credit, bill discounting, etc. They also give demand and demand and term loans to all types of clients against proper security.

Credit creation: It is most significant function of the commercial banks. While sanctioning a loan to a customer, a bank does not provide cash to the borrower Instead it opens a deposit account from where the borrower can withdraw. In other words while sanctioning a loan a bank automatically creates deposits. This is known as a credit creation from commercial bank.

SECONDARY FUNCTIONS OF COMMERCIAL BANKS

Along with the primary functions each commercial bank has to perform several secondary functions too. It includes many agency functions or general utility functions. The secondary functions of commercial banks can be divided into agency functions and utility functions.

Agency Functions: Various agency functions of commercial banks are

- To collect and clear cheque, dividends and interest warrant.
- To make payment of rent, insurance premium, etc.
- To deal in foreign exchange transactions.
- To purchase and sell securities.
- To act as trusty, attorney, correspondent and executor.
- To accept tax proceeds and tax returns.
- General Utility Functions: The general utility functions of the commercial banks include
- To provide safety locker facility to customers.
- To provide money transfer facility.
- To issue traveller's cheque.
- To act as referees.
- To accept various bills for payment *e.g.* phone bills, gas bills, water bills, etc.
- To provide merchant banking facility.
- To provide various cards such as credit cards, debit cards, Smart cards, etc.

MEANING AND DEFINATION OF COMMERCIAL BANK

In modern economy commercial Banks Play an important role in the financial sector. A Bank is an institution dealing in money and credit. Credit money is the major component of money supply in a modern economy. Commercial banks are the creators of credit.

The strength of economy of any country basically depends on a sound and solvent banking system. A Commercial bank is a profit seeking business firms dealing in money or rather claims to money. It safeguards the savings of the public and give loans and advances. The Banking Companies Act of 1949, defines banking company as "accepting for the purpose of lending or investment of deposit money from the public, repayable on demand or otherwise and withdrawable by cheque, drafts, order or otherwise".

FUNCTIONS OF COMMERCIAL BANKS

Modern commercial banks perform a variety of functions. They keep the wheels of commerce, trade and industry always revolving. Major functions of a commercial bank are: - Primary or Banking functions and Secondary or Non-Banking functions.

Primary/ Banking Functions

Commercial banks have two important banking functions. One is accepting deposits and other is advancing loans.

1. *Deposits*: One of the main function of a bank is to accept deposits from the public. Deposits are accepted by the banks in various forms.
   - *Current Account Deposits*: Current Accounts are usually opened by businessmen who have a number of regular transactions with the bank, both deposits and withdrawls. There is no restriction on number and amount of deposits. There is also no restriction on withdrawls. No interest is paid on current deposits. Banks may even charge interest for providing this facility. These accounts are also known as demand deposits as amount can be withdrawn on demand.
   - *Saving Account Deposits*: Saving Accounts are opened by salaried and other less income people. There is no restriction on number and amount of deposits. withdrawls are subject to certain restrictions. It earns Interest but less than fixed deposits. It encourages saving habit among salary earners and others. Saving deposits are an important source of funds for banks.
   - *Fixed Account Deposits*: Deposits in fixed account are time deposits. Money under this account is deposited for a certain fixed period of time varying from 15 days to several years. A high rate of interest is paid. If money is withdrawn before expiry date, the depositor receives lower rate of interest. Deposits can be renewed for further period. Many banks sanction loans against security of fixed deposits.
   - *Recurring Account Deposits*: In Recurring deposit, a specified amount is regularly deposited by account holder, at an internal of usually a month. This is to form the habit of small savings among the people. At the end of maturity period, the account holder gets a substantial amount. Interest on this type of deposit is almost equal to fixed deposits.

Thus by creating variety of deposits, banks motivate people in a variety of ways and encourage savings in the economy.

2. *Loans And Advances*: Banks not only mobilize money but also lend to its credit worthy customers for maximizing profits. Loans and Advances are granted To:-
   - *Business And Trade*: Commercial banks grant short-term loans to business and trade activities in following forms:-
   - *Overdraft*: Commercial banks grant overdraft facility to current account holders Under this system a borrower is allowed to draw more than what is deposited in his account. The borrower is

granted to a fixed additional amount against collateral security. Interest is charged for actual amount drawn.

- *Cash Credit*: Cash credit is given by the bank to any businessman to meet regular working capital needs, against the security of goods or personal security. Interest is charged on actual amount drawn by the customer.
- *Discounting Of Bills*: When the holder of the bill is not in a position to wait till the maturity of the bill and requires cash urgently, he sells the bill of exchange to bank. Bank advance credit by discounting bills of exchange, government securities or any other approved financial instruments. The bank purchases the instruments at a discount.
- *Money At Call*: Banks also grant loans for a very short period, generally not exceeding 7 days. Such advances are repayable immediately at a short notice hence they are called as Money at Call or Call money. These loans are given to dealers or brokers in stock market against Collateral Securities.
- *Direct Loans*: Loans are given to customers against the security of moveable properties. Their maturity varies from 1 to 10 years. Interest has to be paid on entire loan amount sanctioned. Loans are of many types like:- personal loans, term loans, call loans, participative loans, collateral loans etc.
- *Loans to Agriculture*: Banks grant short-term credit to agriculture at a lower rate of interest. Loans are granted for irrigation, purchase of equipments, inputs, cattle etc.
- *Loans To Industries*: Banks grant secured loans to small and medium scale industries to meet their working capital needs. The time period may be from one to five years. It may be in the form of Overdraft, cash credit or direct loan.
- *Loans To Foreign Trade*: Loans are granted to export and import in the form of direct loans, discounting of bills, guarantee for deferred payments etc. Here the rate of interest is low.
- *Consumer Credit/ Personal loans*: Banks also grant credit to household in a limited amount to buy some durable consumer goods like television sets, refrigerators, washing machine etc. Such consumer credit is repayable in installments. Under 20-point programme, the scope of consumer credit has been extended to cover expenses on marriage, funeral etc., as well.
- *Miscellaneous Advances*: Banks also gives advances like packing credits to exporters, export bill purchased or discounted, import finance, finance to self-employed, credit to weaker sections of society at concessional rates etc.

II. *Secondary/ Non-banking Functions:*

Banks gives various forms of services to public. Such services are termed as non- banking or secondary functions:-

1. *Agency Services*: Banks perform certain functions on behalf of their customers. While performing these services, banks act as agents to their customers, hence these are called as agency services. Important agency functions are:-
   - *Collection*: Commercial banks collect cheques, drafts, bills, promissory notes, dividends, subscriptions, rents and any other receipts which are to be received by the customer. For these services banks charge a nominal amount.
   - *Payment*: Banks also makes payments on behalf of their customers like paying insurance premium, rent, taxes, electricity and telephone bills etc for such services commission is charged.
   - *Income – Tax Consultant*: Commercial banks acts as income-tax consultants. They prepare and finalise the income tax returns of their clients.
   - *Sale And Purchase Of Financial Assets*: As per the customers instruction banks undertake sale and purchase of securities, shares and any other financial assets. Nominal charges are charged by a bank.
   - *Trustee, Executor And Attorney*: As a trustee, banks becomes the custodian and manager of customer funds. Bank also acts as executor of deceased customer's will. As an Attorney the banks sign the documents on behalf of customer.
   - *E- Banking*: Through Electronic Banking, a customer can operate his bank account through internet. He can make payments of various bills. He can even transfer money from one place to another.

Utility Services

Modern Commercial banks also performs certain general utility services for the community, such as:

- *Letter of Credit*: Banks also deal in foreign trade. They issue letter of credit and provide guarantee to foreign traders for the soundness of their customers.
- *Transfer of Funds:* Banks arrange transfer of funds cheaply and safely from one place to another. Transfer can be in the form of Demand draft, Mail transfer Travellers cheques etc.
- *Guarantor*: Banks offer a guarantee of payment on behalf of importer to facilitate imports with deferred payments.
- *Underwriting*: This facility is provided to Joint Stock Companies and

to government to enable them to raise funds. Banks guarantee the purchase of certain proportion of shares, if not sold in the market.

- *Locker Facility*: Safe Lockers are provided to the customers. So that they can deposit their valuables like Jewellary, Securities, Shares and otherdocuments.
- *Referee*: Banks may act as referee with respect to financial standing, business reputation and respectability of customers.
- *Credit Cards*: Credit card facility have been introduced by commercial banks. It enables the holder to minimize the use of hard cash. Credit card is a convenient medium of exchange which enables its holder to buy goods and services from member – establishment without using money.

Subsidiary Activities

Many commercial banks also undertakes subsidiary activities such as:

- *Housing Finance*: Housing finance is provided against the security of immoveable property of land and buildings. Many banks such as SBI, Bank of India etc. have set up housing finance subsidiaries.
- *Mutual Funds*: A Mutual fund is a financial intermediary that pools the savings of investors for collective investment in diversified portfolio securities Many banks like SBI, Indian Bank etc. have set up mutual fund subsidiaries.
- *Merchant Banking*: A variety of services are offered by merchant banking like:-
  - Management, Marketing and Underwriting of new issues, project promotion, corporate advisory services, investment advisory services etc.
- *Venture Capital Fund:* Venture capital fund provides start-up share capital to new ventures of little known, unregistered, risky, young and small private business, especially in technology oriented and knowledge intensive business. Many commercial banks like SBI, Canara Bank etc. have set up venture Capital Fund Subsidiaries.
- *Factoring*: Factoring is a continuing arrangement between a financial intermediary (factor) and a business concern (client) where by the factor purchases the clients accounts recieveable. Banks like SBI and Canara Bank have established subsidiaries to provide factoring services.

Thus various services are provided by commercial Banks.

SIGNIFICANCE OF COMMERCIAL BANKS

Commercial banks play such an important role in the economic development of a country that modern industrial economy cannot exist without them. They constitute nerve centre of production, trade and industry of a country. In the words of Wick-sell, "Bank is the heart and central point of modern exchange economy."

The following points highlight the significance of commercial banks:

- They promote savings and accelerate the rate of capital formation.
- They are source of finance and credit for trade and industry.
- They promote balanced regional development by opening branches in backward areas.
- Bank credit enables entrepreneurs to innovate and invest which accelerates the process of economic development.
- They help in promoting large-scale production and growth of priority sectors such as agriculture, small-scale industry, retail trade and export.
- They create credit in the sense that they are able to give more loans and advances than the cash position of the depositor's permits.
- They help commerce and industry to expand their field of operation.
- Thus, they make optimum utilisation of resources possible.

MULTIPLE CREDIT CREATION BY COMMERCIAL BANKS

Creation of credit is an important function of a commercial bank. Prof. Sayers said "Banks are not merely purveyors of money but, also in an important sense manufacturers of money". In a modern economy Bank's deposits form a major proportion of total money supply.

A bank's demand deposits arise mainly from:- Cash deposits by customers and Bank Loans and Investments.

CASH DEPOSITS BY CUSTOMERS

These are termed as primary deposits as they arise from the actual deposits of cash in a bank made by its customers. In receiving such deposits, the bank plays a passive role. The creation of primary deposits, however is nothing but transforming the currency money in to deposit money.

BANK LOANS AND INVESTMENTS

These are termed as derivative or active deposits. The derivative deposits are lent in the form of loans or advances, discounting of bills or used for purchasing securities or other assets.

Deposit account in the name of the customer or seller, credits him with the amount of loan granted or value of security purchased, subject to withdrawl by cheque, as required. Hence loans advanced or purchases of securities creates deposits.

Thus every loan creates a deposit. They increase the quantity of bank money. The size of derivative demand deposits is determined by the banks lending and investment activities. There will be a constant inflow and outflow of cash with the banks. For the sake of liquidity and safety some proportion of total deposit must be maintained in cash, for *e.g.*:- 10 per cent to 20 per cent to meet the demand for cash at the counter. This is known as Cash Reserve Ratio.

Primary deposits serve as a basis for creating derivative deposits, that is credit creation, and for increasing money supply. Commercial banks are profit seeking institutions and when they find that large volume of cash received lies Idle, they use these resources for advancing loans or for making investment in securities, shares etc. there by earning high rate of interest.

The creation of credit also depends on excess cash reserves or cash reserve ratio. The derivative deposits are used as working capital.

When the borrower withdraws money from his loan account by cheque it is deposited by the payee in some other bank. Those banks again create deposit on the basis of fresh deposits received after keeping required reserves. Ultimately, the total volume of credit or derivative deposits or bank money created by all banks would be a multiple of the original amount of new cash reserves in the system. Thus multiple expansion of credit takes place.

Example: Suppose the Cash Reserve Ratio is 20 per cent and a person deposits ₹ 10,000/- with Bank of India. This is primary deposit. The bank keeps ₹ 2000 as CRR and balance of ₹ 8000 is used for granting credit.

Now suppose Bank of India lends ₹ 8000 to Mr. A and Mr. A pays a cheque of ₹ 8000 to Mr. B, who has an account in Bank Of baroda.

Then Bank Of Baroda receives ₹ 8000 as primary deposit. It keeps ₹ 1,600 (20 per cent) as CRR and excess amount of ₹ 6,400 is used for giving credit. Now if, Mr. C is granted this loan and Mr.C gives a cheque of ₹ 6,400 to another person who may deposit it in Bank of Maharashtra. Bank of Maharashtra will keep ₹ 1,280 as CRR and issue a loan of ₹ 5,120. This process continues until the original excess reserves of ₹ 8000 with the first Bank of India, have been parceled out among various banks and have been required resources. As a result, the aggregate of derivative deposits in the entire banking system, approximates 5 times the initial derivative deposit over a period of time.

Let us explain with the help of table:

Table. Process of Multiple Expansion of Credit

Banks	Primary Deposit	CRR20%	Credit Creation or Creation of Derivative Deposits
Bank of India	10,000	2000	8000
Bank of Baroda	8,000	1,600	6,400
Bank of Maharashtra	6,400	1,280	5,120
Total of all Banks	50,000	10,000	40,000

In the above Eg., the credit expansion is five times the initial excess reserve of ₹ 8,000 when CRR is 20%.

$$TC = \frac{PD - PCR}{CRR} x100$$

Symbolically,
Where TC = Total Credit
PD = Primary Deposit.
PCR = Primary cash Reserve.
CCR = Cash Reserve Ratio.

$$\text{Cash Creation } = \frac{10000 - 2000}{20} x100 = \frac{8000x100}{20} = ₹40,000$$

The Credit Multiplier depends on CRR.
r = CRR
If CRR is 20 per cent then, credit multiplier will be
The Multiple expansion of credit is the inverse of CRR maintained by banks. Higher the CRR,
Lower the expansion of credit and vice versa.

LIMITATIONS OF CREDIT CREATION

Commercial banks do not have unlimited powers of deposit or credit creation, because their activities in this direction are subject to a number of restrictions, such as:-

AMOUNT OF CASH

The larger the amount of cash with banking system, the greater will be the excess funds, and that larger will be the credit creation power of the bank. The banks power of creating money or credit is thus limited by cash it can get in its hands on, primarily through primary deposits.

Cash Reserve Ratio

Higher the cash reserve ratio, smaller the volume of credit creation and vice versa. If CRR falls to a certain minimum, then power of the banks to create credit is limited.

External Drain

External drain refers to the withdrawl of cash from the banking system by public. Every rupee in cash that is withdrawn from the banking system, lowers the reserves of the banks and thus checks further deposit expansion.

Willingness to Borrow

Credit creation will be larger during a period of business prosperity and smaller during a depression. Bankers cannot create credit at will. The amount of credit is conditioned by the needs and will of the borrowers.

Supply of Collateral Securities

The availability of good securities places one more limitation on the power of banks to create money. If approved securities are not available, the bank cannot create credit without inviting trouble. "The bank does not create money out of thin air, it transmutes other forms of wealth in to money.

Banking Habits and Banking System

In the absence of banking habits and banking system, credit creation will be impossible. The banking habit will become popular only if there is a sound, developed banking system.

Monetary Policy of Control Bank

The Central bank has the power to influence the volume of money in the country and from time to time, use various methods of credit control and thus its influences the banks to expand or contract credit.

BALANCE SHEET OF COMMERCIAL BANKS

Banks are the most important financial intermediary in an economy. Banks performance can be analysed by its balance sheet and profit and loss account. Bank publish balance sheet in their annual accounts. The balance sheet of a commercial Bank is a statement of its liabilities and Assets at a particular time. Liabilities show the sources of funds through which bank raises funds for its business. Assets represents uses of funds to generate income for bank. Thus, the balance sheet indicates the manner in which bank has raised funds and invested them in various types of assets. It is customary to state liabilities on left and assets on right side. A model of balance sheet of a bank is given below:-

Table. Balance sheet of a commercial bank

Liabilities	Assets
1. Share Capital (paid up)	1. Cash Balances a) With Central Bank b) With other Banks
2. Reserves and surplus	2. Money at call and short notice.
3. *Deposits*: a. Time deposits. b. Demand Deposits c. Saving Deposits	3. Bills discounted, including treasury bills.
4. Borrowings	4. Investments
5. Other Liabilities	5. Loans and Advances
	6. Other Assets.

LIABILITIES OF A COMMERCIAL BANK (LIABILITIES PORTFOLIO)

The liabilities of a commercial bank shos how the bank raises funds for its business.

- *Share Capital (Paid-up):* It is the contribution made by the shareholders of the bank. This indicates the bank's liabilities to its shareholders.

- *Reserves And Surplus:* It is the amount accumulated over the years out of undistributed profits to meet contingencies. Reserves and surplus are liabilities of the bank, as they belong to its shareholders.
- *Deposits:* Deposits from the public constitute the biggest proportion of banks working funds. The deposits accepted by bank in current, fixed and savings account are liabilities of bank to t5heir customers. They are categorized as demand, time and saving deposits. These funds are liabilities of bank to their customers, which have to be returned to them. But at the same time, these funds are also assets to bank since the banker can make use of them to get certain interest yielding assets.
- *Borrowings:* When a bank borrows from other banks liability is created. It consist of borrowing/ refinance obtained from RBI, commercial banks and other financial institutions. It also includes overseas borrowings.
- *Other Liabilities:* In course of its business, miscellaneous liabilities are incurred by bank. They include bills payable like drafts, travelers cheques, pay slips etc. It also includes income tax provision.

Assets of a Commercial Bank (Assets Portfolio)

The assets portfolio shows how the bank uses the funds entrusted to it:

- *Cash Balances:* A bank holds cash to meet the day-today withdrawls of deposits by its customer. This is known as cash reserve. Bank hold cash balances with itself, with other banks and with RBI. In India, Commercial Banks are obliged to keep a certain proportion of total deposits in the form of cash reserve requirement with RBI. Cash has perfect liquidity, but yields no profit.
- *Money at Call and Short Notice*: It refers to short term loans made in money market. Such loans are borrowed by speculators in stock exchange market. Their maturity vary between one day to 15 days. These loans are repayable on demand and at the option of either lender or borrower. Thus, these forms of assets are highly liquid and are interest earning too, though at a comparatively low rate.
- *Bills Discounted*: Banks funds are invested in commercial bills which are short-dated, usually three months. Banks also invest in treasury bills. These assets are self-liquidating in nature.
- *Investments:* Investment in various kinds of securities is a major part of assets of a bank. Mainly commercial banks invest in government securities, shares etc. Securities and bonds are known as banks secondary reserves because they are shiftable and Interest yielding.

Usually banks prefer medium and short term securities. This secondary reserve fails to convert securities in to cash at the same time.

- *Loans And Advances:* The most important asset item in the Balance sheet of a bank is loans advances. The profitability of a bank depends upon the extent to which it grants loans advances to customers. The various types of loans advances provided by banks are: Cash Credit, Overdraft, Loans, Installments, purchase and discounting of Bills. Banks mostly grant short term working capital loans only so that they can have fair liquidity with high profitability.
- *Other Assets:* It includes fixed assets, furniture and fixtures etc. It will also include the net position of inter-office account.

From above assets and liabilities, banks will have to balance their revenues against expenses in such a way to generate income to sustain profitability from business.

Objectives of Portfolio Management (Trade-off Between Liquidity and Profitability)

A commercial bank has to manage its assets and liabilities with three objectives in mind, namely:- Liquidity, profitability and solvency.

Liquidity means the capacity of the bank to give cash on demand in exchange for deposits. But a commercial bank is a profit – seeking institution. It has to arrange its assets in such a way that it makes maximum profits. The bank should also maintain the confidence of public by making cash available on demand. Liquidity and profitability are, therefore, conflicting considerations for bankers. Cash has perfect liquidity but yields no return at all, while other income-yielding assets such as loans are profitable but have no liquidity. The bank should strike a balance between liquidity and profitability. Another consideration of the bank is its own solvency and security. This refers to liquidity and shiftability. Liquidity is the capacity to produce cash on demand. Shiftability means the assets acquired by bank should be easily shiftable to other banks or central bank. Those securities would be preferred by a bank which can be shifted easily without any loss to the bank than the risky and more profitable ones.

A bank which is solvent may not be liquid. Its assets may exceed its liabilities, but the assets may not be in such a form that they are readily convertible in to cash. Thus, the two motives of a bank's liquidity and profitability are contradictory, but have to be reconciled. A good banker is one who follows a wise investment policy and distributes the assets in such a way that both the requirements of liquidity and profitability are satisfied. The assets should bring in maximum profits and should provide maximum security to the depositors. The secret of success of a bank lies in striking a sound balance between liquidity and profitability.

RECONCILING TWIN OBJECTIVES

A good banker is one who follows a wise investment policy and distributes the assets in such a way that both the requirements of liquidity and profitability are satisfied.

The secret of success of a bank lies in striking a balance between liquidity and profitability. The commercial bank arranges its assets in an ascending order of profitability and descending order of liquidity. As we move down the balance sheet the assets become less and less liquid and more and more profitable. The more liquid the assets, the less profitable it is. Let us Explain:

Cash

Cash balance have perfect liquidity, but no profitability. Cash is held to meet the withdrawl needs of depositors.

Money at Call

Surplus cash of commercial banks is lend to each other. This earns some interest and is also very liquid.

Investment in Securities

Statutorily banks have to invest a part of their assets in government securities. These securities have low rate of interest but banks can borrow from RBI against these securities. Thus investment in securities provide returns as well as liquidity to bank.

Loans and Advances

Here liquidity is low but profitability is high.

Thus banks hold various assets in such a way that the requirements of liquidity and profitability are balanced.

FACTORS AFFECTING LIQUIDITY OF BANKS

The amount of liquid assets held by bank, depends upon the following factors:

Statutory Requirements

Every commercial bank has to keep a minimum cash balance by law. The extent of reserves held by bank depends upon the statutory requirements like CRR and SLR. These limits are fixed by central bank. Commercial banks also have to maintain liquid assets in the form of gold and approved securities.

Nature of Money Market

It will be easy for banks to buy and sell securities if the money marketis fully developed. In such case need for cash will be less.

Banking Habits

Banking habits of customers have a direct bearing on banks cash balance and liquidity position. In developed countries for making payments cheques are used hence, the use of cash is less. On other hand, in developing countries banking habits are not fully developed, so banks have to maintain large cash reserves.

Structure of Banks

Under unit banking, every bank is an independent unit and they have to keep a high degree of liquidity. Under branch banking, the cash reserves can be centralized in head office and branches can have smaller liquid reserves.

Business Conditions

In Industrialised countries, business in brisk and speculative activities are undertaken so, the demand for money is large. In agricultural countries, during off season, demand is less so, the banks can manage with small cash balances.

Monetary Transactions

During busy season such as festival times, harvest season, beginning of month etc. banks will have to keep large percentage of cash. Thus, the size of liquid reserves also depend on the number and magnitude of monetary transactions.

Number And Size of Deposits:

When the number and size of deposits rise, banks have to keep more liquidity and vice versa.

Nature of Deposits

The nature of deposits also determines the liquidity requirements of a bank. Deposits are various types such as time deposits, demand deposits etc. Larger the demand and short term deposits, larger will be liquidity.

Clearing House Facility

When clearing house facilities are available, then large transactions can be made through book adjustments. This will reduce cash requirements of commercial banks.

Liquidity Policy of Other Banks

A Bank which decides to hold large cash balances will have more customers due to goodwill. Hence other bank will also try to improve their liquidity position to attract customers. Thus, the liquidity position of one bank depends on the liquidity policy of other banks. On the whole, we can say by looking in to past experience, each bank has to take its own decision on liquidity requirement.

Factors Affecting Profitability of Banks

- *Cost of Funds:* Share capital, reserves, deposits, borrowing and other liabilities are the sources of funds for bank. The cost of funds refers to interest expenses.
- *Yield on Funds:* Banks fund are used for different sources like CRR, SLR requirement, loans and Advances etc. Many of these give rise to yields mainly in terms of interest income. This depends on the portfolio management of banks.
- *Spread:* The difference between interest income and interest expenses in defined as spread. High interest spreads shows the level of efficiency and a relatively less competitive market.
- *Non-Interest Income*: Non-Interest income is income derived from non-financial asset and services and includes commission and brokerage on remittance facilities, guarantees underwriting, contracts etc, locker rentals and other service charges.
- *Amount of Working Capital*: Profitability is directly related to the amount of working funds deployed by banks. Working funds are funds deployed by a bank in its business.
- *Non performing Assets*: Profitability also depends on NPAs. Larger the NPAs lower will be the profitability and vice versa.
- *Competition:* When the level of Competition increases, there is fall in margins and hence it results in lower profitability.
- *Operating cost:* If operating cost are higher, profitability of banks will be lower and vice versa. Operating cost includes:- Salaries, bonus, gratuity, expenses on stationery, printing, rent, depreciation etc.
- *Risk Cost:* Risk cost is the cost which is likely to be incurred on annual loss on assets. For *e.g.*:- provisions for bad and doubtful debts is included under this head. Thus risk cost also affects the profitability of banks.
- *Burden*: The total non-interest expenses representing the transaction cost will generally be more than miscellaneous income. The difference between the two is known as Burden. Higher the burden, lesser will be the profitability of banks.

Thus from above we can say that the objectives of liquidity and profitability have to be reconciled. A successful banker will adopt a prudent investment policy keeping the requirements of liquidity and profitability.

ROLE, STRUCTURES AND IMPORTANCE IN COMMERCIAL BANKS

ROLE AND IMPORTANCE OF COMMERCIAL BANKS

The functions of commercial banks explain their importance in the economic development of a country.

Banks help in accelerating the economic growth of a country in the following ways:

- *Accelerating the Rate of Capital Formation*: Commercial banks encourage the habit of thrift and mobilise the savings of people. These savings are effectively allocated among the ultimate users of funds, *i.e.*, investors for productive investment. So, savings of people result in capital formation which forms the basis of economic development.
- *Provision of Finance and Credit*: Commercial banks are a very important source of finance and credit for trade and industry. The activities of commercial banks are not only confined to domestic trade and commerce, but extend to foreign trade also.
- *Developing Entrepreneurship*: Banks promote entrepreneurship by underwriting the shares of new and existing companies and granting assistance in promoting new ventures or financing promotional activities. Banks finance sick (loss-making) industries for making them viable units.
- *Promoting Balanced Regional Development*: Commercial banks provide credit facilities to rural people by opening branches in the backward areas. The funds collected in developed regions may be channelised for investments in the under developed regions of the country. In this way, they bring aboutmore balanced regional development.
- *Help to Consumers*: Commercial banks advance credit for purchase of durable consumer items like Vehicles, T.V., refrigerator etc., which are out of reach for some consumers due to their limited paying capacity. In this way, banks help in creating demand for such consumer goods.

Structure of Commercial Banks in India

The commercial banks can be broadly classified under two heads:

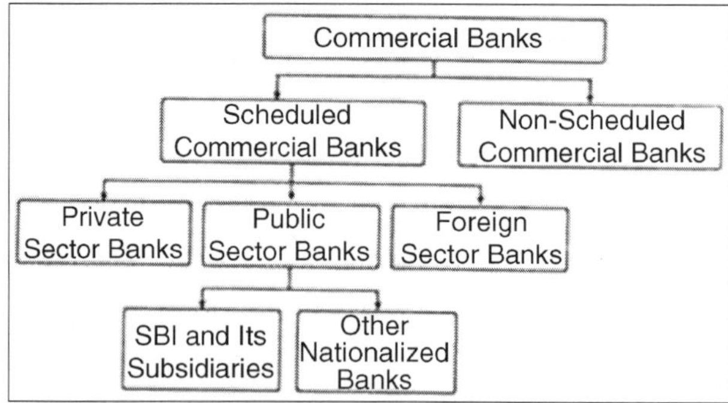

Scheduled Banks

Scheduled Banks refer to those banks which have been included in the Second Schedule of Reserve Bank of India Act, 1934.

In India, scheduled commercial banks are of three types:

- Public Sector Banks: These banks are owned and controlled by the government. The main objective of these banks is to provide service to the society, not to make profits. State Bank of India, Bank of India, Punjab National Bank, Canada Bank and Corporation Bank are some examples of public sector banks.

Public sector banks are of two types:

  - SBI and its subsidiaries;
  - Other nationalized banks.

- Private Sector Banks: These banks are owned and controlled by private businessmen. Their main objective is to earn profits. ICICI Bank, HDFC Bank, IDBI Bank is some examples of private sector banks.
- Foreign Banks: These banks are owned and controlled by foreign promoters. Their number has grown rapidly since 1991, when the process of economic liberalization had started in India. Bank of America, American Express Bank, Standard Chartered Bank are examples of foreign banks.

Non-Scheduled Banks

Non-Scheduled banks refer to those banks which are not included in the Second Schedule of Reserve Bank of India Act, 1934.

TYPES AND FUNCTIONS OF COMMERCIAL BANKS

Commercial Banks: Types and Functions of Commercial Banks of India!

A bank is an institution where debts (usually referred to as bank deposits) are commonly accepted in final settlement of other peoples' debts. Yet another definition defines banking as "the accepting for the purpose of lending,investment of deposits of money from the public, repayable on demand or otherwise and with drawable by cheques, drafts or otherwise." The modern bank thus, carries out several functions. It provides safe custody for those savers who want to put their savings with it and earns an income also, offers facilities to the busy businessmen or professional as the cheque facility, thus making the flow of payments and receipts easier while at the same time acting as the custodian of their funds. It also provides finance for the needy ones by allowing overdraft and loan facilities by creating credit.

TYPES OF BANKING

Banks can be classified into different groups either on the basis of their structure or on the basis of their function. Structurally banking can be divided into Branch banking and Unit Banking. Functionally, banking can be divided into Deposit Banking, Investment Banking and Mixed Banking.

Branch Banking

This refers to a system under which two or more banks are opened under a single ownership. Examples are State Bank of India, Punjab National Bank, Indian Bank etc. which have several branches spread all-over India.

Unit Banking

This refers to that system of banking in which banking operations are carried on through a single organisation, without any branches. This system used to be popular in America.

One great advantage of branch banking is that the same bank can cater to several parts of a large country (through its branches situated in those parts) which a unit bank would find difficult to do. As against this, a unit bank has the advantage that its efforts are concentrated in one area so that it can serve that area well.

Group Banking

This is a system under which two or more banks, separately incorporated, are connected by being controlled by a single holding company as trust.

Chain Banking

This is similar to Group Banking. Here two or more banks are controlled by a single group through the ownership of shares or otherwise.

Deposit Banking

In this category, the banks act as custodian or trustees of the depositors.

Investment Banking

This refers to banks whose main function is to provide finance for investment to industrial concerns. They provide this by purchasing shares and debentures of newly floated companies.

Mixed Banking

Most banks in India play both roles. Deposit Banking and Investment Banking. Such type of banking is called mixed banking.

FUNCTIONS OF COMMERCIAL BANKS

The major functions of Commercial Banks are as follows:

Acceptance of Deposits

The main function of commercial banks is to accept deposits from the public. Banks maintains demand deposits accounts for their customers and converts deposit money into cash and vice versa, at the direction of the latter. Demand deposits are technically accepted in current accounts, which are with draw able any time by the depositor by means of cheques. Deposits are made in fixed deposit accounts which are with draw able only after a specific period. Thus, fixed deposits are time liabilities of the banks. Deposits are also received in saving bank accounts subject to certain restrictions on the amount receivable and with draw able. This is how banks pool the scattered savings of the community and serve as the reserves of its savings.

Giving Loans and Advances

Another function of commercial banks is to extend loans and advances out of the money which comes to them by way of deposits to businessmen and entrepreneurs against approved securities such as gold or silver bullion, government securities, easily saleablestocks and shares and marketable goods.

Bank advances to customers may be made in the following ways:

- Overdrafts,
- Discounting bills,
- Money-at-call and short notice,
- Loans and advances
- Various forms of direct loans to traders and producers.

Using Cheque System

Banks also render important services by providing an expensive medium of exchange, such as cheques. In modern business transactions, the use of cheques to settle debts is found to be much more convenient than the use of cash. In fact, the cheque is also known as the most developed credit instrument.

Other Functions

Commercial banks also perform a multitude of other non-banking functions which may be classified as (a) agency services and (b) general utility services.

- *Agency services*: The bankers perform certain functions for and on behalf of their customers, such as:
  - To act as executor, trustee and attorney for the customer's will.
  - To collect or make payments for bills, cheques, promissory notes, interest, dividends, rents, subscriptions, insurance premium, etc. For these services, some charges are usually levied by the banks.
  - To remit funds on behalf of the clients by drafts or mail or telegraphic transfers.
  - To arrange income-tax experts to prepare income tax returns for their customers, and help them to get refund of income tax in appropriate cases.
  - To work as correspondents, agents or representatives of their clients.
- *General Utility Services*: The modem Commercial banks usually perform certain general utility services for society, such as:

- Bank drafts and traveler's cheques are issued in order to provide facilities for transfer of funds from one part of the country to another.
- Letter of credit may be given by the banks to their customers to enable then to go abroad.
- Dealing with foreign exchange or finance foreign trade by accepting or collecting foreign bills of exchange.
- Shares floated by Government, Public bodies and corporations may be underwritten by banks.
- Banks arrange the safe deposit vaults, to the customers, for their valuables.
- Banks also compile statistics and business information relating to trade, commerce and industry. Some banks may publish valuable journals or bulletins containing research on financial economic and commercial matters.

SECURED LOANS

A secured loan is a loan in which the borrower pledges some asset (*e.g.*, a car or property) as collateral for the loan, which then becomes a secured debt owed to the creditor who gives the loan. The debt is thus secured against the collateral – in the event that the borrower defaults, the creditor takes possession of the asset used as collateral and may sell it to regain some or all of the amount originally lent to the borrower, for example, foreclosed a portion of the bundle of rights to specified property.

If the sale of the collateral does not raise enough money to pay off the debt, the creditor can often obtain a deficiency judgement against the borrower for the remaining amount. The opposite of secured debt/loan is unsecured debt, which is not connected to any specific piece of property and instead the creditor may only satisfy the debt against the borrower rather than the borrower's collateral and the borrower.

A mortgage loan is a very common type of debt instrument, used to purchase real estate. Under this arrangement, the money is used to purchase the property. Commercial banks, however, are given security - a lien on the title to the house - until the mortgage is paid off in full. If the borrower defaults on the loan, the bank would have the legal right to repossess the house and sell it, to recover sums owing to it.

In the past, commercial banks have not been greatly interested in real estate loans and have placed only a relatively small percentage of assets in mortgages. As their name implies, such financial institutions secured their earning primarily from commercial and consumer loans and left the major task of home financing to others. However, changes in banking laws have allowed commercial banks to make more home mortgage loans.

In acquiring mortgages on real estate, these institutions follow two main practices. First, some of the banks maintain active and well-organized departments whose primary function is to compete actively for real estate loans. In areas lacking specialized real estate financial institutions, these banks become the source for residential and farm mortgage loans. Second, the banks acquire mortgages by simply purchasing them from mortgage bankers or dealers.

In addition, dealer service companies, which were originally used to obtain car loans for permanent lenders such as commercial banks, wanted to broaden their activity beyond their local area. In recent years, however, such companies have concentrated on acquiring mobile home loans in volume for both commercial banks and savings and loan associations. Service companies obtain these loans from retail dealers, usually on a non-recourse basis. Almost all bank/service company agreements contain a credit insurance policy that protects the lender if the consumer defaults.

Unsecured Loan

Unsecured loans are monetary loans that are not secured against the borrower's assets (no collateral is involved). There are small business unsecured loans such as credit cards and credit lines to large corporate credit lines.

These may be available from financial institutions under many different guises or marketing packages such as:

- Bank overdrafts
- Corporate bonds
- Credit card debt
- Credit facilities or lines of credit
- Personal loans

A corporate bond is a bond issued by a corporation. It is a bond that a corporation issues to raise money in order to expand its business. The term is usually applied to longer-term debt instruments, generally with a maturity date falling at least a year after their issue date.

Sometimes, the term "corporate bonds" is used to include all bonds except those issued by governments in their own currencies. Strictly speaking, however, it applies only to bonds issued by corporations, not to bonds of local authorities and supranational organizations.

Corporate bonds are often listed on major exchanges (bonds there are called "listed" bonds) and ECNs like Bonds.com and MarketAxess and the coupon (or interest payment) is usually taxable. Sometimes, this coupon can be zero, with a high redemption value. However, despite being listed on exchanges, the vast majority of trading volume in corporate bonds in most developed markets takes place in decentralized, dealer-based, over-the-counter markets.

Some corporate bonds have an embedded call option that allows the issuer to redeem the debt before its maturity date. Other bonds, known as convertible bonds, allow investors to convert the bond into equity. Corporate credit spreads may alternatively be earned in exchange for default risk through credit default swaps, which give an unfunded synthetic exposure to similar risks on the same "Reference Entities". However, quite volatile credit default swaps "basis" make the spreads on credit default swaps and the credit spreads on corporate bonds be significantly different.

Primary Functions

Commercial banks perform various functions:

- Commercial banks accept various types of deposits from public especially from its clients, including saving account deposits, recurring account deposits, and fixed deposits. These deposits are payable after a certain time period
- Commercial banks provide loans and advances of various forms, including an overdraft facility, cash credit, bill discounting, money at call etc. They also give demand and demand and term loans to all types of clients against proper security.
- Credit creation is the most significant function of commercial banks. While sanctioning a loan to a customer, they do not provide cash to the borrower. Instead, they open a deposit account from which the borrower can withdraw. In other words, while sanctioning a loan, they automatically create deposits, known as a credit creation from commercial banks.

Secondary Functions

Along with primary functions, commercial banks perform several secondary functions. The secondary functions of commercial banks can be divided into agency functions and utility functions.

Agency functions include:

- To collect and clear cheques, dividends and interest warrant.
- To make payments of rent, insurance premium, etc.
- To deal in foreign exchange transactions.
- To purchase and sell securities.
- To act as trustee, attorney, correspondent and executor.
- To accept tax proceeds and tax returns.

Utility functions include:

- To provide safety locker facility to customers.
- To provide money transfer facility.
- To issue traveller's cheque.
- To act as referees.
- To accept various bills for payment: phone bills, gas bills, water bills, etc.

- To provide merchant banking facility.
- To provide various cards: credit cards, debit cards, smart cards, etc.

SUPPLEMENTARY ACTIVITIES OF COMMERCIAL BANKS

As a continuation of their main deposit taking and lending activities, banks pursue certain activities to offer a number of services to customers.

They can be put into two broad categories:

1. Other basic banking activities and
2. Para-banking activities.

The former includes provision of remittance facilities including issuance of drafts, mail transfers and telegraphic transfers, issuance of travellers' cheques and gift cheques, locker facility etc. Banks also undertake various para-banking activities including investment banking services, selling mutual funds, selling insurance products, offering depository services, wealth management services, brokerage, etc.

While the services offered assist the banks to attract more depositors and borrowers, they also manage to increase their income in the process. Banks earn fees by offering these services to the customers, as opposed to interest income earned from the lending activities.

OTHER BASIC BANKING ACTIVITIES

FOREIGN EXCHANGE SERVICES

Banks undertake foreign exchange transactions for their customers. The foreign exchange contracts arise out of spot (current) and forward foreign exchange transactions entered into with corporate and non-corporate customers and counter-party banks for the purpose of hedging and trading. Banks derive income from the spread or difference between buying and selling rates of foreign exchange.

Leading banks provide customer specific products and services which cater to risk hedging needs of corporates at domestic and international locations, arising out of currency and interest rate fluctuations. These include products such as options and swaps, which are derived from the foreign exchange market or the interest rate market. These are tailor made products designed to meet specific risk hedging requirements of the customer. In addition to the direct foreign exchange related income on buying and selling of foreign exchange, income is generated in related services while undertaking the main foreign exchange business. These services include the establishment of letters of credit, issuance of guarantees, document collection services, etc.

Some banks, including leading public sector banks, private sector banks and local branches of foreign banks earn significant income from foreign exchange related transactions.

BANKS' SERVICES TO GOVERNMENT

Banks offer various types of services to government departments including direct and indirect tax collections, remittance facilities, payments of salaries and pensions, etc. Banks also undertake other related businesses like distribution of Government and RBI bonds and handling public provident fund accounts. Government departments pay fees to banks for undertaking this business. Banks such as State of Bank of India, with a wide network of branches, are able to earn significant income by offering these services to government departments.

PAYMENT AND SETTLEMENT SYSTEMS

In any economy, banks are at the core of the payment and settlement systems, which constitute a very important part of the commercial banks' functions. The payment and settlement systems, as a mechanism, facilitate transfer of value between a payer and a beneficiary by which the payer discharges the payment obligations to the beneficiary. The payment and settlement systems enable two-way flow of payments in exchange of goods and services in the economy. This mechanism is used by individuals, banks, companies, governments, etc. to make payments to one another.

The RBI has the power to regulate the payment system under the provisions of the Payment and Settlement Systems (PSS) Act 2007, and the Payment and Settlement Systems Regulations 2008. The Board for Regulation and Supervision of Payment and Settlement Systems (BPSS) is a sub-committee of the Central Board of RBI and is the highest policy making body on the payment system. The Board is assisted by a technical committee called National Payments Council (NPC) with eminent experts in the field as members.

There are two types of payments: paper based and electronic. Payments can be made in India in paper based forms (in the forms of cash, cheque, demand drafts), and electronic forms (giving electronic instructions to the banker who will make such a payment on behalf of his customers; credit card; debit card).

Paper Based Clearing Systems

The primary paper based payment instrument is the cheque. The process of cheque payment starts when a payer gives his personal cheque to the beneficiary. To get the actual payment of funds, the receiver of the cheque has to deposit the cheque in his bank account. If the beneficiary has an account in the same bank in the same city then the funds are credited into his account through internal arrangement of the bank. If the beneficiary has an account with any other bank in the same or in any other city, then his banker would ensure that funds are collected from the payer's banker through the means of a 'clearing house'. A clearing house is an association of banks that facilitates payments through cheques between different bank branches within a city/ place.

It acts as a central meeting place for bankers to exchange the cheques drawn on one another and to claim funds for the same. Such operations are called 'clearing operations'. Generally one bank is appointed as in-charge of the clearing operations. In the four metros and a few other major cities, however, RBI is looking after the operations of the clearing house.

The paper based clearing systems comprise:

- MICR Clearing,
- Non- MICR clearing and
- High Value clearing.

MICR stands for Magnetic Ink Character Recognition (MICR). MICR is a technology for processing cheques. This is done through information contained in the bottom strip of the cheque where the cheque number, city code, bank code and branch code are given. Generally, if a cheque is to be paid within the same city (local cheque), it takes 2-3 days for the money to come to the beneficiary's account. In case of High Value Clearing, however, which is available only in some large cities, cheque clearing cycle is completed on the same day and the customer depositing the cheque is permitted to utilise the proceeds the next day morning. The introduction of 'Speed Clearing' in June 2008 for collection of outstation cheques has significantly brought down the time taken for realisation of outstation cheques from 10-14 days; now the funds are available to customers on T+1 (transaction day + 1 day) or T+2 (transaction day + 2 days) basis.

Cheque Truncation

Cheque Truncation is a system of cheque clearing and settlement between banks based on electronic data/ images or both without physical exchange of instrument. Cheque truncation has several advantages. First, the bank customers would get their cheques realised faster, as T+0 (local clearing) and T+1 (inter-city clearing) is possible in Cheque Truncation System (CTS). Second, faster realisation is accompanied by a reduction in costs for the customers and the banks. Third, it is also possible for banks to offer innovative products and services based on CTS. Finally, the banks have the additional advantage of reduced reconciliation and clearing frauds.

Electronic Payment Systems

Payments can be made between two or more parties by means of electronic instructions without the use of cheques. Generally, the electronic payment systems are faster and safer than paper based systems. Different forms of electronic payment systems are listed here. Real Time Gross Settlement (RTGS) system, introduced in India in March 2004, is a system through which electronic instructions can be given by banks to transfer funds from their account to the account of another bank.

The RTGS system is maintained and operated by RBI and provides a means of efficient and faster funds transfer among banks facilitating their financial operations. As the name suggests, funds transfer between banks takes place on a 'real time' basis. Therefore, money can reach the beneficiary instantaneously. The system which was operationalised with respect to settlement of transactions relating to inter-bank payments was extended to customer transactions later. Though the system is primarily designed for large value payments, bank customers have the choice of availing of the RTGS facility for their timecritical low value payments as well. More than 60,000 branches as at end-September 2009 are participants in the RTGS.

Electronic Funds Transfer (EFT) is a system whereby anyone who wants to make payment to another person/ company etc. can approach his bank and make cash payment or give instructions/ authorisation to transfer funds directly from his own account to the bank account of the receiver/ beneficiary. RBI is the service provider for EFT. The electronic payment systems comprise large value payment systems as well as retail payment mechanisms.

In addition, there are some electronic payment systems which are exclusively for retail payments. The retail payment system comprises Electronic Clearing Services (ECS), National Electronic Funds Transfer (NEFT) and card based payment systems including ATM network. Electronic Clearing Service (ECS) is a retail payment system that can be used to make bulk payments/ receipts of a similar nature especially where each individual payment is of a repetitive nature and of relatively smaller amount. This facility is meant for companies and government departments to make/ receive large volumes of payments rather than for funds transfers by individuals. The ECS facility is available at a large number of centres. The ECS is further divided into two types - ECS (Credit) to make bulk payments to individuals/ vendors and ECS (Debit) to receive bulk utility payments from individuals.

Under ECS (Credit), one entity/ company would make payments from its bank account to a number of recipients by direct credit to their bank accounts. For instance, companies make use of ECS (Credit) to make periodic dividend/ interest payments to their investors. Similarly, employers like banks, government departments, etc make monthly salary payments to their employees through ECS (Credit). Payments of repetitive nature to be made to vendors can also be made through this mode.

The payments are affected through a sponsor bank of the Company making the payment and such bank has to ensure that there are enough funds in its accounts on the settlement day to offset the total amount for which the payment is being made for that particular settlement. The sponsor bank is generally the bank with whom the company maintains its account. ECS (Debit) is mostly used by utility companies like telephone companies, electricity companies etc. to receive the bill payments directly from the bank accounts of their customers.

Instead of making electricity bill payment through cash or by means of cheque, a consumer (individuals as well as companies) can opt to make bill payments directly into the account of the electricity provider/ company/ board from his own bank account.

For this purpose, the consumer has to give an application to the utility company (provided the company has opted for the ECS (Debit) scheme), providing details of the bank account from which the monthly/ bi-monthly bill amount can be directly deducted. Thereafter, the utility company would advise the consumer's bank to debit the bill amount to his account on the due date of the bill and transfer the amount to the company's own account. This is done by crediting the account of the sponsor bank, which again is generally the bank with whom the company receiving the payments, maintains the account. The actual bill would be sent to the consumer as usual at his address.

The settlement cycle under the ECS has been reduced to T+1 day from earlier T+3 days across the country. To widen the geographical coverage of ECS beyond the existing ECS centres and to have a centralised processing capability, the National Electronic Clearing Service (NECS) was operationalised with effect from September 29, 2008. The NECS is a nationwide system in which as many as 114 banks with 30,780 branches participated as at the end of September, 2009.

National Electronic Funds Transfer (NEFT) system, introduced in November 2005, is a nationwide funds transfer system to facilitate transfer of funds from any bank branch to any other bank branch. The beneficiary gets the credit on the same day or the next day depending on the time of settlement. Ninety one banks with over 61,000 branches participated in NEFT as at end of September 2009.

The banks generally charge some processing fees for electronic fund transfers, just as in the case of other services such as demand drafts, pay orders etc. The actual charges depend upon the amount and the banker-customer relationship. In a bid to encourage customers to move from paper-based systems to electronic systems, RBI has rationalised and made transparent the charges the banks could levy on customers for electronic transactions. RBI on its part has extended the waiver of its processing charges for electronic modes of payment up to the end of March 2011. In order not to be involved with day-to-day operations of the retail payment system, RBI has encouraged the setting up of National Payment Corporation of India (NPCI) to act as an umbrella organisation for operating the various retail payment systems in India. NPCI has since become functional and is in the process of setting up its roadmap. NPCI will be an authorised entity under the Payment and Settlement Systems Act and would, therefore, be subjected to regulation and supervision of RBI.

Credit/ Debit cards are widely used in the country as they provide a convenient form of making payments for goods and services without the use of cheques or cash. Issuance of credit card is a service where the customer is provided with credit facility for purchase of goods and services in shops, restaurants, hotels, railway bookings, petrol pumps, utility bill payments, etc. The merchant establishment who accepts credit card payments claims the amount subsequently from the customer's bank through his own bank.

The card user is required to pay only on receipt of the bill and this payment can be either in full or partially in instalments. Banks issuing credit cards earn revenue from their customers in a variety of ways such as joining fee, additional card fee, annual fee, replacement card fee, cash advance fee, charge slip/ statement retrieval fee, charges on over limit accounts and late payment fee, interest on delayed payment, interest on revolving credit, etc. The fees may vary based on the type of card and from bank to bank. Banks earn income not only as issuers of credit cards, but also as acquirers where the transaction occurs on a point of sale terminal installed by the bank. As the Indian economy develops, it is expected that the retail market will increasingly seek shortterm credit for personal uses, and to a large extent, this rising demand would be met by the issuance of credit cards.

Debit Card is a direct account access card. Unlike a credit card, in the case of a debit card, the entire amount transacted gets debited from the customer's account as soon as the debit card is used for purchase of goods and services. The amount permitted to be transacted in debit card is to the extent of the amount standing to the credit of the card user's account. Automated Teller Machines (ATMs) are mainly used for cash withdrawals by customers. In addition to cash withdrawal, ATMs can be used for payment of utility bills, funds transfer between accounts, deposit of cheques and cash into accounts, balance enquiry and several other banking transactions which the banks owning the ATMs might want to offer.

NRI REMITTANCES

NRI, as an individual, can remit funds into India through normal banking channels using the facilities provided by the overseas bank. Alternately, an NRI can also remit funds through authorised Money Transfer Agents (MTA). Further, a number of banks have launched their inward remittance products which facilitate funds transfer on the same day/ next day.

CASH MANAGEMENT SERVICES AND REMITTANCES

Many banks have branches rendering cash management services (CMS) to corporate clients, for managing their receivables and payments across the country. Under cash management services, banks offer their corporate clients custom-made collection, payment and remittance services allowing them to reduce the time period between collections and remittances, thereby streamlining their cash flows. Cash management products include physical cheque-based clearing, electronic clearing services, central pooling of country-wide collections, dividend and interest remittance services and Internet-based payment products. Such services provide customers with enhanced liquidity and better cash management.

PARA-BANKING ACTIVITIES

The Reserve Bank of India (RBI) has allowed the Scheduled Commercial Banks (SCBs) to undertake certain financial services or para-banking activities and has issued guidelines to SCBs for undertaking these businesses. The RBI has advised banks that they should adopt adequate safeguards so that para-banking activities undertaken by them are run on sound and prudent lines. Banks can undertake certain eligible financial services either departmentally or by setting up subsidiaries, with prior approval of RBI.

PRIMARY DEALERSHIP BUSINESS

Primary Dealers can be referred to as Merchant Bankers to Government of India. In 1995, the Reserve Bank of India (RBI) introduced the system of Primary Dealers (PDs) in the Government Securities Market, which comprised independent entities undertaking Primary Dealer activity. In order to broad base the Primary Dealership system, banks were permitted to undertake Primary Dealership business in 2006-07. To do primary dealership business, it is necessary to have a license from the RBI.

The primary objectives of the PD system are to:

- Strengthen the infrastructure in the government securities market to make it vibrant, liquid and broad based.
  - Improve secondary market trading system, which would (a) Contribute to price discovery,
  - Enhance liquidity and turnover and (c) encourage voluntary holding of government Securities.

A bank can do PD business either through a subsidiary or departmentally. A subsidiary of a scheduled commercial bank dedicated predominantly to the securities business (particularly, the government securities market) can apply for primary dealership. To do PD business departmentally, only banks which do not have a partly or wholly owned subsidiary undertaking PD business and fulfill the following criteria can apply:

- Minimum net owned funds (NOF) of ₹.1,000 crores
- Minimum CRAR of 9 per cent
- Net NPAs of less than 3 per cent and a profit making record for the last three years

INVESTMENT BANKING/ MERCHANT BANKING SERVICES

Investment Banking is not one specific function or service but rather an umbrella term for a range of activities. These activities include issuing securities (underwriting) for companies, managing portfolios of financial assets, trading securities (stocks and bonds), helping investors purchase securities and providing financial advice and support services. It can be seen that all these services are capital market related services. These services are offered to governments, companies, non-profit institutions and individuals. A number of commercial banks have formed subsidiaries to undertake investment banking services. Here, it is important to draw the distinction between Merchant Banking and Investment Banking.

As per the Securities and Exchange Board of India (SEBI) (Merchant Bankers) Rules, 1992 and SEBI (Merchant Bankers) Regulations, 1992, merchant banking service is any service provided in relation to issue management either by making arrangements regarding selling, buying or subscribing securities as manager, consultant, advisor or rendering corporate advisory service in relation to such issue manage-ment.

This, inter alia, consists of preparation of prospectus and other information relating to the issue, determining financial structure, tie up of financiers and final allotment and refund of the subscription for debt/ equity issue management and acting as advisor, consultant, co-manager, underwriter and portfolio manager. In addition, merchant banking services also include advisory services on corporate restructuring, debt or equity restructuring, loan restructuring, etc. Fees are charged by the merchant banker for rendering these services. Banks and Financial Institutions including Non Banking Finance Companies (NBFCs) providing merchant banking services are governed by the SEBI Rules and Regulations.

On the other hand, the term 'Investment Banking' has a much wider connotation and has gradually come to refer to all types of capital market activity. Investment banking thus encompasses not merely merchant banking but other related capital market activities such as stock trading, market making, broking and asset management as well as a host of specialized corporate advisory services in the areas of mergers and acquisitions, project advisory and business and financial advisory. Investment banking has a large number of players: Indian and foreign. The large foreign investment banks such as Goldman Sachs and Merrill Lynch (which are standalone investment banks) have entered India attracted by India's booming economy. However, the Indian investment banking firms (including investment banking arms of Indian commercial banks) have generally succeeded in holding their own as they are able to service both small and large customers. However, one area foreign banks still dominate is global mergers and acquisitions.

MUTUAL FUND BUSINESS

A number of banks, both in the private and public sectors have sponsored asset management companies to undertake mutual fund business. Banks have entered the mutual fund business, sometimes on their own (by setting up a subsidiary) and sometimes in joint venture with others. Other banks have entered into distribution agreements with mutual funds for the sale of the latter's mutual fund products, for which they receive fees. The advantage that banks enjoy in entering the mutual fund businesses is mainly on account of their wide distribution network.

Money Market Mutual Funds (MMMFs) come under the purview of SEBI regulations. Banks and Financial Institutions desirous of setting up MMMFs would, however, have to seek necessary clearance from RBI for undertaking this additional activity before approaching SEBI for registration.

PENSION FUNDS MANAGEMENT (PFM) BY BANKS

Consequent upon the issue of Government of India Notification dated May 24, 2007, banks have been advised that they may now undertake Pension Funds Management (PFM) through their subsidiaries set up for the purpose. This would be subject to their satisfying the eligibility criteria prescribed by Pensions Fund Regulatory and Development Authority (PFRDA) for Pension Fund Managers. Banks intending to undertake PFM should obtain prior approval of RBI before engaging in such business.

The RBI has issued guidelines for banks acting as Pension Fund Managers. According to the guidelines, banks will be allowed to undertake PFM through their subsidiaries only, and not departmentally. Banks may lend their names/ abbreviations to their subsidiaries formed for PFM, for leveraging their brand names and associated benefits thereto, only subject to the banks maintaining 'arm's length' relationship with the subsidiary.

In order to provide adequate safeguards against associated risks and ensure that only strong and credible banks enter into the business of PFM, the banks complying with the following eligibility criteria (as also the solvency margin prescribed by PFRDA) may approach the RBI for necessary permission:

- Net worth of the bank should be not less than ₹.500 crores.
- CRAR should be not less than 11% during the last three years.
- Bank should have made net profit for the last three consecutive years.
- Return on Assets (ROA) should be at least 0.6% or more.
- Level of net NPAs should be less than 3%.
- Performance of the bank's subsidiaries, if any, should be satisfactory.

DEPOSITORY SERVICES

In the depository system, securities are held in depository accounts in dematerialized form. Transfer of securities is done through simple account transfers. The method does away with the risks and hassles normally associated with paperwork. The enactment of the Depositories Act, in August 1996, paved the way for the establishment of National Securities Depository Limited (NSDL) and later the Central Depository Services (India) Limited (CDSL). These two institutions have set up a national infrastructure of international standards that handles most of the securities held and settled in dematerialised form in the Indian capital markets.

As a depository participant of the National Securities Depository Limited (NSDL) or Central Depository Services (India) Limited (CDSL), a bank may offer depository services to clients and earn fees.

Custodial depository services means safe keeping of securities of a client and providing services incidental thereto, and includes:

- Maintaining accounts of securities of a client;
- Collecting the benefit of rights accruing to the client in respect of the securities;
- Keeping the client informed of the action taken or to be taken by the issuer of securities, having a bearing on the benefits or rights accruing to the client; and
- Maintaining and reconciling records of the services referred to in sub-clause (a) to (c).

WEALTH MANAGEMENT/ PORTFOLIO MANAGEMENT SERVICES

A number of banks and financial institutions are seeking a share in the fast-growing wealth management services market. Currently, a high net worth individual can choose from among a number of private sector and public sector banks for wealth management services. In addition to high net worth resident Indians, non-resident Indians (NRIs) form a major chunk of the customer base for personal wealth management industry in India.

Banks that do portfolio management on behalf of their clients are subject to several regulations. No bank should introduce any new portfolio management scheme (PMS) without obtaining specific prior approval of RBI. They are also to comply with the guidelines contained in the SEBI (Portfolio Managers) Rules and Regulations, 1993 and those issued from time to time.

The following conditions are to be strictly observed by the banks operating PMS or similar scheme:

- PMS should be entirely at the customer's risk, without guaranteeing, either directly or indirectly, a pre-determined return.
- Funds should not be accepted for portfolio manage-ment for a period less than one year.
- Portfolio funds should not be deployed for lending in call/ notice money; inter-bank term deposits and bills rediscounting markets and lending to/ placement with corporate bodies.
- Banks should maintain clientwise account/ record of funds accepted for management and investments made and the portfolio clients should be entitled to get a statement of account.

- Banks' own investments and investments belonging to PMS clients should be kept distinct from each other, and any transactions between the bank's investment account and client's portfolio account should be strictly at market rates.
- PMS clients' accounts should be subjected by banks to a separate audit by external auditors.

BANCASSURANCE

With the issuance of Government of India Notification dated August 3, 2000, specifying 'Insurance' as a permissible form of business that could be undertaken by banks under Section 6(1) (o) of the BR Act, banks were advised to undertake insurance business with a prior approval of the RBI. However, insurance business will not be permitted to be undertaken departmentally by the banks.

A number of banks (both in public and private sectors) have entered into joint venture partnerships with foreign insurance companies for both life and non-life insurance business. At present, Indian partners (either alone or jointly) hold at least 74% of Indian insurance joint ventures. This is because the maximum holding by foreign companies put together cannot exceed 26% of the equity of Indian insurance ventures. Laws and regulations governing insurance companies currently provide that each promoter should eventually reduce its stake to 26% following the completion of 10 years from the commencement of business by the concerned insurance company.

The advantage that banks have in entering the insurance business is mainly on account of their wide distribution network. Banks are able to leverage their corporate and retail customer base for cross selling insurance products. Banks collect fees from these subsidiaries for generating leads and providing referrals that are converted into policies.

In addition, some banks distribute Third Party Insurance Products. With a view to provide "one stop banking" to their customers, banks distribute life insurance products and general insurance products through their branches. Banks have entered into agency agreements with life and non-life companies to distribute their various insurance products, for which they are paid a commission. The personnel involved in selling these insurance products have to be authorised by the IRDA regulations to act as specified persons for selling insurance products.

8

Banking Theory and Practice

DEVELOPMENT OF BANKING

The History of Banking begins with the first prototype banks of merchants of the ancient world, which made grain loans to farmers and traders who accepted goods flanked by municipalities. This began approximately 2000 BC in Assyria and Babylonia. Later, in ancient Greece and throughout the Roman Empire, lenders based in temples made loans and added two significant innovations: they carried deposits and changed money. Archaeology from this era in ancient China and India, also illustrates proof of money lending action.

Banking, in the contemporary sense of the word, can be traced to medieval and early Renaissance Italy, to the rich municipalities in the north such since Florence, Venice, and Genoa. The Bardi and Peruzzi families dominated banking in 14th century Florence, establishing branches in several other sections of Europe. Possibly the mainly well-known Italian bank was the Medici bank, recognized through Giovanni Medici in 1397.

The growth of banking spread from northern Italy by Europe and a number of significant innovations took lay in Amsterdam throughout the Dutch Republic in the 16th century, and in London in the 17th century. Throughout the 20th century, growths in telecommunications and computing caused major changes to banks operations and let banks dramatically augment in size and geographic spread. The Late-2000s financial crisis caused several bank failures, including of some of the world's main banks, and much debate in relation to the bank regulation.

PRECEDENTS

Monetary

The history of banking depends on the history of money—and on grain-money and food cattle-money used from at least 9000 BC, two of the earliest things understood since accessible to barter (Davies), Anatolian obsidian since a raw material for stone-age apparatus being distributed since early since 12,500

B.C., with organized deal occurring in the 9th millennia. In Sardinia one of the four largest locations for sourcing the material deposits of obsidian within the Mediterranean, deal of this were replaced in the 3rd millennia through deal in copper and silver. The community adapted from relating from one fixed material since valued deposits accessible for deal to another.

The possibility of stable economic dealings was much improved with the transform from the reliance on hunting and gathering of foods to agricultural practice, throughout eras dated since beginning sometime after 12,000 BC, at almost 10,000 years ago in the Fertile Crescent, in northern China in relation to the 9,500 years ago, in relation to the 5,500 years ago in Mexico and almost 4,500 in the eastern sections of the United States of the continent of the lay now know since northern America.

Structural

Through the fifth millennium B.C. the settlements of Sumer, such since Eridu, were shaped approximately a central temple. In the fifth millennium, people began to build and live in the culture of municipalities, providing a building for the construction of organizations and establishments. Tell Brak and Uruk were two early urban settlements.

EARLIEST SHAPES OF BANKING

Wealth is deposited and kept in temples; in thêsaurus (treasure homes) and treasuries, where safety is afforded through the will of the gods. The earliest banks were used exclusively through rulers to finance the more significant and superior festivals and for structure expenses. All close knowledge of the origin of the abacus is lost. Through the time of the ancient Hindus, Greeks and Romans a shape of counting calculation was in exploit, initially the dust abacus and later the counting table. The condition originally referred to table, bench, or board.

Archaeological Proof

Substances described tokens made of clay have been recovered from within Close to East excavations dated to a era beginning 8000 B.C.E and ending 1500 B.C.E., presumed to have been made since records of the counting of agricultural produce.

Commencing the late fourth millennia mnemonic representations were in exploit through members of temples and palaces to serve to record stocks of produce. Kinds of records accounting for deal exchanges of payments were being made firstly in relation to the 3200. A extremely early writing on clay tablet described the Code of Hammurabi, refers to the regulation of a banking action of sorts within the culture (Armstrong), throughout the period, dating to ca. 1700 BCE, banking was well sufficient urbanized to justify laws governing banking operations. Later throughout the Achaemenid Empire (after 646 BC.), further proof is establish of banking practices in the Mesopotamia area.

Mesopotamia

Banking since understood since in an archaic state (or quasi-banking), is idea to have begun throughout a era since early since the second section of the fourth millennia to since late since the third to second millennia BC. Some sources for a beginning time since within the 4th millennia are establish in sources published in the year 2005 and 1999, in the 4th to 3rd millennia, 1996, since the 3rd, based on depository action in temples the 2nd or the 1st millennia, published throughout 1958. Certainly an individual measured perhaps active since a banker was alive throughout the eighteenth century.

Temple

Prior to the reign of Sargon I of Akkad (2335-2280) the occurrence of deal was limited to the internal boundaries of each municipality-state of Babylon and the temple situated at the centre of economic action there-in; deal at the time for citizens external to the municipality was forbidden.

In Babylonia of 2000, people depositing gold were required to pay amounts since much since one sixth of the total deposited. Both the palaces and temple are recognized to have provided lending and issuing from the wealth they held—the palaces to a lesser extent. Such loans typically involved issuing seed-grain, with re-payment from the harvest. These vital social agreements were documented in clay tablets, with an agreement on interest accrual. The habit of depositing and storing of wealth in temples sustained at least until 209 B.C., since evidenced through Antioch having ransacked or pillaged the temple of Aine in Ecbatana (Media) of gold and silver.

Family

Cuneiform records of the home of Egibi of Babylonia define the families financial behaviors dated since having occurred sometime after 1000 BC and ending sometime throughout the reign of Darius I, illustrate a “lending home”, a family engaging in “professional banking...” and economic behaviors same to a degree to contemporary deposit banking, although another states the families behaviors bigger called since entrepreneurship rather than banking. The provision of credit is apparently also something the Murashu family participated in.

Egypt

In relation to the time of the eighteenth century B.C.E. amounts of gold were deposited within the boundaries of the temple structures of Egypt for causes of security. In Egypt from early times, grain having an intrinsic value since food functioned, in addition to valuable metals, since money. The local granaries were used to store and loan the grain of societies, functions same to banking services although not the similar. Under the dynastic rule of the Greek Ptolemies, the numerous scattered government granaries were transformed into a network of grain banks, centralized in Alexandria where the largest accounts from all the state granary banks were recorded. This centralized management was the first recognized governmental bank, functioning since a deal credit organization that transferred payments flanked by accounts without passing money. Documents made to illustrate the banking of taxes were recognized since peptoken-records. The recording of the gathering of money to buy grain in pharaoh's kingdom since ordered through Joseph, is written within Genesis of the Torah of the Holy Bible, and this money was placed within the Home of the pharaoh. Joseph brought with the money of the pharaoh a big amount of corn, having this then laid in the public granaries.

India

In ancient India there is proof of loans from the Vedic era (beginning 1750 BC). Later throughout the Maurya dynasty (321 to 185 BC), an instrument described adesha was in exploit, which was an order on a banker desiring him to pay the money of the note to a third person, which corresponds to the definition of a bill of swap since we understand it today. Throughout the Buddhist era, there was considerable exploit of these instruments. Merchants in big cities gave letters of credit to one another.

China

In ancient China, starting in the Qin Dynasty (221 to 206 BC), Chinese currency urbanized with the introduction of standardized coins that allowed easier deal crossways China, and led to growth of letters of credit. These letters were issued through merchants who acted in ways that today we would understand since banks.

Greece Money-changing

Ancient Grecian bankers were in the first case moneychangers and pawnbrokers, present in the marketplace or festival locations, changing coinage of foreign merchants into the regional currency. Those idea the earliest spaces of storage were the money-boxes containments made same to the construction of a bee-hive, since of the Mycenae tombs of 1550-1500 BC.

Palace & Temple-banking

Private and civic entities within ancient Grecian community; especially Greek temples performed financial transactions. These consisted of deposits, currency swap, validation of coinage, and loans. The temples were the spaces where treasure was deposited for safe-keeping. The three temples idea the mainly significant was the temple to Artemis in Ephesus, and temple of Hera within Samos and within Delphi, the temple to Apollo.

The first treasury to the Apollonian temple was built before the end of the seventh century BC, a treasury of the temple was constructed through the municipality of Siphnos throughout the sixth century. The task of keeping the deposited wealth provided to the temple of Asklepios were allotted often to the neokoros or zakoros; or at Kos the hierophylakes, who were also the mnemones or record keepers of such exchanges.

Before the destruction through Persians throughout the 480 invasion the Athenian Acropolis temple specialized to Athena stored money; Pericles rebuilt a depository afterward contained within the Parthenon. Athens received the Delian leagues treasury throughout 454.

The municipality-states of Greece after the Persian Wars in 323 produced a government and civilization sufficiently organized for the birth of a private citizenship and so an embryonic capitalist community, allowing for the separation of wealth from exclusive state ownership to the possibility of ownership through the individual.

Non-temple & State-banking

Throughout the reign of the Ptolemies state depositories replaced temples since the site of security-deposits, records exist to illustrate this having occurred through the end of the reign of Ptolemy I (305-284). The first person to have participated in ancient community to some degree since a banker was named Philostephanos (of Corinth).

Loans

Several loans are recorded in writings from the classical age, although an extremely little proportion was provided through banks. Provision of these was likely an occurrence of Athens, with loans recognized to have been provided at some time at an annual interest of 12%. Within the boundaries of Athens, banker's loans are recorded since having been issued on eleven occasion's altogether. A loan was made through a Temple of Athens to the state throughout 433-427 BCE.

Metic-class

Several early bankers in Greek municipality-states belonged to the metic classification of citizenship. A slave named Pasion, for a time owned through Archestratos and Antisthenes who were partners of a banking firm in Peiraieus, was at some time Athens' mainly significant banker. Having gained comparative freedom to the metic class he was subsequently involved in banking from 394 BC, a business inherited through his slave named Phormio.

Banking Sites

Since require for new structures to home operations increased, construction of these spaces within the municipalities began approximately the courtyards of the agora (markets). In the late 3rd and 2nd century BC, the Aegean island of Delos, became a prominent banking center. Throughout the second century, there were for sure three banks and one temple depository within the municipality. Thirty five Hellenistic municipalities incorporated private banks throughout the 2nd century. Of the settlements of the Greco-Roman world of the 1st century AD, three were of pronounced wealth and centers of banking, Athens, Corinth and Patras.

Asia Minor

From the fourth millennia previously agricultural settlements began administrative behaviors. The temple of Artemis at Ephesus was the main depository of Asia. A pot-hoard dated to 600 B.C. was establish in excavations through the British Museum throughout the year after 1904. Throughout the time at the cessation of the first Mithridatic war the whole debt record at the time being held, was annulled through the council. Spot Anthony is recorded to have stolen from the deposits on an occasion. The temple served since a depository for Aristotle, Caesar, Dio Chrysostomus, Plautus, Plutarch, Strabo and Xenophon. The temple to Apollo in Didyma was constructed sometime in the sixth century. A big sum of gold was deposited within the treasury at the time through king Croesus.

Rome

The Roman Empire inherited the spirit of capitalism from Greece (Parker). Throughout the time of the Empire, public deposits slowly ceased to be held in temples, and instead were held in private depositories. The earliest recorded proof showing banking practices is given through one source since throughout 325 BC. On explanation of being in debt, the Plebians were required to borrow money. At that time newly appointed quinqueviri mensarii were commissioned to give services to those that had security to give in swap for money from the public treasury. Another source has the shops of banking of Ancient Rome firstly opening in the public forums throughout the era 318 to 310 BC. In early Ancient Rome deposit bankers were recognized since argentarius and at a later time (from the second century anno domini onward) since nummularius or mensarii. The banking-homes were recognized since Taberae Argentarioe and Mensoe Numularioe.

Bankers operated from either appointment through the government so tasked with collecting taxes, or were instead self-governing and practicing banking for individual ends. Statutes (AD 125/126) of the Empire called "letter from Caesar to Quietus" illustrate rental monies to be composed from persons by land belonging to a temple and given to the temple treasurer, since decreed through Mettius Modestus governor of Lycia and Pamphylia. Money-lenders would set up their stalls in the transitional of enclosed courtyards described macella on an extensive bench described a bancu, from which the languages banco and bank are derived. Since a moneychanger, the merchant at the bancu did not therefore much invest money since merely convert the foreign currency into the only legal tender in Rome – that of the Imperial Mint. The Roman empire at some time formalized the administrative aspect of banking and instituted greater regulation of financial organizations and financial practices. Charging interest on loans and paying interest on deposits became more highly urbanized and competitive. The growth of Roman banks was limited, though, through the Roman preference for cash transactions. Throughout the reign of the Roman emperor Gallienus (AD 260–268), there was a temporary breakdown of the Roman banking organization after the banks rejected the flakes of copper produced through his mints. With the ascent of Christianity, banking became subject to additional restrictions, since the charging of interest was seen since immoral. After the fall of Rome, banking temporarily ended in Europe and was not revived until the time of the crusades.

RELIGIOUS RESTRICTIONS ON INTEREST

Mainly early religious organizations in the ancient Close to East, and the secular codes arising from them, did not forbid usury. These communities regarded inanimate matter since alive, like plants, animals and people, and capable of reproducing itself. Hence if you lent 'food money', or monetary tokens of any type, it was legitimate to charge interest. Food money in the form of olives, dates, seeds or animals was lent out since early since c. 5000 BCE, if not earlier. In the middle of the Mesopotamians, Hittites, Phoenicians and Egyptians, interest was legal and often fixed through the state.

Judaism

The Torah and later parts of the Hebrew Bible criticize interest-taking, but interpretations of the Biblical prohibition modify. One general understanding is that Jews are forbidden to charge interest upon loans made to other Jews, but obliged to charge interest on transactions with non-Jews, or Gentiles. Though, the Hebrew Bible itself provides numerous examples where this provision was evaded.

- Deuteronomy 23:19 Thou shalt not lend upon interest to thy brother: interest of money, interest of victuals, interest of any thing that is lent upon interest. Deuteronomy 23:20 Unto a foreigner thou mayest lend upon interest; but unto thy brother thou shalt not lend upon interest; that the LORD thy God may bless thee in all that thou puttest thy hand unto, in the land whither thou goest in to possess it.

Israelites were forbidden to charge interest on loans made to other Israelites, but allowed to charge interest on transactions with non-Israelites, since the latter were often amongst the Israelites for the purpose of business anyway, but in common, it was seen since advantageous to avoid debt at all, to avoid being bound to someone else. Debt was to be avoided and not used to fund consumption, but only when in require. Though, laws against usury were in the middle of several the prophets condemn the people for breaking.

Christianity

Originally, the charging of interest recognized since usury was banned through Christian churches meaning the charging of interest at any rate was banned. This incorporated charging a fee for the exploit of money, such since at a bureau de transform. Though in excess of time the charging of interest became acceptable, the condition came to be used for interest above the rate allowed through law.

Islam

In Islam it is strictly prohibited to take interest; the Quran strictly prohibits lending money on Interest. "O you who have whispered, do not consume usury, doubled and multiplied, but fear Allah that you may be successful" and Allah has permitted deal and has forbidden interest". Riba (usury)) is forbidden in Islamic economic jurisprudence fiqh. Islamic jurists talk about two kinds of riba: an augment in capital with no services provided, which the Qur'an prohibits— and commodity exchanges in unequal quantities, which the Sunnah prohibits.

Medieval Europe

Banking, in the contemporary sense of the word, is traceable to medieval and early Renaissance Italy, to rich municipalities in the north such since Florence, Venice, and Genoa.

Emergence of Merchant Banks

The original banks were "merchant banks" that Italian grain merchants first invented in the Transitional Ages. Since Lombardy merchants and bankers grew in stature based on the strength of the Lombard plains cereal crops, several displaced Jews fleeing Spanish persecution were attracted to the deal. They brought with them ancient practices from the Transitional and Distant East silk circuits. Originally designed to fund extensive trading journeys, they applied these methods to fund grain manufacture and trading. Jews could not hold land in Italy, therefore they entered the great trading piazzas and halls of Lombardy, alongside regional traders, and set up their benches to deal in crops. They had one great advantage in excess of the locals. Christians were strictly forbidden the sin of usury, defined since lending at interest (Islam creates same condemnations of usury). The Jewish newcomers, on the other hand, could lend to farmers against crops in the field, a high-risk loan at what would have been measured usurious rates through the Church; but the Jews were not subject to the Church's dictates. In this method they could close the grain-sale rights against the eventual harvest. They then began to advance payment against the future delivery of grain shipped to far ports. In both cases they made their profit from the present discount against the future price. This two-handed deal was time-consuming and soon there arose a class of merchants who were trading grain debt instead of grain. The Jewish trader performed both financing (credit) and underwriting (insurance) functions. Financing took the shape of a crop loan at the beginning of the rising season, which allowed a farmer to develop and production (by seeding, rising, weeding, and harvesting) his annual crop. Underwriting in the shape of a crop, or commodity, insurance guaranteed the delivery of the crop to its buyer, typically a merchant wholesaler. In addition, traders performed the merchant function through creation arrangements to supply the buyer of the crop by alternative sources—grain stores or alternate markets, for example—in the event of crop failure. He could also stay the farmer (or other commodity producer) in business throughout a drought or other crop failure, by the issuance of a crop (or commodity) insurance against the hazard of failure of his crop.

Merchant banking progressed from financing deal on one's own behalf to settling deals for others and then to holding deposits for resolution of "billette" or notes written through the people who were still brokering the actual grain. And therefore the merchant's "benches" (bank is derived from the Italian for bench, banca, since in a counter) in the great grain markets became centers for holding money against a bill (billette, a note, a letter of formal swap, later a bill of swap and later still a cheque).

These deposited finances were designed to be held for the resolution of grain deals, but often were used for the bench's own deals in the meantime. The condition bankrupt is a corruption of the Italian banca rotta, or broken bench, which is what happened when someone lost his traders' deposits. Being "broke" has the similar connotation.

Crusades

In the 12th century, require to transfer big sums of money to fund the Crusades stimulated the re-emergence of banking in western Europe. In 1162, King Henry the II levied a tax to support the crusades—the first of a series of taxes levied through Henry in excess of the years with the similar objective. The Templar's and Hospitallers acted since Henry's bankers in the Holy Land. The Templar's' wide flung, big land holdings crossways Europe also appeared in the 1100–1300 time frame since the beginning of Europe-wide banking, since their practice was to take in regional currency, for which a demand note would be given that would be good at any of their castles crossways Europe, allowing movement of money without the usual risk of robbery while traveling.

Discounting of Interest

A sensible manner of discounting interest to the depositors against what could be earned through employing their money in the deal of the bench soon urbanized; in short, selling an "interest" to them in a specific deal, therefore overcoming the usury objection. Once again this merely urbanized what was an ancient way of financing extensive-aloofness transport of goods. Medieval deal fairs, such since the one in Hamburg, contributed to the development of banking in a curious method: moneychangers issued documents redeemable at other fairs, in swap for difficult currency. These documents could be cashed at another fair in a dissimilar country or at a future fair in the similar site. If redeemable at a future date, they would often be discounted through an amount comparable to a rate of interest. Eventually, these documents evolved into bills of swap, which could be redeemed at any office of the issuing banker. These bills made it possible to transfer big sums of money without the complications of hauling big chests of gold and hiring armed guards to protect the gold from thieves.

Foreign Swap Contracts

In 1156, in Genoa, occurred the earliest recognized foreign swap contract. Two brothers borrowed 115 Genoese pounds and agreed to reimburse the bank's mediators in Constantinople the sum of 460 bezants one month after their arrival in that municipality. In the following century the exploit of such contracts grew rapidly, particularly as profits from time variations were seen since not infringing canon laws against usury.

Italian Bankers

The first bank to be recognized was recognized in Venice with guarantee from the State in 1157. Just as to Macardy this was due to the commercial agency of the Venetians, acting in the interest of the Crusaders of Pope Urban the Second. The cause is given elsewhere since due to costs of the expansion of the empire of Duke Basic Mitchel II, and to relieve the subsequent financial burden on the republic "a forced loan" was made necessary. To this end the Chamber of Loans, was created to control the affairs of the forced loan, since to the loans repayment at four percent interest. Changes in the enterprises of the Chamber, firstly through the commencing of exploit of discounting exchanges and later through the receipt of deposits, there urbanized the functioning of the organisation into The Bank of Venice, with an initial capital of 5,000,000 ducats. In any case, banking practice proper began in the mid-sections of the 12th century, and sustained until the bank was caused to cease to operate throughout the French invasion of 1797. The bank was the first national bank to have been recognized within the boundaries of Europe. There were banking failures from 1255-62.

In the transitional of the 13th century, clusters of Italian Christians, particularly the Cahorsins and Lombards, invented legal fictions to get approximately the ban on Christian usury; for instance, one way of effecting a loan with interest was to offer money without interest, but also need that the loan is insured against possible loss or injury, and/or delays in repayment. The Christians effecting these legal fictions became recognized since the pope's usurers, and reduced the importance of the Jews to European monarchs; later, in the Transitional Ages, a distinction evolved flanked by things that were consumable (such since food and fuel) and those that were not, with usury permitted on loans that involved the latter.

Florence inhabited the mainly powerful of families occupied in banking. Amongst all of these including the Acciaiuoli and Mozzi, the Bardi and Peruzzi families possibly dominated, establishing branches in several other sections of Europe. Almost certainly the mainly well-known Italian bank was the Medici bank, set up through Giovanni di Bicci de' Medici in 1397 and continuing until 1494.

It was the Italian bankers that would take their lay and through 1327, Avignon had 43 branches of Italian banking homes. In 1347, Edward III of England defaulted on loans. Later there was the bankruptcy of the Bardi (1343) and Peruzzi (1346). The accompanying development of Italian banking in France was the start of the Lombard moneychangers in Europe, who moved from municipality to municipality beside the busy pilgrim circuits significant for deal. Key municipalities in this era were Cahors, the birthplace of Pope John XXII, and Figeac.

Through the later Transitional Ages, Christian Merchants who lent money with interest were without opposition, and the Jews lost their privileged location since money-lenders;

After 1400, political forces did, in information, somewhat turn against the methods of the Italian free enterprise bankers, In 1401 King Martin I of Aragon had some of these bankers expelled. In 1403, Henry IV of England prohibited them from taking profits in any method in his kingdom. In 1409, Flanders imprisoned and then expelled Genoese bankers. In 1410, all Italian merchants were expelled from Paris. In 1407, the Bank of Saint George, the first state-bank of deposit, was founded in Genoa and was to control business in the Mediterranean.

Silver Crisis

Through the 1390s silver was in short supply all in excess of Europe, except in Venice. The silver mines at Kutná Hora had begun to decline in the 1370s, and finally closed down after being sacked through King Sigismund in 1422. Through 1450 approximately all of the mints of northwest Europe had closed down for lack of silver. The last money-changer in the major French port of Dieppe went out of business in 1446. In 1455 the Turks overran the Serbian silver mines, and in 1460 captured the last Bosnian mine. Since currency became scarce, many Venetian banks failed since did the Strozzi bank of Florence, the second main in the municipality.

EXPANSION

Throughout this time Geneva is the mainly significant and active in banking within the central Europe area.

Italy

In the times flanked by 1527 - 1572 the Genoese people produced a number of significant banking family clusters, the Grimaldi, Spinola and Pallavicino families were especially influential and prosperous, also the Doria, although possibly less influential, and the Pinelli and the Lomellini.

Spain and the Ottoman Empire

In 1401 the magistrates of Barcelona recognized in the municipality the first replication of the Venetian model of swap and deposit, Taula de Canvi - the Table of Swap. Halil Ýnalcik suggests that, in the sixteenth century, Marrano Jews (Doña Gracia from Home of Mendes) fleeing from Iberia introduced the techniques of European capitalism, banking and even the mercantilist concept of state economy to the Ottoman empire. In the sixteenth century, the leading financiers in Istanbul were Greeks and Jews. Several of the Jewish financiers were Marranos who had fled from Iberia throughout the era leading up to the expulsion of Jews from Spain. Some of these families brought great fortunes with them. The mainly notable of the Jewish banking families in the sixteenth century Ottoman Empire was the Marrano banking home of Mendes, which moved to Istanbul in 1552, under the defense of Sultan Suleyman the Magnificent. When Alvaro Mendes arrived in Istanbul in 1588, he is accounted to have brought with him 85,000 gold ducats. The Mendès family soon acquired a dominating location in the state funds of the Ottoman Empire and in commerce with Europe. They thrived in Baghdad throughout the eighteenth and nineteenth centuries under Ottoman rule, performing critical commercial functions such since money lending and banking. Like the Armenians, the Jews could engage in necessary commercial behaviors, such since money lending and banking, that were proscribed for Moslems under Islamic law.

Emergence of the Court Jew

Court Jews were Jewish bankers or businessmen who lent money and handled the funds of some of the Christian European noble homes, primarily in the seventeenth and eighteenth centuries. Court Jews were forerunners to the contemporary financier or Secretary of the Treasury. Their occupations incorporated raising revenues through tax cultivation, negotiating loans, master of the mint, creating new sources for revenue, negotiating loans, floating debentures, devising new taxes and supplying the military. In addition, the Court Jew acted since personal bankers for nobility: he raised money to cover the noble's personal diplomacy and his extravagances. Court Jews were skilled officers and businessmen who received privileges in return for their services. They were mainly commonly establish in Germany, Holland, and Austria, but also in Denmark, England, Hungary, Italy, Poland, Lithuania, Portugal, and Spain. Just as to Dimont, virtually every duchy, principality, and palatinate in the Holy Roman Empire had a Court Jew.

Germany and Poland

The Fuggers were financiers from 1485 to 1560 and are recognized since a particularly significant banking family in Southern Germany. Dutch bankers played a central role in establishing banking in the Northern German municipality states. Berenberg Bank is the oldest private bank in Germany, recognized in 1590 through Dutch brothers, Hans and Paul Berenberg in Hamburg. The bank is still owned through the Berenberg dynasty.

Holland

During 17th century, valuable metals from the New World, Japan and other locales have been channeled into Europe, with corresponding price increases. Thanks to the free coinage, the Bank of Amsterdam, and the heightened deal and commerce, Netherlands attracted even more coin and bullion. These concepts of Fractional-reserve banking and payment organizations went on and spread to England and elsewhere.

England

In the Municipality of London there weren't any banking homes operating in a manner established since therefore today until the 17th century, although the London Royal Swap was recognized in 1565.

The 17th and 18th Centuries

Through the end of the 16th century and throughout the 17th, the traditional banking functions of accepting deposits, money lending, money changing, and transferring finances were combined with the issuance of bank debt that served since a substitute for gold and silver coins. New banking practices promoted commercial and industrial development through providing a safe and convenient means of payment and a money supply more responsive to commercial requires, since well since through "discounting" business debt. Through the end of the

17th century, banking was also becoming significant for the funding necessities of the relatively new and combative European states. This would lead on to government regulations and the first central banks. The success of the new banking techniques and practices in Amsterdam and also the thriving deal municipality of Antwerp help spread the concepts and thoughts to London and helped the growths elsewhere in Europe.

Goldsmiths of London

The largest developers of banking in London were the goldsmiths, who transformed from easy artisans to becoming depositories of gold and silver holdings. Measures such at the appropriation of £200,000 of private money through King Charles I from the royal mint, in 1640 caused merchants to lose trust in the existing organizations and drive them to discover more trusted alternatives such since the goldsmiths.

Goldsmiths soon establish themselves with money they had no immediate exploit for, and they began to lend it out at interest to merchants and the government. Finding substantial profit in this business, they began to solicit deposits and pay interest on them. The goldsmiths eventually exposed that the deposit receipts they provided were passing from person to person in lieu of payment in coin. This prompted them to begin lending paper receipts rather than coins. Through promoting acceptance of the receipts since a means of payment, the goldsmiths exposed they could lend more than the gold and silver coin they had on hand, a practice that became recognized since fractional-reserve banking.

Debt since a New Type of Money

These practices created a new type of "money" that was actually debt, that is, goldsmiths' debt rather than silver or gold coin, a commodity that had been regulated and controlled through the monarchy. This growth required the acceptance in deal of the goldsmiths' promissory notes, payable on demand. Acceptance in turn required a common belief that coin would be accessible; and a fractional reserve normally served this purpose. Acceptance also required that the holders of debt be able legally to enforce an unconditional right to payment; it required that the notes (since well since drafts) be negotiable instruments. The concept of negotiability had appeared in fits and starts in European money markets, but it were well urbanized through the 17th century. Nevertheless, an act of Parliament was required in the early 18th century (1704) to overrule court decisions holding that the gold smith's notes, despite the "customs of merchants", were not negotiable.

Meanwhile, the credit of the British Crown had been diminished through default in 1672. The monarchy's urgent require for finances at rates lower than those charged through the goldsmiths, and the instance of the public Bank of

Amsterdam, which had been able to create an ample supply of credit accessible at low interest rates, led in 1694 to the establishment of the Bank of England. The Bank of England succeeded in raising money for the government at relatively low rates.

Growth of Central Banking

The Bank of Amsterdam became a model for the functioning of a bank in the capability of monetary swap and started the growth of central banks. The first such bank was the Sveriges Riksbank, recognized in 1668. This was followed through the Bank of England which was recognized in 1694 and was initially founded specifically to assist the English government in funding the sustained war against France.

In London the Bank of England had a monopoly in excess of corporate banking, and even big partnerships were prohibited. But private banks, however relatively little, personal enterprises, sustained to discover profitable business in discounting merchants' bills. In the latter half of the century little banks in country cities grew rapidly in number and needed "correspondent" banks in London with which they could deposit and invest finances. The London banks in turn settled accounts in Bank of England notes, and through the end of the century several kept their own deposit accounts with the Bank of England.

Central Banking in North America

The management of the government of the State of Massachusetts issued the first bill of credit in the history of America in 1690. In 1784 John Colman proposed the thought of bank that would issue paper but this is since distant since the "Colman bank" concept went. The Bank of North America was recognized in 1784 and started growths that led to a national banking organization.

There was opposition to the making of a central bank in the United States when the United States was first founded. But the First Bank of the United States was founded in 1791, though its charter was left to expire in 1811 because of the on-going disagreements. A second effort was made with the establishment of Second Bank of the United States in 1816, again its charter was not renewed in 1836. It was only in 1913 with the making of the Federal Reserve Organization that a de facto central bank was created in the United States.

Royal Banking

Throughout the 13th century and early fourteenth both the French and English monarchies were still by temple banking. Early in the reign of King George IIIrd, sometime in the eighteenth century, the English monarchy began to bank with a private bank recognized since Coutts. The French kings were by banking homes of Geneva sometime after the beginning of the French Revolution in 1789, a procedure of transition with a footing sometime throughout 1713.

Removal of Religious Restrictions on Earning Interest

The rise of Protestantism, freed several European Christians from Rome's dictates against usury. In the late 18th century, Protestant merchant families began to move into banking, especially in trading countries such since the United Kingdom (Barings), Germany (Schroders) and the Netherlands (Hope & Co.) At the similar time, new kinds of financial behaviors broadened the scope of banking distant beyond its origins. The merchant-banking families dealt in everything from underwriting bonds to originating foreign loans. For example, bullion trading and bond issuance were two of the specialties of the Rothschilds. In 1803, Barings teamed with Hope & Co. to facilitate the Louisiana Purchase.

LATE 18TH AND 19TH CENTURIES

In the late eighteenth and nineteenth century, spurred at first through financing required for the Napoleonic wars and then through the expansion of railroads, banks evolved for the first time to operate through method of commerce, that is to accept demand deposits and give business loans, instead of only functioning for the good of the state. Before 1776 there were only three commercial banks on the landmass recognized then since America. Throughout this era a big number of commercial banks were recognized in a number of dissimilar countries. This incorporated banks such since the Commercial Bank of Scotland which was founded in 1810 and the Bank of New South Wales which was dated to 1817. Jews were founders and leaders of several of the significant early European banks, since well since important banks in the United States. Many Jewish bankers became very influential, successfully competing with non-Jewish banking homes in the floating of government loans.

Europe

Rothschild family banking businesses pioneered international high fund throughout the industrialization of Europe and were instrumental in supporting railway organizations crossways the world and in intricate government financing for projects such since the Suez Canal. The family bought up a big proportion of the property in Mayfair, London. Major businesses directly founded through Rothschild family capital contain:

- Alliance Assurance (1824) (now Royal & Sun Alliance);
- Chemin de Fer du Nord (1845);
- Rio Tinto Cluster (1873);
- Société Le Nickel (1880) (now Eramet); and
- Imétal (1962) (now Imerys).

The Rothschilds financed the founding of De Beers, since well since Cecil Rhodes on his expeditions in Africa and the making of the colony of Rhodesia. From the late 1880s onwards, the family controlled the Rio Tinto mining company. The Japanese government approached the London and Paris families for funding throughout the Russo-Japanese War. The London consortium's issue of Japanese war bonds would total £11.5 million.

The United States of America

In the 19th century, the rise of deal and industry in the US led to powerful new private merchant banks, culminating in J.P. Morgan & Co. Throughout the 20th century, though, the financial world began to outgrow the possessions of family-owned and other shapes of private-equity banking. Corporations came to control the banking business. For the similar causes, merchant banking behaviors became presently one region of interest for contemporary banks.

Globalization

In the late 19th century there was a huge development in the banking industry. Banks played a key role in moving from gold and silver based coinage to paper money, redeemable against the bank's holdings. Within the new organization of ownership and investment, the state's role since an economic factor grew considerably.

20TH CENTURY

The first decade of the 20th century saw the Panic of 1907 in the US, which led to numerous runs on banks and became recognized since the bankers panic.

1930s Great Depression

Throughout the Crash of 1929 preceding the Great Depression, periphery necessities were only 10%. Brokerage firms, in other languages, would lend $9 for every $1 an investor had deposited. When the market fell, brokers described in these loans, which could not be paid back. Banks began to fail since debtors defaulted on debt and depositors attempted to withdraw their deposits en masse, triggering multiple bank runs. Government guarantees and Federal Reserve banking regulations to prevent such panics were ineffective or not used. Bank failures led to the loss of billions of dollars in assets. Outstanding debts became heavier, because prices and incomes fell through 20–50% but the debts remained at the similar dollar amount. After the panic of 1929, and throughout the first 10 months of 1930, 744 US banks failed. Through April 1933, approximately $7 billion in deposits had been frozen in failed banks or those left unlicensed after the March Bank Holiday.

Bank failures snowballed since desperate bankers described in loans those borrowers did not have time or money to repay. With future profits looking poor, capital investment and construction slowed or totally ceased. In the face of bad loans and worsening future prospects, the surviving banks became even more conservative in their lending. Banks built up their capital reserves and made fewer loans, which intensified deflationary pressures. A vicious cycle urbanized and the downward spiral accelerated. In all, in excess of 9,000 banks failed throughout the 1930s.

In response, several countries significantly increased financial regulation. The U.S. recognized the Securities and Swap Commission in 1933, and passed the Glass–Steagall Act, which separated investment banking and commercial banking. This was to avoid more risky investment banking behaviors from ever again causing commercial bank failures.

World Bank and the Growth of Payment Technology

Throughout the post second world war era and with the introduction of the Bretton Woods organization in 1944, two institutions were created: the International Monetary Finance (IMF) and the World Bank. Encouraged through these organizations, commercial banks started to lend to sovereign states in the third world. This was at the similar time since inflation started to rise in the west. The Gold average was eventually abandoned in 1971 and a number of the banks were caught out and became bankrupt due to third world country debt defaults.

This was also a time of rising exploit of technology in retail banking. In 1959, banks agreed on an average for machine readable characters (MICR) that was patented in the United States for exploit with cheques, which led to the first automated reader-sorter machines. In the 1960s, the first Automated Teller Machines (ATM) or Cash machines were urbanized and first machines started to seem through the end of the decade. Banks started to become heavy investors in computer technology to automate much of the manual processing, which began a shift through banks from big clerical staffs to new automated organizations. Through the 1970s the first payment organizations started to be develop that would lead to electronic payment organizations for both international and domestic payments. The international SWIFT payment network was recognized in 1973 and domestic payment organizations were urbanized approximately the world through banks working jointly with governments.

1980s Deregulation and Globalization

Global banking and capital market services proliferated throughout the 1980s after deregulation of financial markets in a number of countries. The 1986 'Large Bang' in London allowing banks to access capital markets in new ways, which led to important changes to the method banks operated and accessed capital. It also started a trend where retail banks started to acquire investment banks and stock brokers creating universal banks that offered a wide range of banking services. The trend also spread to the US after much of the Glass–Steagall Act was repealed in the 1980s, this saw US retail banks embark on large rounds of mergers and acquisitions and also engage in investment banking behaviors.

Financial services sustained to grow by the 1980s and 1990s since a result of a great augment in demand from companies, governments, and financial organizations, but also because financial market circumstances were buoyant and, on the entire, bullish. Interest rates in the United States declined from in relation to the 15% for two-year U.S. Treasury notes to in relation to the 5% throughout the 20-year era, and financial assets grew then at a rate almost twice the rate of the world economy.

This era saw an important internationalization of financial markets. The augment of U.S. Foreign investments from Japan not only provided the finances to corporations in the U.S., but also helped fund the federal government. The dominance of U.S. financial markets was disappearing and there was a rising interest in foreign stocks. The extraordinary development of foreign financial markets results from both big increases in the pool of savings in foreign countries, such since Japan, and, especially, the deregulation of foreign financial markets, which enabled them to expand their behaviors. Therefore, American corporations and banks started seeking investment opportunities abroad, prompting the growth in the U.S. of mutual finances specializing in trading in foreign stock markets.

Such rising internationalization and opportunity in financial services changed the competitive landscape, since now several banks would demonstrated a preference for the "universal banking" model prevalent in Europe. Universal banks are free to engage in all shapes of financial services, create investments in client companies, and function since much since possible since a "one-stop" supplier of both retail and wholesale financial services.

21ST CENTURY

The early 2000s were marked through consolidation of existing banks and entrance into the market of other financial intermediaries: non-bank financial organization. Big corporate players were beginning to discover their method into the financial service society, offering competition to recognized banks. The largest services offered incorporated insurances, pension, mutual, money market and hedge finances, loans and credits and securities. Indeed, through the end of 2001 the market capitalization of the world's 15 main financial services providers incorporated four non-banks.

The procedure of financial innovation advanced enormously in the first decade of the 21 century rising the importance and profitability of non-bank fund. Such profitability priory restricted to the non-banking industry, has prompted the Office of the Comptroller of the Currency (OCC) to encourage banks to explore other financial instruments, diversifying banks' business since well since improving banking economic health. Hence, since the separate financial instruments are being explored and adopted through both the banking and non-banking industries, the distinction flanked by dissimilar financial organizations are slowly vanishing. The first decade of the 21st century also saw the culmination of the technological innovation in banking in excess of the previous 30 years and saw a major shift absent from traditional banking to internet banking.

Late-2000s Financial Crisis

The Late-2000s financial crisis caused important stress on banks approximately the world. The failure of a big number of major banks resulted in government bail-outs. The collapse and fire sale of Bear Stearns to JP Morgan Chase in March 2008 and the collapse of Lehman Brothers in September that similar year led to a credit crunch and global banking crises. In response governments approximately the world bailed-out, nationalized or arranged fire sales for a big number of major banks. Starting with the Irish government on 29 September 2008, governments approximately the world provided wholesale guarantees to underwriting banks to avoid panic of systemic failure to the entire banking organization. These measures spawned the condition 'too large to fail' and resulted in a lot of discussion in relation to the moral hazard of these actions.

MAJOR MEASURES IN BANKING HISTORY

- Florentine banking – The Medicis and Pittis in the middle of others.
- 1100–1300 – Knights Templar run earliest Euro wide/Mideast banking.
- 1542–1551 – The Great Debasement refers to the English Crown's policy of coement throughout the reigns of Henry VIII and Edward VI.
- 1553 – First joint-stock company, the Company of Merchant Adventurers to New Lands, is chartered in London.
- 1602 – The Amsterdam Stock Swap was recognized through the Dutch East India Company for relations in its printed stocks and bonds.
- 1609 – The Amsterdamsche Wisselbank (Amsterdam Swap Bank) was founded.
- 1656 - The first European bank to exploit banknotes opened in Sweden for private clientele, throughout 1668 the organization converted to a public bank.
- 1690s – The Massachusetts Bay Colony was the first of the Thirteen Colonies to issue permanently circulating banknotes.
- 1694 – The Bank of England was set up to supply money to the King.

- 1695 – The Parliament of Scotland makes the Bank of Scotland.
- 1716 – John Law opens Banque Générale
- 1717 – Master of the Royal Mint Sir Isaac Newton recognized a new mint ratio flanked by silver and gold that had the effect of driving silver out of circulation (bimetalism)and putting Britain on a gold average.
- 1720 – The South Sea Bubble and John Law's Mississippi Scheme, which caused a European financial crisis and forced several bankers out of business.
- 1775 – The first structure community, Ketley's Structure Community, was recognized in Birmingham, England.
- 1782 – The Bank of North America opens.
- 1791 – The First Bank of the United States was a bank chartered through the United States Congress. The charter was for 20 years.
- 1800 – the Rothschild family establishes European wide banking.
- 1800 (January 18) Napolean Bonaparte founds the Bank of France.
- 1816 – The Second Bank of the United States was chartered five years after the First Bank of the United States lost its charter. This charter was also for 20 years. The bank was created to fund the country in the aftermath of the War of 1812.
- 1817 - The New York Stock and Swap Board are recognized.
- 1818 - the first savings bank of Paris
- 1862 – To fund the American Civil War, the federal government under U.S. President Abraham Lincoln issued a legal tender paper money, the "greenbacks".
- 1870 - Establishment of the Deutsche Bank
- 1874 – The Specie Payment Resumption Act provided for the redemption of United States paper currency ("greenbacks"), in gold, beginning in 1879.
- 1913 – The Federal Reserve Act created the Federal Reserve Organization, the central banking organization of the United States of America, and granted it the legal power to issue legal tender.
- 1930–33 – In the wake of the Wall Street Crash of 1929, 9,000 banks secure, wiping out a third of the money supply in the United States.
- 1933 – Executive Order 6102 signed through U.S. President Franklin D. Roosevelt forbade ownership of Gold Coin, Gold Bullion, and Gold Certificates through U.S. citizens beyond a sure amount, effectively ending the convertibility of US dollars into gold.
- 1971 – The Nixon Shock was a series of economic events taken through U.S. President Richard Nixon which canceled the direct convertibility of the United States dollar to gold through foreign nations. This essentially ended the existing Bretton Woods organization of international financial swap.

- 1986 – The "Large Bang" (deregulation of London financial markets) served since a catalyst to reaffirm London's location since a global centre of world banking.
- 2007 – Start of the Late-2000s financial crisis that saw the credit crunch that led to the failure and bail-out of a big number of the worlds major banks.
- 2008 – Washington Mutual collapses. It was the main bank failure in history.

BRIEF BUILDING OF BANKS

BRANCH BANKING

A branch, banking center or financial center is a retail site where a bank, credit union, or other financial organization (and through extension, brokerage firms) offers a wide array of face-to-face and automated services to its customers. Throughout the 3rd century banks in Persia (now Iran) and in other territories started to issue letters of credit recognized since Sakks, simply checks in today's language that could be traded in cooperative homes or offices during the Persian territories. In the era from 1100-1300 banking started to expand crossways Europe and banks began opening 'branches' in remote, foreign sites to support international deal. In 1327, Avignon in France had 43 branches of Italian banking homes alone.

The practice of opening satellite branches was popularized in the early 20th century through Amadeo Giannini, then head of the Bank of America. Historically, branches were housed in imposing structures, often in a neoclassical architecture approach. Today, branches may also take the shape of smaller offices within a superior intricate, such since a shopping mall.

Traditionally, the branch was the only channel of access to a financial organization's services. Services provided through a branch contain cash withdrawals and deposits from a demand explanation with a bank teller, financial advice by a specialist, safe deposit box rentals, bureau de transform, insurance sales (where it is allowed through law), etc. In the early 21st century, characteristics such since automated teller machines (ATM), telephone and online banking, allow customers to bank from remote sites and after business hours. This has caused financial organizations to reduce their branch business hours and to merge smaller branches into superior ones. Conversely, they converted some into *mini-branches* with only ATMs for cash withdrawal and depositing; computer terminals for online banking and cheque depositing machines. Some mini-branches may have one or no human staff with only telephone support.

Some financial organizations, in an effort to illustrate a friendlier image, offer a boutique or coffeehouse-like habitation in their branches, with sit-down counters, refreshments, interactive displays, music and playing regions for children. Some branches also have drive-by teller windows or ATM's. Other financial organizations reduce their costs and location their offerings through having no branches and are sometimes recognized since virtual banks.

Legal Restrictions

Historically, branch banking in the United States - especially interstate branch banking - was viewed unfavorably through regulatory authorities, and this was codified with the enactment of the McFadden Act of 1927, which specifically prohibited interstate banking. In excess of the after that few decades, some banks attempted to circumvent McFadden's provisions through establishing bank holding companies that operated therefore-described self-governing banks in multiple states.

To address this, The Bank Holding Company Act of 1956 prohibited bank holding companies headquartered in one state from having branches in any other state. Mainly interstate banking prohibitions were repealed through the Riegle-Neal Interstate Banking and Branching Efficiency Act of 1994. Some states have also had restrictive bank branch laws; for instance, Illinois outlawed branches (other than the largest office) until 1967, and did not allow an unlimited number until 1993.

KINDS OF BRANCHES

Traditional or Brick-and-mortar

These are typically stand alone branches of a financial organization that often are contained in its own structure. These branches typically offer full service banking including safe deposit boxes. They may contain access to drive-by teller windows.

In-store

These are typically branches situated in a retail space such since a grocery or discount store. They may be full service branches or limited service branches. They usually do not contain a drive-by teller windows or safe deposit boxes. These branches have limited staff and typically contain technology since a means to deliver banking services such since the exploit of automated teller machines, videoconferencing, and video banking organizations.

Green Branch

Green Branch is a federally registered trademark to denote the environmentally friendly construction and design of retail banking sites. This condition was granted since a trademark through the U.S. Patent and Trademark Office on 16 January 2007 to the PNC Financial Services Cluster, Inc. (NYSE: PNC). The foundation for the federal patent office's approval of PNC's trademark application incorporated the determination that financial and banking services are not usually associated with environmentally friendly or ecologically efficient aspects.

CLUSTER BANKING

In fund, "cluster banking" can refer either to banking provided to a specific cluster of people with modified services for requires or to the formation of a holding company in manage of many banks. The kind of banking is generally apparent from the context, since the two concepts are extremely dissimilar.

In the first sense, cluster banking often comes up in the context of employees who join a bank or credit union jointly. The employer jobs with the bank to make a stimulus program encouraging people to sign up. Members of the cluster may get discounts on fees, access to special services, and greater manage in excess of retirement accounts beside with offers for insurance and other products. While people are not required to participate in cluster banking, the benefits of the program are often a compelling argument to join.

For banks, cluster banking gives a ready-made cluster of customers, a separate benefit. The bank does not have to recruit customers, because they sign up on their own. In addition, bureaucratic costs associated with things like direct deposit of paychecks are greatly reduced when employers and employees bank in the similar site. Banks get access to capital by the deposits of cluster banking participants and the participants get benefits like special interest rates, explanation characteristics like free traveler's checks, and therefore forth.

Cooperatives involved in cluster banking do not have to be employees of the similar company. Housing cooperatives may exploit same organizations and people can also bank since a cluster affiliated with a church or another institution. Bank policies modify, and people interested in the possibility of setting up a cluster banking program should create arrangements to meet with a bank representative to discover out in relation to the accessible options and necessities, such since a minimum number of members. Cluster banking in the sense of holding companies in manage of banks consists of a holding company with a majority share in two or more banks. The banks have their own boards and are run since self-governing entities, but the holding company dominates their behaviors and has the domination to outvote other shareholders. Depending on local laws and the percentage of shares owned, the holding company's ownership may require to be approved through government regulators to address concerns in relation to the potential for creating a banking monopoly, where free market competition is limited through having a single company manage the bulk of the companies offering banking services.

CHAIN BANKING

Chain banking is a situation in which three or more banks that are independently chartered are controlled through a little cluster of people. The mechanisms used to set up this kind of arrangement normally involve securing sufficient stock flanked by the individuals to have a controlling interest in each of the bank corporations involved. The arrangement can also be supervised with the establishment of interlocking directorates or boards of directors that effectively make a network flanked by the banks without require for some kind of central holding company.

The concept of chain banking is dissimilar from cluster banking, in that the entities involved in the chain bank arrangement remain autonomous and are not owned through a single holding company. Through contrast, the cluster banking model needs a holding company to own all the banks involved, effectively creating an umbrella under which all the banks operate. Chain banking is also dissimilar from branch banking, a situation where all regional branches of a bank are owned through a single banking organization.

In years past, chain banking afforded many benefits for investors. The strategy made it possible to earn steady returns from many banks that operated in the similar society, without any fears of a great trade of competition from other banks in the region. The network style made it possible for investors to exploit their cumulative power to stay bank services and their attendant fees same from one enterprise to another, therefore ensuring that returns remained constant. The chain banking procedure also made it possible for investors to make a network where each bank in the chain served a dissimilar section of the market within the region. For instance, one bank may focus on business accounts while another specialize in personal accounts, and the third bank in the chain provided services related to the purchase and sale of securities.

In excess of time, the chain banking style has become less popular in a number of nations. This is due to changes in banking laws in several spaces that helped to redefine the procedure of interstate banking since well since international banking. This redefinition has made it possible for some banks that were once somewhat restricted in what they could offer customers to be able to offer a wider range of services. With more liberalized banking laws in several jurisdictions, the benefits afforded through the chain banking model can now be realized by other approaches, sometimes with a greater degree of efficiency and without the require for establishing this kind of investor network.

FUNCTIONS OF COMMERCIAL BANKS

Commercial banks engage in the following behaviors:

- Processing of payments through method of telegraphic transfer, EFTPOS, internet banking, or other means
- Issuing bank drafts and bank cheques
- Accepting money on condition deposit
- Lending money through overdraft, installment loan, or other means
- Providing documentary and standby letter of credit, guarantees,

performance bonds, securities underwriting commitments and other shapes of off balance sheet exposures

- Safekeeping of documents & other things in safe deposit boxes
- Sales, sharing or brokerage, with or without advice, of: insurance, element trusts and same financial products since a "financial supermarket"
- Cash administration and treasury
- Merchant banking and private equity financing
- Traditionally, big commercial banks also underwrite bonds, and create markets in currency, interest rates, and credit-related securities, but today big commercial banks generally have an investment bank arm that is involved in the mentioned behaviors.

SIGNIFICANCE OF BANKING IN AN ECONOMIC ORGANIZATION

Banks in the contemporary economy are profit maximizing businesses. The easy account is that banks allow for the close depositing of money for individuals and businesses. Though, when banks receive a substantial amount of deposits, it becomes irrational to basically let the money sit there. Since a result, banks then invest this money and have it earn interest for the bank and the depositor. From this, banks became central actors in the contemporary economic organization.

Characteristics

By an extremely easy model, when banks collect deposits, they seek to create this money "job" for them by investing it through lending it out to others. As it is unlikely that depositors will demand their money all back at once, the bank can leverage its deposit collection to back superior and superior risks. In other languages, they will exploit their deposit money to leverage superior loans and investments, therefore keeping only a fraction of their deposits actually on hand. This is described "fractional reserve" banking.

Significance

The largest region of significance for banks in contemporary financial organizations is since agents of risk. Banks are for-profit institutions that seek to exploit depositors finances since backing for extensive condition investment. The brief formula is that banks collect deposits from individuals, these deposits are used since collateral for raising finances on money markets, and these finances are then put into extensive condition investments.

Function

Banks lend a portion of depositors' money to businesses that the bank considers will create money, hence creation money for their depositors. There is no good cause for deposit money to merely collect dust in vaults, therefore it is lent out to those who the bank has approved in advance since a good credit risk. This means that banks oversee investments, by depositors' money since backing. As bank loans are the largest source of funding for businesses, banks actually have a huge role in overseeing investments globally.

Effects

The largest effect of the significance of banks is that they have a hand in almost all investments made in the contemporary economy. When one takes out a mortgage to buy a home, the bank has determined that the borrower is a good credit risk and is likely to pay the money back, including the interest which is the bank's "cut," for taking the risk in the first lay. The major concept is that as mainly capital is raised by banks, banks then manages mainly investments.

Thoughts

When banks lend money to investors, this loan means many things:

- That the bank actually owns the enterprise (home, business, car, etc.) until the money is paid off; and
- These investments are all mediated through the bank, which means that banks measure and approve (or reject) the risks investors take.

If too several investments fail, the bank fails, and the depositors' money goes to the entity that takes in excess of the failing or failed bank. As the 1930s, though, deposits are backed through the federal government, guaranteeing individual deposits up to $250,000 up until 2014, when the sheltered maximum per explanation goes back to $100,000.

Making of Credit

One of the significant functions of commercial bank is the making of credit. Credit making is the multiple expansions of banks demand deposits. It is an open secret now that banks advance a major portion of their deposits to the borrowers and stay smaller sections of deposits to the customers on demand. Even then the customers of the banks have full confidence that the depositor's lying in the banks is quite safe and can be withdrawn on demand. The banks use this trust of their clients and expand loans through much more time than the amount of demand deposits possessed through them. This tendency on the section of the commercial banks to expand their demand deposits since a multiple of their excess cash reserve is described making of credit.

The single bank cannot make credit. It is the banking organization since an entire which can expand loans through several times of its excess cash reserves. Further, when a loan is advanced to an individuals or a business concern, it is not given in cash. The bank opens a deposit explanation in the name of the borrower and allows him to attract upon the bank since and when required. The loan advanced becomes the gain of deposit through some other bank. Loans therefore create deposits and deposits create loans.

COMMERCIAL BANKING IN INDIA

Banking in India originated in the last decades first banks were The Common Bank of India, which started in 1786, and Bank of Hindustan, which started in 1770; both are now defunct. The oldest bank in subsistence in India is the State Bank of India, which originated in the Bank of Calcutta in June 1806, which approximately immediately became the Bank of Bengal. This was one of the three presidency banks, the other two being the Bank of Bombay and the Bank of Madras, all three of which were recognized under charters from the British East India Company. For several years the Presidency banks acted since quasi-central banks, since did their successors. The three banks merged in 1921 to shape the Imperial Bank of India, which, upon India's independence, became the State Bank of India in 1955.

STATE BANK OF INDIA

State Bank of India (SBI) is the main banking and financial services company in India through revenue, assets and market capitalization. It is a state-owned corporation with its headquarters in Mumbai, Maharashtra. Since of March 2012, it had assets of US$360 billion and 14,119 branches, including 173 foreign offices in 37 countries crossways the globe. Including the branches that belong to its associate banks, SBI has 21,500 branches.

The bank traces its ancestry to British India, by the Imperial Bank of India, to the founding in 1806 of the Bank of Calcutta, creation it the oldest commercial bank in the Indian Subcontinent. Bank of Madras merged into the other two presidencies banks—Bank of Calcutta and Bank of Bombay—to shape the Imperial Bank of India, which in turn became the State Bank of India. The Government of India nationalized the Imperial Bank of India in 1955, with the Reserve Bank of India taking a 60% stake, and renamed it the State Bank of India. In 2008, the government took in excess of the stake held through the Reserve Bank of India. SBI has been ranked 285th in the Fortune Global 500 rankings of the world's major corporations for the year 2012.

SBI gives a range of banking products by its huge network of branches in India and overseas, including products aimed at non-resident Indians (NRIs). The State Bank Cluster has the main banking branch network in India. SBI has 14 regional head offices located at:

- Chandigarh (Punjab & Haryana),
- Delhi, Lucknow (Uttar Pradesh),
- Patna (Bihar),
- Kolkata (West Bengal),

- Guwahati (North East Circle),
- Bhubaneswar (Orissa),
- Hyderabad (Andhra Pradesh),
- Chennai (Tamil Nadu),
- Trivandrum (Kerala),
- Bengaluru (Karnataka),
- Mumbai (Maharashtra),
- Bhopal (Madhya Pradesh)
- Ahmedabad (Gujarat) and
- 57 Zonal Offices that is situated at significant municipalities during the country.

SBI is a local banking behemoth and is one of the main financial organizations in the world. It has a market share in the middle of Indian commercial banks of in relation to the 20% in deposits and loans. The State Bank of India is the 29th mainly reputed company in the world just as to *Forbes*. Also, SBI is the only bank featured in the coveted "top 10 brands of India" list in an annual survey mannered through Brand Fund and *The Economic Times* in 2010.

International Attendance

Since of 31 March 2012, the bank had 173 overseas offices spread in excess of 34 countries. It has branches of the parent in Moscow, Colombo, Dhaka, Frankfurt, Hong Kong, Tehran, Johannesburg, London, Los Angeles, Male in the Maldives, Muscat, Dubai, New York, Osaka, Sydney, and Tokyo. It has offshore banking elements in the Bahamas, Bahrain, and Singapore, and representative offices in Bhutan and Cape City. It also has an ADB in Boston, USA.

SBI operates many foreign subsidiaries or affiliates. In 1990, it recognized an offshore bank: State Bank of India (Mauritius).

In 1982, the bank recognized a subsidiary, State Bank of India (California), which now has ten branches – nine branches in the state of California and one in Washington, D.C. The 10th branch was opened in Fremont, California on 28 March 2011. The other eight branches in California are situated in Los Angeles, Artesia, San Jose, Canoga Park, Fresno, San Diego, Tustin and Bakersfield.

The Canadian subsidiary, State Bank of India (Canada) also dates to 1982. It has seven branches, four in the Toronto region and three in British Columbia.

In Nigeria, SBI operates since INMB Bank. This bank began in 1981 since the Indo-Nigerian Merchant Bank and received permission in 2002 to commence retail banking. It now has five branches in Nigeria.

In Nepal, SBI owns 55% of Nepal SBI Bank, which has branches during the country. In Moscow, SBI owns 60% of Commercial Bank of India, with Canara Bank owning the rest. In Indonesia, it owns 76% of PT Bank Indo Monex.

The State Bank of India already has a branch in Shanghai and plans to open one in Tianjin. In Kenya, State Bank of India owns 76% of Giro Commercial Bank, which it acquired for US$8 million in October 2005...

Associate Banks

SBI has five associate banks; all exploit the similar logo of a blue circle and all the associates exploit the "State Bank of" name, followed through the local headquarters' name:

- State Bank of Bikaner & Jaipur
- State Bank of Hyderabad
- State Bank of Mysore
- State Bank of Patiala
- State Bank of Travancore

Earlier SBI had only seven associate banks that constituted the State Bank Cluster. Originally, the then seven banks that became the associate banks belonged to princely states until the government nationalized them flanked by October 1959 and May 1960. In tune with the first Five Year Plan, emphasizing the growth of rural India, the government integrated these banks into the State Bank of India organization to expand its rural outreach. There has been a proposal to merge all the associate banks into SBI to make a "mega bank" and streamline operations.

The first step towards unification occurred on 13 August 2008 when State Bank of Saurashtra merged with SBI, reducing the number of state banks from seven to six. Then on 19 June 2009 the SBI board approved the merger of its subsidiary, State Bank of Indore, with itself. SBI holds 98.3% in State Bank of Indore. (Individuals who held the shares prior to its takeover through the government hold the balance of 1.77%.)

The acquisition of State Bank of Indore added 470 branches to SBI's existing network of branches. Also, following the acquisition, SBI's total assets will inch extremely secure to the ₹10 trillion spot. The total assets of SBI and the State Bank of Indore stood at ₹9,981,190 million since of March 2009. The procedure of merging of State Bank of Indore was completed through April 2010, and the SBI Indore branches started functioning since SBI branches on 26 August 2010.

Non-banking Subsidiaries

Separately from its five associate banks, SBI also has the following non-banking subsidiaries:

- SBI Capital Markets Ltd
- SBI Finances Administration Pvt Ltd
- SBI Factors & Commercial Services Pvt Ltd
- SBI Cards & Payments Services Pvt. Ltd. (SBICPSL)
- SBI DFHI Ltd

- SBI Life Insurance Co. Ltd.
- SBI Common Insurance

In March 2001, SBI (with 74% of the total capital), joined with BNP Paribas (with 26% of the remaining capital), to shape a joint venture life insurance company named SBI Life Insurance company Ltd. Now-a days SBI Life Insurance Co. Ltd ranks in the middle of the top and mainly trusted Life Insurance Companies in India and also abroad. In 2004 SBI DFHI Ltd(DISCOUNT AND FUND HOME OF INDIA) was founded with its headquarter in MUMBAI, MAHARASHTRA.SBI DFHI Ltd is primary dealer that deals in Fixed income securities(treasury bills, state growth loans, government securities, non SLR bonds, corporate bonds) and Short Condition Money Market instruments(certificates of deposits, commercial paper, inter-corporate deposits, call and money notice deposits).IT is an organization shaped through RBI to support the book structure procedure in primary auctions of Government securities and give necessary depth and liquidity to the Secondary market in Government securities.

Current Board of Directors

After the end of O. P. Bhatt's reign since SBI chairman on 31 March 2011, the post was taken in excess of through Pratip Chaudhuri, who is the former deputy managing director of the international division of SBI. Since of 4 August 2011, there are twelve members in the SBI board of directors, including Subir Gokarn, who is also one of the four deputy governors of the Reserve Bank of India. The complete list of the Board members is:

- Pratip Chaudhuri (Chairman)
- Hemant G. Contractor (Managing Director)
- Diwakar Gupta (Managing Director)
- A Krishna Kumar (Managing Director)
- S. Venkatachalam (Managing Director)
- Dileep C Choksi (Director)
- D. Sundaram (Director)
- Parthasarathy Iyengar (Director)
- G. D. Nadaf (Officer Employee Director)
- Rashpal Malhotra (Director)
- D. K. Mittal (Director)
- Subir V. Gokarn (Director)

Other SBI Service Points

- SBI has in relation to the 27,000+ ATMs (25,000th ATM was inaugurated through the then Chairman of State Bank Shri O.P. Bhatt on 31 March 2011, the day of his retirement); and SBI cluster(including associate banks) has in relation to the 45,000 ATMs.

SBI has become the first bank to install an ATM at Drass in the Jammu & Kashmir Kargil area. This was the banks 27,032 and ATM on 27 July 2012.

- SBI has 99000 offices in India.

NATIONALIZATION OF COMMERCIAL BANKS

Despite the provisions, manage and regulations of Reserve Bank of India, banks in India except the State Bank of India or SBI, sustained to be owned and operated through private persons. Through the 1960s, the Indian banking industry had become a significant tool to facilitate the growth of the Indian economy. At the similar time, it had appeared since a big employer, and a debate had ensued in relation to the nationalization of the banking industry. Indira Gandhi, then Prime Minister of India, expressed the intention of the Government of India in the annual conference of the All India Congress Meeting in a paper entitled *"Stray considerations on Bank Nationalization."* The meeting received the paper with enthusiasm.

Thereafter, her move was swift and sudden. The Government of India issued an ordinance ('Banking Companies (Acquisition and Transfer of Undertakings) Ordinance, 1969')) and nationalized the 14 main commercial banks with effect from the midnight of July 19, 1969. These banks contained 85 percent of bank deposits in the country. Jayaprakash Narayan, a national leader of India, called the step since a *"masterstroke of political sagacity."* Within two weeks of the issue of the ordinance, the Parliament passed the Banking Companies (Acquisition and Transfer of Undertaking) Bill, and it received the presidential approval on 9 August 1969.

A second dose of nationalization of 6 more commercial banks followed in 1980. The stated cause for the nationalization was to provide the government more manage of credit delivery. With the second dose of nationalization, the Government of India controlled approximately 91% of the banking business of India. Later on, in the year 1993, the government merged New Bank of India with Punjab National Bank. It was the only merger flanked by nationalized banks and resulted in the reduction of the number of nationalized banks from 20 to 19. After this, until the 1990s, the nationalized banks grew at a pace of approximately 4%, closer to the standard development rate of the Indian economy.

Banking Growth as Nationalization

The partition of India in 1947 adversely impacted the economies of Punjab and West Bengal, paralyzing banking behaviors for months. India's independence marked the end of a regime of the Laissez-faire for the Indian banking. The Government of India initiated events to play an active role in the economic life of the nation, and the Industrial Policy Settlement adopted through the government in 1948 envisaged a mixed economy. This resulted into greater involvement of the state in dissimilar segments of the economy including banking and fund. The major steps to regulate banking incorporated:

- The Reserve Bank of India, India's central banking power, was recognized in April 1935, but was nationalized on January 1, 1949 under the conditions of the Reserve Bank of India (Transfer to Public Ownership) Act, 1948.
- In 1949, the Banking Regulation Act was enacted which empowered the Reserve Bank of India (RBI)"to regulate, manage, and inspect the banks in India".
- The Banking Regulation Act also provided that no new bank or branch of an existing bank could be opened without a license from the RBI, and no two banks could have general directors.

CENTRAL BANKING

WHAT IS A CENTRAL BANK?

A central bank, reserve bank, or monetary power is a public organization that manages a state's currency, money supply, and interest rates. Central banks also generally oversee the commercial banking organization of their respective countries. In contrast to a commercial bank, a central bank possesses a monopoly on rising the nation's monetary foundation, and generally also prints the national currency, which generally serves since the nation's legal tender. Examples contain:

- The European Central Bank (ECB),
- The Federal Reserve of the United States, and
- The People's Bank of China.

The primary function of a central bank is to control the nation's money supply (monetary policy), by active duties such since managing interest rates, setting the reserve requirement, and acting since a lender of last resort to the banking sector throughout times of bank insolvency or financial crisis. Central banks generally also have supervisory dominations, designed to prevent bank runs and to reduce the risk that commercial banks and other financial organizations engage in reckless or fraudulent behavior. Central banks in mainly urbanized nations are institutionally intended to be self-governing from political interference.

FUNCTIONS OF CENTRAL BANK

Bank of Note Issue

The central bank has the sole monopoly of note issue in approximately every country. The currency notes printed and issued through the central bank become unlimited legal tender during the country. In the languages of De Kock, "The privilege of note-issue was approximately everywhere associated with the origin and growth of central banks." Though, the monopoly of central bank to issue the currency notes may be incomplete in sure countries. For instance, in India, one rupee notes are issued through the Ministry of Fund and all other notes are issued through the Reserve Bank of India.

The largest advantages of giving the monopoly right of note issue to the central bank are given below:

- It brings uniformity in the monetary organization of note issue and note circulation.
- The central bank can exercise bigger manage in excess of the money supply in the country. It increases public confidence in the monetary organization of the country.
- Monetary administration of the paper currency becomes easier. Being the supreme bank of the country, the central bank has full information in relation to the monetary necessities of the economy and, so, can transform the quantity of currency accordingly.
- It enables the central bank to exercise manage in excess of the making of credit through the commercial banks.
- The central bank also earns profit from the issue of paper currency.
- Granting of monopoly right of note issue to the central bank avoids the political interference in the matter of note issue.

Banker, Agent and Adviser to the Government

The central bank functions since a banker, agent and financial adviser to the government,

- Since a banker to government, the central bank performs the similar functions for the government since a commercial bank performs for its customers. It maintains the accounts of the central since well since state government; it receives deposits from government; it creates short-condition advances to the government; it collects cheques and drafts deposited in the government explanation; it gives foreign swap possessions to the government for repaying external debt or purchasing foreign goods or creation other payments,
- Since an Agent to the government, the central bank collects taxes and other payments on behalf of the government. It raises loans from the public and therefore manages public debt. It also symbolizes the government in the international financial organizations and conferences,
- Since a financial adviser to the lent, the central bank provides advise to the government on economic, monetary, financial and fiscal ^ natters such since deficit financing, devaluation, deal policy, foreign swap policy, etc.

Bankers' Bank

The central bank acts since the bankers' bank in three capacities:

- Custodian of the cash preserves of the commercial banks;
- Since the lender of the last resort; and
- Since clearing agent. In this method, *the* central bank acts since a friend, philosopher and guide to the commercial banks

Since a *custodian of the cash reserves* of the commercial banks the central bank maintains the cash reserves of the commercial banks. Every commercial bank has to stay a sure percentage of its cash balances since deposits with the central banks. These cash reserves can be utilized through the commercial banks in times of emergency. The centralization of cash reserves in the central bank has the following advantages:

- Centralized cash reserves inspire confidence of the public in the banking organization of the country.
- Centralized cash reserves give the foundation of a superior and more elastic credit building than if these amounts were scattered in the middle of the individual banks.
- Centralized reserves can be used to the fullest possible extent and in the mainly effective manner throughout the eras of seasonal strains and financial emergencies.
- Centralized reserves enable the central bank to give financial accommodation to the commercial banks which are in temporary difficulties. In information the central bank functions since the lender of the last resort on the foundation of the centralized cash reserves.
- The organization of centralized cash reserves enables the central bank to power the making of credit through the commercial banks through rising or decreasing the cash reserves by the technique of variable cash-reserve ratio.
- The cash reserves with the central bank can be used to promote national welfare.

Lender of Last Resort

Since the supreme bank of the country and the bankers' bank, the central bank acts since the lender of the last resort. In other languages, in case the commercial banks are not able to meet their financial necessities from other sources, they can, since a last resort, style the central bank for financial accommodation. The central bank gives financial accommodation to the commercial banks through rediscounting their eligible securities and swap bills. The largest advantages of the central bank's functioning since the lender of the last resort are:

- It increases the elasticity and liquidity of the entire credit building of the economy.

- It enables the commercial banks to carry on their behaviors even with their limited cash reserves.
- It gives financial help to the commercial banks in times of emergency.
- It enables the central bank to exercise it's manage in excess of banking organization of the country.

Clearing Agent

Since the custodian of the cash reserves of the commercial banks, the central bank acts since the clearing home for these banks. As all banks have their accounts with the central bank, the central bank can easily settle the claims of several banks against each other with least exploit of cash. The clearing home function of the central bank has the following advantages:

- It economies the exploit of cash through banks while settling their claims and counter-claims.
- It reduces the withdrawals of cash and these enable the commercial banks to make credit on a big level.
- It keeps the central bank fully informed in relation to the liquidity location of the commercial banks.

BEHAVIORS AND RESPONSIBILITIES

Functions of a central bank may contain:

- Implementing monetary policies.
- Determining Interest rates
- Controlling the nation's whole money supply
- The Government's banker and the bankers' bank ("lender of last resort")
- Managing the country's foreign swap and gold reserves and the Government's stock register
- Regulating and supervising the banking industry
- Setting the official interest rate – used to control both inflation and the country's swap rate – and ensuring that this rate takes effect via a diversity of policy mechanisms

Monetary Policy

Central banks implement a country's chosen monetary policy. At the mainly vital stage, this involves establishing what shape of currency the country may have, whether a fiat currency, gold-backed currency (disallowed for countries with membership of the International Monetary Finance), currency board or a currency union. When a country has its own national currency, this involves the issue of some shape of standardized currency, which is essentially a shape of promissory note: a promise to swap the note for "money" under sure conditions. Historically, this was often a promise to swap the money for valuable metals in some fixed amount. Now, when several currencies are fiat money, the "promise to pay" consists of the promise to accept that currency to pay for taxes.

A central bank may exploit another country's currency either directly (in a currency union), or indirectly (a currency board). In the latter case, exemplified through Bulgaria, Hong Kong and Latvia, the regional currency is backed at a fixed rate through the central bank's holdings of a foreign currency. In countries with fiat money, the expression "monetary policy" may refer more narrowly to the interest-rate targets and other active events undertaken through the monetary power.

GOALS OF MONETARY POLICY

HIGH EMPLOYMENT

Frictional unemployment is the time era flanked by occupations when a worker is searching for, or transitioning from one occupation to another. Unemployment beyond frictional unemployment is classified since unintended unemployment. For instance, structural unemployment is a shape of unemployment resulting from a mismatch flanked by demand in the labour market and the skills and sites of the workers seeking employment. Macroeconomic policy usually aims to reduce unintended unemployment. Keynes labeled any occupations that would be created through a rise in wage-goods (i.e., a decrease in real-wages) since involuntary unemployment:

- Men are involuntarily unemployed if, in the event of a little rise in the price of wage-goods relatively to the money-wage, both the aggregate supply of labour willing to job for the current money-wage and the aggregate demand for it at that wage would be greater than the existing volume of employment.

Price Continuity

Inflation is defined either since the devaluation of a currency or equivalently the rise of prices comparative to a currency. As inflation lowers real wages, Keynesians view inflation since the solution to involuntary unemployment. Though, "unanticipated" inflation leads to lender losses since the real interest rate will be lower than expected. Therefore, Keynesian monetary policy aims for a steady rate of inflation.

Economic Development

Economic development can be enhanced through investment in capital, such since more or bigger machinery. A low interest rate implies that firms can loan money to invest in their capital stock and pay less interest for it. Lowering the interest is so measured to encourage economic development and is often used to alleviate times of low economic development. On the other hand, raising the interest rate is often used in times of high economic development since a contra-cyclical device to stay the economy from overheating and avoid market bubbles.

- Interest rate continuity
- Financial market continuity
- Foreign swap market continuity
- Conflicts in the middle of goals

Goals regularly cannot be separated from each other and often clash. Costs necessity so is cautiously weighed before policy implementation.

Currency Issuance

Same to commercial banks, central banks hold assets (government bonds, foreign swap, gold, and other financial assets) and incur liabilities (currency outstanding). Central banks make money through issuing interest-free currency notes and selling them to the public in swap for interest-bearing assets such since government bonds. When a central bank wishes to purchase more bonds than their respective national governments create accessible, they may purchase private bonds or assets denominated in foreign currencies. The European Central Bank remits its interest income to the central banks of the member countries of the European Union. The US Federal Reserve remits all its profits to the U.S. Treasury. This income, derived from the domination to issue currency, is referred to since seignior age, and generally belongs to the national government. The state-sanctioned domination to make currency is described the Right of Issuance. During history there have been disagreements in excess of this domination, as whoever dominates the making of currency dominates the seignior age income.

Interest Rate Interventions

Typically a central bank dominates sure kinds of short-condition interest rates. These power the stock- and bond markets since well since mortgage and other interest rates. The European Central Bank for instance announces its interest rate at the meeting of its Governing Council; in the case of the U.S. Federal Reserve, the Board of Governors. Both the Federal Reserve and the ECB are collected of one or more central bodies that are responsible for the largest decisions in relation to the interest rates and the size and kind of open market operations, and many branches to execute its policies. In the case of the Federal Reserve, they are the regional Federal Reserve Banks; for the ECB they are the national central banks.

Limits on Policy Effects

Although the perception through the public may be that the "central bank" dominates some or all interest rates and currency rates, economic theory (and substantial empirical proof) illustrates that it is impossible to do both at once in an open economy. Robert Mundell's "impossible trinity" is the mainly well-known formulation of these limited dominations, and postulates that it is impossible to target monetary policy (broadly, interest rates), the swap rate (by a fixed rate) and uphold free capital movement. As mainly Western economies are now measured "open" with free capital movement, this essentially means that central banks may target interest rates or swap rates with credibility, but not both at once.

In the mainly well-known case of policy failure, Black Wednesday, George Soros arbitraged the pound sterling's connection to the ECU and (after creation $2 billion himself and forcing the UK to spend in excess of $8bn defending the pound) forced it to abandon its policy. As then he has been a harsh critic of clumsy bank policies and argued that no one should be able to do what he did.

The mainly intricate relationships are those flanked by the yuan and the US dollar, and flanked by the Euro and its neighbors. The situation in Cuba is therefore exceptional since to need the Cuban peso to be dealt with basically since an exception, as the United States forbids direct deal with Cuba. US dollars were ubiquitous in Cuba's economy after its legalization in 1991, but were officially removed from circulation in 2004 and replaced through the convertible peso.

POLICY INSTRUMENTS

The largest monetary policy instruments accessible to central banks are:

- Open market operation,
- Bank reserve requirement,
- Interest rate policy,
- Re-lending and re-discount (including by the condition repurchase market), and
- Credit policy (often coordinated with deal policy).

While capital adequacy is significant, it is defined and regulated through the Bank for International Settlements, and central banks in practice usually do not apply stricter rules.

To enable open market operations, a central bank necessity hold foreign swap reserves (generally in the shape of government bonds) and official gold reserves. It will often have some power in excess of any official or mandated swap rates: Some swap rates are supervised, some are market based (free float) and several are somewhere in flanked by ("supervised float" or "dirty float").

Interest Rates

Through distant the mainly visible and obvious domination of several contemporary central banks is to power market interest rates; contrary to popular belief, they rarely "set" rates to a fixed number. Although the mechanism differs from country to country, mainly exploit a same mechanism based on a central bank's skill to make since much fiat money since required.

The mechanism to move the market towards a 'target rate' (whichever specific rate is used) is usually to lend money or borrow money in theoretically unlimited quantities, until the targeted market rate is sufficiently secure to the target. Central banks may do therefore through lending money to and borrowing money from (taking deposits from) a limited number of qualified banks, or through purchasing and selling bonds. Since an instance of how this functions, the Bank of Canada sets a target overnight rate, and a group of plus or minus 0.25%. Qualified banks borrow from each other within this group, but never above or below, because the central bank will always lend to them at the top of the group, and take deposits at the bottom of the group; in principle, the capability to borrow and lend at the extremes of the group are unlimited. Other central banks exploit same mechanisms.

It is also notable that the target rates are usually short-condition rates. The actual rate that borrowers and lenders receive on the market will depend on (perceived) credit risk, maturity and other factors. For instance, a central bank might set a target rate for overnight lending of 4.5%, but rates for (equivalent risk) five-year bonds might be 5%, 4.75%, or, in cases of inverted yield curves, even below the short-condition rate. Several central banks have one primary "headline" rate that is quoted since the "central bank rate". In practice, they will have other apparatus and rates that are used, but only one that is rigorously targeted and enforced.

"The rate at which the central bank lends money can indeed be chosen at will through the central bank; this is the rate that creates the financial headlines." – Henry C.K. Liu. Liu explains further that "the U.S. central-bank lending rate is recognized since the Fed finances rate. The Fed sets a target for the Fed finances rate, which its Open Market Committee tries to match through lending or borrowing in the money market... a fiat money organization set through command of the central bank. The Fed is the head of the central-bank because the U.S. dollar is the key reserve currency for international deal. The global money market is a USA dollar market. All other currencies markets revolve approximately the U.S. dollar market." Accordingly the U.S. situation is not typical of central banks in common. A typical central bank has many interest rates or monetary policy apparatus it can set to power markets.

- Marginal lending rate (currently 1.5% in the Euro zone) – a fixed rate for organizations to borrow money from the central bank. (In the USA this is described the discount rate).
- Largest refinancing rate (0.75% in the Euro zone) – the publicly visible interest rate the central bank announces. It is also recognized since *minimum bid rate* and serves since a bidding floor for refinancing loans. (In the USA this is described the federal finances rate).

- Deposit rate (0.00% in the Euro zone) – the rate parties receive for deposits at the central bank.

These rates directly affect the rates in the money market, the market for short condition loans.

Open Market Operations

By open market operations, a central bank powers the money supply in an economy directly. Each time it buys securities, exchanging money for the security, it raises the money supply. Conversely, selling of securities lowers the money supply. Buying of securities therefore amounts to printing new money while lowering supply of the specific security. The largest open market operations are:

- Temporary lending of money for collateral securities ("Reverse Operations" or "repurchase operations", otherwise recognized since the "repo" market). These operations are accepted out on a regular foundation, where fixed maturity loans (of one week and one month for the ECB) are auctioned off.
- Buying or selling securities ("direct operations") on ad-hoc foundation.
- Foreign swap operations such since forex swaps.

All of these interventions can also power the foreign swap market and therefore the swap rate. For instance the People's Bank of China and the Bank of Japan have on occasion bought many hundred billions of U.S. Treasuries, presumably in order to stop the decline of the U.S. dollar versus the rennin and the yen.

Capital Necessities

All banks are required to hold a sure percentage of their assets since capital, a rate which may be recognized through the central bank or the banking supervisor. For international banks, including the 55 member central banks of the Bank for International Settlements, the threshold is 8% of risk-adjusted assets, whereby sure assets (such since government bonds) are measured to have lower risk and are either partially or fully excluded from total assets for the purposes of calculating capital adequacy. Partly due to concerns in relation to the asset inflation and repurchase agreements, capital necessities may be measured more effective than reserve necessities in preventing indefinite lending: when at the threshold, a bank cannot extend another loan without acquiring further capital on its balance sheet.

Reserve Necessities

Historically, bank reserves have shaped only a little fraction of deposits, an organization described fractional reserve banking. Banks would hold only a little percentage of their assets in the shape of cash reserves since insurance against bank runs. In excess of time this procedure has been regulated and insured through central banks. Such legal reserve necessities were introduced in the 19th century since an effort to reduce the risk of banks overextending themselves and suffering from bank runs, since this could lead to knock-on effects on other overextended banks.

Since the early 20th century gold average was undermined through inflation and the late 20th century fiat dollar hegemony evolved, and since banks proliferated and occupied in more intricate transactions and were able to profit from relations globally on a moment's notice, these practices became mandatory, if only to ensure that there was some limit on the ballooning of money supply. Such limits have become harder to enforce. The People's Bank of China retains (and exploits) more dominations in excess of reserves because the yuan that it manages is a non-convertible currency.

Loan action through banks plays a fundamental role in determining the money supply. The central-bank money after aggregate resolution –"final money" – can take only one of two shapes:

- Physical cash, which is rarely used in wholesale financial markets,
- Central-bank money which is rarely used through the people

The currency component of the money supply is distant smaller than the deposit component. Currency, bank reserves and institutional loan agreements jointly create up the monetary foundation, described M1, M2 and M3. The Federal Reserve Bank stopped publishing M3 and counting it since section of the money supply in 2006.

Swap Necessities

To power the money supply, some central banks may need that some or all foreign swap receipts (usually from exports) be exchanged for the regional currency. The rate that is used to purchase regional currency may be market-based or arbitrarily set through the bank. This tool is usually used in countries with non-convertible currencies or partially convertible currencies. The recipient of the regional currency may be allowed to freely dispose of the finances, required to hold the finances with the central bank for some era of time, or allowed to exploit the finances subject to sure restrictions. In other cases, the skill to hold or exploit the foreign swap may be otherwise limited.

In this way, money supply is increased through the central bank when it purchases the foreign currency through issuing (selling) the regional currency. The central bank may subsequently reduce the money supply through several means, including selling bonds or foreign swap interventions.

Periphery Necessities and other Apparatus

In some countries, central banks may have other apparatus that job indirectly to limit lending practices and otherwise restrict or regulate capital markets. For instance, a central bank may regulate periphery lending, whereby individuals or companies may borrow against pledged securities. The periphery requirement establishes a minimum ratio of the value of the securities to the amount borrowed.

Central banks often have necessities for the excellence of assets that may be held through financial organizations; these necessities may act since a limit on the amount of risk and leverage created through the financial organization. These necessities may be direct, such since requiring sure assets to bear sure minimum credit ratings, or indirect, through the central bank lending to counterparties only when security of a sure excellence is pledged since collateral.

BANKING SUPERVISION AND OTHER BEHAVIORS

In some countries a central bank by its subsidiaries dominates and monitors the banking sector. In other countries banking supervision is accepted out through a government department such since the UK Treasury, or a self-governing government agency (for instance, UK's Financial Services Power). It examines the banks' balance sheets and behaviour and policies toward consumers.

Separately from refinancing, it also gives banks with services such since transfer of finances, bank notes and coins or foreign currency. Therefore it is often called since the "bank of banks".

Several countries such since the United States will monitor and manage the banking sector by dissimilar agencies and for dissimilar purposes, although there is generally important cooperation flanked by the agencies. For instance, money center banks, deposit-taking organizations, and other kinds of financial organizations may be subject to dissimilar (and occasionally overlapping) regulation. Some kinds of banking regulation may be delegated to other stages of government, such since state or provincial governments.

Any cartel of banks is particularly closely watched and controlled. Mainly countries manage bank mergers and are wary of concentration in this industry due to the danger of groupthink and runaway lending bubbles based on a single point of failure, the credit civilization of the few big banks.

RESERVE BANK OF INDIA

The Reserve Bank of India (RBI) is India's central banking organization, which dominates the monetary policy of the Indian rupee. It was recognized on 1 April 1935 throughout the British Raj in accordance with the provisions of the Reserve Bank of India Act, 1934. The share capital was divided into shares of 100 each fully paid which were entirely owned through private shareholders in the beginning. Following India's independence in 1947, the RBI was nationalized in the year 1949.

The RBI plays a significant section in the growth strategy of the Government of India. It is a member bank of the Asian Clearing Union. The common superintendence and direction of the RBI is entrusted with the 21-member-strong Central Board of Directors—the Governor (currently Duvvuri Subbarao), four Deputy Governors, two Fund Ministry representative, ten Government-nominated Directors to symbolize significant units from India's economy, and four Directors to symbolize Regional Boards headquartered at Mumbai, Kolkata, Chennai and New Delhi. Each of these Regional Boards consists of five members who symbolize local interests, since well since the interests of co-operative and indigenous banks. The Bank is also active in promoting financial inclusion policy and is a leading member of the Alliance for Financial Inclusion (AFI) View the Bank on AFI's member map.

HISTORY

1935–1950

The Reserve Bank of India was founded on 1 April 1935 to respond to economic problems after the First World War. It came into picture just as to the guidelines laid down through Dr. Ambedkar. RBI was conceptualized since per the guidelines, working approach and outlook presented through Dr Ambedkar in front of the Hilton Young Commission. When this commission came to India under the name of "Royal Commission on Indian Currency & Fund", each and every member of this commission were holding Dr Ambedkar's book named "The Trouble of the Rupee – its origin and its solution." The Bank was set up based on the recommendations of the 1926 Royal Commission on Indian Currency and Fund, also recognized since the Hilton–Young Commission. The original choice for the seal of RBI was The East India Company Double Mohr, with the sketch of the Lion and Palm Tree. The Preamble of the RBI defines its vital functions to regulate the issue of bank notes, stay reserves to close monetary continuity in India, and usually to operate the currency and credit organization in the best interests of the country. The Central Office of the RBI was initially recognized in Calcutta (now Kolkata), but was permanently moved to Bombay (now Mumbai) in 1937. The RBI also acted since Burma's central bank, except throughout the years of the Japanese job of Burma (1942–45), until April 1947, even however Burma seceded from the Indian Union in 1937. After the Partition of India in 1947, the Bank served since the central bank for Pakistan until June 1948 when the State Bank of Pakistan commenced operations. However originally set up since a shareholders' bank, the RBI has been fully owned through the Government of India as its nationalization in 1949.

1950–1960

In the 1950s, the Indian government, under its first Prime Minister Jawaharlal Nehru, urbanized a centrally intended economic policy that focused on the agricultural sector. The management nationalized commercial banks and recognized, based on the Banking Companies Act of 1949 (later described the Banking Regulation Act), a central bank regulation since section of the RBI. Furthermore, the central bank was ordered to support the economic plan with loans.

1960–1969

Since a result of bank crashes, the RBI was requested to set up and monitor a deposit insurance organization. It should restore the trust in the national bank organization and was initialized on 7 December 1961. The Indian government founded finances to promote the economy and used the slogan Developing Banking. The Government of India restructured the national bank market and nationalized a lot of institutes. Since a result, the RBI had to play the central section of manage and support of this public banking sector.

1969–1985

In 1969, the Indira Gandhi-headed government nationalized 14 major commercial banks. Upon Gandhi's return to domination in 1980, a further six banks were nationalized. The regulation of the economy and especially the financial sector was reinforced through the Government of India in the 1970s and 1980s. The central bank became the central player and increased its policies for a lot of tasks like interests, reserve ratio and visible deposits. These events aimed at bigger economic growth and had a vast effect on the company policy of the institutes. The banks lent money in selected sectors, like agri-business and little deal companies. The branch was forced to set up two new offices in the country for every newly recognized office in a city. The oil crises in 1973 resulted in rising inflation, and the RBI restricted monetary policy to reduce the effects.

1985–1991

A lot of committees analyzed the Indian economy flanked by 1985 and 1991. Their results had an effect on the RBI. The Board for Industrial and Financial Reconstruction, the Indira Gandhi Institute of Growth Research and the Security & Swap Board of India investigated the national economy since an entire, and the security and swap board proposed bigger methods for more effective markets and the defense of investor interests. The Indian financial market was a leading instance for therefore-described "financial repression" (Mackinnon and Shaw). The Discount and Fund Home of India began its operations on the monetary market in April 1988; the National Housing Bank, founded in July 1988, was forced to invest in the property market and a new financial law improved the versatility of direct deposit through more security events and liberalization.

1991–2000

The national economy came down in July 1991 and the Indian rupee was devalued. The currency lost 18% comparative to the US dollar, and the Narsimahmam Committee advised restructuring the financial sector through a temporal reduced reserve ratio since well since the statutory liquidity ratio. New guidelines were published in 1993 to set up a private banking sector. This turning point should reinforce the market and was often described neo-liberal. The central bank deregulated bank interests and some sectors of the financial market like the trust and property markets. This first stage was a success and the central government forced a variety liberalization to diversify owner buildings in 1998.

The National Stock Swap of India took the deal on in June 1994 and the RBI allowed nationalized banks in July to interact with the capital market to reinforce their capital foundation. The central bank founded a subsidiary company—the Bharatiya Reserve Bank Note Mudran Limited—in February 1995 to produce banknotes.

As 2000

The Foreign Swap Administration Act from 1999 came into force in June 2000. It should improve the foreign swap market, international investments in India and transactions. The RBI promoted the growth of the financial market in the last years, allowed online banking in 2001 and recognized a new payment organization in 2004–2005 (National Electronic Finance Transfer). The Security Printing & Minting Corporation of India Ltd., a merger of nine organizations, was founded in 2006 and produces banknotes and coins. The national economy's development rate came down to 5.8% in the last quarter of 2008–2009 and the central bank promotes the economic growth.

BUILDING

Central Board of Directors

The Central Board of Directors is the largest committee of the central bank. The Government of India appoints the directors for a four-year condition. The Board consists of a governor, four deputy governors, fifteen directors to symbolize the local boards, one from the Ministry of Fund and ten other directors from several meadows. The Government nominated Arvind Mayaram, since a director of the Central Board of Directors with effect from August 7, 2012 and vice R Gopalan, RBI said in a report on August 8, 2012..

Governors

The current Governor of RBI is Duvvuri Subbarao. The RBI extended the era of the present governor up to 2013. There are four deputy governors, Deputy

Governor K C Chakrabarty, Subir Gokarn, Shri Anand Sinha, and Shri H.R. Khan. Deputy Governor K C Chakrabarty's condition has been extended further through 2 years.

Supportive Bodies

The Reserve Bank of India has ten local symbols: North in New Delhi, South in Chennai, East in Kolkata and West in Mumbai. The symbols are shaped through five members, appointed for four years through the central government and serve—along the advice of the Central Board of Directors—since a forum for local banks and to trade with delegated tasks from the central board. The organization has 22 local offices.

The Board of Financial Supervision (BFS), shaped in November 1994, serves since a CCBD committee to manage the financial organizations. It has four members, appointed for two years, and takes events to strength the role of statutory auditors in the financial sector, external monitoring and internal controlling organizations.

The Tarapore committee was set up through the Reserve Bank of India under the chairmanship of former RBI deputy governor S. S. Tarapore to "place the road map" to capital explanation convertibility. The five-member committee recommended a three-year time frame for complete convertibility through 1999–2000. On 1 July 2007, in an effort to enhance the excellence of customer service and strengthen the grievance redresses mechanism, the Reserve Bank of India created a new customer service department.

LARGEST FUNCTIONS

Bank of Issue

Under Part 22 of the Reserve Bank of India Act, the Bank has the sole right to issue bank notes of all denominations. The sharing of one rupee notes and coins and little coins all in excess of the country is undertaken through the Reserve Bank since agent of the Government. The Reserve Bank has a distinct Issue Department which is entrusted with the issue of currency notes. The assets and liabilities of the Issue Department are kept distinct from those of the Banking Department.

Originally, the assets of the Issue Department were to consist of not less than two-fifths of gold coin, gold bullion or sterling securities provided the amount of gold was not less than 40 crore in value. The remaining three-fifths of the assets might be held in rupee coins, Government of India rupee securities, eligible bills of swap and promissory notes payable in India. Due to the exigencies of the Second World War and the post-war era, these provisions were substantially customized. As 1957, the Reserve Bank of India is required to uphold gold and foreign swap reserves of Rs.200 crore (Rs.2 billion), of which at least Rs.115 crore (Rs.1.15 billion) should be in gold and Rs.85 crore (Rs.850 million) in the shape of Government Securities. The organization since it exists today is recognized since the minimum reserve organization.

Monetary Power

The Reserve Bank of India is the largest monetary power of the country and along that the central bank acts since the bank of the national and state governments. It formulates, implements and monitors the monetary policy since well since it has to ensure an adequate flow of credit to productive sectors. Objectives are maintaining price continuity and ensuring adequate flow of credit to productive sectors. The national economy depends on the public sector and the central bank promotes an expansive monetary policy to push the private sector as the financial market reforms of the 1990s.

Regulator and Supervisor of the Financial Organization

The organization is also the regulator and supervisor of the financial organization and prescribes broad parameters of banking operations within which the country's banking and financial organization functions. Its objectives are to uphold public confidence in the organization, protect depositors' interest and give cost-effective banking services to the public. The Banking Ombudsman Scheme has been formulated through the Reserve Bank of India (RBI) for effective addressing of complaints through bank customers. The RBI dominates the monetary supply, monitors economic indicators like the gross domestic product and has to decide the design of the rupee banknotes since well since coins.

Managerial of Swap Manage

The central bank manages to reach the goals of the Foreign Swap Administration Act, 1999. Objective: to facilitate external deal and payment and promote orderly growth and maintenance of foreign swap market in India.

Issuer of Currency

The bank issues and exchanges or destroys currency notes and coins that are not fit for circulation. The objectives are giving the public adequate supply of currency of good excellence and to give loans to commercial banks to uphold or improve the GDP. The vital objectives of RBI are to issue bank notes, to uphold the currency and credit organization of the country to utilize it in its best advantage, and to uphold the reserves. RBI maintains the economic building of the country therefore that it can achieve the objective of price continuity since well since economic growth, because both objectives are diverse in themselves.

Banker of Banks

RBI also jobs since a central bank where explanation holders (are commercial bank's) can deposit money. RBI maintains banking accounts of all scheduled banks. Commercial banks make credit. It is the duty of the RBI to manage the credit by the CRR, bank rate and open market operations. Since banker's bank, the RBI facilitates the clearing of checks flanked by the commercial banks and helps inter-bank transfer of finances. It can grant financial accommodation to schedule banks. It acts since the lender of the last resort through providing emergency advances to the banks. It supervises the functioning of the commercial banks and take action against it if require arises.

DISCOVERY OF FAKE CURRENCY

Developmental Role

The central bank has to perform a wide range of promotional functions to support national objectives and industries. The RBI faces a lot of inter-sectoral and regional inflation-related troubles. Some of these troubles are results of the dominant section of the public sector.

Related Functions

The RBI is also a banker to the government and performs merchant banking function for the central and the state governments. It also acts since their banker. The National Housing Bank (NHB) was recognized in 1988 to promote private real estate acquisition. The organization maintains banking accounts of all scheduled banks, too. RBI on 7 August 2012 said that Indian banking organization is resilient sufficient to face the stress caused through the drought like situation because of poor monsoon this year.

POLICY RATES AND RESERVE RATIOS

Bank Rate

RBI lends to the commercial banks by its discount window to help the banks meet depositor's demands and reserve necessities for extensive condition. The interest rate the RBI charges the banks for this purpose is described bank rate. If the RBI wants to augment the liquidity and money supply in the market, it will decrease the bank rate and if RBI wants to reduce the liquidity and money supply in the organization, it will augment the bank rate.

Reserve Requirement Cash Reserve Ratio (CRR)

Every commercial bank has to stay sure minimum cash reserves with RBI. Consequent upon amendment to sub-Part 42(1), the Reserve Bank, having regard to the requires of securing the monetary continuity in the country, RBI can prescribe Cash Reserve Ratio (CRR) for scheduled banks without any floor rate or ceiling rate, Before the enactment of this amendment, in conditions of Part 42(1) of the RBI Act, the Reserve Bank could prescribe CRR for scheduled banks flanked by 5% and 20% of total of their demand and time liabilities]. RBI exploits this tool to augment or decrease the reserve requirement depending on whether it wants to effect a decrease or an augment in the money supply. An augment in Cash Reserve Ratio (CRR) will create it mandatory on the section of the banks to hold a big proportion of their deposits in the shape of deposits with the RBI. This will reduce the size of their deposits and they will lend less. This will in turn decrease the money supply. The current rate is 4.75%. 25 foundation points cut in Cash Reserve Ratio(CRR) on 17 September 2012, It will release Rs 17,000 crore into the organization/Market. The RBI lowered the CRR through 25 foundation points to 4.25% on 30 October 2012, a move it said would inject in relation to the 175 billion rupees into the banking organization in order to pre-empt potentially tightening liquidity. 1476732,web.web.pvt-India,patfuly of world bank]

Liquidity Ratio (SLR)

Separately from the CRR, banks are required to uphold liquid assets in the shape of gold, cash and approved securities. Higher liquidity ratio forces commercial banks to uphold a superior proportion of their possessions in liquid shape and therefore reduces their capability to grant loans and advances, therefore it is an anti-inflationary impact. A higher liquidity ratio diverts the bank finances from loans and advances to investment in government and approved securities. In well-urbanized economies, central banks exploit open market operations—buying and selling of eligible securities through central bank in the money market—to power the volume of cash reserves with commercial banks and therefore power the volume of loans and advances they can create to the commercial and industrial sectors. In the open money market, government securities are traded at market related rates of interest. The RBI is resorting more to open market operations in the more recent years. Usually RBI exploits three types of selective credit dominate:

- Minimum margins for lending against specific securities.
- Ceiling on the amounts of credit for sure purposes.
- Discriminatory rate of interest charged on sure kinds of advances.

Direct credit dominates in India are of three kinds:

- Section of the interest rate building i.e. on little savings and provident finances, are administratively set.
- Banks are mandatory required to stay 23% of their deposits in the shape of government securities.
- Banks are required to lend to the priority sectors to the extent of 40% of their advances.

INDIAN MONEY MARKET

The Indian money market is "a market for short-condition and Extensive condition finances with maturity ranging from overnight to one year and comprises financial instruments that are deemed to be secure substitutes of money." It is diversified and has evolved by several levels, from the conventional platform of treasury bills and call money to commercial paper, certificates of deposit, repos, FRAs and IRS more recently.

The Indian money market consists of diverse sub-markets, each dealing in a scrupulous kind of short-condition credit. The money market fulfills the borrowing and investment necessities of providers and users of short-condition finances, and balances the demand for and supply of short-condition finances through providing an equilibrium mechanism. It also serves since a focal point for the Central Bank's intervention in the market.

BUILDING

The Indian money market consists of the unorganized sector: moneylenders, indigenous bankers, chit finances; organized sector: Reserve Bank of India, private banks, public sector banks, growth banks and other Non Banking Financial Companies(NBFCs) such since:

- Life Insurance Corporation of India (LIC),
- Element Trust of India (UTI),
- The International Fund Corporation,
- IDBI, and
- The co-operative sector.

INSTRUMENTS

Call Money Market

The call money market trades in short condition fund repayable on demand, with a maturity era varying from one day to 14 days. S.K. Muranjan commented that call loans in India are provided to the bill market, rendered flanked by banks, and given for the purpose of dealing in the bullion market and stock exchanges. Commercial banks, both Indian and foreign, co-operative banks, Discount and Fund Home of India Ltd.(DFHI), Securities trading corporation of India (STCI) participate since both lenders and borrowers and Life Insurance Corporation of India (LIC), Element Trust of India(UTI), National Bank for Agriculture and Rural Growth (NABARD)can participate only since lenders. The interest rate paid on call money loans, recognized since the call rate, is highly volatile. It is the mainly sensitive part of the money market and the changes in the demand for and supply of call loans are promptly reflected in call rates. There are now two call rates in India: the Inter bank call rate and the lending rate of DFHI. The ceilings on the call rate and inter-bank condition money rate were dropped, with effect from May 1, 1989. The Indian call money market has been transformed into a pure inter-bank market throughout 2006–07. The major call money markets are in Mumbai, Kolkata, Delhi, Chennai, Ahmedabad.

Treasury Bill Market

Treasury bills are instrument of short-condition borrowing through the Government of India, issued since promissory notes under discount. The interest received on them is the discount which is the variation flanked by the price at which they are issued and their redemption value. They have assured yield and smallest risk of default. Under one classification, treasury bills are categorized since ad hoc, tap and auction bills and under another classification it is classified on the maturity era like 91-days TBs, 182-days TBs, 364-days TBs and two kinds of 14-days TBs. In the recent times (2002–03, 2003–04), the Reserve Bank of India has been issuing only 91-day and 364-day treasury bills. the auction format of 91-day treasury bill has changed from uniform price to multiple prices to encourage more responsible bidding from the market players. the bills are two types:

- Ad hoc and
- Regular.

The *ad hoc* bills are issued for investment through the state governments, semi government departments and foreign central banks for temporary investment. they are not sold to banks and common public. The treasury bills sold to the public and banks are described regular treasury bills. they are freely marketable. Commercial bank buys whole quantity of such bills issued on tender they are bought and sold on discount foundation.

Ready Forward Contract (Repos)

Repo is an abbreviation for Repurchase agreement, which involves a simultaneous "sale and purchase" agreement. When banks have any shortage of finances, they can borrow it from Reserve Bank of India or from other banks. The rate at which the RBI lends money to commercial banks is described repo rate, a short condition for repurchase agreement. A reduction in the repo rate will help banks to get money at a cheaper rate. When the repo rate increases borrowing from RBI becomes more expensive.

Money Market Mutual Finances

Money market mutual finances invest money in specifically, high-excellence and extremely short maturity-based money market instruments. The RBI has approved the establishment of extremely few such finances in India. In 1997, only one MMMF was in operation, and that too with extremely little amount of capital.

RESERVE BANK OF INDIA

The power of the Reserve Bank of India's domination in excess of the Indian money market is confined approximately exclusively to the organized banking building. It is also measured to be the major regulator in the markets. There are sure rates and data which are released at regular intervals which have a vast impact on all the financial markets in INDIA. The unorganized sector, which consists mostly of indigenous bankers and non-banking financial companies, although occupying an significant location in the money market have not been properly integrated with the rest of the money market.

Reforms

The recommendations of the Sukhmoy Chakravarty Committee on the Review of the Working of the Monetary organization, and the Narasimham Committee Statement on the Working of the Financial Organization in India, 1991, The Reserve Bank of India has initiated a series of money market reforms simply directed towards the efficient discharge of its objectives. The bank reduced the ceiling rate on bank advances and on inter-bank call and short-notice money. There has been an important lowering of the minimum lending rate of commercial banks and public sector growth financial organizations from 18% in 1990–91 to 10.5% in 2005–06.

Bibliography

Alak Ghosh: *Emerging Money Market in India*, Deep & Deep Publication, Delhi, 2001.

Amitabh Shukla: *International Money Market and Indian Economic Reforms*, Kanishka Publication, Delhi, 2000.

B.N. Dash: *Commercial Banking : Risk and Credit Management*, Arise Publication, Delhi, 2011.

B.R. Nanda: *Indian Banking : Its Fraud and Crime*, Surendra Publication, Delhi, 2011.

B.S. Sharma: *Analysis of Commercial Banking*, Vista International Publication House, Delhi, 2011.

Benton E. Gup and James W. Kolari: *Commercial Banking: The Management Of Risk*, Wiley, 2001.

Bijay Kumar Sinha: *Indian Banking and Economic Reforms : Problems and Prospects*, Classical Publication, Delhi, 2007.

Deepak Tandon, Neelam Tandon and Kanhaiya Ahuja: *Indian Banking : Technology Innovations and Key Concerns*, Kunal Books, Delhi, 2011.

G P Kapoor: *Commercial Banking*, APH Publication, Delhi, 2004.

Harbans Lal Sharma: *Commercial Banking Development : A Study*, Rajat Publication, Delhi, 2003.

K.R. Gupta: *Economics : For UGC-NET/SLET and Other Competitive Examinations*, Atlantic Publication, Delhi, 2011.

Keshava, S R.: *Economics*, New Age International, Delhi, 2009.

M.S. Gopalan: *Indian Money Market : Structure, Operation and Developments*, Deep & Deep Publication, Delhi, 2000.

N.K. Sharma: *Economics : Theory and Practice*, DND Publications, Delhi, 2015.

PAUL: *No Money Marketing*, Tata McGraw-Hill, 2009.

R K Uppal and Rimpi Kaur: *Indian Banking : Transformation Through Information Technology*, Mahamaya Publishing House, Delhi, 2008.

R K Uppal: *Indian Banking Industry and Information Technology*, New Century Publication, Delhi, 2006.

R.K. Uppal: *Indian Banking : A New Vision*, Mahamaya Publication, Delhi, 2009.

R.K. Uppal: *Indian Banking : Scaling New Heights*, Kunal Books, Delhi, 2009.

R.K. Uppal: *Indian Banking and Contemporary Issues*, Kunal Books, Delhi, 2011.

R.K. Uppal: *Indian Banking in New Global Order*, Sarup Publication, Delhi, 2012.

R.K. Uppal: *Indian Banking in the Globalised World*, New Century Publications, Delhi, 2008.

R.K. Uppal: *Indian Banking Industry : Issues Challenges and Opportunities*, Sarup Publication, Delhi, 2013.

Rajesh Pal: *Indian Banking and Globalization*, Adhyayan Publication, Delhi, 2009.

Ravishankar Kumar Singh: *Indian Banking and Financial Sector Reforms : Realising Global Aspirations (2 Vols-Set)*, Abhijeet Publication, Delhi, 2006.

Richard Lipsey and Alec Chrystal: *Economics*, Oxford University Press, Delhi, 2007.

Index